ALONG THE PATH

ALONG THE PATH

STUDIES IN KABBALISTIC MYTH, SYMBOLISM, AND HERMENEUTICS

Elliot R. Wolfson

State University of New York Press

Published by
State University of New York Press, Albany

Printed in the United States of America

For information, address State University of New York
Press, State University Plaza, Albany, N.Y., 12246

Production by Marilyn P. Semerad
Marketing by Fran Keneston

Library of Congress Cataloging-in-Publication Data

Wolfson, Elliot R.
Along the path : studies in Kabbalistic myth, symbolism, and Hermeneutics / Elliot R. Wolfson.
p. cm.
Includes index.
ISBN 0-7914-2407-3 (alk. paper). — ISBN 0-7914-2408-1 (pbk. : alk. paper)
1. Mysticism—Judaism—History. 2. Cabala—History. 3. Sefer ha —bahir. 4. Hasidism—History. I. Title.
BM723.W645 1995
296.1'6—dc20 94-18317
CIP

10 9 8 7 6 5 4 3 2 1

C, 1

For Tsvi,
fellow traveler on the path

Thinking itself is a way. We respond to the way only by remaining underway. To be underway on the way in order to clear the way. . . . Nevertheless if we are to remain underway we must first of all and constantly give attention to the way. The movement, step by step, is what is essential here. Thinking clears its way by its own questioning advance.

—Martin Heidegger, *What Is Called Thinking?*

◆ CONTENTS ◆

◆ PREFACE ◆

The first chapter included in this work, "The Image of Jacob Engraved upon the Throne: Further Reflection on the Esoteric Doctrine of the German Pietists," is a revised and much expanded English version of a study written in Hebrew in 1989 but just recently published in 1994. In addition to the path that it opens up with respect to the esoteric doctrines of the circle of Rhineland Pietists of the twelfth and thirteenth centuries, this study raises many questions about the transmission and evolution of esotericism in Judaism from Late Antiquity to the Middle Ages. In a fundamental sense it challenges certain conventionally held beliefs and the superficial boundaries that scholars have drawn in their attempt to chart the history of Jewish mysticism. At the very least, the study of this one motif exposes the depth of a core myth of ancient Jewish esotericism and its subsequent metamorphosis in the religious imagination of the German Pietists.

The second chapter, "The Tree That Is All: Jewish-Christian Roots of a Kabbalistic Symbol in *Sefer ha-Bahir*," is arguably a work of imaginative reconstruction. I present this study, a slightly revised version of a text originally published in 1993, as a working hypothesis that calls for further investigation on the part of myself and other scholars. The *Sefer ha-Bahir*, generally thought to be the first work of theosophic kabbalah to appear on the literary scene in twelfth-century Provence, is a notoriously difficult and frustrating text. If my conjecture regarding the possible Jewish-Christian provenance of the motif of the cosmic tree proves to be unacceptable, the merit of my study nevertheless lies in the fact that I have forced a methodological issue about the textual parameters of this work into the open. In short, my essay challenges the view that the most pervasive and innovative theosophic structure in this work is the doctrine of the ten *sefirot*. This challenge, in turn, raises fundamental questions about the taxonomy of medieval kabbalah accepted by many scholars. In order to locate the origins of the kabbalah, it simply may not be sufficient to trace the trajectory of the theosophic interpretation of the ten *sefirot.* If one is to assume that the bahiric text is the first work of kabbalah in a proper sense, then this document itself explodes the aforementioned definition of kabbalah insofar as it incorporates a variety of different theosophic systems based on various numerical systems. To place the *Bahir,* then, at the beginning of the search for the origins of kabbalah necessitates a much more expanisve and flexible hypothesis regarding the nature of the phenomenon at hand. Indeed, the very posing of the inquiry in this way may prove to be grossly inadequate, for kabbalah is no one thing for which an obvious origin in historical time or geographical place can be determined.

The third chapter, "Walking as a Sacred Duty: Theological Transformation of Social Reality in Early Hasidism," originally written in 1988, provides an in-depth analysis of one of the central motifs in the formative texts of eighteenth- and nineteenth-century east European Hasidism. The sustained reflection on the theme of walking indicates how this one motif played an essential part in the formation of early Hasidic spirituality both in the realms of ideology and in praxis. Indeed, the basic issues of Hasidic mysticism all coalesce about the motif of walking which expresses in a symbolic manner the theurgical, magical, and soteriological role of the charismatic master in relation to his disciples. The religious texture of Hasidism, I submit, is enframed by the image of walking and the basic elements that it entails, to wit, the foot, the shoe, and the path. From a phenomenological vantage point walking may thus be considered a ground concept, for it allows one to grasp the foundation of Hasidism in an originary way.

In sum, it can be said that the three chapters contained in this volume amply demonstrate the complexity of kabbalistic hermeneutics, symbolism, and myth. In my scholarly work I always have avoided the temptation to impose typological categories on the wide variety of sources that constitute the basic texts studied under the rubric of Jewish mysticism. My aim rather is to provide a morphology of these texts and thereby allow the deep structures of thought to appear from within philological concealedness. The task of scholarship, as I conceive it, is to provide an opening through which those structures become manifest as markers on the path of inquiry. Those accustomed to the path well understand that the journey is always underfoot, for indeed the path is laid by the traces of walking. To reach a final destination is the way of one who comes no more, not the journeyman whose way is predicated on staying on the path. On the pathways of thinking there are no preconceived notions or fixed determinations, only the unfolding of questions that open up the way. As Martin Heidegger put it, "Thinking keeps to its way of thinking. It is the way toward what is worthy of questioning, problematical." These studies truly are steps along the path.

◆ 1 ◆

THE IMAGE OF JACOB ENGRAVED UPON THE THRONE: FURTHER REFLECTION ON THE ESOTERIC DOCTRINE OF THE GERMAN PIETISTS

Verily, at this time that which was hidden has been revealed
because forgetfulness has reached its final limit;
the end of forgetfulness is the beginning of remembrance.

—Abraham Abulafia, ʾ*Or ha-Sekhel,* MS Munich, Bayerische Staatsbibliothek 92, fol. 59b

I

One of the most interesting motifs in the world of classical rabbinic aggadah is that of the image of Jacob engraved on the throne of glory. My intention in this chapter is to examine in detail the utilization of this motif in the rich and varied literature of Eleazar ben Judah of Worms, the leading literary exponent of the esoteric and mystical pietism cultivated by the Kalonymide circle of German Pietists in the twelfth and thirteenth centuries. The first part of the chapter will investigate the ancient traditions connected to this motif as they appear in sources from Late Antiquity and the Middle Ages in order to establish the basis for the distinctive understanding that evolves in the main circle of German Pietists to be discussed in the second part.

As I will argue in detail later, the motif of the image of Jacob has a special significance in the theosophy of the German Pietists, particularly as it is expounded in the case of Eleazar. The amount of attention paid by previous scholarship to this theme is disproportionate in relation to the central place that it occupies in the esoteric ruminations of the Kalonymide Pietists.[1] From several passages in the writings of Eleazar it is clear that the motif of the image of Jacob is covered and cloaked in utter secrecy. I will mention here two of the more striking examples that illustrate my point: in his commentary on the liturgy Eleazar concludes a section in which he discusses several issues related to this image with the assertion *ʾein lefaresh yoter,* "the matter cannot be further explained."[2] In a second passage from a text that is essentially a commentary on the *ʿAmidah,* the traditional standing prayer of eighteen benedictions, Eleazar again mentions the image of Jacob engraved on the throne and quickly notes: *we-ʾein lefaresh ha-kol ki ʿim be-ʿal peh la-ʾish ha-yareʾ borʾo be-khol ʾet,* "the matter cannot be fully explained except orally to one who fears his Creator at all times."[3] The reluctance on the part of Eleazar to disclose matters pertaining to the motif of the image of Jacob is not something incidental or inconsequential. On the contrary, I assume that there is a profound secret here that may provide the scholar with an important key with which to discern the esoteric doctrine of the German Pietistic theosophy. A precise textual analysis should enable us to uncover this secret.

The thesis that I put forth here is that in the circle of Judah the Pious—as is known in particular from the writings of Eleazar of Worms—there was transmitted an esoteric doctrine predicated on bisexuality in the divine realm. As Alexander Altmann,[4] Joseph Dan,[5] and more recently Asi Farber,[6] have already noted, in the composition entitled the "Secret of the Nut" (*sod ha-ʾegoz*), contained in Ashkenazi sources, a composition that according to all three scholars preserves an older esoteric tradition of *merkavah* speculation, the nut that symbolizes the divine chariot is described in bisexual images. More specifically, the bisexuality was expressed in terms of the symbolism of the nut depicting the structure of the chariot, in the description of the throne itself, as well as in the distinction between the *ḥashmal* and *ḥashmalah* (scripturally, the two are identical in meaning—the word *ḥashmal* appears in Ezekiel 1:4 and 27, and *ḥashmalah* in 8:2—but in the various recensions of the *sod ha-ʾegoz* text and the Pietistic literature influenced by it, they are two distinct entities).[7] Farber suggested that the origin of this sexual symbolism is not to be sought in the Ashkenazi reworking of the composition, but in the "ancient proto-kabbalistic form of the secret" that circulated from the Orient.[8] Rather than adding these sexual images to the secret of the nut, the Pietists weakened or actually removed them by altering the text. Farber thus takes issue with Dan's hypothesis that the Pietists themselves added these sexual references to the received texts, a hypothesis that stands in marked contrast, as Dan himself acknowledges, with his view that

Pietistic theosophy is to be distinguished from kabbalistic on the grounds that they did not advocate a male-female polarity within the divine.[9] Notwithstanding the obvious tendency on the part of the Pietists to minimize or even obscure the sexual nature of these images,[10] a careful reading of their writings shows that there are veiled allusions to the bisexual nature of the throne world.[11] According to Farber, therefore, we must distinguish between the "exoteric" side of the Pietistic theology that attempted to attenuate or even supress sexual images and the "esoteric" side that described aspects of the divine world in overtly sexual terms. This esoteric aspect was not fully committed to writing but was transmitted orally from master to disciple.[12] Another illustration of the esoteric side of the Pietistic theology, also related to the bisexual nature of the glory, can be found in the use of the aggadic motif of the image of Jacob engraved upon the throne in the writings of Eleazar of Worms.

More precisley, the thesis that I propose to demonstrate is that the relation between the upper and the lower glory according to the esoteric theology of the German Pietists must be understood in terms of the union of male and female potencies. I will set out to show, moreover, that for the Pietists the lower of these potencies—identified as the cherub in the theosophic texts attributed to Judah and the compositions of Eleazar and as the image of Jacob engraved on the throne by Eleazar—is itself equated with the union of two cherubim that correspond to the divine names (YHWH and Adonai) and the two attributes (mercy and judgment); through a complicated numerological exegesis (discussed later) the two names are said to comprise the 613 commandments or the Torah in its totality. The Pietists draw the obvious theurgical implications: by performing the 613 commandments one unites the two names within the lower glory, an act that prepares it for its union with the upper glory.[13] This implies that in the esoteric doctrine of the German Pietists one can find an exact parallel to two of the cornerstones of theosophical kabbalah: mythologization of the divine realm as male and female, on the one hand, and the theurgical understanding of the commandments, on the other.[14] This doctrine, in my opinion, must be viewed as part of the truly "esoteric" teaching cultivated by Judah and Eleazar and their followers, that can be reconstructed from the texts largely buried in manuscripts. To be sure, the Pietists were extremely cautious about disclosing these matters in print. Yet, once disclosed it can be seen that this theosophic doctrine may provide the ideational basis for the pietistic worldview including notions of the divine will,[15] divine love,[16] communion with God (*devequt*),[17] performance of the *miṣwot*,[18] especially prayer,[19] and the subjugation of sexual desire.[20] These are matters that lie outside my immediate concern, but it is clear to me on the basis of my research that one could fruitfully re-examine the whole question of the relationship between theosophy and pietism in the case of the Ḥaside Ashkenaz. Finally, it is evident that in contrast to the theosophic kabbalah that developed in Provence and northern Spain, the bisexual nature of the glory in the religious thought of the Pietists remains in the realm of the esoteric in the exact sense of the term, that is, something that cannot be disclosed in writing to the populace. Even so, the assumption that the divine world in the writings of the German Pietists comprises masculine and feminine elements, and that the task of every Jew is to unite the two names of God that correspond to the divine attributes or the two glories, brings their secret teaching into close proximity to the orientation of the kabbalists, a view that has been affirmed by a number of contemporary scholars.[21]

II

The motif of Jacob's image engraved on the throne is mentioned in Targum Yerushalmi to Genesis 28:12,[22] and in slightly different terminology in the Targum Pseudo-Jonathan on the same verse.[23] According to the targumic rendering, the angels who accompanied Jacob ascended to notify the angels above that Jacob, whose icon (*ʾiqonin*) was engraved on the throne, was below; the angels thus descended to have a look at the earthly Jacob. The midrashic elaboration in the targumim thus provides a motivation for the angels' movement as well as an explanation for the strange locution, "ascending and descending." The same motif appears in *Genesis Rabbah* 68:12[24] and in B. Ḥullin 91b. In both of these sources the matter is placed in the context of another well-known motif regarding the enmity or envy of the angels toward human beings.[25] That is, according to the statements in *Genesis Rabbah* and B. Ḥullin, the angels, who beheld Jacob's image above, were jealous and sought to harm Jacob below. The influence of the talmudic reworking of this motif is apparent in several later midrashic sources as well.[26]

The specific background of this image is not entirely clear.[27] Some scholars have suggested that Jacob represents primordial Adam and hence the icon engraved on the throne is to be construed as the universal image of humanity.[28] Other scholars have intimated that the aggadic image of Jacob engraved on the throne is connected with speculation on the demiurgic angel or the Logos as it appears in Philo (one of the standard names for the Philonic Logos is Israel, the firstborn of God[29]) or the fragment of the Jewish apocryphal text, *Prayer of*

Joseph, cited by the church father, Origen.[30] The notion of an angel named Jacob-Israel is also known from Jewish Christian texts, as reported mainly by Justin,[31] and appears as well in Gnostic works such as the Nag Hammadi treatise *On the Origin of the World,*[32] and in Manichean texts.[33] Such a tradition, perhaps through the intermediary of Philo, passed into Christian sources wherein the celestial Jacob or Israel was identified with Jesus who is depicted as the Logos and Son of God.[34] A reference to the demiurgic quality of Jacob may be found in the following comment in *Genesis Rabbah* 98:3 on the verse, "Hearken to Israel your father" (*we-shimʿu ʾel yisraʾel ʾavikhem* [Gen. 49:3]). According to R. Yudan the verse should be recast as "hearken to the God of Israel your father" (*shimʿu le-ʾel yisraʾel ʾavikhem*), but an even more daring reading is proposed by R. Pineḥas: *ʾel huʾ yisraʾel ʾavikhem,* that is, Israel your father is a God, for "just as the Holy One, blessed be He, creates worlds so too your father creates worlds, just as the Holy One, blessed be He, divides the worlds so too your father divides the worlds."[35] The demiurgic role accorded Jacob is highlighted as well in a passage from another midrashic collection: "'But now thus said the Lord—Who created you, O Jacob, Who formed you, O Israel' (Isa. 43:1): R. Pineḥas said in the name of R. Reuben: the Holy One, blessed be He, said to His world, My world, My world, who created you and who formed you? Jacob created you and Israel formed you, as it is written, 'Who created you, O Jacob, Who formed you, O Israel.' "[36] From another passage in *Genesis Rabbah* 78:3 it is clear that the image of Jacob is a divine or at the very least an angelic power. In this context the expression *sarita* in the verse, *ki sarita ʿim ʾelohim,* "for you have striven with divine beings" (Gen. 32:28), is thought to be derived from the word *serarah* (rule, authority or dominion). According to the midrashic reading of the verse, therefore, Jacob is an archon (*sar*) together with God, and thus his image is engraved above on the throne.[37] Simply put, this verse is understood by the anonymous midrashist as imparting information about the apotheosis or divinization of Jacob. Interestingly enough, evidence for such a reading of the verse is found as well in Jerome's commentary on Genesis: "Sarith enim, quod ab Israel vocabulo derivatur, principium sonat. Sensus itaque est: Non vocabitur nomen tuum supplantator, hoc est, Jacob; sed vocabitur nomen tuum princeps cum Deo, hoc est, Israel."[38] Support for my interpretation of the *demut yaʿaqov* motif is found in a passage attributed to R. Joshua ben Naḥman in *Lamentations Rabbah* 2:2, commenting on the verse, *hishlikh mi-shamayim ʾareṣ tifʾeret yisraʾel,* "He cast down from heaven to earth the majesty of Israel" (Lam. 2:1).[39] In that context the image of Jacob engraved on the throne is named on the basis of the verse just cited *tifʾeret yisraʾel* and is compared parabolically to a king's crown (*ʿaṭarah*).[40] This image was transformed, as we shall see, in Eleazar's writings from a literary motif to a theosophic symbol.

Other aggadic passages could be quoted to prove the point that in the rabbinic tradition, especially as expressed in Palestinian amoraic sources, Jacob was treated as a divine or angelic being. Thus, for example, in an aggadic statement attributed to R. Berachiah in the name of R. Simon the name Jeshurun in Deuteronomy 33:26 is interpreted as a reference to *yisraʾel sabbaʾ*, Israel the elder, that is, Jacob, thus prompting a comparison (supported by relevant scriptural texts) of God and Jacob.[41] An even bolder reading of this verse in another midrashic setting emphasizes the angelic or divine status of Israel-Jeshurun: "'There is none like God, O Jeshurun': Israel says, there is none like God, and the Holy Spirit responds, except Jeshurun."[42] As Michael Fishbane has noted, the theologoumenon preserved here in an extraordinary fashion subverts through the voice of the Holy Spirit the standard theological assertion attributed to Moses regarding the utter incomparability of God. In contrast to the seemingly normative claim of Scripture, the midrashic text affirms that there is one who is like God, namely, Jeshurun.[43] The divinization of Israel-Jeshurun is underscored by the semantic ambiguity of the response of the Holy Spirit, *ʾel yeshurun,* which, as Fishbane observed, "may be read either as an ellipsis for *ʾel(ah) yeshurun* ('except Jeshurun'), or as the more daring assertion, *ʾel yeshurun* ('Jerushun is (like) God')."[44] In any event, the underlying theological assumption of this pericope, like the other midrashic statement referred to above, is that Jeshurun represents the angelic Jacob who is comparable to the deity. Along similar lines in another passage we find the following interpretation of Genesis 33:20, "He set up an altar there and called it El-elohe-Yisrael": "He said to Him: You are God in relation to the beings above and I am god in relation to the beings below."[45] It would appear that Jacob is the one who addresses God and thus makes the analogy that just as God is the divine authority above so he is the one who rules below. However, in a baraita in B. Megillah 18a it seems that God is the one who addresses Jacob:

> R. Aḥa said in the name of R. Eleazar: Whence do we know that the Holy One, blessed be He, calls Jacob "god"? As it is written, "He called him El, the God of Israel" (Gen. 33:20). If you suppose that Jacob called the altar by the name "god," then it would have been necessary to read "Jacob called it." Rather it says, "He called him," i.e., Jacob, and who called him? El, the God of Israel.

It is worth noting in passing that a variety of medieval commentators understood the midrashic passage in light of the talmudic one.[46] Although from a scholarly vantage point it is necessary to distinguish between these two sources, there is no doubt that in both of them one can find traces of the older myth regarding the divine or angelic status of Jacob.[47]

A reverberation of this aggadic tradition concerning the angelic status of Jacob is discernible in the *Hekhalot* corpus related to the celestial *ḥayyah* whose name is Israel.[48] The connection between the aggadic tradition regarding the image of Jacob engraved on the throne and the esoteric conception of an angelic creature named Jacob or Israel is evident in the *qerovah* of Yannai to Genesis 28:12,[49] wherein one reads an elaborate description of the angels, who surround the throne, seeing the image of Jacob and sanctifying God who is called the "Holy One of Israel" or the "God of Israel," terms that indicate the special relationship between God and the people who are symbolized by the persona of Jacob.[50] This notion is attested to as well in several midrashic sources of which I will here cite two examples. The first comes from a fragment of *Midrash Yelammedenu*:

> Another explanation, "Behold the angels of God were ascending and descending upon it" (Gen. 28:12). From the day that the Holy One, blessed be He, created the world, the angels were praising the Holy One, blessed be He, saying "Bless the Lord, God of Israel" (Ps. 41:14), but they did not know who was Israel. When Jacob reached Bet-El the angels who accompanied him ascended to heaven and said to the ministering angels, "If you wish to see the man in whose name we bless the name of the Holy One, blessed be He, descend and see that very man." The angels descended and saw his image. They said, "Certainly this is the form (*ṣurah*) and this is the image (*demut*) engraved upon the throne of glory." All of them responded and said, "Bless the Lord, God of Israel."[51]

The second example is from a parallel in *Numbers Rabbah*: "The Holy One, blessed be He, said to Jacob: 'Jacob, you have increased the glory in My eyes for, as it were, I have set your icon on My throne, and in your name the angels praise Me and say, 'Bless the Lord, God of Israel' (Ps. 41:14), 'That which is glorious in My eyes is honorable' (Isa. 43:4)."[52] Yannai has added to the midrashic view the idea that the angels too are called by the names Jacob and Israel. Hence, the image of Jacob simultaneously alludes to the earthly man and the heavenly angel. The same motif can be found in a host of *piyyuṭim,* for example, the poem recited liturgically as the *yoṣer* for Shavuot, *ʾereṣ maṭah we-raʿashah* of Eleazar Qallir,[53] and the *qerovah* for the afternoon service on Yom Kippur, *ʾetan hikkir ʾemunotekha*, by Elijah bar Mordecai.[54]

In this connection it is worthwhile to note that David Halperin has called our attention to an ancient targum to Ezekiel 1:26, preserved in manuscript, that explains the reference to the "semblance of a human form" upon the throne in terms of Jacob's image.[55] That is to say, according to the targumic author, the anthropomorphic glory who sits on the throne is in the image of Jacob. Put differently, the image of Jacob serves as a symbol for the human form of the glory. This notion too is clearly reflected in the *piyyuṭ* literature, for example, the *qerovah* of Qallir that begins with the words, *we-ḥayyot ʾasher henah merubbaʿot kisseʾ*. The *payyeṭan* mentions all the details of the chariot in the appropriate order, following the biblical text, with one striking exception: in lieu of mentioning the image of the human form on the throne, Eleazar writes: *tavnit tam yifen ḥaquqah ba-kisseʾ*.[56] In other words, the aggadic image of Jacob engraved upon the throne replaces the biblical image of the human form seated upon the throne.

A related but somewhat different view is enunciated in a passage from *Pirqe Rabbi ʾEliʿezer*: "The ministering angels ascended and descended upon it and they saw the face of Jacob and said, 'This face is like the face of the creature (*ḥayyah*) that is in the throne of glory."[57] According to this text, then, the image of Jacob refers to the angelic creature that comprises all four creatures who bear the throne. An allusion to this tradition is found in the *Midrash Sekhel Ṭov* of Menaḥem bar Solomon who cites the aforementioned passage from *Genesis Rabbah* describing the icon of Jacob engraved on the throne of glory. However, in his description of the angels ascending to glance upon this icon, he diverges in one significant detail from the received text of the earlier source: "They ascended and saw the fourth creature that was in the throne of glory whose name was like his, i.e., Israel."[58] Echoing this tradition, Judah ben Barzillai makes the following observation in his *Commentary on Sefer Yeṣirah:* "The Holy One, blessed be He, created the face of Jacob by means of a great splendor (*hadar gadol*), and it is explained in the aggadah that the face of Jacob is engraved on the throne. It is explained as well in the dream of Jacob our patriarch, with respect to the matter, 'Behold the angels of God were ascending and descending upon it,' that those [angels] above would descend to see the face of Jacob our patriarch, how it resembled the face of the creature that was under the throne of glory."[59] A slightly different version of this tradition is found in *Midrash ʾOtiyyot de-R. ʿAqivaʾ*: "'And the image of their face was an image of a man' (Ezek.

1:10), this is the image of Jacob engraved on the throne of glory."[60] In this passage the image of Jacob is related to the four creatures who bear the throne described collectively as the image of man. It appears that the words of this midrashic text influenced the eleventh-century exegete Solomon ben Isaac of Troyes (Rashi)[61] who thus described the four creatures in his commentary to Ezekiel 1:5: " 'An image of a man,' this is the image of the countenance (*demut parṣufo*) of Jacob our patriarch." Similarly, in his commentary to the words in B. Ḥullin 91b, "they looked upon his icon above," Rashi wrote: "The human countenance (*parṣuf ʾadam*) that is in the four creatures is in the image of Jacob." The four creatures comprise one form that is described as an image of a human in the appearance of Jacob. The relationship between this image and the glory that sits on the throne, also described as an image of an anthropos, is not sufficiently clear. It is possible, however, that underlying a particular layer of esoteric tradition is the notion that the glory interchanges with the anthropomorphic form that comprises all four creatures.[62]

Confirmation of this possibility is found in the teaching of the German Pietists of the Kalonymide circle. Thus, for example, one reads in the *Hilkhot ha-Merkavah* of Eleazar of Worms, which is part of his comprehensive work, *Sode Razayyaʾ*:

> Thus the prophet must see the throne of glory and upon it an angel, and of necessity the four creatures are one creature. . . . "Each one had four faces, the face of the first had the face of a cherub, the face of the second had the face of a human, the third had the face of a lion, and the fourth the face of an eagle" (Ezek. 10:14). The face of the first was the face of a cherub and the face of the second the face of a human.[63] The word "face" is [repeated] twice (*pene pene*) with respect to the cherub and twice with respect to the face of a human, but with respect to the face of the lion and that of the eagle [the word] "face" (*pene*) is written once, for it is written, "Let us make man in our image and in our likeness. God created man in His image, in the image of God He created him" (Gen 1:26–27). "This is the book of the generations of man on the day that God created man, in the likeness of God He made him," (ibid., 5:1) "for in the image of God He made man" (ibid., 9:6). [The word] *pene* is written four times with respect to the human and the cherub. . . . Thus there are four [occurrences of the word] "likeness" (*demut*) and twice "appearance" (*marʾeh*). . . . Corresponding to them are [the words] "in our image and

> in our likeness" (*be-ṣalmenu ki-demutenu*), "man in His image in the image" (*ha-ʾadam be-ṣalmo be-ṣelem*). Therefore, with respect to the human face and that of the cherub [the word] *pene* [is written] four times. Therefore, Ezekiel and Daniel were called the "son of man" (*ben ʾadam*), i.e., one who knows that you have seen the image of a human (*demut ʾadam*).[64]

It follows that, according to Eleazar, the four creatures of the chariot are but one creature,[65] and the principle image of that creature is that of an anthropos or a cherub—the two are related to the same form.[66] Thus, in another passage Eleazar writes:

> "They had the figures of human beings" (Ezek. 1:5), i.e., the essence of their appearance was that of a human, the cherub of the creatures. "They had the figures of human beings," the most cherished is their beginning, i.e., the cherished image is that of an anthropos. "The figures of human beings," their beginning is an anthropos. "The figures of human beings. However, each had four faces" (ibid., 5–6), their beginning was the head, i.e., the anthropos who was the head and most important amongst them. This is [the meaning of] "in the direction in which one of the heads faced" (ibid., 10:11), that is the cherub.[67]

The principle form of the four creatures, which collectively comprise one entity, is that of an anthropos, also identified as the cherub. Thus, in another work, commenting on the attribution of a human face to the celestial creatures who bear the throne, Eleazar writes that "the essence of their appearance was that of a human who is a cherub."[68] The latter is identified specifically as the singular creature (*ḥayyah*) that comprises all four creatures.[69] It is noteworthy that a view very similar to that of Eleazar is expressed in writings that were composed in the Pietistic circle of the Special Cherub (*ḥug ha-keruv ha-meyuḥad*).[70] In the case of these writings there is no doubt that the form that comprises all four creatures is identified as the cherub who sits upon the throne. I will cite here three examples that illustrate the point. The first is a passage from one of the main texts of this circle, the *Baraita of Joseph ben Uziel*:

> Concerning that which is written, "Then the glory of the Lord left the platform of the House and stopped above the cherubim" (Ezek. 10:18), the glory of the Lord is the cherub, and the cherub is the creatures (*ḥayyot*), "and the glory of the God of Israel was above them, and this is the same

> creature (*ḥayyah*) that I had seen below the God of Israel" (ibid., 19–20). . . . The cherubim, wheels, and all the work of the chariot are called one creature, and this creature is the cherub. Adam was created in its image and likeness, as it says, "and on top, upon this semblance of a throne, there was the semblance of a human form" (ibid., 1:26).[71]

The second example is taken from the *Sod ha-Sodot* of Elḥanan ben Yaqar of London: "The Presence of the Lord moved from the cherub,[72] the creature (*ḥayyah*) is called the cherub, it is the entirety of the chariot, for the whole chariot is one creature (*kol ha-merkavah ḥayyah ʾaḥat*), and there is one life force for all of them, as it says, 'for the spirit of the creatures was in the wheels' (Ezek. 1:20), and all of them are one just as the limbs of a person."[73] The third example is drawn from the *Sefer ha-Qomah*, the commentary on the ancient work, *Shiʿur Qomah*, composed by Moses ben Eleazar ha-Darshan,[74] a work that has obvious affinity to the *keruv ha-meyuḥad* material: "One creature rises above the Seraphim and that creature is the cherub . . . and the Presence has authority over the cherub."[75] From this passage it is evident that an ontic distinction between the divine Presence (*Shekhinah*) and the cherub is upheld, even though the latter is accorded the highest angelic status.[76] However, from other passages in this work the distinction is more ambiguous as the cherub is described in terms that are appropriately predicated of the Presence itself.

> The cherub sits on the throne and it is the image (*demut*) of the Holy One, blessed be He, as long as His shadow is upon him, and this is [the import of] what is said, "in the hands of the prophet I was imaged" (Hosea 12:11). . . . This is the cherub that changes and is seen in all these aspects.[77]

> Concerning the cherub it is said, "Your stately form is like the palm" (Song of Songs 7:8), the a"t ba"sh [of the expression, "like the palm," *damtah le-tamar*] is numerically equal to [the expression] *ha-keruv*.[78] . . . And that which is written, "Great is our Lord and full of strength" (Ps. 147:5), ["full of strength," *we-rav koaḥ*, equals 236 which stands for one of the standard measurements of the Creator in the *Shiʿur Qomah* tradition] and this is the cherub. [The expression] *we-rav koaḥ* has the letters of *keruv*. . . . This cherub is called in the Torah the Lord and the one.[79] Thus one must say that this cherub appeared to the prophets. Having proven that the cherub appeared to the prophets, it must be said that the glory of God is the cherub, as it says,

> "the glory of the Lord [appeared in a cloud]" (Exod. 16:10), i.e., [the word] *nirʾah* ("appeared") is numerically *zeh ha-keruv* ("this is the cherub"),[80] as it says, "It is the glory of God to conceal a matter" (Prov. 25:2), one must conceal it and not reveal it except to the modest.[81]

According to these passages, in marked contrast to the former, the cherub is identified with the Presence or glory, at the very least in its visible aspect upon the throne. Let me mention yet another passage in this work wherein one may discern some effort to harmonize the two positions without, however, completely obliterating the distinction between the angelic cherub and the divine glory: "It is always called a cherub when there is not an abundance of the emanation of the Presence (*hamshakhat ha-shekhinah*) upon it, even though all is one. Therefore, it is called 'king of all kings' (*melekh malkhe ha-melakhim*), for it enthrones kings like the angel of the countenance (*sar ha-panim*), Moses our master, and his disciples, i.e., prophets who were like him, for the Presence rested upon the angel of the countenance and the prophets, and through his influence it enthroned them, but God forbid that the children should be like the father."[82]

In the passages from Eleazar that I have cited above, the image of Jacob was not mentioned at all, but in other places in his writings he does mention this motif explicitly in conjunction with the four creatures who bear the throne. Thus, for example, in his commentary on Ezekiel's chariot he writes:

> "Each of them had a human face" (Ezek. 1:10), this is the face of Jacob. . . . An archon from the supernal archons wrestled with him and Jacob prevailed.[83] . . . Therefore he was placed first in the verse, "Each of them had a human face," *u-demut penehem pene ʾadam*, which is numerically equal to "and they had the image of the face of Jacob," *u-vi-demut pene yaʿaqov hem*.[84] And the final letters [of *u-demut penehem pene ʾadam*] are *tamim* on account of Jacob, the "mild man," *ʾish tam* (Gen. 25:27).[85]

In another work of Eleazar we find the following passage that parallels the one just cited:

> "Each of them had a human face" (Ezek. 1:10), for the man is the most glorious of all countenances since he rules over them all. . . . He created Adam two-faced (*du-parṣufin*) and the male went first. So too the human face, which is the essence, goes first for the human image is the image of Jacob. . . . Therefore it comes first in the verse *u-demut*

> *penehem pene ʾadam*, the final letters are *tamim* on account of Jacob, the "mild man," *ʾish tam*. [The expression] *u-demut penehem pene ʾadam* numerically equals *u-vi-demut pene yaʿaqov hem*.[86]

The appearance of the anthropoid creature that comprised the four celestial creatures of the chariot is that of Jacob. Indeed, the creatures constitute the heavenly Jacob. A brief allusion to this motif is discernible in one of Eleazar's liturgical poems wherein the divine voice proclaims: *gaʾawati le-tifʾarti yisraʾel menashsheq be-ʾorah/ demut pene ʾadam meḥabbeq le-toʾarah*.[87] The word *gaʾawah*, grandeur, reflects more specifically the use of this term in older Jewish esoteric literature where it connotes the luminous form of the enthroned glory.[88] Hence, Eleazar poetically conveys the image of the divine form kissing the illuminated splendor of Israel. *Prima facie*, it may seem that the latter expression simply refers to the mundane community of Israel.[89] From the continuation of the poem, however, it is evident that the "majesty of Israel," *tifʾeret yisraʾel*, is a technical designation of the form (*toʾar*) that has the appearance of a human. In this context, therefore, as in the passage from *Lamentations Rabbah* mentioned above, the biblical expression "majesty of Israel" is transformed into a symbol for the icon of Jacob engraved on the throne.[90] The double image of kissing (*menashsheq*) and hugging (*meḥabbeq*) reflects the particular locution of a passage in *Hekhalot Rabbati*, discussed below, wherein the glory is said to embrace (*megappef*), fondle (*meḥabbeq*), and kiss (*menashsheq*) the visage of Jacob engraved on the throne at the time that Israel below utters the Trisagion (Isa. 6:3) in prayer.[91] Support for my interpretation may be gathered from another passage from Eleazar that is an exegesis of the verse, "I am my beloved's, and his desire is for me" (Song of Songs 7:11): "This is to teach that the desire of the chariot (*maʿaseh merkavah*) is upon the image of Israel (*demut yisraʾel*), and this is what is written 'upon Israel is His grandeur,' *ʿal yisraʾel gaʾawato* (Ps. 68:35)."[92] From the context it is clear that the expression *maʿaseh merkavah* is employed here in a rather unconventional way as a designation of the divine glory that is enthroned upon the chariot;[93] I have therefore rendered it simply as the "chariot" rather than the more literal translation "work of the chariot." It seems, moreover, that the *demut yisraʾel*, the image of Israel towards whom the desire of the glory is directed, is the icon of Jacob engraved on the throne.[94] The erotic passion conveyed in the verse from Song of Songs is alluded to as well in the liturgical refrain, "upon Israel is His grandeur," that is, the grandeur, *gaʾawah*, is synonymous with *maʿaseh merkavah*, the enthroned glory, and Israel is a shortened way of referring to the image of Israel, *demut yisra᾽el,* the iconic representation of Jacob upon the throne that represents the anthropomorphic form of the angelic creatures. In the following section I will deal at much greater length with the meaning of the icon of Jacob in the esoteric teaching of Eleazar and the particular nuance of the aforementioned erotic imagery. Suffice it here to say that, for Eleazar, the four creatures constitute one creature that is in appearance like Jacob and thus may be identified as the iconic form of Jacob engraved on the throne.

The theosophic implications of Eleazar's thought are drawn out and elaborated upon in the commentary on Ezekiel's chariot by Jacob ben Jacob ha-Kohen of Castile, a text whose literary dependence upon the commentary of Eleazar has been well noted in scholarly literature[95]: "The four creatures are one creature that is divided into four, and it is the creature whose name is Israel on account of the face of Jacob engraved in it, for his name was Israel."[96] In another composition, the *Perush ha-᾽Otiyyot,* Jacob alludes to the identification of the image of Jacob and the heavenly creature whose name is Israel: "The name of the one creature that is in the four creatures is Israel and it is in the image of the icon of Jacob, our patriarch, peace be upon him, as it says, 'Your name shall no longer be Jacob, but Israel etc.' (Gen. 32:29)."[97] In another passage from this work the matter is reiterated: "The head of the holy creatures is in the image of the icon of Jacob, our patriarch, peace be upon him, for he was the head of the creatures of the chariot."[98] As will be explained more fully below, the theosophic recasting of the esoteric tradition preserved in the Ashkenazi material entails that the creature whose name is Israel is identified with the image of Jacob, the lower glory in relation to the attribute of *Tif᾽eret,* which is the upper glory. It emerges from the texts of Jacob ha-Kohen that the creature divided into four creatures is the glory that is below in the world of angels corresponding to the divine gradation that is the glory above in the sefirotic pleroma.

The words of Jacob are repeated, albeit in slightly different language, in the *Sefer ha-᾽Orah* of his student, Moses of Burgos: "The four creatures are one creature that is divided into four, and this is the creature whose name is *Tif᾽eret Yisra᾽el* on account of the fact that the face of Jacob, whose name was Israel, is engraved in it."[99] A parallel version to that of Jacob ha-Kohen is also found in an anonymous commentary on the tenth chapter of Ezekiel called *Sod ha-Merkavah ha-Sheniyyah,* that apparently was composed by a participant in the circle of Jacob and Isaac ha-Kohen[100]: "That which he mentioned in the four creatures that he saw in each appearance the form of an anthropos refers to the small countenance (*᾽appe zuṭre*), and this is the icon of

Jacob engraved in the four holy creatures, concerning whom it says, 'How will Jacob survive? He is so small (*qaṭon*)' (Amos 7:2). However, the upper glory (*ha-kavod ha-ʿelyon*) that stands upon the throne, the great majesty (*ha-yaqar ha-gadol*) that is the large countenance (*ʾappe ravreve*), is not seen by the *ḥashmal*, angel, seraph, or even the throne."[101] This passage is based on Eleazar's commentary on the chariot, which is discussed below in more detail. In the theosophic setting of the kabbalistic reworking of the Pietistic work, the image of Jacob, which is the form of the anthropos that comprises the four celestial creatures,[102] is the lower glory that parallels the upper glory or the sixth emanation, *Tifʾeret*. Utilizing the distinction attributed to R. Papa in B. Ḥagigah 13b between the face of the cherub (*pene keruv*) that is the small countenance (*ʾappe zuṭre*) and the face of an anthropos (*pene ʾadam*) that is the large countenance (*ʾappe ravreve*),[103] this author implies that the lower glory is the cherub and the upper glory the human form. The matter is expressed more clearly in a second passage: "Just as in the supernal chariot [i.e., the sefirotic realm] there is the image of the four creatures and the image of Jacob amongst them . . . the large countenance, so this great light passes with increased might at the end of the splendor [*sof zohar*, i.e., the last emanation or the *Shekhinah*] until from that great light and mighty splendor is made the image of the second chariot in the likeness of the four creatures, and He created there the small countenance, the icon of Jacob, the mild man."[104]

It is worthwhile to cite in this context a tradition that appears in one of the recensions of *Sefer ha-ʿIyyun*, the thirteenth-century pseudepigraphic work of mystical contemplation[105]: "Afterwards the Holy One, blessed be He, created an image using the four primal elements,[106] like the image of a real man. These are the four camps of the Divine Presence. They are: Michael, Gabriel, Uriel, and Raphael."[107] In her discussion of this passage, Farber suggested that perhaps there is an identification here of the angelic creatures and the glory or the body of the Presence (*guf ha-shekhinah*) mentioned immediately preceding the aforecited text.[108] An alternative interpretation is offered by Moshe Idel who suggested that in this passage the expression "body of the Presence" refers not to the four angelic camps, but rather to the seven archangels who are also called "soul" (*neshamah*) in relation to God who is the "soul of the soul" (*neshamah la-neshamah*).[109] According to this explanation, the image of the Presence (*demut ha-shekhinah*) is not the glory itself but rather an angelic form in the structure of an anthropos made up of eight angels, the lower seven constituting the body, and the eighth one the head.[110] The relation between the body of the Presence and the image that comprises the four camps is that of the body to the soul as is attested by a version of *Sefer ha-ʿIyyun*, apparently deriving from Moses of Burgos[111]: "The Holy One, blessed be He, created an image in the form of the four elements, for the Presence is in them like a soul and they are in the image of a body, the image of an anthropos, and they are the four camps of the Presence. They are: Michael, Gabriel, Uriel and Raphael."[112] Confirmation of this understanding, as both Farber and Idel noted,[113] can be found in the commentary of Moses of Burgos to the chariot-vision of Ezekiel: "Four camps of angels . . . [they are] spiritual bodies . . . in the image of a spiritual anthropos. . . . The four camps are in the image of spiritual bodies and the [*Shekhinah*] is in the image of a soul within the body."[114] The same viewpoint appears in zoharic literature. Thus, for example, one reads in the following passage:

> These four creatures are contained one within the other for they correspond to the four directions. . . . When they are contained one within the other one body is made from them, and this is the secret that is called Adam. Several different types of [angelic] camps go out from those that are the inner secret in relation to the Point[115] that stands upon them. Adam: male and female. The letter that is the secret of the male is the letter *nun*, the secret of Adam in his perfection, and this letter rules over the Point, which is a *dalet*, above the four creatures. . . . When they looked momentarily it is written, "Each of them had a human face" (Ezek. 1:10), and afterwards the image of each one separated in accordance with its quality. When they all hid so that they would not look above within the secret that was upon them, no image was seen at all except the image of an anthropos, the image that comprises all images.[116]

A similar tradition regarding the four angels in the image of an anthropos is mentioned in the introduction to *Tiqqune Zohar*. However, in that context the anonymous author connects the anthropomorphic image in the angelic world specifically to Meṭaṭron who is described as the body of the Presence[117]:

> The lower Presence . . . her chariot is Meṭaṭron, the body of the Presence. The Presence is [designated by the word] *mah*[118] . . . her chariot is Meṭaṭron. Concerning him it is said, "God's chariots are myriads upon myriads, thousands upon thousands" (Ps. 68:18). What is [the meaning of] "thousands," *shinʾan*? [This is an acrostic for the four creatures] ox (*shor*), eagle (*nesher*), lion (*ʾaryeh*), and human (*ʾadam*).[119] This is the secret of the chariot (*merkavah*), *rekhev mah*[120] precisely.[121]

It is difficult to decide definitively if this matter reached the kabbalists from ancient sources preserving an older form of theosophic speculation according to which Meṭaṭron was identified as the divine chariot inasmuch as he comprised all four living creatures or even represented the enthroned glory itself. In any event, the fact that one stream of tradition connects the image of Jacob with the glory, and a second stream connects that image with the creatures that bear the throne, in my view strengthens the supposition that the kabbalists were elaborating in novel ways upon an ancient tradition concerning the anthropomorphic form of the chariot.

It is important for our discussion to note that, according to the targumic author cited by Halperin, the motif of the image of Jacob is mentioned in the context of the chariot-vision of Ezekiel, whereas in the other sources discussed above it is connected with Jacob's dream-vision of the ladder.[122] Interestingly enough, in one of the major textual units of the corpus of mystical speculation on the chariot, the *Hekhalot* literature, the ladder becomes a clear symbol for the ascent to the chariot. Thus, in a key passage in *Hekhalot Rabbati* we read that the one who is free from the cardinal sins of idolatry, lewdness, bloodshed, slander, false oaths, profanation of the divine name, impudence, and baseless hatred, and who observes all of the ritual proscriptions and prohibitions, is worthy to ascend to the chariot "to gaze upon the King and His glorious throne," and such a person is like "a man who has a ladder in his house."[123] The possibility that the ladder mentioned here is related to the ladder of Jacob is strengthened, in my opinion, by a second passage in *Hekhalot Rabbati* wherein the descent of the angels to the world and their ascent back to heaven is described in terms reminiscent of the image of the angels descending and ascending upon Jacob's ladder.[124] Similarly, in a later text, the *Sefer ha-ʾOrah* of Moses of Burgos, the author cites a passage in the name of his teacher, Jacob ha-Kohen, concerning the throne and the world of the chariot. *Inter alia*, Jacob ha-Kohen describes the angels in terms reflecting the aforementioned text in *Hekhalot Rabbati*: "They ascend upon the ladder of the streams of fire, one with the permission of the other . . . until they reach the hosts of ʿAravot."[125] The connection between the ladder of Jacob and the chariot figures prominently in a tradition that appears in one of the Pietistic compositions that Dan attributed to Judah the Pious[126]:

> There are angels who are not worthy to see the body of the chariot, but sometimes there is an illumination below like the sun that shines by way of a window as a pillar, so there are visions upon the river[127] and the stream. So it was in the case of Jacob, our patriarch, for an opening corresponding

> to the chariot was opened, facing the throne of glory, and there was an illumination of the visions from heaven to earth, referred to as the "ladder that was set on the ground and its top reached to the sky" (Gen. 28:12).[128]

This passage attests that in the circle of Judah the Pious there was a tradition that assumed that the ladder beheld by Jacob referred to an illumination that shone upon him from an opening before the throne of glory. This illumination is described as a ladder connecting heaven and earth, for by means of it Jacob saw what he did in the world of the chariot. There is also an allusion in this passage to a technique known from other Pietistic sources that involved a body of water as a medium of visualization.[129] That is, the illumination cast from above and beheld below is comparable to a vision of something as reflected in a river or stream. Jacob's vision of the chariot was an indirect one. No mention is made here of the image of Jacob engraved on the throne, although it is reasonable to assume that underlying this passage is some such motif; that is, Jacob is granted a vision of the chariot that is described as the ladder set on the ground and whose head reached the heavens. The link that connects heaven and earth is Jacob, for he is in both places insofar as he is below but his image is engraved above. In a passage from Eleazar of Worms' comprehensive compedium of esoteric and mystical secrets, *Sode Razayya*ʾ, cited by Nathan Naṭa ben Solomon Spira in his *Megalleh ʿAmuqot*, one can discern a further development of the aggadic motif such that Jacob is himself the ladder: "From the earth to the throne of glory above there are twenty-two matters . . . and this is what is written, 'he lay down in that place' (Gen. 28:11), read in it [a reference to] twenty-two [*kaf-bet* in the word *wa-yishkav*, he lay down] in that place, from the image of Jacob below to the image of Jacob on the throne, for 'its top reached the sky,' for there were twenty-two steps."[130] Another and earlier example for this development, that indeed may have influenced Eleazar's formulation, may be found in the *Midrash Leqaḥ Ṭov* of Tobias ben Eliezer: "'A ladder was set on the ground,' this refers to Jacob our patriarch himself, 'and its top reached the sky,' for the image of his icon was engraved on the throne of glory."[131]

To review the evidence that has been examined up to this point, in the earliest sources the motif of the icon of Jacob engraved on the throne may have been related to the hypostatization of the Logos. The appropriateness of the persona of Jacob to represent the Logos is due to a merging of two factors: first, this biblical patriarch, the ideal Israel, symbolically and typologically replaces Adam; and, second, the Logos is typically portrayed as the macroanthropos. It is thus entirely plausible that the adamic figure of Jacob should symbolize the Logos. Moreover, in some of the relevant sources I have uncovered another stream of tradition according to which the icon of Jacob is identified as the angelic creature that has the face of a human and comprises all four creatures who bear the throne. It is possible that the celestial image of Jacob is a mythic portrayal of the demiurgic angel who is most commonly referred to as Meṭaṭron in Jewish esoteric sources.[132] In this connection it is of interest to mention a tradition expressed in a later mystical treatise, a commentary on the seventy-two-letter name of God, apparently from the circle of *Sefer ha-Temunah*;[133] the text has been printed in *Sefer Razi ͗el* and is extant in several manuscripts.[134] In one passage reference is made to the "palace of Meṭaṭron" described further as the "pure intellect that overflows to the soul of the innocent, pure, and perfect man."[135] The pure intellect obviously alludes to the Active Intellect that is the supernal anthropos as is explicitly mentioned in another passage from that very text. The identification of Meṭaṭron and the Active Intellect is known from many sources—both philosophical and mystical—written in the High Middle Ages.[136] In the text that I am presently discussing the anonymous author identifies the palace of the intellects, which are angelic beings, and the supernal world. Yet above that world is another realm of existence referred to by the technical rabbinic eschatological term, the world-to-come, which is also identified as the "palace of Jacob, the palace of Meṭaṭron, for the souls of the righteous from the lower world come there. Meṭaṭron is the Active Intellect, and this is the power of Shaddai,[137] everything is one power."[138] From here it may be inferred that Jacob is identified with Meṭaṭron who is the Active Intellect. Even though the author employs standard medieval philosophical terminology, it is reasonable to assume that there is an echo here of an ancient tradition based on the identification of the heavenly Jacob and Meṭaṭron who stands in the position of the Logos or the divine Intellect depicted mythically as the supernal anthropos. In the text under discussion there is no mention of the image of Jacob engraved upon the throne. However, the connection between the image of Jacob and Meṭaṭron is alluded to in a passage that apparently belongs to the older *Hekhalot* literature copied by Aaron ben Yeḥiel in his book, *Qorban ͗Aharon*, from a manuscript of the commentary on liturgical poems by Eliezer ben Nathan of Mainz in the possession of Ephraim Zalman Margaliot.[139] In that passage Meṭaṭron, the angel of the countenance (*sar ha-panim*), is identified as Jacob who is said to be inscribed upon the throne and upon the heart of Meṭaṭron.[140] One of the clearest indications of this tradition is found in the Ashkenazi Pietistic commentary on the names of Meṭaṭron extant in various manuscripts and printed as *Sefer ha-Ḥesheq* in Lemberg in 1865.[141] Commenting on one of the names of Meṭaṭron, the anonymous Pietist writes: "חסידה is numerically equal to 'upon the throne' (בכסא, i.e., both expressions = 83), for he [Meṭaṭron] is engraved above on the throne of glory."[142] While the aggadic notion of Jacob's image engraved upon the throne is not mentioned here, it is obvious that precisely this theme has been appropriated by the author of this text and applied to Meṭaṭron. It is likely that such an appropriation was made possible by the fact that in the older merkavah sources, the name Israel is associated with Meṭaṭron, specifically his crown.[143]

In my opinion, an echo of this tradition is reflected as well in the writings of Abraham ibn Ezra when he mentions the aggadic motif of the image of Jacob engraved upon the throne. Thus, for example, in one place in his commentary on the Torah he writes: "The explanation of '[He fixed the boundaries of peoples] in relation to Israel's numbers' (Deut. 32:8): the sages, blessed be their memory, said that the form of Jacob, our patriarch, is engraved on the throne of glory, and this is a great secret. The attestation to this is 'For the Lord's portion is His people' (ibid., 9), this is the great level that 'He did not do for any other nation' (Ps. 147:20)."[144] Ibn Ezra notes that there is a great secret in the words of the sages, but he does not explain the content of the secret. The key to the allusion is the matter of the throne upon which the image is engraved. In the writings of ibn Ezra the term "throne" has at least two significations: it refers either to the world of the heavenly spheres in general[145] or to the tenth sphere in particular.[146] It appears to me that in the context of the aforecited passage the throne alludes to the tenth sphere.[147] If this supposition is correct, then it follows that the image of Jacob engraved upon the throne should be identified as the first intellect that comprises within itself the intelligible world. Moreover, as I have argued elsewhere, in the philosophical thought of ibn Ezra, the first intellect in the chain of being is Meṭaṭron, also called *yoṣer bereʾshit*, the demiurge.[148] Thus, the secret to which ibn Ezra alludes is the identification of the image of Jacob with Meṭaṭron who is the form of the intellect that stands above the tenth sphere. Whereas the governance of every nation depends upon the stars and zodiacal signs, the providence of Israel depends solely upon the very image that is the first intellect, the macroanthropos in whose image the microanthropos (represented ideally by Israel) is created.[149]

Further evidence for the identification of the image of Jacob as Meṭaṭron can be found in the literary corpus of Abraham Abulafia. Thus, for example, let us consider the following passage in the latter's *ʾOr ha-Sekhel*:

> The secret of "And [the angel of God] moved" (Exod. 14:19), he is the end even though he is the beginning. The secret is that he is the end of the angels, but he is still the beginning. He alone is the angel (*malʾakh*) who is called by the name of God (*ha-ʾelohim*). This is the secret of the "jealous God" (*ʾel qannaʾ*) and he comprises the seven *sefirot* of the name (*zayyin sefirot ha-shem*). Therefore, the image of Jacob engraved on the throne of glory comprises the seven *sefirot*. This is a great secret and from it you can understand the secret of the warp and you can discern in it as well its opposite.[150] Thus the secret of Jacob (*yaʿaqov*) is "my heel" (*ʿaqevi*),[151] and the secret of Israel (*yisraʾel*) is "to my head" (*le-roʾshi*).[152]

My intention here is not to analyze this passage in all of its complex details, but only to emphasize the most important issues related to the figure of Meṭaṭron. Without doubt the main topic in this text is Meṭaṭron who is referred to as the only angel to be called Elohim. Through a series of numerical equations various terms and concepts are linked in a continuous chain. The word *malʾakh* has the same numerical value as *ha-ʾelohim*, both equal 91, and together they make up the sum 182, which is the respective value of the expressions *ʾel qannaʾ*, *yaʿaqov*, and seven times the four-letter name YHWH (i.e., 7 x 26) conveyed in the expression *zayyin sefirot ha-shem*. In the ontological scheme of Abulafia, based on Maimonides, Meṭaṭron is the Active Intellect or the last of the ten separate intellects.[153] On the other hand, Meṭaṭron is also described as the first of the created entities outside the divine.[154] Abulafia alludes to this dual status of Meṭaṭron in his comment that the angel of God "is the end of the angels, but he is still the beginning." The two aspects of Meṭaṭron are alluded to as well in the names Israel and Jacob; the secret of the former is conveyed in the transposition of the consonants *yisraʾel* to form the word *le-roʾshi*, "to my head,"[155] and the latter in the letters *yaʿaqov* that are transposed into *ʿaqevi*, "my heel."[156] The aspect of Meṭaṭron as the first is conveyed in the physical image of the head, and as the last, in the image of the heel. (As shall be noted in the following section, the precise symbolism is discernible in the theosophic speculation of Eleazar of Worms.) Just as Israel and Jacob are two names for one and the same person, so too the two aspects are unified in the one angelic personality. Meṭaṭron is described, therefore, as possessing opposite qualities, the first and last, beginning and end, which parallels the description of the two functions of Meṭaṭron in other passages in Abulafia by use of the terms *naʿar* and *zaqen*; that is, this angel is the *na ᶜar*, the youngest of the angels in the sense of being last in the ontic chain, as well as the *zaqen*, the oldest or the first in that chain.[157] The passage that I have cited above illustrates that the aggadic motif of the image of Jacob engraved upon the throne is clearly transferred in Abulafia to Meṭaṭron.[158] It is worthwhile to note that in a list of seventy-two intelligible powers (*koḥot sikhliyyim*) that appears in the introduction to the collection of Jacob ha-Kohen's teachings, *Sefer ha-ᵓOrah*,[159] the fifth power is described as the

> pure intellect[160] that is the form fixed on the throne of glory, and Jacob, peace be upon him, comprehended its knowledge, and he was constantly conjoined to that attribute, to the point that he and it became one thing.[161] His image was like his image above, and from the abundance of His love the Holy One, blessed be He, called him a god in the lower entities[162] for it was done according to his will, as it says, "He called him El-elohe-yisrael" (Gen. 33:20).[163] Thus you will find that his name has the computation of the explicit name [YHWH] which is 186. How is this so? Jacob is numerically 182, and when you join together to it the four letters of His name, YHWH, this name adds up to 186. You find that numerically it is [like the word] *maqom* [literally "place" but also a designation for God] that is 186.[164]

There is no reason to assume that in this passage the pure intellect is identified as Meṭaṭron or the first intellect. On the contrary, Meṭaṭron is enumerated as a separate power, the second in the list, and to him is attributed the designation "fixed intellect" (*sekhel qavuᶜa*), reflecting the technical terminology of the Iyyun circle.[165] It appears, therefore, that preserved here is another tradition that assumed that the form fixed on the throne of glory represented one of the powers in the intelligible world but not Meṭaṭron. It is interesting to note that in other places in this anthology of esoteric teachings the pure intellect is described by Jacob ha-Kohen himself in terms that are very close to the description of Meṭaṭron. I will emphasize in particular the correlation between Jacob and the Tetragrammaton that relates specifically to the immanence of the divine in the world. The numerical value of Jacob is 182, to which must be added 4, representing the 4 letters of the name, to get a sum of 186. This figure is the numerical value of the word *maqom*, "place," one of the traditional designations of God, and it is alluded to as well in the Tetragrammaton when the numerical value of each of the letters is squared: $10 \times 10 + 5 \times 5 + 6 \times 6 + 5 \times 5 = 100 + 25 + 36 + 25 = 186$. It is noteworthy that in *Sefer ha-ᶜIyyun* one finds the same numerological connection between the word *maqom* and the squaring of each letter of the Tetragrammaton, but in that context the matter is linked specifically to Meṭaṭron:

> All of this is an allusion to acknowledging the sovereignty of the Holy One, blessed be He, over all of His powers. The start is with Meṭaṭron. . . . Concerning this it was said, "Blessed is the glory of God from His place" (Ezek. 3:13). He is the domain (*maqom*) of the world, but the world is not His domain.[166] Moreover, the numerical value of *maqom* is 186, and the Tetragrammaton is also 186. How so? *Yod* is numerically ten, and when you calculate ten times ten, it is one hundred. *Heh* is numerically five, and when you calculate five times five, it is twenty-five. *Vav* is numerically six, and when you calculate six times six, it is thirty-six. The final *heh* of the Name yields a sum of twenty-five. Accordingly, you shall find that the Name yields a sum of 186. This is the calculation which has been completely squared, when you calculate the numerical value of each individual letter and word in a correct computation.[167]

The source for this numerology is the literature of the German Pietists where the matter too is connected with the immanence of the divine in the world. Thus, for example, Eleazar of Worms writes in his *Sefer ha-Ḥokhmah*: "Thus, when the Tetragrammaton is squared, i.e., ten times ten, five times five, six times six, and five times five, it equals the numerical value of *maqom*, for He is the place of the world."[168] It is not a coincidence that the use of the same numerology appears in a similar context in the *Sefer ha-ᶜIyyun* and in the introduction to Jacob ha-Kohen's *Sefer ha-ᵓOrah*. Even though in the latter case the name of Meṭaṭron is not mentioned explicitly, it is reasonable to assume that here too such a tradition is implicit. Perhaps related to this nexus of ideas is the fact that the image of Jacob fulfills one of the roles assigned to Meṭaṭron in the older sources.

My conjecture is confirmed by additional textual evidence. In several places in the writings of Jacob ha-Kohen, the creature named "Israel" is identified as the image of Jacob engraved upon the throne.[169] I have already alluded to this matter above, and here I will cite some further illustrations. Thus, for example, in his commentary on Ezekiel's vision of the chariot he writes:

> The face of a human [in the creatures] is the glory of Jacob called the creature whose name is Israel, and he is called

> the back of God, blessed be He . . . Moses was able to see the glory below the supernal glory for it is the back [of God] and it is the face of Jacob engraved in the four creatures. . . . Now, my son, consider [the expression] "you will see My back," *we-ra'ita 'et 'aḥorai* (Exod. 33:23), there are eleven letters whose numerical value is that [of the expression] "with the image of Jacob that is engraved on the throne," *bi-demut ya'aqov she-ḥaquq ba-kisse'*,[170] which consists of nineteen letters.[171]

Jacob ha-Kohen distinguishes between two glories—in the passage before the one that I cited, he employs the well-known expression used by Nathan ben Yeḥiel of Rome in his talmudic lexicon, *Sefer he-'Arukh*, the "glory above the glory"[172]—the great glory that consists of the face of God that Moses did not see, and the lower glory that is the hinder part of God that is seen through prophetic vision. The words of Jacob ha-Kohen are based on those of Eleazar of Worms in his own commentary on Ezekiel's vision of the chariot as will be seen in more detail in the following section. However, the Castilian kabbalist has clothed the words of Eleazar of Worms in the technical language of the theosophic doctrine of the *sefirot*: the upper glory is identified as *Tif'eret*, the sixth of ten emanations; and corresponding to him in the world of the chariot beneath the divine realm is the lower glory that is symbolized as the image of Jacob. Thus he writes in the continuation of this discussion:

> Just as the Holy One, blessed be He, brought forth for His supernal glory, which is close to Him, nine appearances that are nine gradations, for the glory is the median line called His Majesty (*tif'arto*), and the nine gradations are *Keter, Ḥokhmah, Binah, Ḥesed, Gevurah, Neṣaḥ, Hod, Ṣaddiq,* and *'Aṭarah* . . . so too He brought forth for the glory that is beneath Him, that is the Majesty of Israel (*Tif'eret Yisra'el*), nine appearances that are the nine images of the creatures that are fixed in the nine spheres, and these Ezekiel saw. Thus, these are alluded to in the final letters of the words *mar'ot 'elohim* (visions of God), [*taw* and *mem* that spell] *tam* [a reference to Jacob on the basis of Gen. 25:27], for these are the nine images that are found in relation to the glory of Jacob, the mild man that is engraved upon the chariot, who is called the glory that stands beneath the supernal glory.[173]

The point is reiterated in another section of the same text:

> Know, my son, that the upper glory that is called the middle line is that which is called *Tif'eret Yisra'el*, and the image

> of Jacob engraved in the holy creatures is the glory that is below the upper glory, and it is likewise called *Tif᾿eret Yisra᾿el*. . . . This is to teach that there is a glory above the glory. Since the face of the anthropos is that of Jacob who is engraved upon the throne, thus you find the word Adam repeated twice, once in the last letters of the words, "O throne of glory exalted [from of old]," *kisse᾿ khavod marom* (Jer. 17:12) and once in the last letters of the words "granting them seats of honor," *we-khisse᾿ khavod yanḥilem* (1 Sam. 2:8).[174]

It may be concluded from these passages that the angelic creature named Israel is the image of Jacob, also named *Tif᾿eret Yisra᾿el,* for it is the lower glory that corresponds to the upper glory, that is, the sixth emanation likewise called *Tif᾿eret Yisra᾿el.* Furthermore, according to Jacob ha-Kohen, this creature is described in language that is used in ancient Jewish esoteric sources to describe Meṭaṭron.[175] One may infer, therefore, that there is a blurring of boundaries separating Meṭaṭron and the creature that is named Israel. To put the matter in somewhat different terms, the name Israel is an appropriate designation for Jacob, and thus the image of Jacob is applied to Meṭaṭron and/or the celestial creature.

In all the sources that I have discussed up to this point there is no explicit mention of the gender of the icon of Jacob, but it stands to reason that it is masculine like the figure below, of which it is an image. This would concur, moreover, with other images associated with the demiurgic Logos that are decidedly masculine in character. There is, however, one text in *Hekhalot Rabbati,* to which I made a passing reference above, wherein it appears that the image of Jacob assumes a feminine characterization. The relevant passage relates in graphic terms the drama that unfolds before the throne at the moment that the Jewish people utter the Trisagion below. The mystics are implored to narrate what they have seen:

> Bear witness to them[176]
> of the testimony you see in Me
> regarding what I do to the visage of Jacob, your father,
> which[177] is engraved[178] upon My throne of glory,
> for when you say before Me, "Holy,"
> I bend down over it,[179] embrace it, fondle it, and kiss it,
> and My hands are on its arms,[180]
> thrice daily,
> for you say before Me "Holy,"
> as it says, "Holy, holy, holy."[181]

There is no question that in the above text the image of Jacob, or more precisely the visage (*qelaster panav*) of Jacob, is described vis-à-vis the divine king who sits upon the throne in terms befitting a feminine persona.[182] It is possible that the visage of Jacob is here feminized on account of the throne, which is described in this literature in feminine terms.[183] However, it is also possible to explain the feminine characterization in another way: if we assume that the image of Jacob symbolizes the ecclesia of Israel, and we assume further that the latter is feminine, then it follows that the image above is feminine.[184] This reconstruction fits well with the thematic context of the passage in *Hekhalot Rabbati*: when Israel utters the Trisagion below, God descends from His throne to embrace, fondle, and kiss the visage of Jacob. However, it is possible that even in this passage the face of Jacob symbolizes the heavenly or ideal Adamic figure without any connection to the feminization of the ecclesia of Israel. If this is the case, then the feminine language used in describing the image must be construed as a metaphorical expression of God's love for Israel, but it does not signify a dynamic in the divine world between the masculine king and the feminine form engraved on the throne.[185] The utilization of gender imagery in a metaphorical context is not uncommon in aggadic and midrashic sources; referring to a specific reality as male or female does not necessarily imply a hypostatic orientation. Thus, for example, the influence of the text from *Hekhalot Rabbati* is apparent in a passage from *Midrash ʾOtiyyot de-R. ʿAqivaʾ* (version B), but in that context the image of Jacob should be described precisely as a male potency:

> *HLQ* refers to Jacob who is called smooth-skinned (*ḥalaq*) . . . and He engraved his image upon His throne of glory.[186] When his descendants recite the Trisagion the Holy One, blessed be He, lowers His mouth from above and kisses him on his head that is engraved on the throne of glory, as it says, "For the Lord has chosen Jacob for Himself" (Ps. 135:4). Whence do we know that Jacob is called smooth-skinned (*ḥalaq*)? As it says, "and I am smooth-skinned" (Gen. 27:11). "For the Lord's portion (*ḥeleq*) is his people, Jacob His own allotment" (Deut. 32:9).[187]

In this redactional setting, it does not seem that the decisively feminine aspect of the original image in *Hekhalot Rabbati* is an essential element. On the contrary, I would suggest that the issue of the feminine gender is effectively neutralized here for it is clearly the masculine character of the icon of Jacob that is stressed. Indeed, the homoeroticism reaches a fervent pitch in this text insofar as the decidedly male nature both of God and of the image of Jacob is underscored. Further proof of my contention can be found in an anonymous text, based on the aforecited words of *Midrash ʾOtiyyot de-R. ʿAqivaʾ*, which reflects in my opinion the ambivalent relationship regarding the gender of the image of Jacob engraved upon the throne:

> *HLQ*: do not read *hlq* but rather *ḥlq*, this is Jacob, our patriarch, who is called smooth-skinned (*ḥalaq*), for in him the name of the Holy One, blessed be He, is renewed. The Holy One, blessed be He, engraved his image on the throne of glory, and when Israel recite the Trisagion the Holy One, blessed be He, lowers His face above and kisses the mouth of Jacob and his image that is on the throne, as it says, "For the Lord has chosen Jacob for Himself" (Ps. 135:4).[188]

Even though the images in *Hekhalot Rabbati* are unquestionably erotic, the authors of the two texts cited above understood the relevant passage as an allusion to God's relationship to Jacob's image, which is clearly male. The eroticism, therefore, is set within the framework of a relationship between two masculine personalities. As will be seen shortly, the image of Jacob receives a definite feminine character in the esoteric theosophy of the German Pietists, especially as it is formulated in the writings of Eleazar of Worms. In great measure, this development is based on the passage from *Hekhalot Rabbati* that I have been discussing. The distinctive quality of Eleazar's usage is highlighted by a comparison of his works with kabbalistic literature from roughly the same period. By the mid-thirteenth century or so the image of Jacob becomes a standard symbol for the masculine potency in the sefirotic realm, either the sixth gradation, *Tifʾeret*, or the ninth, *Yesod*, although there are occasional references in the pertinent sources that indicate that Jacob was employed specifically as a symbol for the feminine potency, the divine Presence.[189] An exception to the established framework can be found in the following comment of Judah ben Yaqar on the words *moṣiʾ ḥamah mimeqomah u-levanah mimekhon shivtah* ("He brings forth the sun from its place and the moon from its dwelling") in the standard morning liturgy for Sabbath, *ha-kol yodukha we-ha-kol yeshabbeḥukha*:

> It says "its place" (*meqomah*) by the sun and "its dwelling" (*mekhon shivtah*) by the moon to allude to the fact that the nations count [days and months] according to the sun . . . but Israel count according to the moon for the image of Jacob is engraved in it.[190] Even though we have not found in the aggadah that his name or form is engraved in the moon,

> still it must be said that the moon is called *ma᾿or qaṭan* (the "lesser light"),[191] and on account of her name the verse says, "How will Jacob survive? He is so small," *mi yaqum ya῾aqov ki qaṭon hu᾿* (Amos 7:2, 5).[192] It says in the *Hekhalot*[193] that there is a creature whose name is Israel and engraved upon its forehead is Israel, and it stands in the middle of the firmament, and it says, "Bless the Lord who is blessed." All the archons above respond after it, "Bless the Lord who is blessed forever." Each and every one of the angels, hosts, and all the camps utters to this creature while standing, "Hear, O Israel, the Lord our God, the Lord is one."[194] Therefore, it is explained that the creature, whose name is Israel and upon whose forehead is inscribed Israel, sees the moon upon which is engraved the image of Jacob. She is called small (*qaṭan*) on account of Jacob who is Israel, and the moon draws the name Jacob to her and unites with it, and the moon sits next to the creature. This is [the meaning of the expression] "its dwelling" (*mekhon shivtah*). Similarly, it is written there,[195] "what I do to the visage of Jacob, your father, which is engraved upon the throne of glory, for when you say before the Holy One, blessed be He, "Holy, holy, holy," I bend down over it, embrace it, fondle it, and kiss it, and My hands are on My arms." All this is by way of parable and secret (*derekh mashal we-sod*).[196]

It is reasonable to assume that Judah ben Yaqar was influenced directly by German Pietistic traditions or a shared source that expanded upon the relevant *Hekhalot* passages[197]: in the teaching of Judah ben Yaqar, as in the case of Eleazar of Worms as will be seen below, the image of Jacob is a feminine form that is engraved upon the moon and upon the throne of glory. The change in symbolism began in the thirteenth-century kabbalistic sources, and a striking example of this phenomenon is Naḥmanides, a student of Judah ben Yaqar. In the teaching of Naḥmanides, as it is explicated by several of the commentators on the secrets contained in his Torah commentary, the image of Jacob symbolizes the masculine potency in the sefirotic pleroma, either *Tif᾿eret* or *Yesod.*[198] It is no suprise, therefore, that in the writings of the Ashkenazi sages who were influenced by the Provençal-Spanish theosophic kabbalah, for example, Shem Ṭov ben Simḥah ha-Kohen[199] and Abraham of Cologne,[200] the image of Jacob was interpreted as a symbol for *Tif᾿eret* or *Yesod,* masculine potencies of the divine. Hence, in Jewish esoteric literature of the thirteenth century there were at least two ways to explain the aggadic motif of the image of Jacob:

either as the ideal male as was prevalent in the theosophic kabbalah or as a feminine potency as it appeared in the esoteric teaching of the German Pietists, an echo of which is heard as well in some kabbalistic sources. Despite the difference between the approach of the German Pietists, especially Eleazar of Worms, in relation to the image of Jacob and the dominant kabbalistic interpretation, I contend that a careful examination of the signification of that image in the Ashkenazi material demonstrates that the theosophy of the latter exhibits a striking conceptual kinship to kabbalistic myth and symbolism.

III

From a detailed investigation of the use of this motif in the German Pietistic literature from the main circle of Judah the Pious, and especially in the works of Eleazar of Worms, the possibility arises that already in the Ashkenazi doctrine of the glory there appears a pronounced theosophic position that describes the glory in masculine and feminine terms. The dynamic in the divine realm between the two glories—male and female—is quite close to the bisexual theology expressed in the theosophic kabbalah. What is most suprising is that this closeness is not simply phenomenological, but it is terminological as well. That is, Eleazar of Worms at times describes the relationship between the two glories in the very terms and expressions utilized by the kabbalists.

Before turning to a detailed textual analysis to substantiate my hypothesis, it is in order to pose the question, Was the image of Jacob employed as a technical designation of a divine hypostasis in the early theosophic writings of German Pietistic provenance that served as the sources for Eleazar's teachings, including those texts that Dan has attributed to Judah the Pious himself? As far as I am able to discern, it can be assumed that in these texts the image of Jacob does symbolize a distinct power in the throne world. Thus, for example, we read in a passage from a text entitled *Sefer ha-Kavod*, although, as Dan has noted,[201] this is not to be identified with the text by the same name composed by Judah the Pious and cited by other authors: "The spirit of Jacob was created on the fifth day, for on the fifth day [Ps. 81 is uttered which includes the verse] 'Raise a shout for the God of Jacob,' and his form (*to*ʾ*aro*) is engraved on the throne of glory."[202] From this text it is difficult to ascertain if the image of Jacob engraved upon the throne is to be identified with the glory itself. It will be noted, however, that in another passage from this text it appears that the name Jacob when written in the plene form (*yod-*ʿ*ayin-qof-waw-bet*), and not the image of Jacob, symbolizes the glory in a state of aggrandizement and multiplicity:

> "Not like these is the Portion of Jacob, for it is He who formed all things" (Jer. 51:19).... *Ya*ʿ*aqov* is written in the plene form with a *waw*, for they say six words, *Shema*ʿ *yisra*ʾ*el yhwh* ʾ*elohenu yhwh* ʾ*eḥad* ["Hear, O Israel! The Lord is our God, the Lord is One"] (Deut. 6:4), and corresponding to them *barukh shem kevod malkhuto le-*ʿ*olam va*ʿ*ed* ["Blessed is the name of His glorious kingdom forever"] and corresponding to them *yhwh hu*ʾ *ha-*ʾ*elohim yhwh hu*ʾ *ha-*ʾ*elohim* ["The Lord alone is God, the Lord alone is God"] (1 Kings 18:39). Know that they said six words, for it is written, "[Then Elijah took twelve stones] corresponding to the number of the tribes of the sons of Jacob—to whom the word of the Lord has come: Israel shall be your name" (ibid., 31). *Shema*ʿ *yisra*ʿ*el yhwh* ʾ*elohenu yhwh* ʾ*eḥad* and corresponding to it is the plene form [of Jacob] with a *waw*. Moreover, the *Shema*ʿ is recited during the day in proximity to [the blessing] *yoṣer* ʾ*or u-vore*ʾ *ha-kol*, and it is recited at night in proximity to [the blessing] *ma*ʿ*ariv* ʿ*aravim*. Therefore, the plene form is used in the case of *yoṣer ha-kol, ya*ʿ*aqov*, and *yoṣer* ʾ*or u-vore*ʾ *ha-kol.*[203]

It is likely that in this passage there is a trace of an older tradition regarding Jacob or Israel as the divine power called the demiurge (*yoṣer bere*ʾ*shit*). This matter is alluded to in the words from the opening verse of the citation, "the Portion of Jacob, for it is He who formed all things," *ḥeleq ya*ʿ*aqov ki yoṣer ha-kol hu*ʾ (Jer. 51:19), as well as in the liturgical formulation based on Isaiah 45:7, "He who forms light and creates all," *yoṣer* ʾ*or u-vore*ʾ ʾ*et ha-kol.* It seems to me, moreover, that the demiurge is here identified with the *kavod;* this is alluded to in the prayer, "Blessed is the name of His glorious kingdom forever," *barukh shem kevod malkhuto le-*ʿ*olam va*ʿ*ed.* In this passage there is also an allusion to the containment of two attributes within the demiurge or the *kavod.* This is alluded to in the name Jacob when it is written in the plene form, *yod-*ʿ*ayin-qof-waw-bet,* that is, Jacob plus the extra letter *waw.*[204] Jacob receives this addition by means of the recitation of the three specified liturgical expressions, for in each of these there are six words: (a) *Shema*ʿ *yisra*ʾ*el yhwh* ʾ*elohenu yhwh* ʾ*eḥad,* (b) *barukh shem kevod malkhuto le-*ʿ*olam va*ʿ*ed,* and (c) *yhwh hu*ʾ *ha-*ʾ*elohim yhwh hu*ʾ *ha-*ʾ*elohim.* Moreover, the sum of the words of the *Shema*ʿ and the *barukh shem* equal twelve, which corresponds to twelve celestial tribes, that is, the angels that surround the glory,[205] alluded to in the image that appears in the verse from 1 Kings 18:31 concerning the "tribes of the sons of Jacob" (Jacob= Israel= the glory). On the other hand, the last liturgical expression, *yhwh hu᾿ ha-᾿elohim*, signifies the unity of the two names of God that symbolize the attributes of mercy and judgment within the glory. According to this text, therefore, the form of Jacob written with a *waw* alludes to the *kavod* that is surrounded by twelve angelic beings and comprises within itself the unity of the two names or two attributes. There is no explicit indication in this text that Jacob is a feminine hypostasis nor is there a hint of an upper glory that influences the lower glory. Nevertheless, there are obvious allusions in this passage that Jacob is the glory that in its state of fullness comprises the two names, YHWH and Elohim, which correspond to the two divine attributes. As will be seen below, in another passage from this same composition, the "glory of the God of Israel" (*kevod ᾿elohe yisra᾿el*) is described in similar terms. Furthermore, many of the views of Eleazar that I shall mention are clearly based on passages in these texts still largely buried in manuscript.

Let me now turn to the development of this motif in the writings of Eleazar of Worms. I will begin with a passage that is found in the pseudo-Hai commentary on the forty-two-letter name of God included in Eleazar's *Sefer ha-Ḥokhmah*[206]: "*PZQ* is numerically equal to *yofi nikhbad* ('glorious beauty') as well as the numerology of *ʿal kiss᾿o* ('upon His throne')[207] as well as *ʿal levanah* ('upon the moon') for He sits upon His throne and the beauty of His Presence (*yofi shekhinato*) illuminates the image of Jacob that is engraved on His throne in the image of the moon."[208] Two aggadic traditions are combined here—one concerning the image of Jacob engraved on the throne, and the other concerning that image engraved in the moon.[209] The word *PZQ*, one of the combinations of the forty-two-letter name of God, is numerically equal to the expression *yofi ha-nikhbad* ("glorious beauty"), that is, 187, which is also the numerical equivalent of the expressions *ʿal kiss᾿o*, "upon His throne" and *ʿal levanah*, "upon the moon." The use of the term *yofi* here resembles the technical connotation of that term in the *Hekhalot* literature, and hence its signification is the luminous beauty of the enthroned form of the Presence.[210] The latter two expressions, *ʿal kiss᾿o* and *ʿal levanah*, convey the notion that the luminous splendor of the *Shekhinah*—the glorious beauty—shines upon the image of Jacob that is said to be engraved either upon the throne or upon the moon. According to this text, the image of Jacob is ontically below the *Shekhinah* that shines upon it, but it is not clear to what potency, attribute, or gradation this image is related. In a second passage from this composition there is a reference to the image of Jacob based on the relevant passages in *Hekhalot Rabbati*[211]:

> When Israel say the *qedushah* and the *shema ͑ yisra ͗el* each day, He says to the ministering angels: See how Israel sanctify, enthrone and unify Me. Immediately He hugs and kisses (*meḥabbeq u-menashsheq*) the face of Jacob engraved upon the throne of glory as we have found in the "Book of the Palaces" (*sefer hekhalot*) and in the "Book of the Glory" (*sefer ha-kavod*) where He says each day when the [time of the] morning and afternoon services arrives, "Blessed are you to Me, those who enter before the chariot (*yorde merkavah*)[212] (you have made Me one unit in the world as it says, "Who is like You, O Lord, among the celestials" [Exod. 15:11], blessed are you to Me, those who enter before the chariot; until here is the *Sefer Yirqaḥ*[213]) if you tell My children what I do to Jacob, your patriarch, when they lift their eyes heavenward and utter the Trisagion.[214]

In order to enter into the depth of the symbolism of the image of Jacob in the thought of Eleazar of Worms, it is necessary to examine carefully additional passages of his own writings in which he mentions and elaborates upon this matter. I will begin with a passage from Eleazar's commentary on Ezekiel's chariot that will be cited according to two manuscript witnesses:

> We have known that the human being is the most glorious of the creatures, and the head is the most glorious of all. Thus it is above with respect to the image of Jacob, the chosen of God, and he is engraved upon the throne of glory. "[The Lord] has cast down from heaven to earth the majesty of Israel" (Lam. 2:1). And it is written, "[You are My servant] Israel in whom I glory" (Isa. 49:3). Jacob is called small (*qaṭan*), for the cherubim have small faces (*͗appe zuṭre*) . . . and the face of Jacob is engraved on the throne. Thus the last letters [of the expression] "O throne of glory, exalted," *kisse͗ khavod marom* (Jer. 17:12) are *͗adam*, as well as [the last letters of] "granting them seats of honor," *we-khisse͗ khavod yanḥilem* (1 Sam 2:8). Since he is unique the image of man precedes all the countenances, as it is written, "For the Lord has chosen Jacob for Himself" (Ps. 135:4), and it is written, "Jacob His own allotment" (Deut. 32:9). It is written, "You will see My back," *we-ra͗ita ͗et ͗aḥorai* (Exod. 33:23)—that is numerically equivalent to [the expression] "like the image of Jacob that is engraved on the throne," *ki-demut ya͑aqov ḥaquqah ba-kisse͗*[215]. . . . It is written that Jacob said, "Am I (*͗anokhi*) under God?" (Gen. 30:2), [the

word ʾanokhi] is numerically equivalent to *kisse*ʾ (throne). Thus, Jacob receives the splendor when the prayer rises upward. It is written, "And they saw the God of Israel" (Exod. 24:10), it should be read as "Israel under His feet."[216]

It is known that the human being is the most glorious of the creatures, and the head of a human is the most glorious of all the limbs, and so it is above. This head is in the image of Jacob, our patriarch, may peace be upon him, who is engraved upon the throne of glory. Concerning him it is said, "[The Lord] has cast down from heaven to earth the majesty of Israel" (Lam. 2:1), "[You are My servant] Israel in whom I glory" (Isa. 49:3). Therefore, it says in Song of Songs, "His left hand was under my head" (2:6), transpose [the letters of *le-ro*ʾ*shi*, "my head"] and read *yisra*ʾ*el* [Israel].[217] Therefore, the diadem of the glory is called Israel . . . for it is made from the praise of Israel and ascends to the throne of glory. . . . "And the Lord was standing above him" (Gen. 28:13), as upon the throne above. Thus [it is written], "He mounted a cherub" (2 Sam. 22:11; Ps. 18:11). And it is written, "[Moses] would hear the Voice addressing him from [above the cover that was on top of the Ark of the Pact] between the two cherubim" (Num. 7:89). Jacob is called small (*qaṭan*), and similarly the cherubim have small faces (ʾ*appe zuṭre*). . . . Since the human countenance is that of Jacob engraved on the throne, thus you find the word ʾ*adam* in the last letters [of the expression] "O throne of glory, exalted," *kisse*ʾ *khavod marom* (Jer. 17:12), as well as in the last [letters of] "granting them seats of honor," *we-khisse*ʾ *khavod yanḥilem* (1 Sam 2:8). Concerning them He said [to] Moses, "You will see My back," *we-ra*ʾ*ita* ʾ*et* ʾ*aḥorai* (Exod. 33:23), that is the power that is in him. Jacob said, "Am I (ʾ*anokhi*) under God?" (Gen. 30:2), [the word] ʾ*anokhi* is numerically equivalent to *kisse*ʾ (throne). Therefore, Jacob receives the splendor when the prayer rises upward. It is written, "And they saw the God of Israel and under His feet etc." (Exod. 24:10), it should be read as "Israel under His feet."[218]

In accord with his usual exegetical manner, Eleazar connects seemingly disparate issues through word associations and numerological equivalences. The first and most surprising connection is that between the back of God revealed to Moses and the image of Jacob engraved on the throne.[219] There is no doubt that, in the teaching of Eleazar, the image of Jacob alludes to an actual divine hypostasis. Thus, for example, he writes in his commentary on the secrets of the liturgy: "The Lord, God of Abraham, Isaac, and Israel . . . it mentions Israel and not Jacob for Israel is the archon together with God that is engraved upon the throne."[220] The words of Eleazar are based on the aggadic passage from *Genesis Rabbah* cited above on the verse, "for you have striven with God" (Gen. 32:29): "You are the one whose icon is engraved above." That is to say, Jacob is the archon (*sar*) who is together with the divine and whose image is engraved upon the throne. Further support for my contention is found in the passages that I cited above from Eleazar's commentary on the chariot in which the image of Jacob is called the "splendor of Israel" (a tradition, as we have seen, that already appears in earlier midrashic sources, including *Lamentations Rabbah*) and also, "God of Israel," which is the visionary object of the nobles of Israel at the Sinaitic epiphany described in Exodus 24. According to the second version cited above, from the MS Mussajoff, Eleazar also identified the image of Jacob with the crown made from the liturgical praises of Israel. This association reflects the ancient tradition that Israel is the name of the crown composed of the prayers of Israel that the archangel—according to some literary sources Sandalphon and according to others Meṭaṭron[221]—binds to the head of the glory.[222] It is worth noting that already in early Pietistic texts, attributed by Dan to Judah the Pious, the image of the crown from ancient Jewish mysticism evolves into a hypostatic power in the divine realm.[223] Eleazar adds to this idea the comparison between the image of Jacob and the crown whose name is Israel, based, of course, on the fact that Jacob is Israel.

From the passage cited it seems, moreover, that the image of Jacob is identified as the cherub alluded to in the expression "small face" (*ʾappe zuṭre*).[224] Eleazar reached this identification through the conjunction of two matters related to the concept of smallness (*qaṭnut*). On the one hand, in B. Ḥullin 60b Jacob is designated "Jacob the small one," *yaʿaqov qaṭan*, apparently on the basis of the verse, "How will Jacob survive? He is so small," *mi yaqum yaʿaqov ki qaṭon huʾ* (Amos 7:2),[225] which itself may be based on the words of Jacob, "I am unworthy of all the kindness," *qaṭonti mi-kol ha-ḥasadim* (Gen. 32:10). On the other hand, in a second talmudic passage, B. Ḥagigah 13b, the face of the cherub is described as the "small face" (*ʾappe zuṭre*) in contrast to the human face that is the "great face" (*ʾappe ravreve*).[226] Eleazar combines these two motifs and thereby forges an identification of Jacob's image with the cherub. This identification is alluded to in the verse, "He mounted a cherub," that is, God rode upon the image of Jacob (the exact meaning of this will become clear at a subsequent stage in this analysis). From the other passages cited by Eleazar it also emerges that Jacob's image, which is that of a cherub, is the throne upon which the upper glory sits.[227] To this Eleazar alludes in his words: "And the Lord was upon him [i.e., Jacob] as upon a throne from above." And in more detail: "Thus you will find [the word] *ʾadam* in the last letters of the words, 'O throne of glory, exalted,' *kisseʾ khavod marom* (Jer. 17:12), as well as in the last [letters of the expression] 'granting them seats of honor,' *we-khisseʾ khavod yanḥilem* (1 Sam 2:8). . . . Jacob said, 'Am I (*ʾanokhi*) under God?' (Gen. 30:2), [the word] *ʾanokhi* is numerically equivalent to *kisseʾ* (throne)."[228] This is the allusion as well at the end of the passage in which Eleazar informs us that Jacob's image bears the title "God of Israel," for the name Israel designates the lower power in the divine realm, symbolized in Scripture by the expression "And under His feet."[229] Eleazar has this in mind in the following passage in his commentary on the secrets of prayer: "'Bow down to His footstool' (Ps. 99:5), the face of the cherub. 'They saw the God of Israel' (Exod. 24:10), 'under my head' (Song of Songs 2:6). The holy one of Jacob, this is what is said, 'He has cast down from heaven to earth the majesty of Israel' (Lam. 2:1)."[230] The description of the lower aspect of the glory as that which is beneath the feet is echoed in the *Sefer Ḥakhmoni* of Shabbetai Donnolo, acknowledged as one of the most important sources for Ḥaside Ashkenaz:

> Even though it says "I beheld the Lord" (Isa. 6:1), he did not see the image of His face, he saw the throne. He did not see the glory of the Lord upon the throne, but rather the skirts [of His robe] as the skirts of a coat. Thus we have learned that Moses saw the glory of His back standing and Isaiah saw in a vision His glory seated on a throne. From the vision of the throne and the seraphs standing above Him, he understood that [the throne] was that of God. He saw, however, the glory of His skirts that is the glory under His feet. When [the glory] was seen by Moses, Aaron, Nadab and Abihu, and the seventy elders of Israel, [even though it is written, "And they saw the God of Israel"], they saw only His glory that is under His feet, by means of a sign and symbol, as it says, "And under His feet was the likeness of a pavement of sapphire" (Exod. 24:10).[231]

In Eleazar's thought, the following items are identified through a chain of symbolic associations: the image of Jacob, the back of God, the God of Israel, the majesty of Israel (*tifʾeret yisraʾel*), the crown of the glory of Israel (*ʿaṭeret kevod yisraʾel*), the small face (*ʾappe zuṭre*), the cherub, and the throne of glory. Let me cite another passage from the *Sod Ma ͑aseh Bereshit* (Secret of the Work of Creation), the first part of the compendium, *Sode Razayya ͗*, in which the image of Jacob is identified with the crown (*͑aṭarah*), the cherub, and the throne:

> We know that there is nothing more glorious amongst the creatures than man, for he is above in the image of Jacob, the one selected by God, and he is engraved on the throne of glory, as it is written, "He has cast down from heaven to earth the majesty of Israel" (Lam. 2:1), and it is written, "Israel in whom I glory" (Isa. 49:3). . . . Thus in Song of Songs it is written, "His left is under my head" (2:6), [*le-ro ͗shi* read as] *yisra ͗el.* Thus it is called *͑aṭeret kavod,* glorious crown, the mantle of Israel, that is made from the praises of Israel, and rises to the head of the glory. . . . [The people of] Israel have their name [from the verse] "because you have striven with Elohim" (Gen. 32:28). Thus, "And the Lord was standing above him" (ibid., 28:13) as upon the throne of glory above. Thus, "He rode upon a cherub" (2 Sam. 22:11; Ps. 18:11), and it is written, "[When Moses went into the Tent of Meeting to speak with Him,] he would hear the Voice addressing him from above the cover that was on top of the Ark of the Pact between two cherubim" (Num. 7:89). Jacob is called small, because the cherubim are small-faced. . . . Since the face of man is Jacob who is engraved on the throne, the word *͗adam* is [in the consonants] at the end of these words, *kisse ͗ khavod marom,* "O throne of glory exalted from of old" (Jer. 17:12) as well as *we-khisse ͗ khavod yanḥilem,* "granting them seats of honor" (1 Sam 2:8). Thus, the image of man goes with all the countenances, for it is written, "For the Lord has chosen Jacob for Himself" (Ps. 135:4), and it is written, "Jacob His own allotment" (Deut. 32:9). It is written, *we-ra ͗ita ͗et ͗aḥorai,* "and you shall see My back" (Exod. 33:23)—that is numerically equal to *bi-demut ya ͑aqov she-ḥaquqah ba-kisse ͗*, "in the image of Jacob that is engraved on the throne." Afterwards it is written, "And Jacob said, Am I under Elohim" (Gen. 30:2). *͗Anokhi* numerically equals *kisse ͗*. Thus, Jacob receives the splendor when the prayers rise above.[232]

It is noteworthy that, in another passage from this work, Eleazar attributes to the image of Jacob the title, "Israel, the elder," *yisra ͗el sabba ͗*, an expression that appears already in *midreshe ͗aggadah* as a name for Jacob.[233] In the passages of Eleazar, however, the expression manifestly is an epithet for a divine hypostasis identified concomitantly as the letter *shin* of the head phylacteries. There is no doubt that for Eleazar the reference is to the phylacteries of God, and one may see in this symbol an allusion to the crown made from the prayers of Israel, which is compared to the phylacteries.[234]

> Why is the *shin* on the compartments of the head phylacteries that correspond to Jacob, as it is written, *yisraʾel ʾasher bekha ʾetpaʾar*, "Israel in whom I glory" (Isa. 49:3), and the phylacteries are called the glory (*peʾer*)[235], as it says, *peʾerkha ḥavosh ʿalekha*, "Put on your turban" (Ezek. 24:17)? At the time of the destruction [of the Temple] He cast them to the earth, as it is written, "He cast down from heaven to earth the majesty of Israel" (Lam. 2:1). . . . It is said in *Sefer Yeṣirah*[236]: He enthroned the letter *shin* [in fire] and placed upon it a crown, and drew upon it the heavens, for they are of fire . . . Moreover, the *shin* is on the compartments near the written verses (*ha-ketivah*)[237] for the image of his icon is fixed upon the throne of glory, and the image of the cherub resembles him. This was the cherub upon which He rose and came to Egypt, as it is written, "He rode a cherub and flew" (2 Sam. 22:11; Ps. 18:11).[238] This is [the implication of] "And when Israel saw the great hand" (Exod. 14:31), i.e., Israel the elder (*yisraʾel sabbaʾ*).[239] When Israel saw the image of Jacob upon the sea they uttered the song. From [the verse] "Then [Moses and the Israelites] sang [this song to the Lord]" (ibid., 15:1) until [the verse] "The Lord will reign for ever and ever!" (ibid., 18), there are 182 words [corresponding to the numerical value of the consonants in the name "Jacob"].[240]

The relationship between the splendor of Israel, the image of Jacob, and the phylacteries is established in the commentary to Lamentations 2:1 attributed to Eleazar: " 'The majesty of Israel,' the image of the icon of Jacob is the majesty of Israel. Another explanation: the majesty refers to the phylacteries of the Master of the world. . . . The majesty of Israel [the consonants of the word *yisraʾel* can be read as] *le-roʾshi* ('to my head') . . . *tifʾeret yisraʾel* is numerically equal to *demut diyoqan shel yaʿaqov ʾavinu she-be-kisseʾ ha-kavod ḥaquqah le-maʿalah* ('the image of the icon of Jacob, our patriarch, engraved upon the throne of glory above')."[241] While there is ample reason to doubt the attribution of this text to Eleazar himself,[242] there is equally good evidence to assume that the text was authored by one close to the Kalonymide circle of Pietists. If that is the case, then the text can edify something of the nature of the esoteric teaching cultivated by

Judah or Eleazar. The conclusion that this text was not authored by Eleazar does not diminish its significance in constructing the views accepted by him.

Up to this point we have seen that in the compositions of Eleazar the image of Jacob symbolizes the crown and the cherub, and it is even identified as the back of God, also called "God of Israel," "splendor of Israel," and "Israel the elder." This image is also the cherub upon which God descended to the Red Sea, alluded to in Scripture by the description of the great power (literally, great hand, *ha-yad ha-gedolah*) that Israel saw upon the sea.[243] These examples indicate that in the esoteric doctrine of Eleazar the image of Jacob is transformed into a distinct hypostasis in the divine world. Moreover, from a comparison of the conclusion of the passage cited above and another text it can be shown that in the teaching of Eleazar the image of Jacob is the glory (to be more precise, as will be seen further below, the lower glory). In the first instance Eleazar mentions the twelve stitchings that surround the letter *shin* of the phylacteries and that correspond to the twelve tribes. On the other hand, in his *Sefer ha-Shem* (Book of the Name) Eleazar speaks of the "twelve tribes that camp in four corners like the twelve tribes that surround the throne."[244] Even more detail is given in Eleazar's commentary on the secrets of prayer:

> Twelve times daily the word "holy" (*qadosh*) is said corresponding to the twelve tribes who are referred to [by the words] "You shall be holy," *qedoshim tehiyu* (Lev. 19:2), and corresponding to the twelve holy ones (*qedoshot*) that surround the throne of glory, three on each side. . . . Corresponding to them were the three tribes of Israel for each and every banner and the Ark in the middle. Similarly, in the case of the phylacteries, there are three stitchings on each of the four sides and the writings [of the scriptural passages upon parchment] in the middle. The twelve tribes of Jacob correspond to the twelve zodiac signs and the twelve stones of the Ephod.[245]

The letter *shin*, therefore, symbolizes the crown and the image of Jacob or the cherub that is identified with the glory. The relationship between the letter *shin* and the glory can be explained in light of other passages in Ashkenazi texts in which the numerical equivalence of the letter *shin* (300) is said to equal that of the letters of the Tetragrammaton, YHWH, written in the code of a"t ba"sh, that is, MṢP"Ṣ (40 + 90 + 80 + 90). Thus, for example, one reads in the pseudo-Hai commentary on the forty-two-letter name of God included in Eleazar's *Sefer ha-Ḥokhmah*: "This is the numerical value of [the expression] *yofi ʿal ha-yeriʿah*, and the numerical value of *yofi ʿal Hadarniʾel*, and likewise the numerical value of *yofi ʿal MṢP"Ṣ*, for the beauty and splendor of the Holy One, blessed be He, who is called MṢP"Ṣ, rests upon the curtain and a great splendor surrounds His throne. Therefore, we must praise the supernal name that is MṢP"Ṣ whose numerical value is that of [the letter] *shin* [i.e., 300], and *shin-yod-nun* [i.e., the letters that make up the word *shin* = 360] is numerically equal to *shimkha* ['your name' that likewise = 360] and the [word] *shin* is an acrostic for *shem yhwh niqraʾ*, 'the name of the Lord is proclaimed' (Deut. 28:10), and the name YHWH through a"t ba"sh is numerically equal to *shin* and these are the letters MṢP"Ṣ."[246] In slightly different words Eleazar himself expresses this nexus of motifs in his commentary on Ezekiel's chariot vision: "Every person knows . . . that there is a *shin* on the phylacteries for the glorious name [YHWH] in a"t ba"sh is MṢP"Ṣ and MṢP"Ṣ has the numerical value of 300 [represented by the letter *shin*]. Therefore, the name is placed between the eyes, for the eyes are like the two cherubim."[247] "The scriptural expression, *yoshev ha-keruvim*, indicates that just as when the righteous of Israel have phylacteries on their heads the name is upon them, so too on the foreheads of the cherubim is the explicit name, as it says, '[the Ark of God] to which the Name was attached, the name Lord of Hosts Enthroned on the Cherubim' (2 Sam. 6:2); since the name is on their foreheads it says *yoshev ha-keruvim*, the one who is enthroned on the cherubim."[248] At a later point in this study I shall deal at greater length with the subject of the cherubim in the esoteric teaching of Eleazar and their relationship to the glory and the explicit name of God. Presently, it is important to note that the image of Jacob is identified as the crown that is the glory or the Tetragrammaton symbolized by the letter *shin*. In another manuscript passage attributed to Eleazar, the connection between the glory or the cherub and the image of Jacob engraved upon the throne of glory is emphasized with greater clarity:

> Those thirteen attributes correspond to the twelve tribes and Jacob who is engraved upon the throne of glory. The twelve tribes stand around the glory just as they stood in the Tabernacle. Corresponding to this there are thirteen occurrences in Scripture of *ʾor panekha* ("light of Your countenance") and *haʾer panekha* ("shine Your countenance"),[249] for through the merit of Jacob the tribes shall recall the thirteen attributes and He shall shine upon us in that very attribute that Moses our master chose. *Marʾeh keruvim* ("the appearance of the cherubim") is numerically equal to *marʾeh kavod* ("the appearance of the glory").[250] Accordingly, the

> Holy One, blessed be He, commanded that the cherubim be made, for this is the attribute of mercy. [The word] *keruvim* is numerically equal to *raḥamekha* ("Your mercy"),[251] as it is written, "There I will meet with you, and I will impart to you—from above the cover, from between the two cherubim" (Exod. 25:22).[252]

The identification of the image of Jacob with the crown, on the one hand, and with the cherub, on the other, raises the possibility that in the esoteric theosophy of Ḥaside Ashkenaz, particularly in Eleazar, this hypostasis is feminine.[253] The feminine characteristic of the crown is especially prominent in the frequently discussed passage in the pseudo-Hai text included in Eleazar's *Sefer ha-Ḥokhmah*,[254] referred to above.[255]

> When the crown is upon the head of the Creator, it is then called Akatriel, and then the crown is hidden from all the holy angels . . . then they ask one another, Where is the place of His glory?[256] Concerning it David said, "O you who dwell in the shelter of the Most High and abide in the protection of Shaddai," *yoshev be-seter ʿelyon be-ṣel shaddai yitlonan* (Ps. 91:1). [The word] *be-seter* has the numerical value of Akatriel.[257] [The expression] *be-ṣel shaddai yitlonan* has the letters of *bi-ṣelot shaddai nalun*[258] as well as the letters *ṣelot denan yesh lo*,[259] for the prayer is the *ṣelota*ʾ of the Holy One, blessed be He. It sits to the left of the Holy One, blessed be He, like a bride by the bridegroom, and it is called the daughter of the king (*bat melekh*). Occasionally, on account of the mission it is called the daughter of the voice (*bat qol*) . . . this is the tenth kingship (*malkhut ʿasirit*) and it is the secret of all secrets (*sod kol ha-sodot*).[260]

In his discussion of this text, Scholem mentioned a second passage in which it is asserted that the "Presence of the Creator is called daughter . . . and it is the tenth *sefirah* and the kingship (*malkhut*) for the crown of kingship (*keter malkhut*) is upon His head."[261] Although in the revised English version of Scholem's *Origins of the Kabbalah* there is a parenthetical remark that introduces this second passage as found "in a commentary on the name of forty-two letters, attributed to Hai Gaon,"[262] the fact of the matter is that this passage is found in the section of *Sefer ha-Ḥokhmah* written by Eleazar himself and not in the introduction that comprises the pseudepigraphic commentaries on the divine names.[263] It should be noted that in another context in the same work Scholem cites the relevant passage and correctly asserts that it is part of *Sefer ha-Ḥokhmah* in which the seventy-three gates of interpretation are explained.[264] It is worthwhile to cite a third passage from this text noted as well by Scholem[265]:

> When Moses our master requested before the Holy One, blessed be He, "Show me Your glory" (Exod. 33:18), He said to him: "No man shall see Me and live" (ibid., 20). Even so you have found favor in My eye and thus I will reveal to you My shoe (*pazmeqe*) that I have not shown to any prophet. This is the import of the verse, "With him I speak mouth to mouth, plainly and not in riddles, and he beholds the likeness of the Lord" (Num. 12:8), for He showed him by way of the luminous speculum His shoe, and it is the supernal crown (*keter ᶜelyon*) called the tenth kingship (*malkhut ᶜasirit*).[266]

From these three passages it may be concluded that the crown is described in concepts and motifs characteristic of theosophic kabbalistic symbolism.[267] More precisely, according to the different Ashkenazi traditions transmitted in the pseudo-Hai commentary on the forty-two-letter name of God that is included in *Sefer ha-Ḥokhmah* one may derive the following chain of symbolic images: the diadem (*ᶜaṭarah*) = Presence (*Shekhinah*) = glory (*kavod*) = prayer (*tefillah* or *ṣelotaʾ*) = bride (*kallah*) = king's daughter (*bat melekh*) = voice of revelation (called by the technical expression, *bat qol*, daughter of the voice) = tenth kingship (*malkhut ᶜasirit*) or *sefirah* = shoe of God (*pazmeqe*) = angel of the Lord (*malʾakh yhwh*) = image of God (*temunat yhwh*) = supernal crown (*keter ᶜelyon*). It is important to emphasize, as I have already intimated, that several of these protokabbalistic images recur in other passages in *Sefer ha-Ḥokhmah* that were unquestionably authored by Eleazar of Worms, as well as in other texts written by Eleazar or the disciples that were closest to him.[268] Thus, for example, there is the key passage in *Sefer ha-Ḥokhmah* that, as I noted above, Scholem himself had cited. The fuller text reads as follows:

> Thus [the word *bereʾshit* can be read as] *roʾsh bat*, for the *Shekhinah* of the Creator is called daughter (*bat*), as it says, "I was with Him" (Prov. 8:30),[269] [this refers to the] *Shekhinah*. [The Aramaic] *mitravyah* has the letters of *barteih*[270] and she is called the tenth *sefirah* and *malkhut*, for the crown of royalty (*keter malkhut*) is upon His head. So too [the word *bereʾshit* can be read as] *yirʾat shav*, this is the Torah, as it says, "The fear of the Lord is pure" (Ps. 119:10), and it is written, "I was with Him a confidant"

> (Prov. 8:30). She was moving about in the heights, and she rose and sat upon His lap like a daughter . . . [the word] *ʾehyeh* through a"t ba"sh is TṢMṢ that numerically equals *keter* (crown)[271]. . . . This is the import of the verse, "His head is finest gold," *roʾsho ketem paz* (Song of Songs 5:11) . . . the word *ketem* is an acrostic for *keter* (crown), *torah* (teaching), *malkhut* (kingship). The Holy One, blessed be He, is glorified by His people, Israel . . . and when they answer [in the *qaddish*], "Amen, let Your great name [be blessed]," then the prayer rises to be a crown on the head of the Holy One, blessed be He, and the Holy One, blessed be He, says to her: Sit at My right side, and for her sake the world was created.[272]

A similar sequence of images is repeated in a second passage in *Sefer ha-Ḥokhmah*, again from the part of the text written by Eleazar himself: "[The word] *bereʾshit* [the first and last] letters [*bet* and *taw*] spell *bat* (daughter), and she is the community of Israel (*kenesset yisraʾel*) who is called daughter (*bat*) . . . as well as *bat qol* (daughter of the voice) for the voice of the prayer of the daughter of Israel (*qol tefillat bat yisraʾel*) ascends to the head of the Creator and sits next to Him like a daughter that is called the *Shekhinah*. This is the import of the verse, 'O you who dwell in the shelter of the Most High,' *yoshev be-seter ʿelyon* (Ps. 91:1), [the word] *be-seter* has the letters *bat sar*, for he is the archon (*sar*) who receives the daughter (*bat*)."[273] In another Ashkenazi text, already discussed by Idel,[274] the protokabbalistic motifs are equally salient:

> The prayer ascends to the firmament that is upon their heads[275] and goes and sits upon the head of the Holy One, blessed be He, and becomes a crown for Him . . . for the prayer sits as a crown. . . . The crown of the Holy One, blessed be He, is 600,000 parasangs, corresponding to the 600,000 Israelites, and the name of the crown is "Sariel" (the letters *yisraʾel*, Israel) and its numerical value is that [of the expression] *tefillah ʾav ʾeḥad*,[276] for one father arranges a crown out of the prayers. When the crown ascends they run and bow down, and rush to place their crowns on [the firmament of] ʿAravot, and offer Him kingship. "Above the expanse over their heads was the semblance of a throne, in appearance like sapphire; and on top, upon this semblance of a throne, there was the semblance of a human form" (Ezek. 1:26). Thus the prayers [that are] crowns that ascend to the throne are like a throne, and the throne is made out of sapphire stone.[277]

The content of this passage is based on ancient traditions regarding the crown of glory whose name is Israel insofar as it is made of the prayers of Israel. The name given to the crown according to the Ashkenazi tradition cited above is Sariel, which is composed of the same letters as the name Israel.[278] We have already seen that in several places in his writings Eleazar identifies the crown made from the prayers of Israel as the image of Jacob engraved upon the throne. It may be surmised that the crown is called Jacob inasmuch as the latter is another name for Israel, the accepted name for the crown in the older sources. It is noteworthy as well that in the anonymous Ashkenazi text cited above, the crown itself is described as a throne in a way that parallels the description in Eleazar's writings of Jacob's image as a throne.[279] Insofar as the crown and the throne are characterized respectively as feminine, and the image of Jacob is the crown and/or the throne, it follows that the image of Jacob assumes a feminine personality in the esoteric doctrine espoused by Eleazar of Worms. Confirmation of my interpretation is found in a second motif that Eleazar employs to describe the image of Jacob. I am referring to the identification of Jacob's image as the cherub, alluded to particularly by the expression *ʾappe zuṭre*, as noted above. It is clear from a careful reading of Eleazar's compositions that the relationship between the supernal glory and the image of Jacob, which is the cherub, is instructive of the relationship between the upper and the lower glories. Can it be concluded, therefore, that according to the esoteric teaching of Eleazar the relation of the two glories should be explained as the union of male and female? In my opinion, it is indeed possible that this is the esoteric doctrine to which Eleazar alludes on several occasions, but always in language that is sufficiently concealing.

Before I offer proof for my reading of the Ashkenazi sources, it is important to bear in mind the talmudic tradition attributed to R. Qaṭina regarding the masculine and feminine natures of the cherubim.[280] One of the key passages in which Eleazar utilizes this imagery is his commentary on the expression *u-khe-milat maʿor*, "like the circumcision of the foreskin," in *Sefer Yeṣirah* 1:3: "The foreskin, as it is written, 'In order to gaze upon their nakedness,' *lemaʿan habiṭ ʿal meʿorehem* (Hab. 2:15), 'as the clear space on each allowed with spirals roundabout,' *ke-maʿar ʾish we-loyot saviv* (1 Kings 7:36), for [the cherubim] were in the Temple to increase the procreation of Israel."[281] There is no doubt that behind the words of Eleazar stands the talmudic tradition according to which the cherubim were both masculine and feminine. However, according to Eleazar, the formulation regarding the cherubim that is more appropriate to commit to writing is the passage in *Midrash Tadshe* that establishes the correlation between the cherubim and the two names of God, YHWH and Elohim.[282] Thus, for example, in the conclusion of his commentary on *Sefer Yeṣirah* he writes: "The two cherubim correspond to YHWH and Elohim."[283] Similarly, in a passage from *Hilkhot Ḥasidut,* published in the beginning of *Sefer ha-Roqeaḥ,* Eleazar mentions the text from *Midrash Tadshe,* but he adds the connection between the cherubim and the divine names and attributes:

> "I make Myself known to him in a vision" (Num. 12:6). [The word] *keruvim* ("cherubim") has the numerical value of *mar'eh kavod* ("appearance of the glory"). In *Midrash Tadshe* [it says] the two cherubim correspond to YHWH Elohim, the unity of His name (*yiḥud shemo*) . . . YHWH through a"t ba"sh is MṢP"Ṣ. MṢP"Ṣ has the numerical value of *be-raḥamim* ("with mercy"). This unity is the attribute of mercy (*yiḥud zo middat ha-raḥamim*). . . . YW"D H"Y W"W H"Y AL"F DL"T NW"N YW"D[284] has the numerical value of [the expression] *zeh hu' ha-raḥamanut* ("this is mercifulness")[285] . . . Elohim has the numerical value of *zeh dayyan* ("this is the judge").[286] Elohenu ("our God") has the numerical value of *ha-dan yeḥidi* ("the one who judges alone").[287] Know that the Lord (YHWH) is God (Elohim).[288]

It appears from this that the cherubim correspond to the two divine names, the Tetragrammaton and Elohim, and they symbolize the attributes of mercy and judgment. The unity of the two names—and presumably the unity of the two cherubim—symbolizes the unity of the two attributes. Furthermore, Eleazar maintains that within this unity the attribute of judgment is itself changed into mercy.[289] Eleazar alludes to this in his statement that the *shem ha-meforash* (Tetragrammaton) and the *kinnuy* (Adonai) both refer to mercy. Complete and perfect unity is alluded to as well in the last comment that YHWH is Elohim: the attribute of mercy is the attribute of judgment. It is appropriate to note that Eleazar understood the function and being of the cherubim in light of the numerical equivalence of the word *keruvim* and the expression *mar'eh kavod,* the appearance of the glory, a numerology whose source is in the writings attributed to Judah the Pious;[290] the implication of this numerology is that the glory is revealed through the cherubim. The unity of the divine names—and one may suppose that alluded to here as well is the unity of the two cherubim—signifies the unity of the attributes of mercy and judgment. In this unity the attribute of judgment is transformed into mercy. Eleazar alludes to this notion as well in *Sefer ha-Ḥokhmah*: "YHWH in a"t ba"sh is MṢP"Ṣ whose numerical value is *be-raḥamim*,[291] so too Elohim written out in full is AL"F LM"D H"Y YW"D M"M whose numerical value is *be-raḥamim*.[292] Thus the name is one."[293] A careful examination indicates that Eleazar has combined the tradition that appears in *Midrash Tadshe*, based on a correlation between the cherubim and the names YHWH and Elohim, with another tradition according to which the cherubim correspond to the name YHWH repeated twice or to the name YHWH and the appellation Adonai. Eleazar, like his earlier Ashkenazi sources, expressed this correlation as well in terms of the image of the name being engraved on the forehead of each cherub. Sometimes this is expressed in terms of the Tetragrammaton being engraved on the forehead of both cherubim; other times it is stated that one cherub corresponds to the Tetragrammaton and the other to Adonai. The tradition that I have unfolded is attested in one of the extensive theosophic compositions that Dan[294] attributes to Judah the Pious:

> Moreover, the appellation of the name YHWH is Adonai [spelled in the plene form: ADWNY] on account of the name YW"D H"E, for all the commandments come forth out of the specified letters, such as YW"D H"E WA"W [of the name YHWH] DL"T NW"N YW"D [of the name] Adonai [written out in full]. The only [letters] to be counted are L"F L"T W"N W"D[295] [= 606]. . . . If you place the ᵓ*alef* [= 1] from H"E [of the name YHWH] upon them [together with the *waw* of W"W which = 6] then the sum equals 613 corresponding to all the commandments, the 365 negative commandments and the 248 positive commandments. . . . [The name] is written YW"D H"E [YHWH] and pronounced AL"F DL"T [Adonai] . . . AL"F DL"T NW"N YW"D H"E. . . . This is [the import of the verse] "The Lord God gave me a skilled tongue" (Isa. 50:4).[296] Therefore this name [Adonai YHWH] was mentioned, for all the commandments are alluded to in the explicit name [YHWH] and in the appellation [Adonai] to indicate that His name and the appellation are resting in the ark, and the cherubim are above [it], one corresponding to the name and the other to the appellation, and the commandments are in the ark and the Torah scroll is there. It is written, "the Ark of God to which the Name was attached, the name Lord of Hosts Enthroned on the Cherubim" (2 Sam. 6:2). Therefore, one who studies all the commandments and fulfills them, his soul is bound under the throne of glory,[297] as it is written, "the life of my lord

> will be bound up in the bundle of life" (1 Sam. 25:29)." . . . Therefore, [the expression] *yhwh ʾelohe yisraʾel* ("Lord, God of Israel"), has the numerical value of 613. [This signifies that] He is the God of those who receive the entire Torah.[298]

What is most intriguing about this passage is that the two cherubim correspond to the explicit name and its appellation, respectively the graphic and aural form of the name, and in them are comprised all the 613 traditional commandments. From other passages in the same text, the numerology by means of which this is established is set out more clearly: the hidden letters (*neʿelam*) of the word Adonai (the L"F of *ʾalef,* L"T of *dalet,* W"N of *nun,* and W"D of *yod*) equal 606. To this sum are added the *neʿelam* of two letters of the Tetragrammaton,[299] the *ʾalef* from the *heʾ* and *waw* from the *waw,* that equal 7. Hence, the sum of the two names equals 613, the number of the commandments. From this numerical play it may be deduced that all the commandments are dependent upon the two names that correspond further to the two cherubim. According to another passage of the same work this is the significance of the esoteric tradition that the Torah is entirely the name of God[300]:

> With regard to AL"F DL"T NW"N YW"D, take the hidden letters L"F L"T W"N W"D and you get a sum of 606. Take from the name as it is written [YHWH] the *ʾalef* from *heʾ* and the *waw* from *waw* [1 + 6] and place them upon the others and the result is 613. . . . Why is the number 613 alluded to in the name? On account of the fact that it is written, "If you fail to observe faithfully all the terms of this teaching (*torah*) that are written in this book, to reverence this honored and awesome Name, the Lord your God" (Deut. 28:58). Thus the entire Torah is dependent upon the glorious name . . . and the entire Torah is weighed in the name . . . and this is [the import of the verse] "[the Ark of God] to which the Name was attached, the name Lord of Hosts Enthroned on the Cherubim" (2 Sam. 6:2). The explicit name was written on the forehead of the cherubim,[301] and this is [the meaning of] "the name Lord of Hosts Enthroned on the Cherubim."[302]

According to this Ashkenazi tradition, the 613 commandments contained in the explicit name and the appellation—that correspond to the cherubim—are also alluded to in the expression "Lord, God of Israel," *yhwh ʾelohe yisraʾel,* whose numerical value is 613.[303] As may be gathered from other passages in the same text, this expression is a techinical term that refers to the divine glory when it is visually manifest to human beings. For example, one passage says: "The angel who receives the prayers says a name on the crown and it rises of itself to the head of the glory that appears to the prophets of Israel, 'And they saw the God of Israel' (Exod. 24:10)."[304] It follows that within the glory itself the two cherubim or names are unified, and the unity of the latter comprises the 613 commandments, or the entire Torah. This matter is alluded to in yet another passage where theurgical significance is imparted to human action:

> "Thus says the Lord, the God of Israel:"[305] this name "God of Israel," *yhwh ᵓelohe yisraᵓel,* has the numerical value of 613, [the term "God" appears] together with "Israel" for [God] is not called by this name except when they fulfill the 613 commandments. When there is this name, "God of Israel," He would speak from the glory, for in Ezekiel the glory is united with the God of Israel, even though in one place he mentions this name "God of Israel" corresponding to the glory.[306]

When the glory is in a state of fullness—in the language of Eleazar the "glory that is augmented," *kavod ha-mitrabbeh*[307]—it comprises the two names, YHWH and Adonai, that correspond to the cherubim. The relationship between the glory and the name "God of Israel," on the one hand, and with the cherubim on the other, is established in the following Pietistic commentary on the theophany described in Exod. 24:9–10:

> "Then Moses and Aaron, Nadab and Abihu, and seventy elders of Israel ascended; and they saw the God of Israel." The explanation of this whole matter is that the cherubim were below and the God of Israel above them, for it is written, "Then the glory of the Lord left the platform of the House" (Ezek. 10:18), for without cherubim it is written the "glory of the Lord" (*kevod yhwh*) but afterwards "the glory of the God of Israel above them, that was the creature that I had seen below the God of Israel" (ibid., 19–20). It is written, "And the glory of the God of Israel appeared there, like the vision that I had seen in the valley" (ibid., 8:4). The cherub lifted [its wing] (cf. ibid., 10:19) until [the point that] "the glory of the God of Israel had moved from the cherub on which it had rested" (ibid., 9:3). "And there, coming from the east with a roar like the roar of mighty waters,

> was the glory of the God of Israel" (ibid. 43:2). It is written, "The sound of the cherub's[308] wings could be heard" (ibid., 10:5), "I could hear the sound of their wings like the sound of mighty waters" (ibid., 1:24). Thus [the title] the "glory of the God of Israel" (*kevod ᾿elohe yisra᾿el*) [is used] when He is upon the cherubim, but when He is not upon the cherubim it is written the "glory of the Lord" (*kevod yhwh*). Therefore, "under the feet" of the God of Israel "was the likeness of a pavement of sapphire" (Exod. 24:10). And it is written "in appearance like sapphire" (Ezek. 1:26), for such were the cherubim and the creatures.[309]

The mounting of the glory upon the cherub (called as well by the plural form cherubim or by an alternative designation the creature) transposes the status of the glory from the "glory of the Lord" to the "glory of the God of Israel."[310] In my opinion there is an allusion here to a sexual mythologization of the divine powers[311]: the glory is joined with the cherub upon which he rides.[312] As will be seen below, the sexual connotation of this image is more clearly expressed in the writings of Eleazar. In any event, the number 613, which corresponds to the traditional number of commandments, is alluded to in the Tetragrammaton and its appellation, YHWH and Adonai, associated with the cherubim, and they assume the name "Lord, God of Israel," a special designation of the enthroned glory. Indeed, the glory receives the name "Lord, God of Israel" only when Israel fulfills the commandments. In other words, the unity of the names within the glory—symbolized by the title "Lord, God of Israel"—is dependent upon the actions of Israel below. Even though the author of the above text has not elaborated on the matter, it is entirely clear that operative here is a definite theurgic element: imparted to the Jewish people is the task of influencing the image of the glory. The notion that through the performance of the commandments the Jew unites the two divine names, which correspond to the two cherubim, is alluded to in another passage in the same composition:

> The hidden letters [in the names "YHWH" and "Adonai"] equal 613 corresponding to the positive and negative commandments, for whoever keeps the commandments has a God, and the names [are united] through his assistance, "[the Ark of God] to which the Name was attached, the name Lord of Hosts Enthroned on the Cherubim" (2 Sam. 6:2). The name is found there for the commandments are in the ark, for whoever establishes [the unity of] Adonai [and] YHWH, one name is upon him from the right and one

> name from the left . . . for one of these two names was on the forehead of one cherub and the other on the second cherub. Since they correspond to the commandments it is said, "The Lord God[313] gave me a skilled tongue" (Isa. 50:4).[314]

The containment of the 613 commandments (the representation of the Torah in its entirety from a ritualistic perspective) in the title "Lord, God of Israel" and in the two names, Adonai and YHWH, which correspond to the cherubim, is found as well in the writings of Eleazar. Thus, for example, we read in *Ḥokhmat ha-Nefesh*: "[The expression] 'Lord, God of Israel' (*yhwh ʾelohe yisraʾel*) has the numerical value of 613 for all the commandments should be interpreted in relation to the image (*demut*) above."[315] From the continuation of this text, it is clear that the subject of the discussion is the primordial supernal image that stands before the throne of glory. The correlation between the 613 commandments and the two divine names appears in a passage in Eleazar's *Sefer ha-Shem* that is essentially a reworking of the numerology discussed above as it is found in the text attributed to Judah the Pious:

> AL"F DL"T NW"N W"W YW"D Adonai [spelled ADWNY]. One should not consider the principal but rather that which derives from it. L"F L"T W W"N W"D [30+80+30+400+6+6+50+6+4= 612]. . . . If one places the *ʾalef* from the *heʾ* [of YHWH] upon them then the sum amounts to 613 corresponding to 613 commandments, 365 prohibitions and 248 proscriptions. Why [is the divine name] written *yod-heʾ* [YHWH] and called *ʾalef-dalet* [Adonai]? For they [the two names together] bear the 613 commandments. . . . Therefore all the commandments are alluded to in the explicit name [YHWH] and the appellation [Adonai] to indicate that His name and His appellation were placed in the ark and the cherubim were above, one corresponding to the name and the other to the appellation, and the commandments were in the ark as was the Torah scroll, as it is written, "[the Ark of God] to which the Name was attached, the name Lord of Hosts Enthroned on the Cherubim" (2 Sam. 6:2). Therefore, he who studies all the commandments and fulfills them, his soul is bound in the bundle of life beneath the throne of glory.[316]

As I indicated above, the words of Eleazar are based on the passage that I cited from the anonymous Pietistic text, but his calculation is somewhat different: he counts the full spelling of the word

ADWNY—instead of ADNY—and thus he needs to add only an *ʾalef* from the letter *heʾ* of the Tetragrammaton in order to get the desired sum of 613.[317] In another context Eleazar reiterates this whole theme but cites scriptural verses that in other places he cites in conjunction with the motif of the image of Jacob engraved upon the throne:

> "Do not dishonor Your glorious throne" (Jer. 14:21): the throne of judgment and the throne of mercy for the throne was divided into two. . . . Upon the throne of judgment was inscribed the explicit name and so too upon the throne of mercy as well as upon the foreheads of the cherubim, as it says, "[the Ark of God] to which the Name was attached, the name Lord of Hosts Enthroned on the Cherubim" (2 Sam. 6:2). And corresponding to it are the two names . . . for the name is upon the throne of judgment and the throne of mercy, and corresponding to them [the names are] upon the cherubim. This is [the import of the verse] "He has cast down from heaven to earth the majesty of Israel, He did not remember His footstool" (Lam. 2:1). And this "For Your name's sake, do not disown us; Do not dishonor Your glorious throne" (Jer. 14:21).[318]

The fact that, exegetically, Eleazar cites in this passage in relation to the throne the very verses that he often cites when discussing the motif of the image of Jacob engraved upon the throne is not a coincidental or insignificant point. On the contrary, implicit here, as I have suggested in a number of other texts, is the identification of Jacob's image as the throne. Moreover, as I have also noted above, the image of Jacob engraved on the throne is utilized by Eleazar as a symbol for the union of the two divine names or attributes, both of which are correlated with the cherubim. This motif is also expressed by Eleazar in terms of the throne itself being split into two, one of judgment, and the other of mercy.[319] In other words, according to Eleazar, the image of Jacob is the cherub that comprises two cherubim,[320] the two attributes symbolized by the two names (either YHWH Elohim or YHWH Adonai). Support for my reconstruction may be found in the following comment in *Sefer ha-Shem*: "YHWH has the numerical value of 26 and it is called Adonai, which has the numerical value of 65. Thus the sum is 91. Hence, the two names [i.e., 2 x the 2 names] equals Jacob [*yaʿaqov* = 182]."[321]

The numerology of the name *yaʿaqov* is 182, which is the numerical value of the two names (YHWH and Adonai) multiplied by two (26 and 65= 91 x 2= 182). What Eleazar expressed in this rather simple numerology is that within Jacob the two names, which correspond to the two attributes and the cherubim, are united. This is an alternative way of saying that Jacob is the cherub that comprises the two cherubim or the one throne that is divided into a throne of mercy and a throne of judgment. Eleazar alludes to this matter in his *Perush Sodot ha-Tefillah,* although without any connection to the motif of the image of Jacob:

> Three times [in the *qedushah* prayer is mentioned the word] *barukh* (blessed): *le-ᶜumotam barukh* is one. *Barkuh kevod yhwh* is two. *Barukh ᵓatah yhwh* is three. These correspond to the three verses wherein the glory is mentioned in close proximity to the cherubim, and they are: (1) "Then the glory of the Lord left the platform of the House and stopped above the cherubim" (Ezek. 10:18). (2) "And I saw the cherubim lift their wings and rise from the earth, with the wheels beside them as they departed . . . with the glory of the God of Israel above them" (ibid., 19). (3) "Then the cherubim, with the wheels beside them, lifted their wings, while the glory of the God of Israel rested above them" (ibid., 11:22). . . . The two [references in the *qedushah* to] the glory (*kavod*) are (1) "His glory fills all the earth"[322] and (2) "Blessed be the glory of the Lord." These correspond to two visions, [that of] Elohim [and that of] YHWH, the face of mercy (*panim raḥamanut*) and the face of anger (*panim zeᶜumot*).[323] Two times [the word] glory (*kavod*) is near [the word] cherub (*keruv*),[324] and it is not written cherubim (*keruvim*): (1) "Now the glory of the God of Israel had moved from the cherub" (ibid., 9:8), and (2) "the glory of the Lord moved from the cherub" (ibid., 10:4).[325]

In another passage Eleazar expresses the same idea but compares Jacob to the *ḥashmal,* the latter also symbolizing the appearance of the glory[326] and the cherubim: "'When the Ark was to set out,' *wa-yehi bi-nesoᶜa ha-ᵓaron* (Num. 10:35). [The word] *bi-nesoᶜa* has the numerical value of *yaᶜaqov*.[327] 'They had the figures of human beings' (Ezek. 1:5) . . . and thus [the word] *bi-nesoᶜa* through [the linguistic device of] a"t ba"sh is *ḥashmal,* for everyone follows him and the depth of the *ḥashmal* . . . and the appearance of His glory is in the likeness of the *ḥashmal,* half of him fire and the other half hail."[328] It may be concluded, therefore, that according to the esoteric teaching of Eleazar, the image of Jacob has a masculine and a feminine aspect.[329] As we have seen, the androgynous quality of that image is expressed in terms of the two cherubim and the split throne. Nonetheless, in relation to the supernal glory, the image of Jacob is described in feminine characteristics, and the relationship between the image and the glory is like that of a female to a male.

In the following key passage from Eleazar's commentary on the liturgy, there is, in my opinion, an allusion to the sexual dynamic between the two glories. The relevant comment is an interpretation of the verses, "Blow the horn on the new moon, on the full moon for our feast day. For it is law for Israel, a ruling of the God of Jacob" (Ps. 81:4–5), recited as part of the additional service (*musaf*) on Rosh ha-Shanah:

> "Blow the horn on the new moon" [comprises] thirteen words corresponding to the thirteen attributes . . . for the Holy One, blessed be He, is filled with mercy on account of the ram's horn (*shofar*), through the merit of the thirteen letters in [the names of] the patriarchs of the world. . . . [The] ten commandments [comprise] 172 words, and the ten [verses included in the section known as the] *shoferot* are mentioned in order to recall the merit of Jacob[330] . . . on account of the fact that He kisses the image of Jacob by means of the sound of the ram's horn. Thus did R. Eleazar Qallir compose in the poem in the *qedushah* of Rosh ha-Shanah[331] from the words *we-qaraʾ zeh ʾel zeh we-ʾamar* until *le-ʿumat kisseʾ le-ʿumatam barukh yoʾmeru* 182 [spelled out as *yaʿaqov*] words, for Jacob is in it [the throne]. . . . This is [the allusion of the verse] "His left hand" (Song of Songs 2:6) Israel.[332] . . . Since the image of Jacob is upon the throne, as it is written, "They saw the God of Israel and under His feet" (Exod. 24:10), "like the appearance" (*ke-marʾeh*),[333] i.e., Israel. "Under His feet," this is "He did not remember His footstool on His day of wrath" (Lam. 2:1). Therefore, by means of the blowing of the ram's horn He sees the image of Jacob and changes into His mercy. The divine king sits upon the throne of mercy.[334] "He mounted a cherub" (2 Sam. 22:11; Ps. 18:11), from Jacob (*mi-yaʿaqov*).[335] "A ruling of the God of Jacob" (Ps. 81:5). The glory above the glory. This cannot be explained further.[336]

Again, we see that Eleazar identifies the image of Jacob with the God of Israel and the cherub, but here he adds the motif that this image is the personification of the attribute of mercy. Specifically, when Israel blows the ram's horn below, the divine glory looks upon the image of Jacob and is filled with mercy. The idea that the blowing of the ram's horn effects a transformation of God's attribute of judgment to mercy is a standard rabbinic theme expressed in classical midrashic sources.[337] On the other hand, the connection between the image of Jacob and the attribute of mercy or compassion is a well-known motif in Palestinian-Ashkenazi *piyyuṭ* literature. Thus, for example, the Ashkenazi *payyeṭan,* Simeon bar Isaac wrote in one of his penitential poems (*seliḥot*):

melekh ʿal kisseʾ
le-ʿamo yehi maḥseh
we-yabiṭ be-ṣurat tam ḥaquqah va-kisseʾ.[338]

King upon the throne,
be compassionate toward Your people,
and look upon the form of the mild one[339] engraved on the throne.

In a simliar vein we read in a *silluq* for the morning prayer of the first day of Rosh ha-Shanah:

ʿim yaṣʾah gezerah deḥuqah
leḥabel yoshve ʾarqaʾ
be-vuqah u-mevuqah u-mevullaqah
histakkel ba-tavnit ʾasher be-kisseʾ ḥaquqah.[340]

If a pressing decree goes forth,
to destroy the inhabitants of the earth,
in desolation, devastation, and destruction,[341]
He looks upon the form that is engraved on the throne.

In the poem of Eleazar Qallir incoporated in the additional service (*musaf*) for Rosh ha-Shanah, to which Eleazar of Worms himself referred in the aforecited passage, there is established a precise connection between the image of Jacob and the transformation of God's judgment into mercy by means of the blowing of the ram's horn:

qol shofar le-ʿet yaʿal meʾaḥez pene kisseʾ
raḥamim yaliṣ be-ʿad reshumim ba-kisseʾ
shofeṭ ʾim yirṣeh shevet be-ʾulam ha-kisseʾ
tavnit tam yifen ḥaquqah ba-kisseʾ.[342]

The sound of the ram's horn rises and it holds on to the face of the throne,
It advocates for mercy on behalf of those inscribed on the throne,
If the Judge wishes to sit in the throne portico,[343]
Let Him look at the form of the mild one engraved upon the throne.

There is no doubt that these sources and others influenced Eleazar.[344] However, in Eleazar's writings the image of Jacob is transformed into a mythical depiction of the attribute of mercy. Eleazar returns to this image frequently in his compostions, in some cases without any connection to the issue of blowing the ram's horn on Rosh ha-Shanah. Thus, for example, he writes in *Sefer ha-Shem*: "He sees the face of Jacob opposite Him upon the throne and He is merciful. This is [the import of the verse] 'Do not dishonor Your glorious throne' (Jer. 14:21)."[345] Similarly, he writes in *Sefer ha-Roqeaḥ*: "When Israel pray, the image of Jacob engraved upon the throne advocates [before God on their behalf], 'But You are holy, enthroned upon the praises of Israel' (Ps. 22:4), Israel the elder."[346] And in somewhat different language in his commentary on the chariot: "The [image of the] eagle seeing [indicates] that the glory will be merciful, [as it is written] 'Like an eagle who rouses his nestlings, gliding down to his young' (Deut. 32:11). The glory immediatley looks at the face of the human, the image of Jacob, and has mercy on them."[347]

What is important to note for our deliberation is that Eleazar describes the act of God's looking upon the image of Jacob as equivalent to the process of the glory sitting upon the throne of mercy, here expressed in terms of the liturgical formula: *ʾel melekh yoshev ʿal kisseʾ raḥamim*.[348] This matter is alluded to as well in the verse, "He rode upon a cherub," which means, according to Eleazar, "He rode upon Jacob." That is to say, sitting upon the throne and riding upon the cherub signify the same phenomenon, also characterized as God looking upon the image of Jacob. All of these metaphorical expressions poetically describe a propitious time when the attribute of mercy is aroused before the throne. The full mythos of these poetic images is laid bare in a passage in another anonymous Pietistic work, *Sefer ha-Qolot*,[349] in which the removal of the glory from the cherub is described as the nullification of divine mercy: "'Now the glory of the God of Israel had moved from the cherub on which it had rested' (Ezek. 9:3) when it was [in the state of being] 'enthroned upon the cherub.' It is written 'had moved' so that He would not have mercy."[350] The erotic relationship between God (or the glory) and Jacob's image upon the throne is alluded to in the verse, "a ruling of the God of Jacob," as well as in Nathan ben Yeḥiel's famous statement concerning the "glory above the glory."[351] The upper glory is the king designated as *mishpaṭ*, and the lower glory is the throne or cherub called *ʾelohe yaʿaqov*, "the God of Jacob." It seems to me that the king's sitting upon the throne and the riding upon the cherub are euphemistic depictions of the sexual union between the masculine and the feminine potencies within the divine pleroma.[352] That something secretive is being transmitted in the case of Eleazar is obvious from the concluding remark of the passage, "This cannot be explained further." This formula is highly unusual for Eleazar who, as we know, wrote extensive treatises that run hundreds of folios in manuscript.[353] Eleazar uses this language here because of the highly sensitive matter that he is divulging. I would like to suggest, moreover, that this matter involves the union between the upper and the lower glories (or the glory and the throne or cherub) that may be characterized as the union between male and female. It is appropriate to cite here the other passage of Eleazar to which I referred at the outset of this study, for in that context too the esotericism connected to the motif of the image of Jacob engraved on the throne is emphasized, although without any allusion to a sexual component: "In the Trisagion are nine words corresponding to the nine appearances (*marʾot*) before the great glory [alluded to] in nine places in Scripture,[354] for the image of Jacob is engraved upon the throne. Everything should not be explained except orally to the man who fears his Creator at all times."[355]

It may be concluded, therefore, that Eleazar utilized the image of God riding upon the cherub or that of the king sitting upon the throne to hint at the most subtle and sensitive theosophical secret that involved the erotic union in the realm of the chariot. This secret is intimated in the following passage in *Sefer ha-Shem*:

> "God's chariots are myriads upon myriads, thousands upon thousands" (Ps. 68:18). "[The Lord] mounted on a swift cloud" (Isa. 19:1). "He mounted a cherub and flew" (2 Sam. 22:11), for he flew by the spirit through 18,000 worlds.[356] [The angels] ask that cherub, "Where is the place of His glory?" He rides upon the cherub until the extremity of the worlds, beyond the universe. The cherub flies to those 18,000 worlds. "No eye has seen [them], O God, but You" (Isa. 64:3). [The angels] ask the cherub to which world he has turned for the praises are in accordance with the worlds. [The cherub] shows the prophets the mounting [of the glory] (*we-huʾ marʾeh la-neviʾim rekhivah*). When the high priest enters the innermost [Holy of Holies] his face changes in the manner of "And God created man in His image, in the image of God" (Gen. 1:27). "The Lord, our God, the Lord is one" (Deut. 6:4)—it is not possible for there to be two images (*temunot*) with the glory. "As face answers to face in water so does one man's heart to another" (Prov. 27:19). "I am my beloved's and my beloved is mine" (Song of Songs 6:3). "My beloved is mine and I am his" (ibid., 2:16). "The

> Lord would speak to Moses face to face" (Exod. 33:11), when he was in the innermost [chamber] his face changed. Similarly with respect to the prophets it is written, "Haggai, the angel of the Lord" (Hag. 1:13), and it is written, "But they mocked the angels of God" (2 Chron. 36:16), and it is written, "for he is an angel of the Lord of Hosts" (Mal. 2:7).[357]

In this extraordinary web of exegesis Eleazar expresses both the dynamic relationship of the glory and the cherub and the ontic transformation of the high priest and prophet into an angel.[358] The cherub is the vehicle of the glory's transport through the spiritual realms designated as the eighteen thousand worlds. Accordingly, the cherub alone possesses knowledge of the place of the glory, and only the cherub can show the prophets the secret of *rekhivah*, the mounting of the glory upon the cherub, which I interpret as a symbolic reference to enthronement. Most significant is Eleazar's reflection on the transformation of the face of the high priest that occurs when he enters the *sanctum sanctorum*: at that moment (which takes place only on Yom Kippur[359]) the face of the high priest changes into the angelic form, the image of God with which Adam was created (cf. Gen. 1:27). Although not stated explicitly in this context, one may assume on the basis of other passages in Eleazar's corpus that this transformation ensues as a result of the theurgical impact of the pronunciation of the divine name by the priest.[360] This metamorphosis, which signifies the ontic assimilation of the high priest to the enthroned glory, also is instructive about the unity of God (cf. Deut. 6:4) represented by the pairing of the names YHWH and Elohim. That the reflection of the face of the glory in the face of the high priest (cf. Prov. 27:19) is a form of mystical union is attested by the citation of the relevant verses from Song of Songs, which clearly describe the erotic union between the male lover and the female beloved.[361] The unity of the (female) high priest and the (male) glory is a reflection of the union of the glory and the cherub that the high priest experiences the moment he enters the Holy of Holies.

In my opinion Eleazar alludes to the secret of the sacred union in his commentary on Ezekiel's chariot (according to the version in MS Mussajoff) and in the parallel in *Sod Ma^caseh Bereshit* cited above: "Thus Jacob receives the splendor (*hod*) when the prayer ascends." It can be demonstrated that the word "splendor" is a technical term in Eleazar (to be sure, based on earlier sources) that refers to the upper, invisible glory.[362] Hence, when the prayer ascends, the image of Jacob, the lower glory, receives the splendor, that is, the upper glory. From another perspective, this reception of the splendor from above, which marks the union of the two glories, may be described by the motif of the crown—another symbol for the image of Jacob—ascending to the head of the glory.[363] The unification of the upper male and the lower female is depicted simultaneously by opposite movements, the downward flow of the glorious splendor and the upward ascent of the luminous crown. The union of the two glories is also alluded to in the words of Eleazar in various sources that I have mentioned above: "Therefore it says in Song of Songs, 'His left hand was under my head' (2:6), transpose [the letters of "under my head," *le-ro'shi*] and read Israel (*yisra'el*)." The sexual implication of this exegetical gloss is most striking in a commentary on the relevant verse in Song of Songs attributed to Eleazar: "His left hand was under my head . . . for the glory embraces the image of Jacob on the throne of glory."[364] This comment is obviously based on the passage from *Hekhalot Rabbati* mentioned above.[365] In the authentic writings of Eleazar this passage is often cited or paraphrased.[366] In almost all the relevant cases it seems that Eleazar understood the text from *Hekhalot Rabbati* in terms of the union of the upper masculine glory and the lower feminine glory called the "image of Jacob." On occasion Eleazar combines the passage from *Hekhalot Rabbati* with the verses that he ordinarily cites when discussing the union of the glory and the image of Jacob. To cite one example: "The image of Jacob is on the throne. . . . 'And the Lord was standing above him' (Gen. 28:13). . . . Therefore, He kisses Jacob when [one says] 'Holy, Holy, Holy,' as it is said in the *Hekhalot*. . . . 'He mounts a cherub' (2 Sam. 22:11; Ps. 18:11), i.e., Israel the elder."[367] Another text from *Ḥokhmat ha-Nefesh* is particularly illuminating, for Eleazar combines the motif from *Hekhalot Rabbati* with the talmudic tradition concerning the male and the female cherubim: "He turns to the image and embraces the image of Jacob. And then the two cherubim were turned toward one another, 'they faced each other' (Exod. 25:20, 37:9)."[368] When the supernal glory turns in an erotic embrace toward the lower glory, the image of Jacob engraved on the throne, then the cherubim face one another, and just as the glory and the image of Jacob are male and female above, so too the cherubim below.

An allusion to the sexual dynamic between the glory and Jacob's image is also found in two sources of Eleazar cited above in another context. The first is his poetic utterance *ga'awati le-tif'arti yisra'el menashsheq be-'orah/ demut pene 'adam meḥabbeq le-to'arah*,[369] and the second is his exegetical gloss on "I am my beloved's, and his desire is for me" (Song of Songs 7:11): "This is to teach that the desire of the chariot (*ma'aseh merkavah*) is upon the image of Israel (*demut yisra'el*), and this is what is written 'upon Israel is His majesty,' *'al yisra'el ga'awato* (Ps. 68:35)."[370] Underlying both of these texts, as I have noted above, is the relationship between the glory and the image of Jacob informed by the passage in *Hekhalot Rabbati.* Support for my interpretation can be gathered from another passage in Eleazar's commentary on the liturgy in which he expounds at length on the motif of the image of Jacob, but he again emphasizes that it alludes to a sublime secret that must be concealed. It is noteworthy that in this citation Eleazar relates to the text from *Hekhalot Rabbati* in two ways. On the one hand, he transfers the motif of the image of Jacob from the world of the chariot to the mundane community of Israel, yet, on the other hand, he reads the text in accordance with its contextual sense, that is, as a description of the supernal image of Jacob engraved upon the throne. After enumerating several additional issues pertaining to this motif, he emphasizes the essential secrecy of the matter:

> "Let us stand in awe of You and sanctify You" as [it is written] "Men will hallow the Holy One of Jacob and stand in awe of the God of Israel" (Isa. 29:23). Why does it say the Holy One of Jacob and not the Holy One of Abraham or the Holy One of Isaac? Because Jacob is engraved on His throne of glory. . . . When Israel sanctify their Creator with the intention of their hearts and their eyes are toward Him, He descends from His glorious chariot and kisses the [face of the] human on his mouth. Therefore, joy falls into the heart of the one who fears God during the *qedushah* and prayer, as it says in the *Hekhalot.*[371] . . . Whenever Israel says before Me "Holy," teach them and say to them: Lift your eyes to heaven, corresponding to your houses of worship, when you say before Me "Holy," for there is no other pleasure in all the world that I created like at that time. . . . Bear witness to them regarding what I do to the visage of Jacob, their patriarch, engraved upon My throne of glory, for when they say before Me, "Holy," I bend down over it, embrace it, fondle it, and kiss it, and My hands are on My arms,[372] thrice daily, when you say before Me "Holy, holy, holy is the Lord of Hosts." "Oh, give me of the kisses of your mouth" (Song of Songs 1:2). "His left hand was under my head, His right arm embraced me" (ibid., 2:6). . . . "God, who is in the power of Your strength, we will sancitfy You" regarding the splendor below on the face of Jacob. I will write an example for you: "They saw the God of Israel" (Exod. 24:10), above as, for instance, "stand in awe of the God of Israel" (Isa. 29:23), the head of the crown that is Israel. "And under His feet" (Exod. 24:10), the Holy One of

> Jacob. "I saw something like a *ḥashmal*" (Ezek. 1:27), which the Targum renders, "I saw the likeness of the *ḥashmal*, like the appearance of fire from the midst of it round about, the appearance of the glory that no eye can see and upon which it is impossible to gaze, and below I saw the appearance of fire and a splendor surrounding it." "For man may not see Me and live" (Exod. 33:20). "And you will see My back" (ibid., 23). "And the skirts of His robe filled the Temple" (Isa. 6:1). Blessed be He and blessed be His glory who reveals His secret to those who fear Him, "to conceal a matter" (Prov. 25:2).[373]

There are, finally, several passages where Eleazar alludes to the relationship between the image of Jacob and the upper glory in a definite theurgical context. Thus, for example, in his *Sod ha-Merkavah* he writes: "When Israel fulfill His will He adds splendor and glory upon the image of Jacob above, and when they do not fulfill His will, 'He cast down from heaven to earth the majesty of Israel' (Lam. 2:1)."[374] An exact parallel to this is found in Eleazar's *Perush Sodot ha-Tefillah*, where he alludes as well to the sexual relation between the glory and the image of Jacob: "Thus the final [letters of the words] *kisse*ʾ *khavod marom* (Jer. 17:12) spell Adam, to notify you that the glory is in the appearance of a human. When He is together with Israel in love, then the face of Jacob is shining in the majesty of the splendor of His glory, but when they do not perform according to His will, 'He cast down from heaven to earth the majesty of Israel' (Lam. 2:1)."[375] The glory appears as a human form when it is together with Israel in love, that is, when Israel fulfills the will of God through the proper performance of the commandments. In that moment the cherub or the lower glory—symbolized by the face of Jacob—unites with the upper glory. Eleazar alludes to this in the words: "shining in the majesty of the splendor of His glory." However, when Israel does not fulfill the will of God, then the lower glory— the "majesty of Israel"— is cast down from heaven to earth.

IV

The following conclusions can be drawn from my analysis:

1. The motif in *Hekhalot Rabbati* of the image of Jacob engraved on the throne receives in Eleazar's writings a definite feminine characterization.[376] In an earlier stage, it seems the image of

Jacob symbolized a masculine potency, either the supreme angel or the Logos second only to God. It is possible that already in *Hekhalot Rabbati* the image of Jacob assumes the new signification as a symbol for the feminine hypostasis in the world of the chariot. In any event, it appears that only in the esoteric teaching of the German Pietists, and principally in the writings of Eleazar, does the image of Jacob evolve into a symbol for the lower glory or the cherub.

2. In the esoteric theosophy of Eleazar the image of Jacob is called by various technical terms, including, *tif᾿eret yisra᾿el* (majesty of Israel), *yisra᾿el sabba᾿* (Israel the elder), *᾿elohe yisra᾿el* (God of Israel), *ʿaṭarah* (diadem), *᾿aḥor shel ha-᾿el* (the back of God), or *temunat yhwh* (image of the Lord). Hence, the image of Jacob is the focal point of religious observance—and this includes a theurgical element—and of visionary experience (for prophet and Pietist alike). With respect to the theurgical orientation, I have shown that, according to the esoteric teaching of the German Pietists, the lower glory comprises the 613 commandments, and the task of the religious life is to aggrandize that glory by means of the fulfillment of the commandments. This expansion is also depicted as the unity of the two attributes, mercy and judgment, or the two names, YHWH and Adonai. It follows that, according to the esoteric teaching of the German Pietists, the secret of divine unity is the secret of the commandments: the ultimate purpose of religious ritual is to unify the two names of God that correspond to the two attributes contained in the glory designated as "Lord, the God of Israel."
3. The relation between the upper glory and the image of Jacob is depicted by Eleazar as the relation between male and female. Although he does not elaborate upon this in great detail, there are sufficient allusions in his writings to prove that in his theosophical worldview the dynamic in the divine realm is sexual in nature. Inasmuch as this is the case it may be concluded that in the Pietistic doctrine of the glory there are precise phenomenological and terminological parallels to the theosophic kabbalah. What is surely lacking in the Pietistic literature is a clear charting of the male and female potencies in terms of the *sefirot*, the hallmark of Provençal-Spanish kabbalah. But this should not mislead one into thinking that the main elements of theosophic kabbalah are not found in the Pietistic theology. I propose that the critical structure, informed by earlier Jewish theosophy, involves the double doctrine of the glory—the upper male and the lower female—and the further identification

of these potencies with the divine names and the Torah. This structure is found in Pietistic literature and in the writings of the theosophic kabbalists, although in the case of the latter it is given a new configuration through sefirotic associations. Notwithstanding the affinity of the German Pietists and the theosophic kabbalists, there is a fundamental difference between them: whereas the kabbalists elaborated at great length in their descriptions of the dynamic between the masculine and the feminine hypostases in the divine realm, and occasionally in very bold mythological language, the Pietists intentionally withheld from expanding in writing on the union of the upper glory and the image of Jacob. On the contrary, as I have indicated above, even Eleazar is quick to emphasize the necessity to conceal this matter in the very contexts that he mentions it. The medium of writing can only permit a partial transmission of the secret. The Pietists thus adhered faithfully to a code of esotericism.

4. Even though the members of the circle of Judah the Pious did not utilize the term "special cherub," *keruv ha-meyuḥad*—terminology that characterizes a distinct circle as Dan has shown—the fact is that in the writings produced by the Kalonymide Pietists the cherub assumes an ontic role that well accords with that of the Special Cherub. As we have seen in the texts of Eleazar, the cherub, also called the "image of Jacob," is the divine power revealed to prophets, and it is the glory that sits upon the throne. By contrast, the upper glory, called occasionally by the names "splendor" or "Presence," is not disclosed to human beings. This upper glory sits upon the cherub, itself called for that reason a "throne." I do not wish to challenge the view that from a historical and literary (as well as geographic[377]) perspective in the development of the German Pietists there were distinct and autonomous circles. The important distinction of Dan still stands: the main circle of Judah the Pious is not one with the circle of the Special Cherub.[378] Nevertheless, it is necessary to note that one can find in the compositions of the Kalonymide circle descriptions of the cherub that parallel descriptions in the writings of the circle of the Special Cherub. Indeed, in the theosophy of the circle of Judah the Pious the cherub occupied a prominent position as the enthroned form described in terms of enormous physical measurments as they are transmitted in the *Shiʿur Qomah* tradition. It is impossible to enter into the depths of the esoteric teaching of the German Pietists without turning an attentive ear to the matter of the cherub.

It is possible that the shared emphasis on the enthroned cherub in the different Pietistic circles points to a common motif whose origin is in ancient Jewish esotericism. It is of interest to note in this connection that in his discussion of the doctrine of the cherub in Pietistic literature Scholem suggested that this conception "figures in certain Merkabah tracts which were known to the Hasidim."[379] The implication, then, is that the notion of the enthroned cherub is a much older doctrine that informed the Pietistic theosophy.[380] Scholem did not, however, distinguish between the different circles of Pietists. More recently, the conjecture of Scholem has been affirmed by Farber with respect to the teaching of the cherub in the writings of the circle of the Special Cherub: "It is not impossible that the Ashkenazi doctrine of the cherub derives from some ancient development of the *Shiʿur Qomah* doctrine that sought to place at the head of the theophanic order an angelic anthropomorphic image that is the manifest aspect of the divine anthropos (connected to the notion of the supernal cherub, or Keruviel, derived from Ezekiel's vision and its development in Hekhalot literature)."[381] In my view, her words may be applied as well to the doctrine of the cherub that emerges from the writings of Eleazar of Worms. It is significant to note that in the conclusion of the aforecited discussion, Farber herself cites a critical passage from Eleazar wherein the image of Jacob is identified explicitly with the cherub.[382] Hence, even though Farber did not elaborate upon the matter, it is evident that she sensed with respect to this issue (as in the case of other subjects[383]) some intrinsic connection between the doctrine of the cherub in the circle of the Special Cherub and the motif of the image of Jacob in the writings of Eleazar. Indeed, the shared descriptions may furnish us with knowledge about the possible existence of an early development in Jewish esotericism: the cherub is the divine or angelic power that is revealed upon the throne in an anthropomorphic image.[384] An ancient tradition such as this, as Farber has shown,[385] is reflected as well in later thirteenth-century mystical literature, for example, the writings of the Iyyun circle and the *Sefer ha-Qomah* of Moses ben Eleazar ha-Darshan.[386] These examples, in my opinion, lend considerable support to the assumption that the Pietists, from the main circle of Judah the Pious and the circle of the Special Cherub, either found the images describing the cherub in ancient written texts or they received them orally from some common source.

◆ 2 ◆

THE TREE THAT IS ALL: JEWISH-CHRISTIAN ROOTS OF A KABBALISTIC SYMBOL IN *SEFER HA-BAHIR*

τὰ . . . μεγάλα πάντα ἐπισφαλῆ.
—Plato, *Republic*, 497d, 9

I

Despite the generally accepted claim that *Sefer ha-Bahir* is the "first" theosophic kabbalistic work to appear in medieval Europe, the precise *vorgeschichte* of this text—in a literary and historical sense—is still unclear. Previous scholarship has attempted to illuminate the generally Gnostic or mythic orientation of different textual units and tradition-complexes that were redacted into the literary form of a distinct text in twelfth-century Provence, reflecting the philosophical and theosophical concerns current in that time and place.[1] Some specific Gnostic texts from Late Antiquity that have interesting parallels to the *Bahir*, both conceptually and linguistically, have been singled out by scholars, but for the most part we are still left to conjecture regarding the religiocultural contexts out of which the symbolic and mythic images incorporated in the *Bahir* may have evolved as well as the possible links and channels of transmission of these images to central Europe of the High Middle Ages. Even if one readily acknowledges the parallels between ancient Gnostic sources and *Sefer ha-Bahir*, the larger problem of influence or provenance is not necessarily answered; that is, it is possible, as Moshe Idel has argued, that the Gnostic sources preserve Jewish esoteric doctrines that may have found their way into kabbalistic texts like the *Bahir* through other channels.[2] One would do well here to recall that Gershom Scholem himself, who generally assumed that Gnostic ideas originating in an "Oriental" setting were Judaized in the *Bahir*,[3] also maintained the possibility of an ancient Jewish gnosis antedating the Middle Ages that preserved mythical elements going back to "an internal written and perhaps also oral Jewish tradition," although he is somewhat skeptical about the likelihood of the latter.[4] Indeed, on a number of occasions Scholem characterizes the *Bahir* as a collection of ancient fragments originating in an Oriental gnosis or reflecting a theosophic aggadah, the latter presumably indicating indigenous Jewish sources.[5]

However, several attempts to relate bahiric doctrines to Gnostic ideas (traceable to the Bulgarian Bogomils[6]) that inspired the medieval heresy of Catharism, which flourished in Provence in the twelfth and thirteenth centuries, have not been convincing.[7] While there may be certain elements in Cathar sources that bear a resemblance to views expressed in the *Bahir*, especially with respect to teachings concerning Satan and the force of evil in the world,[8] no scholar has yet demonstrated direct influence in a definitive manner. What is most essential to note in this context is that, from the vantage point of the themes that I will discuss here, there simply is no reason to presume any such influence, since the central ideas of the *Bahir* to be analyzed in detail below have no substantive parallel in Cathar doctrine.[9] On the contrary, my working assumption is that a sustained and nuanced reading of the relevant passages, informed especially by a sensitivity to the redactional process, will verify the claim that the bahiric text preserves older traditions even though in some cases a concerted effort is made to obscure the original context from which these fragmentary traditions derived.[10] *Prima facie*, it may appear, as Scholem concluded, that the homiletical teachings in this collection "are not set forth according to any particular organizational principle," but rather are "jumbled together haphazardly."[11] However, a careful reading warrants a more cautious approach: even if one cannot totally eliminate the seemingly chaotic aspect of the literary organization of these fragments, certain patterns and structures can be discerned in the redactional process. The latter holds the key for helping the scholar unlock older traditions that are both preserved and undermined in the bahiric text.

The point of departure of this brief study is a re-examination of a key motif in the *Bahir* that exerted a profound impact on subsequent kabbalistic theosophy, the symbol of the cosmic tree designated as *kol*, the All. In the view of Scholem, this term signifies that the tree is the concentration of all the powers that comprise the divine pleroma.[12] By contrast, I will suggest that this designation signifies that the tree is the ontic source of all being, or more specifically of human souls. It is this demiurgic connotation that underlies the *terminus technicus* rather than the theosophic idea (related by Scholem to ancient Gnostic myth) of the tree containing the totality of divine powers of the pleroma.[13] The need for re-examination of this critical term was suggested to me when I came upon a passage in John Scotus Eriugena's *Periphyseon* (On the Division of Nature) that provides a most interesting parallel to the *Bahir*. The philosophical text of Eriugena has been discussed previously in kabbalistic scholarship, but mostly in terms of possible Neoplatonic influences on or similarities with Jewish mystics in Provence and Catalonia of the twelfth and thirteenth centuries, especially Azriel of Gerona.[14] It has even been proposed that the pantheistic tendency in the writings of the German Pietists from the same period may have been due to the Neoplatonic influence of Eriugena (perhaps mediated through the anonymous Hebrew paraphrase of Saadiah Gaon's *Book of Beliefs and Opinions*).[15] However, no one before, to the best of my knowledge, has suggested that a mythical motif found in a kabbalistic composition should be evaluated in light of a text of Eriugena.

The significance of my approach, as will become readily apparent, lies in the fact that by following this path one may discern a possible source (in a secondary if not a primary sense) for a critical symbol in bahiric theosophy within the historical framework of Jewish-Christianity.[16] The symbol of the tree that is the All may not be rooted in the soil of ancient Judeo-syncretist Gnosticism, as Scholem surmised,[17] but rather in Jewish-Christian literature. By drawing this distinction I do not mean to deny the likely historical and textual influence of apocalyptic[18] and Gnostic ideas on certain Jewish-Christian groups[19] nor the possibility that Jewish-Christianity was perhaps one of the important channels for the diffusion of Gnostic myths and baptismal rites.[20] Despite the veracity of these claims, a legitimate distinction can and should be drawn between the varied forms of Gnosticism and Jewish-Christianity.[21] More specifically, with respect to the image that is the primary focus of this analysis, the symbol of the cosmic tree, there is an obvious difference between the two: in the case of the Gnostic sources the use of this symbol is negligible[22] whereas it is basic (if not archetypal) to Christian thinking in general and Jewish-Christianity in particular.[23]

Beyond the more limited confines of this study, therefore, the hypothesis that I will present raises the larger issue of the possibility of yet another milieu that may have fostered some aspects of the complicated mythical structures that became formalized in the theosophic kabbalistic tradition. In short, I am suggesting that perhaps within the framework of Jewish-Christianity older Jewish mythologoumena were preserved that are discernible in the Hebrew text of the *Bahir*. The most significant of these mythologoumena involved the identification of the tree designated *ha-kol*, the All, as the *axis mundi*, which is both the fulcrum of the universe and the column that stretches from heaven to earth. The cosmic tree, additionally, is characterized as the redeeming figure (the Savior). This demiurgic aspect of the Godhead, in turn, occupies the central position of the phallus, which corresponds to either the third of a triadic structure (personified as Father, Mother or Daughter [both symbols of Wisdom[24]], and Son) or the seventh power, hypostasized as the Sabbath.[25] This mythologem will be reconstructed from various passages in the *Bahir* since there is no single context where all the elements appear in a clear and delineated way. I presume that the text went through more than one redaction and that the various redactors utilized literary fragments that preserved the older traditions in a way that they found most appropriate for their own theological concerns. Indeed, as it shall become readily apparent in the course of this analysis, the Christological motifs are never openly professed in the bahiric text; on the contrary, they are cleverly obscured. Nevertheless, the discerning ear will hear resonances of Christian motifs that seem not to have been borrowed from the contemporary environment hostile to basic Jewish beliefs and practices. The tone and tenor of these motifs, especially the positive valence accorded Torah, suggest to me an indigenous Judeo-Christian provenance rather than a Jewish adaptation of some Christological idea current in the charged atmosphere of twelfth-century Provence. Moreover, in certain passages from the *Bahir* I have detected what I consider to be an internal challenge to the mythologoumenon that I have labeled "Jewish-Christian." That is, the final redactors of the *Bahir* attempted to qualify this older tradition by emphasizing the androgynous nature of the aspect of the Godhead that corresponds to the demiurgic phallus.[26] These qualifying statements provide critical assistance in the effort to reconstruct the older mythical tradition complex.

It is worthwhile to recall in this context the claim made by the thirteenth-century Narbonnese scholar Meir ben Simeon in his treatise, *Milḥemet Miṣwah*,[27] regarding the heretical nature and imperfect literary style of the *Bahir*. After categorically rejecting the attribution of the work to the tannaitic figure, Neḥuniah ben ha-Qanah, and concluding that the *Bahir* was composed for[28] one of the Geronese kabbalists, Meir ben Simeon sums up the character of the book in the following way: "The language of this book and its whole content prove that it is from someone who does not know literary language or good style,[29] and there is in it words of heresy and apostasy in many places."[30] As Scholem has pointed out, the statement of Meir ben Simeon implies that the origin of the *Bahir* "should be sought in circles that were far removed from the rabbinical culture of those generations and that were susceptible to heretical influences, from whatever side."[31] While I offer an entirely different historical explanation for the Christological elements contained in the *Bahir*, it is of interest that this polemicist perceived heretical ideas beneath the surface of the bahiric text that appears as a strictly rabbinic midrash.[32] The context in which Meir ben Simeon placed this comment against the kabbalists is also significant, namely, the section of his anti-Christian apologetic work that deals with the misinterpretation of talmudic aggadot by Christians to demonstrate the truths of Christianity. From his vantage point, the *Bahir* presents another example of heretical interpretations of aggadah, probably along the lines of Christian theology.[33]

At the outset let me state clearly that at this stage of my research I do not claim to be able to explain the precise avenue of transmission of these motifs into the hands of those Jews responsible for the redaction of the *Bahir* in the different stages.[34] Jewish Christianity in its various forms, most important the Ebionites and Nazarenes, spread from the second to the fourth centuries from Palestine and Egypt to the East, especially Transjordan, Syria, Edessa, and Asia Minor. While there is reason to assume that Jewish Christian groups were active in the earlier medieval period in countries under Moslem rule,[35] related to various Jewish sects including the Karaites as well as those who helped convert the Khazars to Judaism,[36] there is little evidence of a discernible social phenomenon of Jewish Christians surviving into the High Middle Ages in Europe.[37] But even if the living context of Jewish Christianity had long disappeared from the face of history, the older material could have continued to circulate in limited manner in the vein of *megillot setarim*, hidden documents.[38] Fragments of texts that contained Jewish-Christian logia—for example, the "Gospel according to the Hebrews" or the "Gospel of the Nazoraeans," the "Gospel of the Ebionites," and the "Gospel according to the Egyptians"—were transmitted in the writings of the church fathers (Epiphanius, Clement of Alexandria, Didymus the Blind, Origen, Eusebius, Irenaeus, and Jerome) and continued to have a significant impact on orthodox literature of mainstream Christianity well into the Middle Ages.[39] The writings of the church fathers must also be seen as an important receptacle for the preservation of Jewish-Christian traditions that may have been passed on orally. It is plausible that through such orthodox channels Jewish-Christian ideas may have had an impact on medieval Jewry.[40]

It is also possible that Jewish-Christian traditions were transmitted as part of the literary heritage translated from Syriac into Arabic as Shlomo Pines has demonstrated in the case of a tenth-century Muᶜtazilite author, ᶜAbd al-Jabbār al-Hamadānī, in *Tathbīt Dalāʾil Nubuwwat Sayyidinā Muḥammad* (The Establishment of Proofs for the Prophethood of Our Master Mohammed).[41] Moreover, it has been suggested by Pines that the *Gospel of Barnabas,* which preserves Jewish-Christian traditions of an Ebionite provenance, was adapted or translated from Arabic and thus may have served as an important conduit for the transmission of Jewish-Christianity into Islam.[42] These Arabic sources, in turn, may have influenced Jewish authors who would have appropriated the much older Jewish-Christian teachings as part of an authentic esoteric tradition. I see no contradiction in asserting that a medieval Jewish composition preserved older Jewish-Christian traditions through the influence of contemporary Islamic or Christian sources.

Finally, and perhaps most important, it is possible that certain standard Jewish texts either preserved Jewish-Christian views or originated in Jewish circles with affinity for Christian doctrines as has been argued by Yehuda Liebes with respect to the *Midrash ʾOtiyyot de-R. ᶜAqivaʾ*, a work that is particularly germane insofar as it is a repository of themes and approaches that resemble later kabbalistic texts.[43] Even polemical passages against Christianity in this midrashic collection may provide significant clues for older Jewish-Christian beliefs that may have been committed to writing in documents that later influenced the redactors of the *Bahir.* Also relevant is another study by Liebes where he argued for a possible Jewish-Christian background of the image of Yeshua Sar ha-Panim found, together with Elijah and Meṭaṭron, in one of the prayers in the standard Ashkenazi liturgy for Rosh ha-Shanah.[44] The immediate context to locate this liturgical formulation is one of the main circles of German Pietists, the group responsible for the commentary on the names of Meṭaṭron published under the name *Sefer ha-Ḥesheq,*[45] but, according to Liebes, the *Sitz im Leben* of the image goes back to an ancient Jewish esoteric tradition that preserved this Jewish-Christian belief regarding the angelic status of Jesus.[46] It is plausible that sources such as these, and others that presently lie outside the purview of modern scholarship, were instrumental in transmitting Jewish-Christian ideas to the twelfth-century context wherein the *Bahir* was redacted. Whatever the means of transmission, it is my contention that the earlier sources may help one uncover the full meaning of the theosophic symbols and myths found in the *Bahir.*[47]

By suggesting a Jewish-Christian background for motifs in the *Bahir* I do not mean to reject other possible contexts that may have shaped the physiognomy of theosophic kabbalah as it evolved in Provence and northern Spain, including, for instance, the merging of Gnostic and Neoplatonic trends in Islamic circles, especially Ismāʿīlism,[48] on the one hand, and the blending of *merkavah* gnosis and medieval philosophical currents in Pietistic circles of Germany and northern France, on the other.[49] Scholem's predilection to accept the claim of the Castilian kabbalist Isaac ben Jacob ha-Kohen, that the *Bahir* reached Provence from Germany,[50] and his attempt to substantiate that hypothesis by reference to the textual unit the "Great Mystery" (*Razaʾ Rabbaʾ*), cited in the thirteenth century by Moses ben Eleazar ha-Darshan,[51] seems to me basically correct as I have tried to demonstrate elsewhere by providing specific motifs that are common to both the bahiric text and the theosophic writings of the Rhineland Pietists.[52] This does not, however, settle all issues pertaining to earlier sources and cultural contexts that may have produced textual units later woven into the fabric of the work.

To assess properly the "origins" of theosophic kabbalah in the *Bahir* one must first acknowledge the complexity and multiplicity of the phenomenon at hand. Indeed, it is misleading to view kabbalah, even as expressed in this one textual source, as singular and monolithic; it is rather a polymorphous entity informed by distinct patterns and structures conveyed in symbolic and mythical images. To look for the origins of something presupposes that one has identified and determined the essence of that something in a singular way in its incipient stages. It is evident from Scholem's grappling with the *Bahir* in his different studies, especially the magesterial *Origins of the Kabbalah*,[53] that he was clearly attentive to the redactional complexities pertaining to this text, distinguishing the Oriental setting of the work and its Provençal stratum; indeed, Scholem asserted that contradictions in the bahiric text are often so striking that they could be explained only by assuming a juxtaposition of fragments from different sources.[54] The attentiveness to the contradictory nature of the sources redacted in the *Bahir* notwithstanding, Scholem's choice of the title "origins of kabbalah" suggests that he had a clear and working definition of the phenomenon under investigation: the doctrine of a dynamic Godhead manifest in a decade of powers called most frequently in subsequent kabbalistic literature *sefirot*. That Scholem began his inquiry into the origins of kabbalah with the *Bahir* indicates further that he considered this structure the hallmark doctrine of this work.[55] Indeed, for Scholem, the theosophic interpretation of this key term in the *Bahir* represents the fundamental turn to kabbalah in its precise sense,[56] even though he emphasized time and again that the sefirotic system was not formalized or crystallized in all of the fragments redacted in the *Bahir*. I note, parenthetically, that most scholarship on the *Bahir*, following the lead of Scholem, has been marred by a tendency to interpret the text in accord with later kabbalistic doctrine on the ten *sefirot*,[57] a tendency found as well in the thirteenth-century Catalonian kabbalists who are historically the first individuals to cite the *Bahir*.[58] But such an assumption is suspect for two reasons: first, the term *sefirot* only occurs in one redactional setting in this work;[59] second, comprised within the *Bahir* are various theosophies that serve a more critical and recurring role than that of the ten *sefirot* or even the ten *ma*ʾ*amarot* which appear more frequently in the *Bahir*. There simply is no justification to interpret bahiric passages in light of a system of ten hypostases if the relevant texts are based on a different numerical tradition, whether it be a system of three, seven, twelve, or seventy-two potencies. Reading the doctrine of ten *sefirot* into the text reflects a hermeneutical stance predicated on privileging this structure as that which taxonomically marks the phenomenon of kabbalah.[60] This particularly biased interpretation of the *Bahir* is obviously related to the larger project of demarcating the origins of kabbalah in terms of a theosophic doctrine of ten powers or attributes that is most fully expressed in twelfth- and thirteenth-century materials.

In general, it can be said that this search for origins was clearly mediated by the specific cultural concerns of Scholem and his generation[61] and may not be shared by scholars writing in an age that has challenged in fundamental ways the whole notion of origins as some fixed, absolute beginning in time or place.[62] However, it is plausible to assume that there are religious symbols and mythical structures that span the distance of time and thereby forge a chain of intertextual links that bind together mystics living in different periods and geographical localities.[63] Perhaps these structures and symbols rather than historical novelties hold the most important keys for a proper understanding of the intricate phenomena of Jewish mysticism.[64] These structures and symbols, in turn, arise out of specific literary-historical contexts that reflect sociocultural and religious realia. The ideas may have been transmitted to kabbalists in the High Middle Ages through a variety of channels.[65] I wish to consider here one more trajectory that may supply another piece to this intriguing puzzle of cultural and religious history in the Jewish Middle Ages.

II

Let us now turn to the image of the tree in *Sefer ha-Bahir*. The first relevant context in which this image appears is a discussion found in the part of the text that reformulates a passage in *Genesis Rabbah* to the effect that God alone, without the help of any angels, created the cosmos. In the course of this discussion Isaiah 44:24 is cited, "I am the Lord, I stretch out the heavens alone, the earth is spread out before Me." This particular verse is cited to support the claim that God alone is the creator, for the last word *me-ʾiti* is playfully read *mi-ʾiti*, "who is with me," thus rendering the verse a proclammation of God's unique status as creator.[66] At this point the reader comes upon the critical passage that represents the bahiric addition to the midrashic paraphrase:

> I am the one who planted this tree so that I and the whole world would delight in it. I established in it everything and I called it All (*kol*). The explanation [of the verse in Isaiah] is precisely according to its contextual sense (*mamash ki-feshuto*)[67]: I am the Lord who made All and spread out the earth, who was with Me? There was no angel or seraph with Me, but rather I was alone. I called [the tree] All for everything is dependent upon it and everything comes out from it, all need it, they gaze upon it and wait for it. From there the souls fly out. I was alone when I made it; let no angel rise above it and say I preceded you. For at the time that I spread out the earth in which I planted and rooted this tree, and I rejoiced together with them, who was with Me when I revealed to him this secret of Mine?[68]

According to this text the tree is identified as *kol*, the All, for it is the *axis mundi*, the source of all created things. This motif is here contextualized in a monotheistic setting, for it is emphasized that God alone is the creative power who set the cosmic tree in its place. Despite the effort of contextualization, however, the "original" background of the image is transparent enough: the tree is the ontic source, or in the language of the *Bahir*, "everything is dependent upon it, everything goes out from it, everything needs it." Indeed, it is possible that the reworking of the aggadic passage at the beginning of this text served the redactional purpose of obscuring the full force of the older speculation contained in the latter part of the passage, a redactional strategy employed on other occasions in the book.

In subsequent kabbalistic literature, the reference to this All-Tree is usually interpreted as a symbol for *Yesod* (Foundation), the ninth of the ten divine emanations that corresponds to the *membrum virile* and that comprehends within itself all the forces from above. It does appear, as Scholem has noted,[69] that in the *Bahir* itself the tree may symbolize this particular grade, the *Ṣaddiq Yesod ʿOlam*, elsewhere characterized as the seventh power that is the cosmic column that sustains the world by stretching from heaven to earth.[70] Indeed, the appropriateness of the term *kol* as a designation of the cosmic tree derives from the fact that this term can refer to the phallus.[71] However, despite its obvious phallic import, in the bahiric passage under examination the term *kol* does not semantically function as a designation of the pleroma of divine potencies; the attribution of the term *kol* to the tree signifies rather its ontological status as the source of all mundane reality that is localized in the divine phallus.[72] In that sense it may be said that the term *kol* assumes a demiurgic connotation.[73] The point that I am making is more than a trivial semantic distinction. By understanding the term *kol* as a reference to the pleroma, Scholem sought an origin of the bahiric symbol in Gnostic literature. But the signification of *kol* in this text is not based on a distinctively ambivalent or negative attitude toward the physical world that one would typically find in Gnostic sources. On the contrary, the bahiric symbol of the All-Tree expresses a positive attitude toward the world; indeed, the tree is called *kol* precisely because all mundane things come from it.[74] This tree, which is referred to at the end of the passage as God's secret (*sod*), is clearly the Demiurge, the aspect of divinity that corresponds to the phallus. It is likely that the term *sod* in this context has that connotation as well.[75]

A cryptic reference to this demiurgic All, or that which contains the potencies of all being, is found in an earlier fragment of Wisdom speculation preserved in the *Bahir* where the following theosophic reading of Genesis 1:1 is offered:

> The Torah said: I was first to be the head of the world, as it said, "In the distant past I was fashioned" (Prov. 8:23). If you say that the earth preceded it, it is written, "at the beginning, at the origin of the earth" (ibid.). It is as it is said, "In the beginning Elohim created heaven and earth" (Gen. 1:1). What is "created"? He created all the needs of the All (*kol ṣarkhe ha-kol*). Afterwards Elohim, and what is written after it? "The heaven and the earth."[76]

In this intriguing passage, the first verse in the Bible is interpreted as a process of divine autogenesis. Although the term "created" is employed in this context, upon close inspection it is obvious that this bahiric fragment assumes that the verse in question posits a process of emanation whereby the different divine grades come into being. The word *re᾽shit* in the expression *bere᾽shit* refers to *Ḥokhmah* (the subject of Prov. 8:23), which, following standard rabbinic practice, is identified as Torah, here mythologized within the framework of a hypostatic ontology. The next word in the verse, the predicate *bara*ʾ, "created," is understood in terms of the All (*kol*); that is, all the needs of the All (*kol ṣarkhe ha-kol*) were created.[77] It is possible, although this conjecture needs further examination, that there is a play here, attested as well in other medieval Christian and Jewish sources,[78] on the Hebrew word *bara*ʾ and the Aramaic *bera*ʾ, "son," for both words comprise the same consonants. If that is the case, then, according to this exegesis of Genesis 1:1, the word *bara*ʾ refers to the son (the All, *ha-kol*) who comprises in himself everything.[79] Hence, the son would be in the same position as the tree that is the All described in the other bahiric fragment. Indeed, in the passage of the *Bahir* immediately following the one in which the tree that is named the All is mentioned, the expression *ṣorekh ha-ʿolam ha-zeh*, the need of this world, is used in conjunction with the tree that precedes the creation of the heaven and, we may assume, the earth.[80] The third emanated potency is designated as Elohim, but its precise nature is not specified. Even though all the details of the theosophic structure are not clear, it may be concluded that the first verse of Scripture alludes to a triad of powers that emanate prior to the creation of heaven and earth: Wisdom, the All (or the Son), and Elohim.[81]

It is also relevant that in the section of the *Bahir* immediately preceding the passage that describes the All-Tree, there is speculation on the first three letters of the Hebrew alphabet.[82] In this seemingly older fragment the ʾ*alef* symbolizes the masculine potency of God,[83] the *bet* the Torah or Wisdom, which is the feminine potency, and the *gimmel* the third potency that is described as the conduit (*ṣinnor*) that "draws [the efflux] from above and ejaculates it below" (*sho*ʾ*ev mi-le-ma*ʿ*alah u-meriq le-maṭah*).[84] It is obvious from the continuation of this text, "the *gimmel* draws by way of the head and ejaculates by way of the tail," that this reflects the Galenic conception of the sperm originating in the brain, expressed elsewhere in the *Bahir* as well in terms of the seventh of the ten divine potencies.[85] On account of the obvious phallic activity the *gimmel* is associated with the quality of *gomel ḥasadim*, bestowing acts of mercy, an association that is found in earlier sources as well.[86] It is of especial interest to note the following comment attributed to R. Aqiva in the *Bahir*: "Why is the *gimmel* third? Because it bestows (*gomelet*), grows (*mitgaddelet*), and endures (*mitqayyemet*), as it is said, 'The child grew up and was weaned,' *wa-yigddal ha-yelet wa-yiggamal* (Gen. 21:8)."[87] Is this particular prooftext meant to underscore an intrinsic connection between the third divine potency, symbolized by the *gimmel*, and the divine son represented biblically by Isaac, the promised son of Abraham? Is there here an echo of an older Jewish-Christian exegesis that identified Isaac as the typos of Jesus[88] who, incidentally, is sometimes represented in Jewish-Christian sources by the letter *gamma*, perhaps related to the word *gevurah* (*dynamis*)?[89] What may be concluded with relative certainty is that in these units the *Bahir* preserves an older speculation according to which the divine pleroma comprises three potencies symbolized by the first three letters of the Hebrew alphabet. It is likely, although it is not stated explicitly, that the *ʾalef* corresponds to the father (the Godhead that precedes everything), the *bet* to the mother or daughter (the Torah or Wisdom that was there at the beginning of creation),[90] and the *gimmel* to the son (who transmits the divine efflux to all created things). The latter, moreover, is depicted in graphically phallic terms: the three aspects associated with this potency—bestowal, expansion, and endurance—clearly relate to different activities of the male organ.[91] The redactors of the bahiric text chose to place after this tradition complex another one that is based on the demiurgic All-Tree, which also has obvious phallic connotations.[92]

It is significant that in another bahiric passage the pleroma is also represented by three primary hypostases[93] said to be comprised in the word *ʾish*, "man" (exegetically related to Exod. 15:3, "The Lord is a man of war"): the *ʾalef* is the first, the *yod* the second, and *shin* that which contains all the world (*kolel kol ha-ʿolam*), which is described further as *Teshuvah*, Repentance.[94] The divine anthropos is thus depicted in terms of a triad of powers that are said to be stacked one atop the other. It is plausible to suggest that the third potency, here represented by the letter *shin*, is the Demiurge, which is therefore described as containing the entire world. In a subsequent section of the *Bahir* the same biblical text is interpreted in what appears to me to be a later reworking of the earlier tradition based on a triad of divine potencies related to the word *ʾish*: the latter expression is said to be a sign (*siman*), for the three consonants that make up the word signify different aspects of the divine: the *ʾalef*, which is the first, is designated the "holy palace" (both the Aramaic idiom, *hekhalaʾ qadishaʾ*, and the Hebrew equivalent, *hekhal ha-qodesh*, are mentioned),[95] the *yod* alludes to the ten logoi (*maʾamarot*) by means of which the world was created and which are collectively identified as the Torah of truth (*torat ʾemet*) that "comprises all the worlds" (*kolelet kol ha-ʿolamim*); and the *shin* is the root of the tree (*shoresh ha-ʾillan*), for this particular letter is said to be like the root of the tree.[96] In the continuation of that text the tree is characterized further as comprising the powers (*koḥot*) of God, which are arranged one atop the other. The spring of water that sustains the tree is Wisdom (*ḥokhmah*), and the fruit borne by the tree is the souls of the righteous (*neshamot ha-ṣaddiqim*).[97] Almost the precise demiurgical terms used to describe the third potency, the letter *shin*, in the former context are assigned in the latter context to the second potency, the *yod* or the ten logoi comprised within the Torah of truth. In yet another bahiric passage, the *shin* is similarly characterized as the root of the tree, *shoresh ha-ʾillan*, that is bent (*meʿuqam*).[98] It is likely that this description conveys the phallic quality of the root symbolized by the *shin*. The continuation of the passage lends support to this interpretation: "What is the function of the second *shin* [in the word *shoresh*]? This is to teach you that when you take a branch and plant it, it comes back as a root."[99] The two occurrences of the letter *shin* in the word *shoresh* signify that the branch of the tree when planted becomes itself a root that can produce other trees. In an analogous way the *membrum virile* is the organ that produces seeds that may be planted and become in turn roots whence other plants spring forth. The bent root of the tree, the letter *shin*, is thus in the position of the phallus. The immediate context in which this statement occurs is also significant: the image of the root of the tree is brought as support for the notion that the name of something reflects the very nature of that thing, in the language of the *Bahir*, *di-shemo gufo*. Two examples cited to illustrate this idea are that of the righteous person and that of the wicked, for, according to Proverbs 10:7, "[t]he name of the righteous is invoked in blessing, but the name of the wicked rots."[100] It is plausible that implied here is an identification between the tree and the *ṣaddiq*, and just as the name of the *ṣaddiq* indicates something essential about the person, so the root of the tree, the *shin*, in some fundamental sense is the name of the tree.

It seems to me that attested here is an archaic tradition, probably of a Jewish-Christian provenance, that has been broken up by the redactors of the *Bahir* perhaps in a deliberate effort to hide its original setting. Consequently, the entire force of the tradition can only be appreciated if one pieces together the relevant comments as they appear in the different contexts. When that is done then one can reconstruct the following theosophic tradition: the divine anthropos is the tree of powers, and the root of that tree is the letter *shin*, which is the third power in the position of the phallus. Here we have yet another expression of the notion that the divine pleroma—symbolically portrayed as the tree that is an anthropos—is constituted by three powers: the first is the *ʾalef*; the second is the *yod*; and the third is the *shin*, which is the root of the tree, the manifestation of its name.[101] I have proposed that the origins of this mythic teaching lie in Jewish-Christian speculation.

That the letter *shin* in particular may be associated with Jesus is indicated in the following passage from *Midrash ʾOtiyyot de-R. ʿAqivaʾ*:

> Afterwards the *shin* entered and said before the Holy One, blessed be He: "Master of the Universe, let it be Your will to create the world with me for through me is Your explicit name (*shimkha ha-meforash*) called, as it says, "This shall be My name (*shemi*) forever" (Exod. 3:15). Moreover, I am at the beginning of the name Shaddai.[102] The Holy One, blessed be He, responded and said to her: No! She said to Him: Why? He responded: Because the words *shav*ʾ (falsehood) and *sheqer* (deceit) are called by means of you [i.e., both begin with the letter *shin*]. Deceit has no feet (*sheqer ʾein lo raglayim*), and so too you have no feet. How could I create the world with a letter that has no feet? She immediately departed from before Him in disappointment.[103]

Contained in this passage is a subtle polemic against Christianity based on the identification of the letter *shin* as Jesus, no doubt related to his Hebrew name, *yeshuʿa*, or the more common form in Jewish texts, *yeshu*, wherein the consonant *shin* occupies a central position phonetically.[104] It is also possible that the appropriateness of this letter to symbolize Jesus lies in the fact that the *shin* has three branches that could have easily been applied to the Trinity, the hallmark of Christian theology. In any event, it is evident that in the above passage the anonymous midrashist is utilizing this Christian symbol in a polemical context: the letter *shin*, which stands for Jesus, begins the words for falsehood and deceit. It is, therefore, inappropriate for God to have created the world by means of this letter. The anti-Christian stance is underscored by the statement that just as deceit has no feet so the letter *shin* has no feet,[105] a motif that may have been influenced by older midrashic interpretations of Genesis 3:14 to the effect that the serpent's feet were cut off as a punishment for inticing Eve (and Adam indirectly) to eat from the Tree of Knowledge.[106] On one level the proverbial statement that a lie has no feet simply means that something deceitful cannot endure, a point underscored by an earlier rabbinic comment to the effect that "truth stands but a lie does not stand."[107] On another level, however, this statement has a more symbolic connotation based on the fact that the word "feet" can function semantically as a designation for the male genitals.[108] To say that the lie has no feet implies, therefore, that Jesus, to whom is attached the word *sheqer*, is impotent or castrated. This emasculation—in fact a polemical portrayal of the Christian monastic ideal of celibacy[109]—is represented as well orthographically by the letter *shin* that has no feet, or no marks beneath it. Hence, the query placed in the mouth of God, "How could I create the world with a letter that has no feet?" is a direct challenge to the standard Christological idea (expressed, e.g., in John 1:3) that Jesus is the Logos by means of which God created the world.

Support for my reading may be gathered from a second passage in the same midrashic collection:

> Why does the *shin* have three branches from above but it has no root from below? Because it is the first of the letters of [the word] *sheqer*, and *sheqer* has speech (*dibbur*) but no feet (*raglayim*); in the end it is not established. In the future the Holy One, blessed be He, will close the mouth of those who speak lies, as it says, "May the Lord cut off all flattering lips" (Ps. 12:4), and it also says, "He who speaks untruth shall not stand before my eyes" (ibid., 101:7). To what may this be compared? To a tree whose branches are many but its roots are few, and when the wind comes it uproots it and turns it on its face.[110]

It should be evident from this passage, therefore, that the *shin* represents Jesus: the three branches allude to the Trinity, whereas the fact that there is no root (or feet) beneath the letter suggests that there is no basis or foundation to this entity. The reference to Jesus is confirmed by the intriguing passage, "deceit has speech but no feet"; that is, Jesus is the Logos (*dibbur*), but he has no power of endurance. In the final analysis, this force will be uprooted. Utilizing a parable from an entirely different context in an earlier rabbinic source,[111] the author of this text extends the polemic to Christianity more generally: this religion is like a tree that has many branches but very few roots, and like such a tree it will easily be uprooted and overturned in the future.

Assuming the correctness of my interpretation, one may conclude that these polemical passages preserve an indigenous Jewish-Chrisitian tradition whereby Jesus was represented by the letter *shin*, the position against which the midrashist is directing his comments. It is precisely such symbolism that is operative in the *Bahir* as well. The divine anthropos is the tree comprised of three potencies: the *ʾalef*, the *yod*, and the *shin*. This *shin*, moreover, is the root of the tree that corresponds to the phallus. In marked contrast to the midrashic passages explored above, no negative connotation of the *shin* can be detected in the bahiric text. On the contrary, preserved here is an ancient speculation on the cosmic tree from which all being arises. I have argued that this speculation probably originated in a Jewish-Christian milieu. A similiar claim can be made with respect to the description of the All-Tree in the passage discussed above. That too seems to have derived from a Jewish-Chrisitan context.

At this juncture let me cite the text I referred to above from the *Periphyseon* of John Scotus Eriugena, which is, in fact, an exposition of a comment of Gregory of Nyssa's *De hominis opificio* to the effect that the two trees in Paradise are called respectively "all" (πᾶν) and "knowable" (γνωστόν):

> Now, let no follower of our Theologian's doctrine imagine that there were in Paradise a large number of trees of different forms and different fruits, as though it were a forest thick with trees: there were but two, the one *πᾶν*, and the other *γνωστόν*. And the *πᾶν ζύλον*, that is, "the All-Tree," of Paradise is the Word and Wisdom of the Father, Our Lord Jesus Christ, Who is the fruit-bearing All-tree . . . . And this is what the Scripture says: "And the Lord God produced from the earth," that is, from our material nature, "the All-tree," that is, the Incarnate Word, in Which and through Which all things are made, and Which is all things. For it alone is the substantial Good . . . . From this "All-tree," then, that is to say, this plentitude of all goods, the first human beings were ordered to take their food: and the whole human genus until now is bidden to live by it.[112]

In this passage, then, the "all" is identified as the Word (*verbum*) and Wisdom (*sapienta*) of the Father,[113] the source of all goodness and being. It is thus appropriate that Jesus would be symbolized as the "All-Tree" of Paradise, or the Tree of Life that is fruit-bearing. It is evident from this passage as well that the fruits borne by the tree that is the All are human souls.[114] Apparently, Eriugena has utilized a motif known from earlier Christian literature including passages from the New Testament, to wit, the association of the word "all" (πᾶs) with Jesus insofar as he is (as he receives from the Father) the ontic source of all things,[115] and has combined that with the symbolic identification of Jesus as the Tree of Life. This tree is further characterized as the "plentitude of all goods" (*omnium bonorum plenitudine*)[116] from which all human beings were ordered to derive their sustenance. Thus the Tree of Life is here understood in terms of the image of the cosmic tree. In contrast to the more standard identification found in early Christian art, liturgical, and theological texts of the wooden cross and the Tree of Life (μυστήριον τοῦ ζύλον; *sacramentum ligni vitae*), the *axis mundi* or center of the world,[117] Eriugena has identified Jesus himself as that tree.[118] This identification resonates with a motif found in Jewish-Christian literature wherein the cross of wood is personified as a power that emanated from the resurrected Jesus or fully identified as Christ himself.[119]

It is of interest to note in this context that the same identification, indeed in terms remarkably close to Eriugena's reading of Gregory of Nyssa, is found in one of the texts of the Nag Hammadi library of Gnostic sources, *The Teachings of Silvanus*. It has been argued that despite the appearance of this work in the Gnostic corpus, it derives from another milieu, perhaps one markedly not Gnostic (if not anti-Gnostic in some fundamental sense).[120] According to some scholars, *The Teachings of Silvanus* can be traced back to a Greek original of the late second or early third century (perhaps from Alexandrian Egypt[121]) and may indeed reflect a Jewish-Christian provenance.[122] Malcolm Peel and Jan Zandee have succinctly described the tractate as a "rare specimen of Hellenistic Christian Wisdom literature" that "displays a remarkable synthesis of biblical and late Jewish ideas with Middle Platonic and late Stoic anthropological, ethical, and theological concepts."[123] In *The Teachings of Silvanus* the Tree of Life planted in the Garden of Eden (cf. Gen. 2:9) is identified explicitly as Christ who, moreover, is characterized both as Wisdom[124] and as the Word: "For the Tree of Life is Christ. He is Wisdom. For he is Wisdom; he is also the Word."[125] In another passage from the same work, God, who is said to contain everything, is called the "All": "Everything is in God, but God is not in anything. Now what is it to know God? God is all which is the truth."[126] In the continuation of that passage Christ too is identified as the All, having received everything from the Father or the Existent One: "And all is Christ, he who has inherited all from the Existent One . . . Christ is all. He who does not possess all is unable to know Christ."[127]

The statement regarding everything being in God but God's not being in anything has parallels in Hellenistic Jewish (especially Philonic) and early Christian literature, and it is likely to have originated in some such environment.[128] It would appear, moreover, that in this context "all" signifies the totality of created entities; that is, God is said to be the "All" for he contains all things, and, similarly, Christ is designated by this term for the same reason.[129] Consequently, one should distinguish between the identification of Christ as the All in this context and the Valentinian teaching concerning the Savior who is All, for in the latter sense "all" signifies the totality of the divine pleroma.[130] The significant point for this analysis is that in *The Teachings of Silvanus* Jesus is identified as the Tree of Life that is the All (i.e., contains all things), and at the same time he is identified as Wisdom and as the Word. It is reasonable to assume that these identifications stem from a Jewish-Christian environment where Jesus, the cosmic tree, was viewed as the demiurgic power that contained all of reality in an analogous fashion to the World-Soul in Platonic thought.[131] The identical associations are present in the aforecited passage from Eriugena's *Periphyseon*. While the precise lines of transmission still need to be charted, in general terms it has been shown that *The Teachings of Silvanus* exerted an important influence on several Patristic writers who, in turn, had an impact on Eriugena, for example, Origen and Gregory of Nyssa.[132] In the absence of a more precise understaning of the transmission of this older Jewish-Christian mythologoumenon, it can only be asserted that the text of Eriugena, which does not reflect conventional medieval Christian doctrine, presents an extraordinary parallel to the passage in the *Bahir*. Even if the text of Eriugena, or the tradition upon which it is based, did not directly influence the redactors of the *Bahir*, I contend that the correct implications of the latter can be gauged from the former. This is especially relevant in terms of uncovering latent Christological elements in the Jewish source regarding the Demiurge that is the All-Tree.

The possible Jewish-Christian background of the demiurgic speculation connected to the cosmic tree is supported by another passage in the *Bahir* in which the Righteous One who is the Foundation of the World (*Ṣaddiq Yesod ᶜOlam*) is described as possessing in his hand the

> soul of everything living for he is the eternally living one (*ḥei ha-ᶜolamim*),[133] and every expression of creation (*leshon beriʾah*) is performed through him, and concerning him it is written, "He ceased from work and was refreshed," *shavat wa-yinafash* (Exod. 31:17), and he is the attribute of the Sabbath day (*middat yom ha-shabbat*) . . . . And what is the seventh attribute? It is the attribute of goodness (*middat ṭuvo*) of the Holy One, blessed be He.[134]

This very important passage represents one of the older textual units incorporated in the *Bahir* based on a conception of the pleroma comprising seven potencies, attested to elsewhere in the book as well.[135] Significantly, the seventh attribute, also identified as the Sabbath and divine goodness,[136] is explicitly characterized as the Demiurge through whom every (linguistic) expression of creation is performed and in whose hands are the souls of everything living. The latter motif is repeated elsewhere in the *Bahir* where it is stressed that the biblical expression *shavat wa-yinafash* signifies that the "day of Sabbath establishes all souls" or, alternatively, this hypostasis is the source whence the "souls come forth."[137] Here it is relevant to note that there is sufficient textual evidence to show that an archaic Jewish-Christian tradition, which identified the Demiurge and the Sabbath, exerted a pronounced influence upon several different Gnostic authors, particularly those who espoused a form of Valentinian gnosis.[138] In the case of the Gnostic sources, the demiurgic Sabbaton assumes negative characteristics in line with the basic theological orientation of Gnosticism to differentiate between the good God of the pleroma and the evil Demiurge.[139] Yet beneath the layers of Gnostic interpretation lies the Jewish-Christian teaching regarding the demiurgic Sabbath. There is no reason to assume that in this context, in which the traditional Jewish observance of the Sabbath was upheld, the deified Sabbath would have been treated negatively. On the contrary, it would stand to reason that the Jewish-Christian mythologoumenon was predicated on the identification of Jesus as the Sabbath,[140] a motif that is found in New Testament and Patristic sources as well, although in a typological rather than mythical sense; that is, Jesus represents the soteriological fulfillment of the Sabbath, and as such true rest (*anapausis*) is realized through him rather than through observing the ritual.[141]

Particularly relevant is a passage in the Pseudo-Clementine *Homilies* 17 where the mystery of the seven (*hebdemados mysterion*)[142] is described in terms of the six Extensions (*ektaseis*), corresponding to the six days of creation, going out of and returning to the middle, which is the seventh power or God, the beginning and the end (*arkhe kai teleute*), also designated as the Repose of all (*anapausis ton holon*),[143] i.e., the Sabbath, whose image (*eikon*) is the Aeon-to-come (*esomenon aiona*).[144] The seventh power, moreover, is that which grants life to souls through their drawing breath from the participation of the Intellect. Shlomo Pines noted the similarity of this text and a kabbalistic idea found in a zoharic passage[145] that speaks of the Sabbath as God's name, that is, the totality of the sefirotic pleroma.[146] He would have done well, however, to mention the aforecited bahiric passage that characterizes the Sabbath as the seventh power of the divine. Furthermore, from a second passage in the *Bahir,* it is clear that this seventh logos (*ma᾿amar*), the foundation of all souls (*yesod ha-nefashot kulan*) that corresponds to Sabbath, is in the center and the other six logoi, corresponding to the primordial days of creation, surround it, three above and three below.[147] This text presents a striking parallel to the Jewish-Christian passage noted by Pines. The evidence of the ancient tradition that portrays the Sabbath as the Demiurge is essential for evaluating the possible antiquity of the bahiric fragments. Despite occasional references in aggadic and esoteric sources to a hypostasized or even apotheosized Sabbath, in some cases personified as a bride or queen,[148] there is, as far as I am aware, no Jewish source prior to the *Bahir* that depicts the Sabbath as the Demiurge and the *axis mundi,* the cosmic center that is the source of all souls.[149] Moreover, as will be shown more fully below, the demiurgic *Ṣaddiq* in the relevant bahiric passages also has an implicit (and occasionally explicit) messianic dimension. In light of that factor the reference to the earlier Jewish-Christian tradition is the more intriguing: here too one finds that the Demiurge is designated Sabbath and assumes the dual characteristic of cosmic center and messianic redeemer.

As in the text of Eriugena cited above, in the *Bahir* human souls are specifically mentioned in terms of the All-Tree; all souls come from this tree. The cosmic role of the tree as the ontic and demiurgic source is underscored as well: "everything is dependent upon it and everything comes out from it, all need it." This description is followed by the comment: "towards it they set their gaze and wait for it." It may be assumed that the first part of this statement, "towards it they set their gaze" (*u-vo ṣofim*), involves some conception of a mystical comprehension of the cosmic tree depicted in visionary terms (the operative technical word being *ṣefiyyah*).[150] But what is the underlying conception of the latter part of the statement, "all wait for it" (*we-lo mekhakim*)? Do we have here an implicit messianic reference? Or, to put the issue somewhat differently, is the tree imbued with soteriological significance such that the waiting referred to has a distinct eschatological sense as Scholem already noted in passing?[151] The cosmic tree, then, would not only be the ontic source of all souls, but it would also be a messianic figure. This interpretation is suggested by the philological implication of the expression *we-lo mekhakim*, specifically as it is used in Habakkuk 2:3 and in subsequent exegesis based upon it.

Support for my interpretation may be gathered from the other three explicit references to Messiah in the *Bahir*, although these contexts actually challenge, if not directly attack, the earlier Jewish-Christian motif that I have argued is preserved in the bahiric text. Indeed, careful attention to the issue of the nature of the Messiah provides an important key for understanding something of the redactional strategy employed in this very complicated anthology of competing and at times colliding fragments of theosophic traditions. The first reference to the Messiah occurs in the context of an explication of the seven voices of revelation mentioned in Exodus 20:15, "And all the people saw the voices," which is connected with the voices specified in Psalm 29.[152] In classical rabbinic sources the seven occurrences of the expression "voice of the Lord" (*qol YHWH*) are applied to the revelation of Torah at Sinai. What is distinctive about the *Bahir* is that these voices symbolize the divine emanations.[153] It is my assumption, moreover, that the specific passage reflects a later stage in the redactional process of the text. It is apparent that the redactors of this section extended the received tradition concerning the seven (hypostatic) voices to ten, based in part on earlier rabbinic texts that affirm the presence of ten voices of revelation at Sinai. In the aforementioned passage the seven voices correspond to the seven lower emanations, for as we find elsewhere in the *Bahir,* also reflecting a later redactional stage, the tenfold pleroma is divided into two realms, the upper three emanations that constitute a distinct unity, and the seven lower ones.[154] Assuming the correctness of the previous claim we can further assume that the sixth of the seven voices corresponds to the gradation of *Yesod,* the Foundation. Although it is the case, as I have noted, that in other sections of the *Bahir* this particular gradation is clearly identified as the seventh emanation,[155] it seems that in this context the approach that became most typical in subsequent kabbalistic literature is already operative. That is, the seven voices correspond to the seven lower emanations, and the seventh one is the *Shekhinah.*[156] Having correlated the seventh voice with the *Shekhinah,* it is reasonable to posit that the sixth voice corresponds to *Yesod,* the divine phallus that overflows to the *Shekhinah.* If the sixth emanation is indeed *Yesod,* it is significant that the Messiah is mentioned precisely in conjunction with this gradation: the traditional savior (*mashiaḥ*) is identified as the Righteous (*Ṣaddiq*) in the divine pleroma, the cosmic pillar or *axis mundi.* Not only is the redeemer a nationalist, religious, and political hero, he is the element of God that sustains all existence. I would suggest that the redactors of the *Bahir* well understood the messianic aspect of the demiurgic All-Tree, which corresponds to the phallus. Hence, in the redactional setting described above, the gradation of the divine that is linked to the phallus is still associated with messianic qualities.

The correlation of the masculine *Yesod* and the Messiah is underscored in another section of the *Bahir,* which consists of a reworking of the aggadic interpretation[157] of the word *yinnon* in Psalms 72:17 as a reference to the proper name of the Messiah: "[The word *yinnon*] has a double *nun,* the bent *nun* and the straight *nun,* for [the redemption] must come to be through the masculine and the feminine."[158] As Scholem observed,[159] this text indicates that the process of messianic redemption involves the union or the conjunction of the masculine and feminine aspects of the divine related to the double *nun* in the formation of the name *Yinnon* applied to the Messiah; that is, the two forms of the letter *nun,* the straight and the bent, correspond respectively to the masculine and feminine tendencies. Whereas the first bahiric text mentioned the Messiah in connection with the male potency exclusively, in this context the Messiah is portrayed as embracing the union of male and female. While both of these traditions had an impact on subsequent kabbalistic literature,[160] I suggest that the former reflects the older mythologem that I have described as Jewish-Christian in provenance and the latter is the twelfth-century kabbalistic response to it. That is, the demiurgic All that is the *axis mundi* and cosmic tree is not only male but rather comprises both male and female. To be sure, there are earlier sources that affirm the androgynous nature of the redeemer, but a careful redactional study of the appropriate passages in the *Bahir* reveals that this view is presented as a response or a reaction to the tradition regarding the demiurgic and phallic nature of the Messiah. Thus in one passage the androgynous nature of God is in fact localized in the phallus:

> What is the [letter] *ṣaddi*? *Yod nun,* the *ṣaddi* and his mate, *yod* and *nun.* Thus it is written, "Righteous, foundation of the world" (Prov. 10:25).[161]

Orthographically, the letter *ṣaddi* can be broken up into a *yod* and a *nun,* with the former sitting on top of the latter. The explicit identification of the letter *ṣaddi* as Jesus is made in *Midrash ʾOtiyyot de-Rabbi ʿAqivaʾ*, and it is possible that the exegesis on the shape of the letter *ṣaddi* found in the *Bahir* was already implied in the midrashic source and perhaps entered into the *Bahir* from that channel.[162] The bahiric text wishes to inform the reader that comprised within the *ṣaddi,* which clearly represents the aspect of God called *Ṣaddiq,* that is, the *membrum virile,* are the male (*yod*) and the female (*nun*).[163] This is the import of the prooftext: the masculine Righteous is the foundation of the feminine world. It is possible, as Liebes has suggested, that the letter *ṣaddi* in later kabbalistic sources—especially the *Zohar*—based on earlier midrashic texts, may have symbolized Jesus, the *yod* and *nun* perhaps even standing for *yeshu noṣri.*[164] If we are to assume this to be the conceptual underpinning of the bahiric passage, then the idea expressed here would turn the Christian interpretation on its head; that is, the real *Ṣaddiq,* the cosmic foundation and messianic redeemer, is the androgynous phallus and not the celibate male born of a barren womb, which in effect represents the impotent penis. This is precisely the implication of the passage regarding the double *nun* in the messianic name, *Yinnon;* this figure comprises the union of both genders.[165] The bisexual nature of the letter *ṣaddi,* and the messianic *Ṣaddiq* that it symbolizes, seems to me to represent a direct challenge to the messianic claim of Christianity reflected as well, albeit in a very muted form, in some fragments of the *Bahir.*

To appreciate the full force of this internal debate in the *Bahir* between a Jewish-Christian and an anti-Christian stance regarding the nature of Messiah, it is essential to consider carefully the redactional context of the passage under discussion. Immediately preceding the bahiric reflection on the name *Yinnon,* there is an exegetical reflection on the two shapes of the letter *mem.*

> Why is the open *mem* comprised of masculine and feminine and the closed [*mem*] masculine? To teach you that the essence of the *mem* is masculine. The opening [of the *mem*] is added for the sake of the feminine. Just as the male does not give birth through the opening so the closed *mem* is not open, and just as the female gives birth and is open so the *mem* is closed and opened. Why did you include an opened and closed *mem*? For it is said, do not read *mem* but rather *mayyim*. The woman is cold and thus needs to be warmed by the male.[166]

In this passage there is an extraordinary reversal of gender attribution. The closed *mem* symbolizes the sterile male that is also depicted as the barren womb. Indeed, according to one view expressed in this context, the closed *mem* is shaped from above like a womb (the Hebrew word employed is *beṭen,* which in this case should be translated as "womb"). The woman whose womb is closed and thus cannot give birth is masculinized, for she is like the male who does not give birth through his opening. By contrast, the open *mem* comprises both male and female, symbolizing the womb that gives birth, and it is a sign of fertility and virility because it contains both male and female. The fertile womb is represented by the open *mem,* which is linked essentially to the masculine, *ʿiqqar ha-mem huʾ ha-zakhar;* indeed, the latter term may signify more specifically the *membrum virile.*[167] Hence, the male organ is compared to the womb that gives birth, and the masculine is feminized. It is possible, moreover, that the intricate gender symbolism in this text is a historical allusion to Christianity insofar as Jesus was typically portrayed as the son that issued from the womb of the virgin, that is, the closed *mem.* Liebes has shown that in the thirteenth-century Christian work *Pugio Fidei* by Raymond Martinus, the closed *mem* of the messianic expression *le-marbeh ha-misrah,* "in token of abundant authority" (Isa. 9:6), is interpreted as referring to the closed womb from which Jesus was born. Moreover, Liebes also notes that in this work this exegesis is connected with the talmudic statement that the open *mem* refers to a revealed saying (*maʾamar patuaḥ*) and the closed *mem* to a concealed saying (*maʾamar satum*),[168] the word *maʾamar* being translated in the technical Christian sense of *logos.* These motifs are reflected as well in certain zoharic texts that, as Liebes has argued, indicate an ambivalent attitude toward Jesus: on the one hand, the zoharic authorship polemicizes against the messianic claims of Christianity, but, on the other, the *Zohar* clearly draws from Christological images to construct its own messianic posture.[169] What, however, is underlying the exegesis of the letter *mem* in the *Bahir* itself? Is one to think of the closed *mem* in Isaiah 9:6 in conjunction with the bahiric text, as Azriel of Gerona implied in his own interpretation of this passage,[170] thereby strengthening the messianic signification of the open and the closed *mem*? Such a messianic reading would account well for the subsequent discussion on the two shapes of the letter *nun* that are connected with the messianic name *Yinnon*. As noted above, this particular name of the Messiah conveys the androgynous nature of the savior. With this characterization one moves beyond the Jewish-Christian doctrine regarding the phallic nature of the demiurgic redeemer to the twelfth-century kabbalistic idea that the phallus itself comprises both masculine and feminine components. The messianic figure is still located in the aspect of God that corresponds to the phallus, but the latter represents the unity of male and female: the *ṣaddi* is broken into *yod* and *nun*, masculine and feminine, the Righteous one that is the foundation of the world. Indeed, in the bahiric reflection on the two shapes of the letter *nun* that immediately precedes the passage on the two shapes of the letter *mem*, it is precisely the ontic containment of the feminine in the masculine that is affirmed: "the straight *nun* always comes at the end of a word to indicate that the straight *nun* comprises the bent and straight . . . the straight *nun* is comprised of masculine and feminine."[171] Therein lies the mystical secret of redemption that departs from the older Jewish-Christian teaching preserved in certain fragments of the *Bahir* and embraces the essential kabbalistic gnosis that is more fully developed in subsequent literature.[172] It may very well be that in this case the polemical stance vis-à-vis Christianity served as an impetus for the formulation of the kabbalistic view concerning the theosophic nature of the Messiah.[173]

The position that I have articulated is confirmed in a third context in the *Bahir,* in which reference is made to the Messiah. In this case as well it appears that one is dealing with a section of the text that reflects a later redactional stage. In a different context above I referred to the kernel of what I take to be a much older theosophic tradition regarding the *axis mundi*, the *Ṣaddiq*, who is designated the "eternally living one," *ḥei ha-ʿolamim*, for "in his hand are the souls of all living things."[174] According to that tradition, moreover, the demiurgic *Ṣaddiq* was identified further as the seventh attribute, the Sabbath or divine goodness, that stands in the central position of the phallus. After this tradition is enunciated in the bahiric text it is somewhat qualified by a passage that affirms the feminine aspect of Sabbath, a motif expressed in older Jewish sources. The apparent tension between these two depictions is resolved in a third passage that ascribes an androgynous nature to the Sabbath.[175] This redactional pattern is consistent with the passages that I have cited in which the phallic aspect of God is treated as bisexual. The passage that immediately follows the attribution of masculine and feminine qualities to the Sabbath resumes the discussion on the demiurgic potency designated the "eternally living one," *ḥei ha-ʿolamim*:

> Why do we say [in the blessing after food] "On all that He created etc. the eternally living one?" Why don't we say, "On all that You created?" Rather, we bless the Holy One, blessed be He, so that He will bestow His wisdom upon the eternally living one, and it gives everything. What is the reason for saying [in the blessings] "who has made us holy by His commandments and commanded us?" Why do we not say, "that You have made us holy with Your commandments and commanded us"? This teaches us that all the commandments are comprised within the eternally living one. Because of His love for us He has given us [the commandments] to sanctify us and to allow us to be meritorious. Why? For when we are in this world we may merit the world-to-come which is great. In his hand is the treasury of all souls, and when Israel is good the souls are worthy of coming out and entering this world, and if they are not good they do not emerge. Thus is it is said,[176] the son of David will not come until all the souls in the body are consumed. What is [the meaning of] all the souls in the body? That is to say, all the souls in the body of the anthropos (*guf ha-ʾadam*), and then the new ones will merit to emerge. The son of David will then come for he will merit to be born for his soul will emerge anew, together with the others.[177]

It is obvious that these passages follow quite naturally the preceding one that describes the eternally living one as the Sabbath, the seventh attribute and divine goodness. Both of these passages reiterate the demiurgic role of the divine gradation referred to principally as the eternally living one, and the second one underscores its messianic aspect. While that element of the divine is not specifically identified as the Messiah, it is nevertheless instructive that the bahiric authorship interpreted the talmudic reference to the Messiah's coming when all the souls of the body are consumed in the context of discussing the demiurgic potency of God. The enigmatic reference to the body (*guf*) in the Talmud is here identified more specifically as the body of the anthropos (*guf ha-ʾadam*), which is the eternally living one. That is to say, the word *guf* does not signify the body in a generic sense but rather the male organ that was viewed as the center of the body. The Messiah is described as coming forth from this grade when all the other souls have been consumed. A special relationship is thus established between the body of the anthropos, the divine phallus, and the Messiah.

In summation, through a careful redactional study, I have tried to isolate a core tradition complex in the *Bahir* concerning the demiurgic potency that is represented in various ways, including the tree that is All, the Sabbath, the seventh attribute, divine goodness, the Righteous one, the eternally living one, and the Messiah. All of these appellations share one thing: they are related to the aspect of the divine that anatomically correponds to the phallus. In my judgment, the environment that fostered this cluster of symbols was related to some form of Jewish-Christian speculation on the demiurgic son, Jesus, also portrayed as the All-tree, the ontic source of all souls, the Sabbath, and the Messiah. Interestingly enough, I have located a number of bahiric passages where the theosophic system is predicated on a triad of powers in which the third one is characterized in obvious phallic terms and in some cases either explicitly referred to or implicitly alluded to as the son. A close examination of these fragments indicates that the All-Tree, which is the divine anthropos comprised of three powers, has messianic implications. Indeed, the theosophic mythologem that I have reconstructed is based on the divinization of the Messiah and his contextualization as the demiurgic phallus. In a possible attempt to obfuscate or polemicize against this tradition, perhaps due to its resonance with Christian doctrine, the redactors of the *Bahir* have emphasized the androgynous nature of that aspect of God that is the phallus. That is, the emphasis on the masculine and the feminine elements of this potency presents a direct challenge to the Christological view according to which the savior is decidedly male. To put the matter simply, the *yod-nun* derived from the *ṣaddi* is transformed from *yeshu noṣri*, the impotent male without a female counterpart who issued from the barren womb of the virgin, to the masculine (*yod*) and feminine (*nun*) aspects of the divine phallus, the righteous pillar of the world, the Sabbath Queen and her masculine mate, the hypostasized day of Sabbath. By stressing that the *Ṣaddiq* (or Sabbath) is concomitantly male and female the uniquely Jewish dimension is privileged and thereby displaces the older phallic interpretation that lies at the core of the image of the tree that is the All.

◆ 3 ◆

WALKING AS A SACRED DUTY: THEOLOGICAL TRANSFORMATION OF SOCIAL REALITY IN EARLY HASIDISM

Desire itself is movement
Not in itself desirable.
—T. S. Eliot, "Burnt Norton"

I

One of the central images in both the homiletical and the folkloristic traditions in Hasidic literature is that of the itinerant. The importance of this image for the social history of early Hasidism has been well documented in several major studies with special reference to the role played by wandering preachers (*mokhiḥim* and *maggidim*) and exorcists (*ba ͨale shem*) in the formation of pietistic circles in eighteenth-century Ukraine.[1] What has been less carefully studied, however, is the theological significance that this image assumed in subsequent Hasidic thought.[2] Even a cursory glance at the sources from the second and third generations of the Hasidic movement indicates the extent to which this literature is characterized by an impressive preponderance of imagery associated with walking, taking a journey,[3] and the like, images, that is, derived from the itinerant lifestyle. It is the aim of this study to fill that scholarly gap by presenting some crucial aspects of the itinerant motif as it is developed in early Hasidism.

At the outset, let me note that two distinct typologies can be distinguished, although only the latter is rooted in teachings ascribed to the Besht. The first involves the use of the walking motif as a symbol for the spiritual progression through various grades, culminating ultimately in a state of *devequt*, "cleaving" or "attachment" to God. This usage is found in a wide range of authors, including two of the most prominent followers of the Besht, Jacob Joseph of Polonnoye (d. 1782)[4] and Dov Baer, the Maggid of Miedzyrzecz (1704–1772),[5] as well as many of the latter's disciples.[6] One can indeed distinguish between at least two models of cleaving to God in Hasidic sources: (a) the vertical one that entails the metaphor of ascent and descent, and (b) the horizontal one that entails the metaphor of traversing from place to place. Hasidic writers used both models to delineate the individual's intimate relationship with God; it cannot be said, therefore, as it has been recently argued, that the one took precedence over the other.[7] Hence, the image of the itinerant was upheld as a model for the mystic path. It is true, however, that some Hasidic writers viewed the itinerant lifestyle as a distraction and an obstacle for the *ṣaddiq*, drawing him away from a state of cleaving to God through contemplative prayer and Torah study.[8] Yet there is an abundance of textual evidence that demonstrates conclusively that the early writers saw no conflict between walking and the spiritual state leading to *devequt*. On the contrary, the proper worship of God was said to be realized even as one physically walked about and was engaged in social commerce.[9] As such, *halikhah* became a popular metaphor for the spiritual path.

The second typology, which is traceable to the Besht himself, at least as one may gather from the Hasidic sources, is decidedly soteriological[10] in its orientation, emphasizing two acts whose redemptive nature from the kabbalistic perspective is beyond question, namely, the liberation of the sparks of light trapped in demonic shells and the unification of the masculine and the feminine aspects of the divine. While these two themes are connected already in a prominent fashion in the Lurianic mythology, the Hasidim combined Lurianic ideas with still older kabbalistic themes and symbols. With respect to these ideas the Hasidic texts share some phenomenological similarities with Sabbatian circles, but I argue that the similarities stem from the common literary sources of Lurianic kabbalah rather than any direct borrowing. In discussions on the possible messianic and Sabbatian elements in Hasidism this crucial dimension has not been sufficiently noted. It is this latter typology that is the subject of my analysis. I limit my discussion to the treatment of the motif of *halikhah* in three authors, Jacob Joseph of Polonnoye, Menaḥem Naḥum of Chernobyl (1730–1797), and Moses Ḥayyim Ephraim of Sudlikov (ca. 1737–1800).

II

Viewing the act of walking or migration in a soteriological context is not the innovation of the Besht or any of his immediate disciples. Indeed, already in the writings of Moses Cordovero (1522–1570) the peregrinations of the kabbalists were understood as a means to provide some form of temporary dwelling for the *Shekhinah* in her exilic state. Cordovero effectively inverted the zoharic teaching—which, incidentally, provides the mystical backdrop for the narrative of the *Zohar*—that the *Shekhinah* accompanies the righteous in all their wanderings in exile.[11] Paradoxically, according to Cordovero, by means of the *gerushin,* the forced "banishments" or "exile wanderings" from place to place, the kabbalists were elevated above their own state of exile, for they gave support to the weakened *Shekhinah* and received mystical illumination in the form of innovative Scriptural interpretations.[12]

Closer to home for the circle of the Besht is the idea expressed in the eighteenth-century homiletical work *Sha*ʿ*ar ha-Melekh* of Mordecai ben Samuel, regarding the itinerant preachers, designated the "feet of the *Shekhinah,*"[13] whose journeys from town to town symbolized the exile of *Shekhinah.*[14] Out of poverty these preachers were forced to wander about in order to earn a living, but on a more profound level, through their journeying they not only sought to turn the masses to repentenance, but they accompanied the *Shekhinah* in her homeless state. Hence, they were also called the "camp of the *Shekhinah,*"[15] "for they join the *Shekhinah* as she wanders from her place . . . and they are the messengers of God (*sheluḥe de-raḥmana*ʾ)."[16] The socioeconomic status of the preachers is thus transformed in light of the theological belief concerning the exile of *Shekhinah.*

It is within this latter framework that the Hasidic idea of *halikhah* must be evaluated. The significance that the itinerant life assumed for the Hasidim is evident not only from the legendary tales about the Besht—including his own journeys and the journeys of others coming to see him,[17] but also from comments on the nature of travel attributed directly to the Baal Shem Ṭov by some of his disciples. I begin with the writings of Jacob Joseph that are widely acknowledged to be the richest treasure trove of the Besht's teachings.

Jacob Joseph reports that the Besht taught that by means of one's journeying from place to place one uplifts the fallen sparks of his soul root[18] and restores them to their proper source.[19] He thus writes in his *Ketonet Passim*:

> I have written elsewhere the explanation of the passage in Ḥullin (91b): "'The ground on which you [Jacob] are lying I will assign to you' (Gen. 28:13), what is the significance of this comment? R. Isaac said: this teaches that the Holy One, blessed be He, folded all of the land of Israel and placed it under him [i.e., Jacob]." I have heard in the name of my teacher [i.e., the Besht] that traveling from place to place is [for the sake of] purifying the sparks. Jacob, under whom [God] folded all the land of Israel, did not have to travel, but he was able to purify the sparks in his place by means of the study of Torah.[20]

Reflecting on a passage parallel to the above citation in Jacob Joseph's *Ben Porat Yosef,* Joseph Weiss wrote that the

> Besht's theory of the sparks belonging to one person and yet scattered should be understood as conditioned by his own situation, and indeed it precisely reflects the predicament of the peddler in magical amulets and charms who wanders through the Jewish settlements of Eastern Europe, but dreams in Lurianic terms of the possibility of earning a living in a way that would allow him to gather up the sparks of his soul in one place without having to move from village to village. However, this dream of an ideal sedentary existence could not sufficiently be fulfilled in his own lifetime.[21]

Weiss therefore sees in this teaching attributed to the Besht the beginnings of the shift from the itinerant *ba*ᶜ*al shem* to the settled *ṣaddiq,* who holds court and thus earns his living in a way that allows him to gather the sparks in one place. In fact, however, it can be shown from a careful analysis of all the relevant texts in Jacob Joseph's corpus that this was not the intent of the Besht's teaching, or at least the teaching that Jacob Joseph reports in the name of the Besht. The contrast rather is between one who is compelled to go out to earn a living and one who is worthy to study Torah in a more or less stable and secure position.[22] Hence, in the passage from *Ketonet Passim* cited above, Jacob's study of Torah in one fixed place is contrasted with the individual who must move from place to place, although both have the same goal in mind, namely, purification of the fallen sparks. Support for my interpretation may be gathered from Jacob Joseph's own complicated exegesis of Song of Songs 6:1–3 in the continuation of this passage:

> "Whither has your beloved gone, O fairest of women" (Song of Songs 6:1)—this refers to the sage who is called beloved. . . .

> "Whither has your beloved gone," to seek a livelihood for his household. Could the Holy One, blessed be He, not have provided for them in their place?. . . . But [as the next verse says] "My beloved has gone down to his garden" (ibid., 2), i.e., the place wherein my sparks were sown. The meaning of the expression "his garden" is that in that place the holy sparks have fallen. . . . Therefore he has "to browse in many gardens," i.e., in every place where he is, and "to pick lilies," my sparks. This is not the case for [the one thus described] "I am my beloved's and my beloved is mine; he browses among the lilies" (ibid., 3), i.e., one who cleaves (*medabbeq*) to the Torah, which is called "my beloved" (*dodi*) and, consequently, the Torah is [in a state of] "my beloved is mine." For I am one who "browses among the lilies" as is proper in his place, and I do not have to travel hither and thither.[23]

Jacob Joseph thus distinguishes clearly between two classes of men. On the one hand is the sage who must travel from place to place to earn a living. To the question why cannot God provide sustenance for the sage (a position indeed taken by several Hasidim[24]) he answers that there is a deeper, mystical meaning to the journeying of the sage, that is, to purify the sparks of his soul root that have fallen and to restore them to their source. There is, however, a higher level, that of Jacob, who studies Torah in his fixed place and thereby purifies the fallen sparks. The interesting shift in pronouns from the third to first person may indicate that Jacob Joseph identified with the biblical Jacob in this regard.

In a subsequent passage in the same work Jacob Joseph returns to the teaching of the Besht and further elaborates his own distinction between two models of spiritual restoration (*tiqqun*):

> The matter of a person's traveling from this place to that place for the sake of a livelihood or the like is due to the fact that in the place [to which he goes] are found his sparks and he must release them from there and purify them. Thus we can understand why [Jacob] did not have to travel from place to place in order to purify his sparks for all the land of Israel was contained under him and he purified his sparks in his place... just as there is an aspect of restoration (*tiqqun*) by means of action (*maᶜaseh*) for the masses so there is such an aspect [of *tiqqun*] in the diligent study of Torah (*ᶜeseq ha-torah*) of the sage. . . . Jacob was himself the aspect of Torah . . . and therefore Jacob was able to purify [the

> sparks] in his place just as another person accomplishes this by going out to action (*lelekh be-ma ʿaseh).*[25]

There are thus two levels of *tiqqun,* both understood in terms of the traditional Lurianic conception of uplifting the sparks. There is the one who is involved with worldly pursuits, the man of action for whom even mundane journeys have a spiritual value. Such a man must travel from place to place in order to earn a living, but in truth his journeys have a profound mystical significance, for the place to which he journeys contains sparks of his soul root that must be redeemed.[26] On the other hand, the one who is deeply engaged in the study of Torah may perform the *tiqqun* by staying in one fixed place. While Jacob is a paradigmatic example of the latter, Abraham is prototypical of the former as he is commanded, "Rise up and walk about the land" (Gen. 13:17); that is, "he had to walk about the land from place to place in order to purify the sparks." Although Jacob Joseph begins by saying that only Jacob was on the level of purifying the sparks by staying in one place, in a subsequent passage he notes that Moses, who is identified with the "good" and the Torah, "was able to purify [the sparks] in his place by means of diligent study of Torah (*ʿeseq ha-torah*), and he took the good from the bad, but he did not have to be driven from place to place."[27] Moses, therefore, is on the same level as Jacob, a theme that can be traced back to classical kabbalistic sources, most important, the *Zohar.*[28]

In still another passage from his *Ben Porat Yosef,* alluded to above, Jacob Joseph mentions the Besht's teaching and equates the status of Jacob with that of Noah:

> I have heard in the name of my teacher an explanation of [the passage in] the tractate Ḥullin: "[God] folded all of the land of Israel under Jacob." . . . He did not have to travel from place to place to purify his sparks for he could purify them in his place. . . . And according to this the verse, "But Noah found favor with the Lord" (Gen. 6:8), can be understood. . . . Noah was in his place and purified his sparks according to the mystery of "he was a righteous man, blameless in his age" (Gen. 6:9), i.e., to purify the sparks of the generation. For "Noah walked with God" (ibid.), i.e., he meditated on Torah and the worship of God all day, and by means of this he purified [the sparks] in his place.[29]

Here again we find Jacob Joseph elaborating on the Besht's teaching by drawing a comparison between Jacob and Noah. Just as Jacob was able to liberate the sparks while standing in one place, so too was

Noah of whom it was said in Scripture, "Noah walked with God." The essence of walking, from the pietistic perspective, is to purify the holy sparks and release them from their carnal bondage. Noah, paradoxically, accomplished this by standing in one place.[30]

The above passage in which Jacob Joseph extols the virtue of Noah as one who could gather all the divine sparks by standing still contrasts sharply with another interpretation he offers of the verse "Noah walked with God." A comparison of the two interpretations highlights a basic tension in Jacob Joseph's writings between the clashing ideals of separatism or spiritual elitism, on the one hand, and communal responsibility, on the other.[31] The text from *Ben Porat Yosef* is based on a passage in *Shene Luḥot ha-Berit* of Isaiah Horowitz (1565–1630)[32] which, in turn, is based on a passage in *Sefer Ḥaredim* of Eleazar Azikri (1533–1600).[33] Jacob Joseph writes:

> Noah secluded himself (*mitboded*) with God and did not admonish the people of his generation. Therefore [it is written] "he was a righteous man, blameless in his age" (Gen. 6:9). That is, the people of his age considered him righteous for he walked with God; had he admonished his generation, however, he would not have been considered righteous.[34]

One cannot fail to note the irony in Jacob Joseph's statement that in the eyes of the community one who isolates himself and devotes all his energies to perfecting his own spiritual state is considered righteous, whereas one who would show an interest in reproving others and leading them to repentance is not so considered. In fact, the latter, and not the former, is the true *ṣaddiq*.[35] This, of course, reflects the typology developed in many Hasidic texts, based in turn on earlier homiletical and ethical literature, that distinguishes two kinds of *ṣaddiqim*: the *ṣaddiq* who is only concerned for himself, and the one who is concerned for himself and for others.[36] That Noah's walking with God involved the former state, according to Jacob Joseph, is evident from various other comments that he makes in connection to this verse. "This is the meaning of 'Noah walked with God,' in every place where he went he would go 'with God' for he constantly clove his thought to God."[37] Walking with God thus entailed *devequt*, cleaving to God, attained by means of *hitbodedut*, a term that connotes a state of both mental concentration and social isolation.[38] Indeed, in one sermon Jacob Joseph interprets Noah's being locked up in the ark not as a reward for his righteous behavior but rather as a punishment for secluding himself in the worship of God in houses of study and prayer while ignoring the plight of his generation.[39]

The righteousness of Noah is elsewhere contrasted with that of Abraham.[40] While the former was content with perfecting his own lot—thus he is described as walking "with God"—the latter sought to go out to perfect the status of others—thus he walked "before God." For Jacob Joseph, therefore, the communion with God achieved through *hitbodedut* serves only as a preliminary stage, preparing the *ṣaddiq* for his ultimate task. Indeed, on occasion Jacob Joseph attributes this perfection to Noah: "It says that [Noah was] 'a righteous man, he was blameless in his age,' i.e., when he went out into the city amongst the people of his age he was also a righteous man, to fulfill [the verse] 'I am ever mindful of the Lord's presence' (Ps. 16:8). . . . And this caused that at first he 'walked with God,' i.e., he secluded himself (*hitboded*) so that he would bind himself and cleave to God, blessed be He, before he went out into the city."[41] The ideal then is that of the *ṣaddiq* who first achieves communion with God in isolation and then goes out to help others in their spiritual quest.[42] There is some confusion in Jacob Joseph on whether Noah achieved this state. From still other contexts it is clear that, according to Jacob Joseph, Noah falls short of the ideal of the *ṣaddiq*, linked by Hasidic writers to the Besht himself,[43] for whom cleaving to God is not disrupted by entering into social discourse. One of the basic Hasidic principles attributed to the Besht, but formulated succinctly by Jacob Joseph, is that there are two types of *devequt*: one that is realized in a state of isolation from others (*hitbodedut*), mostly through the devotional acts of study and prayer; and the other realized in a state of community even through physical acts such as eating, drinking, and the like. While Noah represented the former type, Moses is the model of the second.[44] Following the teaching attributed both to the Besht and to Naḥman of Kosov,[45] Jacob Joseph thus maintained that the true *ṣaddiq* is not only one who enters the social arena after a state of *devequt*, but one who can maintain that state of religious intensity and devotion in the public arena. The act of communion with God that is realized within the framework of social relations is referred to on occasion as *halikhah*:

> By means of this one can understand [the statement], "R. Yose ben Qisma said, 'One day I was going in the way,' "[46] i.e., I was once in the description of one who goes which is the opposite of *bi'ah*, i.e., one occupied with corporeal matters. In any event, my thought cleaved to God. . . . *Halikhah* applies to one who goes from grade to grade, the opposite of angels who are called standing on one level, and the goal of the upper level is to cleave one's thought to God. He was going in this grade [of *devequt*] even when he went in the way amidst the level of the masses.[47]

From still other passages in Jacob Joseph's writings it is clear that the purpose of the journey of the *ṣaddiq* is not to improve his own situation by gathering the sparks of his soul root, but rather to elevate others to a higher level of spiritual fulfilment. *Halikhah* thus means descending from one's grade in order to rebuke and instruct others, to lead them to repent.

> With this one can understand [the words of] R. Yose ben Qisma: "One time I was going in the way," for *halikhah* means when one descends from his grade, the opposite of *bi'ah*. This is the meaning of "I was going in the way," he knew the aspect of his grade from which he descended, which is called "going in the way" (*mehalekh ba-derekh*).[48]

> It seems that R. Yose said, "I went in the way," in order to instruct sinners in the way, to rebuke them. . . . This is the description of "walking" (*mehalekh*), i.e., to descend from his level. I conducted myself in this way, I would give rebuke to others; this is the meaning of walking in the way (*mehalekh ba-derekh*).[49]

In this case too the task of *halikhah* is to uplift the sparks, for Jacob Joseph, following the teaching attributed to the Besht,[50] includes under the rubric of *ha'alat ha-niṣoṣot* the imperative to attend to the religious and moral welfare of the community. It is in this sense, furthermore, that one can speak of a "social transformation" of the Lurianic idea in early Hasidism, a phenomenon well attested in scholarly literature.[51] Indeed, according to one passage, the *ṣaddiq* who ascends upward must return and descend "to raise the level of the masses who are his sparks (!) and his branches that they all should be rectified."[52] *Halikhah* is, therefore, equated with *yeridah*, for both are understood in terms of the need for the *ṣaddiq* to redeem the fallen sparks.[53]

> This is the meaning of "Go forth (*lekh lekha*) from your native land and from your father's house" (Gen. 12:1)—after you set yourself at a distance from matter [the masses] to make yourself into form [the elite]. . . . Then you are far from evil and strange thoughts called "your father's house." . . . And after you are removed from the corporeality of matter . . . then you attain the level that is known, called "the seeing of the supernal land," i.e., cleaving to God, blessed be He. This [cleaving] is called ascent (*'aliyah*), for one goes from one grade to the upper grade until one returns to the earth in his death,[54] which is called descent from the level of man to the level of inanimate object. It is

> all for the sake of purifying the holy sparks from the depth of the shells that are below.[55]

That the purification of the sparks spoken of here refers to the elevation of the masses can be seen from the following passage:

> This is the import of the verse, "who will give purity from impurity" (Job 14:4), for the *ṣaddiq* is called pure, but on occasion some impurity is found in him so that he may join the impure to elevate them to [a state of] purity. . . . According to this we can explain the words, "Go forth (*lekh lekha*)" (Gen. 12:1). . . . The meaning of "go" (*lekh*) is to be explained by the expression, "Go (*lekhi*) and diminish youself."[56] The word "to yourself" (*lekha*) means for your good and your enjoyment, for by means of this [going] "I will make you a great nation," for you will join them to release them.[57]

There is thus a perfect parallel in Jacob Joseph's writings between walking (*halikhah*) and descent (*yeridah*), on the one hand, and uplifting the sparks of one's soul and elevating the masses, on the other. "'Jacob lifted up his feet' (Gen 49:1) . . . he departed from the physical to the spiritual.[58] . . . In another place I have written, 'Go and diminish yourself so there will be rule in day and night,' i.e., so that you may join the masses in order to raise them up. . . . Accordingly, one can understand Jacob's going down to Egypt, i.e., to the physical in order to purify the sparks, to join the masses."[59]

One can distinguish two approaches in the writings of Jacob Joseph. The one—which he attributes to the Besht—employs the Lurianic term to describe both one who studies Torah in a fixed place and one who journeys about presumably on any type of business trip, and the other approach that applies this same terminology to characterize the religious leader who must descend in order to admonish the masses. From the relevant sources I think it can be said, moreover, that it was Jacob Joseph who translated the Beshtian teaching concerning *halikhah* from the individualistic mode to one of great social and ethical consequence. What is essential to both, however, is the soteriological aspect expressed in Lurianic terminology. Although several scholars, most notably Dinur[60] and Tishby,[61] have duly noted the messianic dimensions in Jacob Joseph, neither scholar has appreciated the unique redemptive aspect of *halikhah* as it relates to the task of the *ṣaddiq* who descends to the level of the masses. That Jacob Joseph in general understood the lifting up of the sparks in its original Lurianic sense as part of an eschatological *tiqqun* on a cosmic level, and not simply in a "strictly personal sphere,"[62] is beyond question.[63] That the messianic implication applies specifically to the case I am examining is also abundantly clear from the fact that discussions about the Besht's teaching are accompanied by a citation of a critical text from *Peri ᶜEṣ Ḥayyim* that deals with the messianic task of redeeming the sparks.[64]

There is, in particular, one telling passage in the *Toledot Yaᶜaqov Yosef* that, in my view, must be examined in the context of the thematic that I am discussing: "It is written in the writings of the Ari[65] with respect to the purification of the sparks until the [time of the] 'footsteps of the Messiah' (*ᶜiqvot meshiḥa*ᵓ), for in each generation one limb from the configuration (*parṣuf*) of the whole world is purified until the end, the time of the Messiah, when the limb of the feet [will be purified] for it is the heels of the Messiah (*ᶜiqvot meshiḥa*ᵓ), when 'the feet will reach the feet' (*de-maṭu raglin be-raglin*)."[66] Jacob Joseph further contends that his is the time of the "footsteps of the Messiah," for in his generation these souls of the feet are to be redeemed.[67] Without entering into a long discussion on the Lurianic theme briefly alluded to in Jacob Joseph's citation, suffice it to say that the Lurianic kabbalists understood the "footsteps of the Messiah" in one of two ways: in some texts this period was described as the time when the sparks of the souls entrapped in the feet of *ᵓAdam Beliᶜal* (the demonic being) in the world of *ᶜAsiyyah* were to be redeemed, when, paraphrasing the zoharic passage, "the feet will reach the feet."[68] Alternatively, *ᶜiqvot meshiḥa*ᵓ was explained as a time when the sparks in the shells lodged in the feet of *ᵓAdam Qadmon* situated in the world of *ᶜAsiyyah* would be redeemed.[69] The version of this motif offered by Jacob Joseph inclines more toward the latter model.[70]

It is in order here to recall that in the relatively early Hasidic commentary on Psalm 107, ascribed erroneously by some later authorities to the Besht himself, the very same language of the Lurianic kabbalah is utilized, approximating, however, the first model that I delineated: "This is the secret of the exile of *Shekhinah* [when she descends to the demonic shells] all six days of the week, and this is the secret of the 'footsteps of Messiah' (*ᶜiqvot meshiḥa*ᵓ) for when she finishes gathering those souls that are in the heels of that impure one [i.e., *ᵓAdam Beliᶜal*] who is the 'end of the impure body' (*sof ha-guf ha-ṭame*ᵓ) then Messiah will come."[71] The centrality of this belief in Hasidic circles is well attested from various sources. While Tishby did not discuss either the passage from the Hasidic commentary on Psalm 107 or that of the *Toledot*, he did note that Aaron ben Moses ha-Levi of Starosielce reported that his teacher, Shneur Zalman of Liadi, received from his teacher, Dov Baer of Miedzyzrecz, who received from his teacher, the Besht, that they were living in the time of the *ᶜiqvot* *meshiḥa*ʾ.[72] Indeed, on several occasions in his writings Shneur Zalman refers to the fact that his generation was that of the "footsteps of the Messiah."[73]

In this connection mention should also be made of the version of the narrative concerning the Besht's attempted journey to the Holy Land reported by Yiṣḥaq Isaac Safrin of Komarno.[74] According to the tale reported by this authority, the Besht, who is described as the soul (*nefesh*) of David in [the world] of *ʾAṣilut*, desired to join together with Ḥayyim ibn Aṭṭar, whose soul (*neshamah*) is described as deriving from the spirit (*ruaḥ*) of David in [the world of] *ʾAṣilut*, so that "the true redemption (*ha-geʾulah ha-ʾamitit*) would occur."[75] The Besht reportedly asked R. Ḥayyim, through Gershon of Kuty, the Besht's brother-in-law, if the time were propitious for the Besht to travel to Jerusalem to see Ḥayyim face-to-face. R. Ḥayyim responded that the Besht should write him if, when he beheld the "image of his form" (*ṣelem demut tavnito*) in the upper worlds, he saw "all his limbs and his image" or not. I assume that this refers to the divine image and form of the Messiah in the celestial realm.[76] The Besht responded that he did not see the heels of this form. R. Ḥayyim then replied that he should not bother going to the land of Israel, for his efforts would prove to be futile, but the Besht did not receive the response and hence decided to undertake the journey. After spending some time in Istanbul,[77] where he performed "great and wondrous" things, he was forced to flee from there and continue his journey. He then suffered much sorrow and pain, including shipwreck and the near-drowning of his daughter, Edel, in the sea, until at last his celestial teacher, Ahijah, the prophet of Shilo,[78] came to save him by bringing him back to Istanbul from where he returned to his home. The critical point for my purposes is the connection made between the act of journeying to Israel and the "heels" of the divine image. Clearly, the implication here is that the Besht's not beholding the heels of the divine figure was a sign that he was not yet ready to undertake this journey; the detail of the heels, I suggest, should be interpreted in light of the standard Lurianic symbolism of the *ʿiqvot meshiḥa*ʾ. Had the Besht seen the full figure, including, most importantly, the heels, then he would have been ready to undertake the journey, for this would have been a sign that the period for the final rectification was at hand.

Although this relatively late embellishment of the tale reveals a marked tendency to "neutralize" the messianic impulse inasmuch as it understands the Besht's failed journey in terms of the traditional notion of pressing for the end, that is, hastening the messianic redemption before its time, it nevertheless demonstrates how crucial the Lurianic notion of *ʿiqvot meshiḥa*ʾ was in early Hasidic circles. There can be no question, moreover, that some of the early Hasidim maintained the belief that they were living close to the messianic era, the *ᶜiqvot meshiḥa ᵓ*, in which time the final *tiqqun* was to be realized before the advent of the Messiah. The same Lurianic ideas served as an important source for the development of the Sabbatian theology of Nathan of Gaza concerning the task of the Messiah to redeem the sparks lodged in the feet, for this very place was the root of his soul.[79] One, of course, should not rule out, *a priori*, a Sabbatian connection in the case of the Hasidic authors, but it does seem to me more likely that what we are dealing with are two distinct interpretative traditions coming out of one source. The phenomenological resemblance may be explained on exegetical rather than historical grounds. In any event, what is critical from my vantage point is Jacob Joseph's particular usage of this Lurianic tradition. This may be gathered from other contexts in which the masses of people are identified as the "feet" of the configuration of the world; the *ṣaddiqim*, by contrast, are the "eyes of the congregation" or the head of the cosmic figure.[80] By means of this symbolism one can understand Jacob Joseph's interpretation of the Lurianic concept of the *ᶜiqvot meshiḥa ᵓ*; that is, the laity who need to be redeemed at this historical juncture. Thus he states explicitly in one place: "This is the [meaning of the] verse, 'holding on to the heel of Esau' (Gen. 25:26), which refers to the masses of people who are called heel (*ᶜaqev*) according to the secret of the footsteps of the Messiah (*ᶜiqvot meshiḥa ᵓ*)."[81] It follows, therefore, that the *tiqqun* of the feet in the period right before the advent of the Messiah consists of the perfection of the masses by the elite, Hasidic leadership. This is made clear in a comment near the end of the introduction to the *Toledot*: "'Jacob lifted up his feet' (Gen 49:1). He lifted up the lower level called 'his feet' to the higher level . . . he lifted up the men of matter called 'his feet' to the upper form."[82] In another passage he puts the matter as follows:

> There is a spiritual characteristic [literally, aspect (*beḥinah*)] of the one who after his ascent returns and descends in order to raise the level of the lower ones, in the mystery of "I have bathed my feet, was I to soil them again?" (Song of Songs 5:3). And this is the secret of "running and returning" (Ezek. 1:14), and it is called [the state of] smallness (*qaṭnut*) and [the state of] greatness (*gadlut*). In each descent there must be a warning regarding how to return and to ascend, so one does not, God forfend, remain [in the lower state] as I have heard from my teacher that there are some who have remained.[83]

III

It must be acknowledged, however, that Jacob Joseph does not connect the Lurianic tradition concerning the *tiqqun* of the feet in the *ᶜiqvot meshiḥaʾ* with the Beshtian teaching concerning the *berur niṣoṣot* by means of one's journeying. What is interesting, however, is that in a comment of a disciple of the Maggid of Miedzyrzecz, Menaḥem Naḥum of Chernobyl, who, according to tradition, also had personal contact with the Besht, the two motifs are indeed brought together:

> The sages, blessed be their memory, said: "Receiving guests is greater than receiving the face of the *Shekhinah*."[84] This is the explanation of, "The guest by his feet does not come" (Isa. 41:3)[85] . . . for the guest does not come for his own sake but he is the messenger of God (*sheluḥaʾ de-raḥmanaʾ*)[86] to raise the sparks that belong to his soul, and he is obligated to raise them. This is [the meaning of] "the son of David [i.e., the Messiah] will not come until there are no more souls in the body." The Ari, blessed be his memory, explained that there is a body of *ʾAdam Beliᶜal* etc. and each Jew must raise the souls from *ʾAdam Beliᶜal*. Therefore a person must go to the place where the sparks are so that he may raise them. This is what the Besht, blessed be his memory, said [with respect to the verse] "The steps of a man are decided by the Lord, when He delights in his way" (Ps. 37:23).[87] The verse is redundant, "the steps of a man" and "his way." The sages, blessed be their memory, said: "The steps of a man are decided by the Lord," for God leads a man to a certain place by means of that desirable thing that is in that place. Yet, "He delights in his way," for God wants to repair (*letaqqen*) the person there by raising the holy sparks that are there. Then there is unity between the two names, YHWH and Adonai.[88]

Here we see quite unambiguously that the Besht's teaching regarding the mystical intent of journeying was understood in the context of the Lurianic idea of raising the sparks entrapped in the demonic realm, a theme that is repeated on several occasions in the *Meʾor ᶜEinayim*. The Besht, as understood by both Jacob Joseph and Menaḥem Naḥum, was not speaking merely about individual salvation. The concern rather was with cosmic rectification that begins on the individual level.[89] Menaḥem Naḥum adds one new element, the well-known kabbalistic tradition of the two divine names that symbolize the masculine and feminine aspects of the sefirotic realm. Elevation of the sparks accomplished by means of one's going to the proper place results in the unity of these two names, the sign of the ultimate redemption.[90] In this regard too the rebbe of Chernobyl was following closely the Lurianic kabbalah, according to which the liberation of the sparks from the shells was intended to assist in the face-to-face reunification of *Zeᶜeir ᵓAnpin* and *Nuqbaᵓ*, the lower two *parṣufim*, although he used the more traditional zoharic terminology, the Holy One, blessed be He, and the *Shekhinah*.

In the case of the Besht's grandson, Moses Ḥayyim Ephraim of Sudlikov, one likewise finds the two soteriological explanations of walking or taking a journey as lifting the sparks or unifying the masculine and feminine aspects of God. In the first instance Moses Ḥayyim cites an interpretation of Psalms 37:23 in the name of his teachers similar to the one cited in the name of the Besht by Menaḥem Naḥum of Chernobyl. Like the latter, Moses Ḥayyim emphasizes that a person thinks he goes to a particular place to attain something he desires, but in truth that person is led to that place by God, so that he may raise "the holy sparks that have fallen and are sunk within the depths of the shells." In particular, Moses Ḥayyim applies the Besht's teaching to the *ṣaddiq*: "Who is like the wise Master, blessed be He, who sends the will (*raṣon*) to a *ṣaddiq* to go in this way, and by means of his holy thoughts and his holy worship he raises the holy sparks to their source and origin."[91]

The redemptive aspect of the journey is affirmed in another comment in *Degel Maḥaneh ᵓEfrayim*, but in that context the aim that is portrayed is not to redeem the sparks entrapped in the demonic realm but to unify the masculine and the feminine aspects of God. Moses Ḥayyim reports that he has heard in the name of the Besht that the forty-two journeys of the Israelite people in the desert "are to [be found] in every person from the day of his birth until he returns to his world [at death]." Each individual's birth is connected to the exodus from Egypt, and the subsequent stages of life are journeys that lead from place to place until one comes to the "supernal world of life," i.e., the *Shekhinah*.[92] Moses wrote down the journeyings of Israel so that "a person may know the way in which he should go." Moses knew that the purpose of these excursions was "to unify the unifications [of the divine names] in each and every place according to its spiritual character" (*leyaḥed yiḥudim be-khol maqom we-maqom lefi beḥinato*), whereas the rest of Israel did not know the inner purpose of their journeys. "Moses knew the content of the inner intent of God in each and every journey, and all the unifications that were done in each and every place (*we-khol ha-yiḥudim she-naᶜasu be-khol maqom we-maqom*). And this is the meaning of *ᶜal pi* [i.e., in the verse, 'Moses recorded the starting points of their various marches as directed by the Lord,' *ʿal pi YHWH* [Num. 33:2]), the numerical value of [the word] *pi* is ninety-one [i.e.,] including the word itself (*ʿim ha-kolel*),[93] and this [represents] the unity of YHWH and Adonai [i.e., twenty-six plus sixty-five]."[94] The purpose of the journey is thus to unify the two names that, as we have seen, symbolize the masculine and the feminine potencies of the divine. By means of the movement of one's feet, therefore, sexual unification above is enhanced.

That walking serves as a metaphor for sexual activity, which itself represents the supreme mode of *tiqqun* on the spiritual plane—an idea well rooted in the kabbalistic sources—can be seen clearly from a tradition recorded in Jacob Joseph as well, explaining why the ritualistic aspect of Torah is called *halakhah*. According to Jacob Joseph, this is to be explained in one of two ways: the word *halakhah* is related, on the one hand, to *halikhah*, walking or going,[95] and, on the other, to *ha-kallah*, the bride.[96] These two explanations correspond in turn to two modes of study. The prior stage of *halikhah* means that one "progresses and ascends from grade to grade," that is, from the level of study for an ulterior motive to study for its own sake, *torah lishmah*.[97] When one attains this latter level, then one studies—literally—for the sake of the name, *li-shemah*,[98] that is, for the sake of the *Shekhinah*; this is alluded to as well in the fact that the expression *ha-kallah*, the bride, comprises the same letters as the word *halakhah*. More specifically, Jacob Joseph employs an older zoharic idea to the effect that the particular halakhic rulings regarding what is permissible and forbidden are akin to embellishments of the bride (*qishshuṭaʾ de-khallah*).[99] *Halikhah* is thus the adornment of the *kallah* through the means of *halakhah*. By contrast, study of Torah for its own sake, without any immediate practical implications, results in the unification of the individual with the "denuded" Torah. In Jacob Joseph's own words:

> This is the meaning [of the rabbinic dictum] "Do not read *halikhah* but rather *halakhah*"[100] for it is the bride (*ha-kallah*). The bride [*Shekhinah*] should not remain embellished, but rather he [the earthly *ṣaddiq*] should go from this grade [i.e., studying for the sake of another end] to the higher grade, which is the unification without garment or adornment, but only the cleaving of his inner essence to the inner essence of the Torah.[101]

Alternatively expressed, the primary mode of study consists of adorning the bride with jewels and garments by means of a detailed analysis of the rules and regulations of normative Jewish practice.

Beyond this stage, however, is the one in which the adornments are removed, when the Torah stands, as it were, "naked without garment."[102] In such a state the individual cleaves to and is united with the letters of the Torah.[103] In any event, from this intriguing web of word-plays, one sees that for Jacob Joseph the word *halikhah* is related to *halakhah,* which, understood in kabbalistic terms, refers to the arousal of the union of the masculine and the feminine aspects of God. As Jacob Joseph puts it in another context:

> By this you can understand the Talmudic statement, "[Since the Temple was destroyed] the Holy One, blessed be He, has only four cubits of *halakhah* in His world."[104] That is, there is no unity (*yiḥud*) between the Holy One, blessed be He, and His *Shekhinah,* who is called "His world," except by means of the four cubits of *halakhah,* in which the persons of knowledge [i.e., the spiritual elite] are engaged. And there is an advantage for the one so engaged, for light and pleasure proceed from the darkness of the people of the world [i.e., the masses], and there is unity between the Holy One, blessed be He, and His *Shekhinah.*[105]

In still other contexts in Jacob Joseph's corpus, it is indicated that walking serves as a metaphor for sexual activity. Thus, commenting on the talmudic interpretation that God came to visit Abraham on the third day after his circumcision,[106] Jacob Joseph distinguishes between three aspects of circumcision. The first aspect is that of one who sits (*yoshev*), that is, "the one who does evil[107];" the second that of one who stands (*ᶜomed*),[108] that is, "the one who does not do evil but needs instruction (*musar*)" about doing good; and the third that of one who walks (*holekh*), that is, "the one who goes from gradation to gradation."[109] Jacob Joseph goes on to identify these three aspects with the three men who came to Abraham (see Gen. 18:2), who in turn symbolize the three lines in the divine realm: the left, the right, and the middle. The aspect of sitting, *yeshivah,* corresponds to the left, that of standing, *ᶜamidah,* to the right, and walking, *halikhah,* to the middle. Although it is not stated explicitly in this context, according to the standard kabbalistic symbolism adopted by the Hasidim, the gradation of the *ṣaddiq* is in the middle. For Jacob Joseph, therefore, the act of walking is applicable to the divine gradation *Yesod* that corresponds to the *ṣaddiq* below. That walking most appropriately characterizes the *ṣaddiq,* who is the mundane correlate of the supernal grade that is in the position of the *membrum virile,* signifies that walking is, in fact, to be understood as a euphemism for the sexual act.[110] That is to say, just as the divine *ṣaddiq* serves as a conduit connecting the

Holy One, blessed be He, and the *Shekhinah*, so by means of walking the earthly *ṣaddiq* unites with the feminine Presence.

Underlying the above conception is the identification of the feet as a phallic symbol.[111] While this euphemistic use is of hoary antiquity, attested in the Bible[112] and the Talmud,[113] the specific interpretation of walking as a sexual act of union can be found in earlier kabbalistic texts. Especially noteworthy is the use of this symbolism in the sixteenth-century kabbalists, such as Moses Cordovero and Abraham Galante,[114] for it is likely that from these sources the motif passed into the hands of the Hasidic writers. It is of interest to note here that it is precisely this dynamic that underlies one of the more well-known, but not fully understood, Hasidic legends concerning Enoch the cobbler. Gershom Scholem has shown that the literary origin of this legend is to be found in the *Me᾿irat ᶜEinayim* of the fourteenth-century kabbalist, Isaac of Acre, who himself attributes the legend to R. Judah ha-Darshan Ashkenazi.[115] According to the text of R. Isaac, Enoch was a cobbler and "with each and every stitch that he made with his awl in the leather he would bless God with a complete heart and with perfect intention, and thereby cause the blessing to flow upon the emanated Meṭaṭron."[116] The legend explains the ancient mystical tradition concerning the ascension of Enoch and his transformation into the angelic Meṭaṭron; however, as may be gathered from the full context of R. Isaac's text, the transformation is here interpreted as Enoch's becoming one with the *Shekhinah*, also referred to as the upper Meṭaṭron. Scholem rightly sees in this story an example of the "sacral transformation of the purely profane," for even the mundane act of cobbling has cosmic ramifications. The theurgical element of this legend, with its implicit sexual nuance, proved to be highly influential in subsequent kabbalistic literature. An especially telling reworking of this legend can be found in the following text of Cordovero:

> By means of his activity man becomes a chariot for one of the *sefirot*. Thus it is with respect to Enoch-Meṭaṭron. They said that he merited this gradation for he was a cobbler, and in each and every stitch that he made with the awl he would bless for the sake of divine need (*le-ṣorekh gavoha*) . . . for he unified *Malkhut*, who is called shoe (*na ᶜal*), with *Tif᾿eret*, by means of all his channels, and to this the stitchings allude. Thus it was appropriate for [Enoch] to be a chariot for *Malkhut*.[117]

Although Cordovero's version is clearly based on that of Isaac of Acre, and the theurgical dimension of the latter is preserved in the former,

Cordovero has significantly elaborated upon the sexual implications of the whole legend. That is to say, by means of the stitching the cobbler works upon the *Shekhinah*, symbolized by the shoe,[118] and thereby unifies the feminine and the masculine potencies of God, *Shekhinah* (or *Malkhut*) and *Tifʾeret*. The cobbler therefore stands in the position of the *ṣaddiq* or *Yesod*, the conduit that connects the masculine and the feminine.[119] As such, Enoch properly merited unification with the *Shekhinah*, for through his activity he united the *Shekhinah* with the masculine aspect of the divine.

In Hasidic circles the sexual import of the legend was highlighted as well. To substantiate this claim one would do well to recall the interpretation that this legend receives in a host of passages in Jacob Joseph's writings. A representative example follows:

> I heard from my teacher [the Besht] an explanation of the verse, "Whatever it is in your power to do, do with all your might" (Eccl. 9:10). Enoch-Meṭaṭron unified with every stitch the Holy One, blessed be He, and the *Shekhinah* . . . and he thus bound together the physical action of the lower world by means of thought, which is "your power," to the upper spiritual world. With this he fulfilled [the verse] "in all your ways," i.e., of a physical nature, "know Him," i.e., unify the *heʾ* [corresponding to the *Shekhinah*] to the *waw* [the Holy One, blessed be He].[120]

Through his stitching, therefore, the legendary Enoch-Meṭaṭron was able to unite the Holy One, blessed be He, and the *Shekhinah*, heaven and earth, the physical and the spiritual, action and thought.[121] Just as the *sefirah* of *Yesod* above serves to unite the *waw* and the *heʾ* of the Tetragrammaton, the masculine and the feminine, so Enoch below. Each stitch that the cobbler makes assists in this unification. That Enoch is indeed in the position of *Yesod* is brought out even more clearly in the following passage in *Keter Shem Ṭov*, which, so far as I can tell, blends together various passages in Jacob Joseph's writings:

> "Whatever it is in your power to do, do with all your might" (Eccl. 9:10). This means to unite the action with the power of thought. And this is the meaning of the words 'do with all your might' which refers to the gradation of Enoch-Meṭaṭron, for he united the Holy One, blessed be He, with each stitch. And this was the level of Moses our master, may peace be upon him, "But you remain standing here with me etc." (Deut. 5:28). "Jacob lifted up his feet" (Gen. 29:1). That is, by means of faith he lifted the feet of *Malkhut*

> "whose feet go down to death" (Prov. 5:5) and binds her with the pillars of truth (*samkhe qeshoṭ*) of *Zeʿeir ʾAnpin.*[122]

According to this passage, then, the level of Enoch-Meṭaṭron is the same as that of Moses and Jacob. That is to say, the act of stitching is further understood from the acts of standing upright (attributed to Moses) and lifting up one's feet to resume a journey (attributed to Jacob). Moreover, all three activities point to the *tiqqun* of the *Shekhinah* or the unification of the feminine and the masculine potencies within the divine. This is expressed at the end of the passage in the technical language of the kabbalah: Jacob bound the feminine *Malkhut* to the pillars of truth—*Neṣaḥ* and *Hod*[123]—of the masculine *Zeʿeir ʾAnpin,* the central *sefirah* of *Tifʾeret.* The acts of standing on one's feet and lifting one's feet have the same symbolic valence as Enoch's cobbling. All of these actions characterize the *ṣaddiq,* and their common denominator is clearly the use of one's feet. It seems fairly obvious, moreover, that all such activity with one's feet is to be taken as a euphemism for sexual action (a usage well attested in earlier kabbalistic literature), for the *ṣaddiq* not only enhances the unification of male and female aspects within God, but he is himself united with the feminine *Shekhinah.*[124] The *tiqqun* performed by Moses who stood up erectly, by Jacob who commenced his walking, and by Enoch who stitched together shoes is the unification of the feminine and the masculine within the divine, the Holy One, blessed be He, and the *Shekhinah.*

It is of interest to note, finally, that the use of *feet* as a euphemism for sexual activity underlies the Hasidic teaching concerning dance. Thus, in one place Jacob Joseph reports the following teaching that he heard from the Besht: "dance (*ha-riqqud*) is for the sake of elevating the sparks and raising the lower gradation to the higher one."[125] From the fuller context, an explication of the talmudic dictum, "how does one dance before the bride,"[126] it can be shown that the purpose of dance as construed in the Beshtian teaching is to elevate the *Shekhinah* from her exilic state so that she will become a "bride" wedded to her masculine consort. This sexually nuanced conception of dancing underlies a passage in *Shivḥe ha-Besht* concerning the poor man, the Besht's daughter, Edel, and the birth of Baruch of Tulchin:

> Once on Simhath Torah the members of the holy group, the disciples of the Besht, were dancing joyfully in a circle and the *Shekhinah* was in flames about them.[127] During the dance the shoe of one of the lesser members of the group was torn. He was a poor man and it angered him that he was prevented from dancing with his friends and from rejoicing

> in the festivity of the *miṣwah*. The Besht's daughter, the pious Edel . . . said to the disciple: "If you promise me that I will give birth to a baby boy this year, I will give you good shoes immediately." She could say this because she had shoes in the store. He promised her that she certainly would have a baby boy. And so it was that the rabbi, our rabbi and teacher, Barukh of the holy community of Tulchin, was born to her.[128]

In this passage it is clear that the act of dancing expresses an intimate relationship between the individual *ḥasid* and the *Shekhinah*.[129] That this activity, moreover, symbolizes the act of union between the *ḥasid* and the *Shekhinah* may be gathered from the otherwise mundane account of the poor man's ceasing to dance on account of his torn shoe. Admittedly, this is an innocuous detail that, *prima facie*, would hardly excite one's interest. Yet, it is precisely such a detail that contains, from the Hasidic point of view, deep metaphysical and spiritual significance. The wearing of the shoe in this case, as in the other instances that I have mentioned above, is the symbolic enactment of the unification of the masculine individual and the feminine aspect of God. When the shoe is torn, then the unification is severed and the individual can no longer dance. The Besht's daughter, Edel, is willing to rectify the situation by supplying the man with new shoes—which, as we are told, she readily has in her possession—but only in exchange for a blessing that she will give birth to a male child. The blessing is thus a perfect reflection of the act that Edel performed for the man. Just as she supplied new shoes enabling the man to continue dancing and thereby to unite the masculine and the feminine, so she would be blessed with a child, the ultimate fruit of sexual unification.

From the various texts that I have examined it has thus become clear that in early Hasidism the physical act of travel or walking was understood not only in a restorative sense (as the Besht taught) but in a generative sense as well. That is, the double task of the *ṣaddiq* in his moving about from place to place is to redeem the fallen sparks and to assist in the unification of the male and the female aspects of God. The two acts are not really distinct, for unification is brought about through liberation of the sparks. In addition, the soteriological implications of both these actions for the early Hasidic authors must be acknowledged. In his capacity as one who walks or journeys, man assists in the redemption both on an individual and on a cosmic level.[130]

◆ Notes ◆

1. The Image of Jacob Engraved upon the Throne: Further Reflection on the Esoteric Doctrine of the German Pietists

1. An exception is A. Farber, "The Concept of the Merkabah in Thirteenth-Century Jewish Esotericism—'Sod ha-ʾEgoz' and Its Development" (Ph.D. dissertation, Hebrew University, 1986), pp. 312–13, 406, 412, 420 (in Hebrew). While it is certainly the case that Farber recognized the significance of the image of Jacob in the writings of Eleazar, she expressed doubt regarding the identification of that image with the glory itself (see p. 406), the position that I have enunciated in this study. According to Farber, the image of Jacob is the reflection of the anthropomorphic form in the chariot by means of which the upper glory is visually apprehended (see esp. pp. 412, 420).

2. MS Paris, Bibliothéque Nationale héb. 772, fol. 159b. See now the printed version of Eleazar's commentary, *Perushe Siddur ha-Tefillah la-Roqeah: A Commentary on the Jewish Prayer Book*, ed. M. and Y. A. Hershler (Jerusalem, 1992), p. 680. The editors of this edition reported having consulted several manuscripts and utilized MS Oxford, Bodleian Library 1204 (all references to Oxford manuscripts correspond to the numbers in Neubauer's catalog) as the base text with variants inserted in brackets or in the notes on the basis of MS Paris, Bibliothéque Nationale héb. 778. See p. 14 of the editor's introduction.

3. MS Munich, Bayerische Staatsbibliothek 232, fol. 7b. The name of the author, Eleazar, is mentioned on fol. 8b. The linkage of transmission of esoteric lore to God-fearers, exegetically related to Ps. 25:14, is a recurring theme in Pietistic literature. See I. G. Marcus, *Piety and Society: The Jewish Pietists of Medieval Germany* (Leiden, 1981), pp. 66, 105.

4. A. Altmann, "Eleazar of Worms' Ḥokhmath Ha-ʾEgoz," *Journal of Jewish Studies* 11 (1960): 105–6, 109–10.

5. J. Dan, "Ḥokhmath Ha-ʾEgoz: Its Origins and Development," *Journal of Jewish Studies* 17 (1966): 77; idem, *The Esoteric Theology of German Pietism* (Jerusalem, 1968), p. 209 (in Hebrew).

6. Farber, "Concept of the Merkabah," pp. 101–23.

7. Ibid., pp. 112–15.

8. Ibid., pp. 108, 113–14, 115, 611–14, 615.

9. See Dan, "Ḥokhmath Ha-ʾEgoz," p. 77; idem, *Esoteric Theology*, pp. 118, 128–29; and idem, "A Re-evaluation of the 'Ashkenazi Kabbalah,' " *Jerusalem Studies in Jewish Thought* 6, 3–4 (1987): 137–38 (in Hebrew). The point is stated emphatically once again by Dan in "The Emergence of Jewish Mysticism in Medieval Germany," in *Mystics of the Book: Themes, Topics and Typologies*, ed. R. A. Herrera (New York, 1993), p. 81: "We do not find in Ashkenazi Hasidism any parallel to the new kabbalistic idea of the bisexuality of the divine pleroma, of the existence of a divine feminine counterpart to the masculine system of the divine powers." Curiously, Dan does not make mention of the alternative approach taken by other scholars, including Scholem, Idel, and, most important, Farber (see below, n. 12) whose dissertation was written under Dan's supervision. Dan mentions her work (see p. 94 n. 84), but demonstrates no attempt whatsoever to respond to the fundamental challenge to his views that her scholarship raises (see, e.g., p. 237, one of the very pages in Farber's dissertation to which Dan refers in his note). My approach, needless to say, is much more in line with hers.

10. Farber, "Concept of the Merkabah," p. 126; see also p. 613.

11. Ibid., p. 115.

12. Ibid., pp. 117, 126, 237, 254, 621, 628, 629–30. See also E. Ginsburg, *The Sabbath in the Classical Kabbalah* (Albany, 1989), p. 176 n. 231.

13. These motifs are developed further in E. R. Wolfson, "The Mystical Significance of Torah Study in German Pietism," *Jewish Quarterly Review* 84 (1993): 43–78.

14. These are precisely the two motifs that Dan, "A Re-evaluation of the 'Ashkenazi Kabbalah,' " pp. 137–39, singles out as those that clearly differentiate German Pietism and Provençal-Spanish kabbalah.

15. I would thus take issue with the following statement of Marcus, *Piety and Society*, p. 23: "Instead of continuing to think of German-Jewish pietism as part of the traditions of Jewish mysticism, it is better to consider the sources in their own terms. When we do, we find that the ideal of the German *ḥasid* is derived not from assumptions about God's being or other theosophical categories. Rather, it rests on a new perception of the divine will." In my opinion, the Pietistic conception of the will is itself rooted in a specific theosophic outlook that, in turn, generates intense religious experiences that should properly be termed "mystical." See Marcus's own statement that the "esoteric lore of the Lord" for

the Pietists included secrets "about the liturgy and theosophy, on the one hand, or about the will of the Creator, on the other" (p. 66). It should be noted, moreover, that Marcus himself concludes that "in some of Eleazar's writings, pietism is a preparation for a mystical experience during prayer" (p. 118). See also p. 16. My approach to the issue of the relationship between the Pietistic ideal and theosophic speculations basically follows that of Scholem. See the review of the latter's position in Marcus, op. cit., pp. 21–23.

16. See G. Scholem, *Major Trends in Jewish Mysticism* (New York, 1956), pp. 95–96; G. Vajda, *L'Amour de dieu dans la théologie juive du moyen age* (Paris, 1957), pp. 149–62; M. Harris, "The Concept of Love in Sepher Hassidim," *Jewish Quarterly Review* 50 (1959): 13–44; and Marcus, *Piety and Society*, pp. 28–36.

17. See Dan, "A Re-evaluation of the 'Ashkenazi Kabbalah,' " pp. 136–37, who notes the fundamental similarity between the Pietistic and the kabbalistic sources with respect to the themes of love of God and of communion. See especially the text from Eleazar of Worms cited by Dan, op. cit., n. 29, which describes the love of the adept for God in highly erotic terms. Although Dan clearly recognized the erotic nature of this fundamental aspect of the Pietistic mentality, he does not relate it to any mythical element in the divine realm.

18. On the centrality of *ṭa ͨame miṣwot*, "reasons for the commandments," in the theosophy of the German Pietists, see comments of Scholem, *Major Trends*, p. 90, and idem, *Kabbalah* (Jerusalem, 1974), pp. 41–42. See also my study referred to above in n. 13.

19. The function of mystical intention of prayer in the theosophy of the German Pietists has been discussed by a number of scholars. See Scholem, *Major Trends*, pp. 100–3; Vajda, *L'Amour de dieu*, pp. 154–55; Marcus, *Piety and Society*, pp. 117–18; J. Dan, "The Emergence of Mystical Prayer," in *Studies in Jewish Mysticism*, ed. J. Dan and F. Talmage (Cambridge, 1982), pp. 85–120; idem, "Pesaq ha-Yirah veha-Emunah and the Intention of Prayer in Ashkenazi Hasidic Esotericism," *Frankfurter Judaistische Beiträge* 19 (1991/92): 185–215; idem, "Prayer as Text and Prayer as Mystical Experience," in *Torah and Wisdom: Essays in Honor of Arthur Hyman*, ed. R. Link-Salinger (New York, 1992), pp. 33–47; and M. Idel, "Intention in Prayer in the Beginning of Kabbalah: Between Germany and Provence," in *Ben Porat Yosef: Studies Presented to Rabbi Dr. Joseph Safran*, ed. B. and E. Safran (Hoboken, 1992), pp. 5–14 (in Hebrew).

20. In this regard it is of interest to consider the following remark in the Pietistic work in MS Oxford, Bodleian Library, 1566, fol. 38a: "This is [the meaning of the verse] *shemi le-ͨolam*, 'This shall be My name forever' (Exod. 3:15), [the word *shemi* signifies] *shem yod* [i.e., the name that begins with *yod*, the Tetragrammaton], it is written *le-ͨolam*, i.e., [the name is transmitted] to the one who in the world (*ͨolam*) is pure of all transgression. . . . *Shemi le-ͨolam*, the unique name (*shem ha-meyuḥad*) is only revealed to one who has abrogated the desire for women from his heart." The second interpretation is based on the fact that the word *le-ͨolam*, written in the defective, can be read as *leͨalem*, to

conceal. (Cf. B. Pesaḥim 50a; Qiddushin 71a.) According to the Pietistic source, transmission of the Tetragrammaton is linked to nullification of sexual desire. Cf. Eleazar's *Sefer ha-Shem*, MS London, British Museum 737, fol. 213a: "The unique name is only revealed to one who has nullified the desire for women and to one whose heart is anxious." Cf. ibid., fol. 279b: "The name is not revealed except to the righteous (*ṣaddiq*)." And ibid., fol. 307a: "The name is not to be transmitted except to one who has children." Cf. ibid., fol. 321b. On the causal link between libidinal control and the indwelling of the *Shekhinah*, cf. ibid., 310b. For a convenient review of the German Pietists' attitude toward sexuality, see D. Biale, *Eros and the Jews: From Biblical Israel to Contemporary America* (New York, 1992), pp. 72–82.

21. See Scholem, *Major Trends*, p. 117; idem, *Origins of the Kabbalah*, trans. A. Arkush and ed. R. J. Zwi Werblowsky (Princeton, 1987), pp. 41–42, 97–123, 180–98, 215–16, 325 n. 261; M. Idel, "The Sefirot above the Sefirot," *Tarbiz* 51 (1982): 274–77 (in Hebrew); idem, *Kabbalah: New Perspectives* (New Haven, 1988), pp. 98–102, 130–31; and idem, "In the Light of Life: An Examination of Kabbalistic Eschatology," in *Sanctity of Life and Martyrdom: Studies in Memory of Amir Yequtiel*, ed. I. Gafni and A. Ravitsky (Jerusalem, 1992), pp. 191–211, esp. 205–7 (in Hebrew). See also study of Idel cited in n. 19. The work of Farber (cited in full in n. 1) shares this orientation and is replete with interesting textual and conceptual parallels. See also H. Pedaya, "'Flaw' and 'Correction' in the Concept of the Godhead in the Teachings of Rabbi Isaac the Blind," *Jerusalem Studies in Jewish Thought* 6, 3–4 (1987): 251–71, esp. 269ff. (in Hebrew). Also relevant are the studies of I. Ta-Shema, "Ashkenazi Ḥasidism in Spain: R. Jonah Gerondi—the Man and His Work," in *Exile and Diaspora: Studies in the History of the Jewish People Presented to Professor Haim Beinart on the Occasion of His Seventieth Birthday*, ed. A. Mirsky, A. Grossman, and Y. Kaplan (Jerusalem, 1988), pp. 165–94 (in Hebrew); E. Kanarfogel, "Rabbinic Figures in Castilian Kabbalistic Pseudepigraphy: R. Yehudah He-Ḥasid and R. Elḥanan of Corbeil," *Journal of Jewish Thought and Philosophy* 3 (1993): 77–109. For a different approach to the relationship of German Pietism and the Provençal-Spanish kabbalah, see Dan, *Esoteric Theology*, pp. 116–29, and idem, "A Re-evaluation of the 'Ashkenazi Kabbalah,' " pp. 125–40. Other studies in Dan's *ouevre* could be cited, but the two examples I have noted are sufficient as there is little change in his position as it is stated in his various publications.

22. M. Klein, *The Fragment-Targums of the Pentateuch* (Rome, 1980), p. 57; see ibid., p. 144 for an alternative version. It is worthwhile to compare the targumic and midrashic explanation of Gen. 28:12 to the words of the apocryphal text *The Ladder of Jacob*, translated in *The Old Testament Pseudepigrapha*, ed. J. H. Charlesworth (New York, 1985), 2: 407: "And the top of the ladder was the face as of a man, carved out of fire."

23. *Targum Pseudo-Jonathan of the Pentateuch*, ed. E. G. Clarke with collaboration by W. E. Aufrecht, J. C. Hurd, and F. Spitzer (Hoboken, 1984), p. 33.

24. *Genesis Rabbah* 68:12, ed. J. Theodor and Ch. Albeck (Jerusalem, 1965), pp. 787–88; see ibid., 82:2, p. 978.

25. See P. Schäfer, *Rivalität zwischen Engeln und Menschen* (Berlin, 1975), pp. 204–7.

26. Cf. *Midrash ᵓAggadah*, ed. S. Buber (Vienna, 1894), p. 73, and *Midrash ha-Gadol on Genesis*, ed. R. Margaliot (Jerusalem, 1975), p. 504.

27. Two of the more recent discussions of this aggadic motif can be found in J. L. Kugel, *In Potiphar's House: The Interpretive Life of Biblical Texts* (San Francisco, 1990), pp. 112–20, and D. M. Stern, *Parables in Midrash: Narrative and Exegesis in Rabbinic Literature* (Cambridge and London, 1991), pp. 110–13.

28. See L. Ginzberg, *The Legends of the Jews* (Philadelphia, 1968), 5:290 n. 134, and A. Altmann, "The Gnostic Background of the Rabbinic Adam Legends," in *Essays in Jewish Intellectual History* (Hanover, 1981), p. 13. Mention should be made in this context of the aggadic tradition that the beauty of Jacob was like that of Adam. See B. Baba Meṣiᶜa 84a. This Jewish conception of Jacob's image engraved on the throne of glory had a decisive influence on the Ismaᶜili tradition concerning the image of Muhammed qua primordial anthropos engraved upon the throne of Allah. See I. Goldziher, "Neuplatonische und gnostische Elemente im Hadit," *Gesammelte Schriften* (Hildesheim, 1970), 5:327–28. Compare the latter development of this motif in *Zohar* 1:23a (this section belongs to stratum of the *Tiqqunim*), 253a. See also Joseph Gikatilla, *Shaᶜare ᵓOrah*, ed. J. Ben-Shlomo (Jerusalem, 1981), 1: 275.

29. See J. Drummond, *Philo Judaeus; or, the Jewish-Alexandrian Philosophy in Its Development and Completion* (London, 1888), 2: 206–7. See below, n. 34.

30. J. Z. Smith, "The Prayer of Joseph," in *Religions in Antiquity: Essays in Memory of Erwin Ramsdell Goodenough*, ed. J. Neusner (Leiden, 1970), pp. 254–94, esp. 284–86. See also J. E. Fossum, *The Name of God and the Angel of the Lord* (Tübingen, 1985), pp. 188, 314–15, and J. H. Charlesworth, "The Portrayal of the Righteous as an Angel," in *Ideal Figures in Ancient Judaism: Profiles and Paradigms*, ed. J. J. Collins and G. W. E. Nickelsburg (Chico, 1980), pp. 135–51, esp. 140. I. Gruenwald, "The Poetry of Yannai and the Literature of the Yorde Merkavah," *Tarbiz* 36 (1967): 271 (in Hebrew), suggests that the source of the aggadic motif of the image of Jacob engraved upon the throne is in the mystical idealization of the patriarchs. Gruenwald mentions in support of his explanation the oft-cited saying attributed to Resh Laqish in Genesis *Rabbah* 82:6, p. 983: "the Patriarchs are the chariot" (*ha-ᵓavot hen hen ha-merkavah*). On the general phenomenon of righteous individuals becoming angelic hypostases of God, see P. W. van der Horst, "Some Notes on the Exagoge of Ezekiel," in *Essays on the Jewish World of Early Christianity* (Göttingen, 1990), p. 82.

31. See J. Daniélou, *Théologie du Judéo-Christianisme*, 2nd ed. (Paris, 1991), pp. 218–20.

32. See J. Doresse, *The Secret Books of the Egyptian Gnostics* (New York, 1960), p. 167. See also H. C. Youtie, "A Gnostic Amulet with an Aramaic Inscription," *Journal of the American Oriental Society* 50 (1930): 214–20, and

Smith, "Prayer of Joseph," pp. 261–62 n. 2. Mention should also be made of the fact that in *Papyri Graecae Magicae*, xxxvi: 68–101, one of the names of the God, Typhon-Seth, is Iakoumbiai, a title that is no doubt related to the biblical Jacob. See D. F. Moke, "Eroticism in the Greek Magical Papyri: Selected Studies" (Ph.D. dissertation, University of Minnesota, 1975), p. 97. That there are Jewish elements in this papyrus, dated to the fourth century, is evident from the appearance of the Tetragrammaton, Iaeo, in the top left corner of a diagram used as a love charm (xxxvi, 102–34). See Moke, op. cit., p. 110. Interestingly enough, the figure of this diagram has six protuberances coming out from between the legs. There is thus an intrinsic connection between the number six and the phallus. On this connection see sources discussed in E. R. Wolfson, "Anthropomorphic Imagery and Letter Symbolism in the *Zohar*," *Jerusalem Studies in Jewish Thought* 8 (1989): 172 n. 112 (in Hebrew).

33. See A. Böhlig, "Jakob als Engel in Gnostizismus und Manichäismus," *Erkenntnisse und Meinungen*, ed. G. Wiessner (Wiesbaden, 1978), pp. 1–14 (English translation in *Nag Hammadi and Gnosis*, ed. R. McI. Wilson [Leiden, 1978], pp. 122–30).

34. See, e.g., Hippolytus, *Against the Heresy of One Noetus*, trans. S. D. F. Salmond in *The Ante-Nicene Fathers*, ed. A. Roberts and J. Donaldson (Grand Rapids, 1981), 5:225: "For who is Jacob His servant, Israel His beloved, but He of whom He crieth, saying, 'This is my beloved Son, in whom I am well pleased; hear ye Him?' (Mat. 17:5). Having received, then, all knowledge from the Father, the perfect Israel, the true Jacob, afterward did show Himself upon earth, and conversed with men. And who, again, is meant by Israel but a man who sees God? and there is no one who sees God except the Son alone [cf. John 1:18, 6:46], the perfect man who alone declares the will of the Father." On the etymology of Israel as "one who sees God," see Smith, "Prayer of Joseph," p. 266 n. 2. Particularly relevant for the passage from Hippolytus is Philo who identifies the Logos as the divine image, God's firstborn, also named Israel, for it is he who sees God; cf. *De Confusione Linguarum*, 146. See the comprehensive study of G. Delling, "The 'One Who Sees God' in Philo," in *Nourished with Peace: Studies in Hellenistic Judaism in Memory of Samuel Sandmel*, ed. F. E. Greenspahn, E. Hilgert, and B. L. Mack (Chico, Ca., 1984), pp. 27–42. See also C. H. Dodd, *The Interpretation of the Fourth Gospel* (Cambridge, 1953), pp. 70–72. Mention should be made of some scholars' observation that John 1:50–52 may already presuppose a transference of a midrashic reading of Gen. 28:12 from Jacob to Jesus. See Kugel, *In Potiphar's House*, p. 115, and other references given on p. 124 n. 39. The resemblance of the motif of the angelic Jacob to traditions about the incarnation of Jesus in Christian sources has been noted by M. Smith, "The Account of Simon Magus in Acts 8," in *Harry Austryn Wolfson Jubilee Volume* (Jerusalem, 1965), 2:748–49. Finally, it is worth considering the possible influence of Jewish esotericism on the identification of Jesus as the "face of the God of Jacob" (perhaps based on Ps. 24:6) that one finds in Clement of Alexandria, *Stromateis* 7:58. The motif of Jesus as the hypostatic face of God in Gnostic sources and its possible relationship to *merkavah* mysticism has been discussed by N. Deutsch, "Gnosticism and Merkabah Mysticism: A Programmatic Study," to appear in a forthcoming volume of *Aufstieg und Niedergang der Römischen Welt*.

35. *Genesis Rabbah* 98:3, p. 1252 (in the original Hebrew version of this chapter, I neglected to mention this very important source as well as the one cited

in the following note). See parallel sources cited in n. 30 ad locum, especially *Midrash Tanḥuma*ʾ, ed. S. Buber (Vilna, 1885), Toledot, § 11, p. 132: "Jacob was a partner with his Creator in everything. R. Pineḥas ha-Kohen bar Ḥamma said in the name of R. Reuben: See what is written, 'Not like these is the Portion of Jacob; For it is He who formed all things' (Jer. 10:16)." As Albeck correctly points out, according to this midrashic reading, the pronoun "he" in the latter part of the verse refers to Jacob, that is, it is Jacob who is the demiurge that forms all things. Cf. the Ashkenazi source cited below in n. 203.

36. *Leviticus Rabbah* 36:4, ed. M. Margulies (Jerusalem, 1933–34), p. 846. For parallel sources cf. the note ad locum, and see especially *Bereshit Rabbati*, ed. Ch. Albeck (Jerusalem, 1940), pp. 254–55. It is of interest to note that the passage from *Leviticus Rabbah* and the passage from B. Megillah 18a noted below are cited by the fourteenth-century apostate Abner of Burgos in his *Sefer Teshuvot la-Meḥaref* (The Book of Responses to the Blasphemer) as proof that the rabbis affirmed the notion of an incarnate God. See J. Hecht, "The Polemical Exchange between Isaac Pollegar and Abner of Burgos / Alfonso of Valladolid According to Parma MS 2440: *Iggeret Teshuvot Apikoros* and *Teshuvat la-Meharef*" (Ph.D. dissertation, New York University, 1993), pp. 183–84, 371–72. Remarkably, the apostate Jew was able to uncover what appears to me to be the underlying significance of the aggadic traditions regarding the demirugic and angelic status of Jacob. The rabbinic sources betray an affinity with the idea of a glorified demiurgic angel cultivated by Judeo-Christians for whom the figure of Jacob blends together with that of Jesus. See n. 347.

37. *Genesis Rabbah* 78:13, p. 921 n. 4. In light of the probability that underlying the aggadic motif of the icon of Jacob engraved upon the throne is the divinization of Jacob, it is of interest to consider the following comment from a medieval source cited in *Tosafot ha-Shalem: Commentary on the Bible*, ed. J. Gellis (Jerusalem, 1984), 3:107 (in Hebrew) from MS Vatican, Biblioteca Apostolica ebr. 45: "'And the Lord was standing above him' (Gen. 28:13), to protect him [cf. *Genesis Rabbah* 69:3, p. 792]. What forced Rashi to explain this in terms of God's protecting him? When the angels came to accompany [Jacob] they saw that his face was like the appearance of the face engraved on the throne of glory. They said, 'Perhaps, God forbid, there are two [divine] powers?' They desired to kill him, but the Holy One, blessed be He, protected him. This is why he explained [the verse] to protect him, for they harmed him and the Holy One, blessed be He, extended His finger and burned them."

38. Jerome, *Liber Hebraicarum Quasetionum in Genesim*, in J.-P. Migne, *Patroliga Latinae* 23:1038. This passage is mentioned by Smith, "Prayer of Joseph," p. 264 n. 3.

39. *Lamentations Rabbah* 2:2, ed. S. Buber (Vilna, 1899), p. 96. Cf. Ṭodros Abulafia, *Shaʿar ha-Razim*, ed. M. Kushnir-Oron (Jerusalem, 1989), p. 129, and the passage from Nathan Naṭa ben Solomon Spira cited below in n. 175.

40. The connection between *tifʾeret yisraʾel* (on the basis of Lam. 2:1) and the crown (*ʿaṭarah*) is made in *Sefer ha-Bahir*, ed. R. Margaliot (Jerusalem, 1978), § 33, without any allusion to the motif of the image of Jacob engraved on the

throne. On the metaphorical connection between Israel and the crown, compare the passage from *Midrash Tanḥuma*ʾ referred to by Idel, *Kabbalah: New Perspectives*, p. 373 n. 168. On the motif of the divine crown that is called "Israel," see M. S. Cohen, *The Shiʿur Qomah: Texts and Recensions* (Tübingen, 1985), pp. 36 n. 38, 128, 149. On the association of the crown and the image of Jacob, however, without any connection to the motif of the crown made from the prayers of Israel, see the poem, *ʾAderet Tilboshet*, in the *Poems of Shlomo ha-Bavli*, ed. E. Fleischer (Jerusalem, 1973), p. 168 (in Hebrew). See also the formulation in Salmon ben Yeruḥim, *The Book of the Wars of the Lord*, ed. I. Davidson (New York, 1934), p. 110. Cf. the passage from Eleazar of Worms' *Sode Razayya*ʾ in *Sefer Raziʾel* (Amsterdam, 1701), 16d: "It is written in the *Sefer Hekhalot* that the Holy One, blessed be He, embraces and kisses the name of the image of Jacob." For another version of this text cf. *Sode Razayya*ʾ, ed. S. Weiss (Jerusalem, 1988), p. 43.

41. *Genesis Rabbah* 77:1, p. 910.

42. *Sifre on Deuteronomy*, ed. L. Finkelstein (Berlin, 1939; 2nd ed., New York, 1969), p. 422. The English rendering follows the translation of R. Hammer, *Sifre: A Tannaitic Commentary on the Book of Deuteronomy* (New Haven, 1986), p. 376.

43. M. Fishbane, "The 'Measures' of God's Glory in the Ancient Midrash," in *Messiah and Christos: Studies in the Jewish Origins of Christianity Presented to David Flusser on the Occasion of His Seventy-Fifth Birthday*, ed. I. Gruenwald, Sh. Shaked, and G. G. Stroumsa (Tübingen, 1992), pp. 55–56.

44. Ibid., p. 56.

45. *Genesis Rabbah* 79:8, pp. 949–50.

46. Cf. *Perush ha-Ramban ʿal ha-Torah*, ed. C. D. Chavel (Jerusalem, 1978), 1:189, ad Gen. 33:20; Ṭodros Abulafia, *ʾOṣar ha-Kavod ha-Shalem* (Warsaw, 1879), 20d; *Rabbenu Baḥya ʿal ha-Torah*, ed. C. D. Chavel (Jerusalem, 1981), 1:288–89, ad Gen. 33:20; and Menaḥem Recanaṭi, *Perush ʿal ha-Torah* (Jerusalem, 1961), 31b–32a, ad Gen. 33:20. See also *Commentary on Talmudic Aggadoth by R. Azriel of Gerona*, ed. I. Tishby (Jerusalem, 1948), pp. 56–57 (in Hebrew).

47. Echoes of this motif can be found as well in Josephus. See M. Mach, *Entwicklungsstadien des jüdischen Engelglaubens in vorrabbinischer Zeit* (Tübingen, 1992), p. 324 nn. 123–24.

48. See *Midrash Konen* in A. Jellinek, *Bet Midrash* (3rd ed., Jerusalem, 1967), 2:39, 6:49; *Synopse zur Hekhalot Literatur*, ed. P. Schäfer, et al. (Tübingen, 1981), § 406; and Scholem, *Major Trends*, p. 62.

49. *The Liturgical Poems of Rabbi Yannai according to the Triennial Cycle of the Pentateuch and the Holidays*, ed. Z. M. Rabinovitz, 2 vols. (Jerusalem, 1985–87), 1:168–69 (in Hebrew). See ibid., p. 171; Z. M. Rabinovitz, *Halakhah and Aggadah in the Liturgical Poems of Yannai: The Sources of the Poet, His Language and His Period* (Tel-Aviv, 1965), p. 104 (in Hebrew); and Gruenwald, "The Poetry of Yannai" (cited above in n. 30).

50. Compare the words of Judah Halevi in *Kuzari* 4:3 and the *piyyuṭ* of Benjamin bar Zeraḥ, *beriyot ʾesh*, in *Maḥzor le-Ḥag Sukkot*, ed. D. S. Goldschmidt (Jerusalem, 1981), p. 88. See L. Zunz, *Literaturgeschichte der synagogalen Poesie* (Berlin, 1865), p. 501.

51. *Batte Midrashot*, ed. S. Wertheimer (Jerusalem, 1980), 1:156.

52. *Numbers Rabbah* 84:1; see also *Midrash Tanḥumaʾ*, Bemidbar, 8.

53. *Maḥzor* (Venice, 1559), 242b, 243b. Cf. the commentary on this *piyyuṭ* from the school of Rashi in S. J. Schachter, "The Liturgical Commentary of Mahzor Ashkenazi (JTSA MS # 4466)," (DHL., Jewish Theological Seminary of America, 1986), p. 95.

54. *Maḥzor la-Yamim Noraʾim*, ed. D. S. Goldschmidt (Jerusalem, 1970), 2:608 (Yom Kippur). See *Seder ʿAvodat Yisraʾel*, ed. I. Baer (Berlin, 1937), p. 776, and the poetic passage of Joseph ben Nissan cited in E. Fleischer, *The Yoẓer: Its Emergence and Development* (Jerusalem, 1984), p. 727 (in Hebrew). The aggadic image of Jacob engraved upon the throne figures prominently as well in one of the old Aramaic *piyyuṭim* for Shavuot. For the Aramaic text and Hebrew translation, see A. Tal (Rosenthal), "The Aramaic Piyyuṭim for Shavuot: Their Dialectal Aspect and Their Contribution to an Aramaic Lexicon" (M.A. thesis, Hebrew University, 1966), pp. 86–93 (in Hebrew). The text is also conveniently printed in M. H. Schmelzer, "Perush Alfabetin by Rabbi Benjamin ben Abraham min Ha-Anavim," in *Texts and Studies: Analecta Judaica*, ed. H. Z. Dimitrovsky (New York, 1977), 1:260–61 (in Hebrew), and see the relevant commentary on pp. 191–92. This *piyyuṭ* is referred to by the Karaite, Judah Hadassi, *ʾEshkol ha-Kofer* (Eupatoria, 1836), par. 362, 133c–d. My thanks to Dr. Richard White for calling my attention to this source and to Prof. Menaḥem Schmelzer for helping me identify the reference.

55. D. Halperin, *The Faces of the Chariot* (Tübingen, 1988), p. 121. Cf. *Zohar* 1:72a, and Hebrew parallel in the untitled fragment of Moses de León extant in MS Munich, Bayerische Staatsbibliothek 47, fol. 338b. Concerning this work, see G. Scholem, "Eine unbekannte mystische Schrift des Mose de Leon," *Monatsschrift für Geschichte und Wissenschaft des Judentums* 71 (1927): 109–23. See also *Zohar Ḥadash*, ed. R. Margaliot (Jerusalem, 1978), 14b (*Midrash ha-Neʿelam*).

56. *Maḥzor la-Yamim Noraʾim*, ed. D. S. Goldschmidt (Jerusalem, 1970), 1:217 (Rosh ha-Shanah). This *piyyuṭ* is mentioned in Goldziher, "Neuplatonische und gnostische Elemente," p. 328 n. 2.

57. *Pirqe R. ʾEliʿezer*, ch. 35.

58. *Midrash Sekhel Ṭov*, ed. S. Buber (New York, 1959), p. 141.

59. *Perush Sefer Yeṣirah*, ed. S. J. Halberstam (Berlin, 1885), p. 43. On the motif of the image of Jacob engraved beneath the throne, see n. 199.

60. *Batte Midrashot* 1:383.

61. On the possibility that Rashi utilized the midrashic anthology *ʾOtiyyot de-R. ʿAqivaʾ*, see I. Ta-Shema, "The Library of the Ashkenazi Sages of the Eleventh and Twelfth Centuries," *Tarbiz* 40 (1985): 307 (in Hebrew).

62. Cf. Abraham Abulafia, *ʾOr ha-Sekhel*, MS Vatican, Biblioteca Apostolica ebr. 233, fol. 100a: "Thus the *ḥashmal* comprises five vowels as one, for below it are the four beasts called by the name of an anthropos according to the forms of their faces, as it says, 'and the image of their faces was the face of a human' (Ezek. 1:10)." Is Abulafia alluding here to a doctrine that affirms that the glory itself, represented as the *ḥashmal*, is constituted by the four beasts below it that make up the anthropomorphic form? Confirmation of this interpretation is found in another work of Abulafia, *Ḥayye ha-Nefesh*, MS Munich, Bayerische Staatsbibliothek 408, fol. 6a:

> Whatever he comprehends with his intellect is closer to his truth, and that is the anthropos in truth, and its gradations are below the throne and above the throne, and he is the category of the beasts (*ḥayyot*) who bear the throne and in the category of the one who sits upon the throne. And this is the likeness (*demut*) with which he was created, the likeness of the four beasts and "the likeness of a human form upon the throne from above" (Ezek. 1:26). This is the divine image (*ṣelem ʾelohim*), and in its likeness and the true matter is this living being that speaks who is called *ḥashmal, ḥai she-mal*, i.e., the living being (*ḥai*) that speaks and converses (*she-memalel u-medabber*)."

See ibid., 15b. See also Judah ben Solomon Campanton, *ʾArbaʿah Qinyyanim*, MS New York, Jewish Theological Seminary of America Mic. 2532, fol. 77a: "This is the image of a human by way of truth and this is the image that the prophet saw upon the throne that was above the firmament on top of the heads of the creatures that were contained in one, as it says, 'this was the creature (*ḥayyah*) that I had seen by the Chebar Canal' (Ezek. 10:15)." See ibid., fol. 11a. Concerning this work and partial transcription thereof, see E. H. Golomb, "Judah ben Solomon Campanton and His Arba'ah Kinyanim" (Ph.D. dissertation, Dropsie College, 1930). I am presently preparing a comprehensive study of the kabbalistic and mystical elements in the two major works of this figure, *ʾArbaʿah Qinyyanim* and *Leqaḥ Ṭov*. On the containment of the whole structure of the chariot in the form of an anthropos, see the formulation of Abraham Lask, *ʿAyin Panim ba-Torah* (Warsaw, 1797), 31a.

63. Cf. B. Ḥagigah 13b.

64. *Sode Razayyaʾ*, ed. I. Kamelhar (Bilgoraj, 1936), p. 33. Cf. Eleazar's *Sefer ha-Shem*, MS London, British Museum 737, fol. 232a. And cf. ibid., fol. 256a, where a similiar exegesis of Ezek. 10:14, focusing on the use of the word "face" (*panim*) with respect to the human and the cherub, is placed in a decidedly ethical context, that is, the face of the cherub is said to refer to the youthful image of one who sins and repents, whereas the face of the anthropos is the elderly image of one who is pure and sinless.

65. See Farber, "Concept of the Merkavah," pp. 348, 421–24. It is worthwhile to note that in several places Eleazar remarks that in addition to the four beasts, there is one beast that rises above the throne of glory. See, e.g., *Perush ha-Merkavah*, MS Paris, Bibliothéque Nationale héb. 850, fols. 58a, 72b–73a, 79b and *Ḥokhmat ha-Nefesh* (Bene-Beraq, 1987), § 41, p. 69: "All the beasts are joined together like a big nut that is divided into sections, below there are four and a middle one. All the beasts are called the beast, 'this is the same creature that I saw' (Ezek. 10:20), all of them were one body." See A. Farber, "The Commentary on Ezekiel's Chariot by R. Jacob ben Jacob ha-Kohen of Castile" (M.A. thesis, Hebrew University, 1978), p. 115 n. 8 (in Hebrew). The image of the four beasts plus the one beast above them appears as well in several recensions of the "Secret of the Nut," *sod ha-ʾegoz*. See Altmann, "Eleazar of Worms' Ḥokhmath ha-ʾEgoz," p. 112 and Farber, "Concept of the Merkabah," pp. 102–3, 536–37, 590–91. See *Perush Rabbenu ʾEfrayim ʿal ha-Torah*, ed. E. Korach, Z. Leitner with Ch. Konyevsky (Jerusalem, 1992), 2:163, ad Deut. 6:4: "'Hear O Israel,' there are four creatures in the chariot and a fifth creature that is called Israel. No angel has permission to utter a song until that creature begins first and afterwards all the hosts above." Compare the words of Ephraim ben Jacob of Bonn cited in the *Siddur of R. Solomon ben Samson of Garmaise Including the Siddur of the Ḥaside Ashkenas*, ed. M. Hershler (Jerusalem, 1971), p. 70 (in Hebrew): "The four beasts that are seen as bearing the throne are circular, i.e., they make themselves into a circle, for they join one to another in a kiss, for the throne of glory is circular and they had to arrange their bodies so that they would be the same as the throne." On the circular shape of the throne see MS Oxford, Bodleian Library 1566, fol. 29b; *Sode Razayyaʾ*, ed. Kamelhar, p. 23; *Perush ha-Merkavah*, MS Paris, Bibliothéque Nationale héb. 850, fol. 67a; *A Commentary on the Passover Haggadah by Eleazar of Worms*, ed. M. Hershler (Jerusalem, 1984), p. 176 (in Hebrew); and *Merkavah Shelemah*, ed. S. Mussajoff (Jerusalem, 1921), 26b. It is evident that the circular shape of the throne, or the semi-circle connected more specifically to the letter *kaf*, conveys the image of the throne being feminine. See nn. 209 and 353.

66. The comparison of the cherub and the human form emerges from the statement attributed to R. Papa in B. Ḥagigah 13b that the face of the cherub is identical to the face of a human, the only difference being that the former is characterized as a "small face," *ʾappe zuṭre*, and the latter as a "great face," *ʾappe ravreve*. Compare the formulation from a manuscript of the commentary on the Torah by Eleazar of Worms cited by M. M. Kasher, *Torah Shelemah* (New York, 1948), 6:1391 n. 25: "The face of this one [Jacob] upon the throne was the human countenance, 'Am I under God,' *ha-taḥat ʾelohim ʾanokhi* (Gen. 30:2) [the word *ʾanokhi* numerically equals *kisseʾ*, i.e., throne], and the face of this one [Joseph] upon the throne was an ox that was replaced by a cherub [cf. B. Ḥagigah 13b], [as it says] 'Am I under God,' *ha-taḥat ʾelohim ʾani* (ibid., 50:19)." Cf. *Commentary on the Passover Haggadah by Eleazar of Worms*, p. 109: "Moreover, the image of Jacob is engraved upon the throne. Therefore it says, 'Am I under God,' *ha-taḥat ʾelohim ʾanokhi* (Gen. 30:2), *ʾanokhi* numerically equals *kisseʾ*. But Joseph had no throne, as it is written, 'only with respect to the throne, will I be superior to you' (ibid., 41:40). Therefore it says, 'Am I

under God,' *ha-taḥat ʾelohim ʾanokhi*. But Joseph resembled Jacob . . . thus it says by both of them, 'Am I under God,' *ha-taḥat ʾelohim ʾanokhi*." See commentary on Torah by Eleazar ben Moses ha-Darshan, *Sefer ha-Gimaṭriʾot*, MS Munich, Bayerische Staatsbibliothek 221, fol. 136a: "Jacob said, 'Am I under God,' *ha-taḥat ʾelohim ʾanokhi* (Gen. 30:2), Joseph said, 'Am I under God,' *ha-taḥat ʾelohim ʾani* (ibid., 50:19). . . . This alludes to [the fact that] Joseph is in the chariot like Jacob." Cf. "Commentary on Ezekiel's Chariot," p. 29: "This is to teach that the faces of Jacob and Joseph are engraved upon the throne, for the face of an anthropos resembles the face of Jacob and the face of a cherub is like the face of Joseph. Just as the face of Joseph resembles the face of Jacob so too the face of the cherub resembles the face of an anthropos. The face of an anthropos is large like the face of Jacob and the face of the cherub is small like the face of Joseph, may peace be upon him." See *Shaʿar ha-Razim*, p. 82, where Ṭodros Abulafia reports as follows: "I have received a bold matter concerning the inwardness of this secret, for there is small and great there, according to what the sages, blessed be their memory, said, the image of Joseph resembled the image of Jacob [cf. *Genesis Rabbah* 84:8, p. 1010]. 'Now Israel loved Joseph' (Gen. 37:3) . . . for the splendor of his image resembled his own." See also Ṭodros Abulafia, *ʾOṣar ha-Kavod*, 23b and *Rabbenu Baḥya ʿal ha-Torah*, 1:306, ad Gen. 37:2: "By way of kabbalah [the meaning of the expression] Jacob Joseph [in the verse, *ʾeleh toledot yaʿaqov yosef*, 'These are the generations of Jacob: Joseph']: Jacob is the cherub and so too is Joseph. This is what has been said concerning the great face and the small face. Each of them is called *naʿar* [youth or servant], as it is written, 'I fell in love with Israel when he was still a child (*naʿar*)' (Hosea 11:1), and it is written with respect to Joseph that 'he was a helper (*naʿar*) [to the sons of his father's wives]' (Gen. 37:2)." In this context it is evident that Jacob symbolizes the sixth of the ten divine attributes, *Tifʾeret*, and Joseph the ninth, *Yesod*. I have found a similar formulation to this in a Genizah fragment in MS New York, Jewish Theological Seminary of America ENA 3174, 16: "Moreover, we have a matter alluded to by the true sages regarding why he is called Joseph the righteous (*yosef ha-ṣaddiq*). It is because his attribute is close to the attribute of his father, and this is [the meaning of] 'for he was the child of his old age' (Gen. 37:3), as the rabbis, may their memory be for blessing, explained that the splendor of his image resembled that of his father, as it is said, truth [the attribute of Jacob] and peace [the attribute of Joseph] are one." Cf. *Zohar* 1:176b, 180a and Moses de León, *Shaʿar Yesod ha-Merkavah*, MS Vatican, Biblioteca Apostolica ebr. 283, fol. 167b, and printed version in Meir ibn Gabbai, *ʿAvodat ha-Qodesh* (Jerusalem, 1973), Sitre Torah, ch. 19, 127b. Cf. Joseph Angeleṭ, *Quppat Rochlin*, MS Oxford, Bodleian Library 1618, fol. 138a, and Judah ben Solomon Campanton, *ʾArbaʿah Qinyyanim*, MSS New York, Jewish Theological Seminary of America Mic. 2532, fols. 44b–45a and Trinity F. 12, 153, fols. 48b–49a.

67. *Sode Razayyaʾ*, ed. Weiss, p. 141. See Farber, "Concept of the Merkabah," pp. 424, 553.

68. *Perush ha-Merkavah*, MS Paris, Bibliothéque Nationale héb. 850, fol. 52a, cited by Farber, "Concept of the Merkabah," p. 424. See idem, "Commentary on Ezekiel's Chariot," p. 103 n. 10.

69. *Perush ha-Merkavah*, MS Paris, Bibliothéque Nationale héb. 850, fol. 61a, also cited by Farber, "Concept of the Merkabah," p. 424.

70. Concerning this autonomous circle of Pietists see Dan, *Esoteric Theology*, pp. 52–53, 156–64, and idem, *Studies in Ashkenazi Ḥasidic Literature* (Ramat-Gan, 1978), pp. 89–111 (in Hebrew). On the similarity between texts from the circle of the Special Cherub and passages in Eleazar's corpus regarding the description of all the creatures being contained in the one creature that is the anthropomorphic cherub, see Farber, "Commentary on Ezekiel's Chariot," p. 115 n. 8, and idem, "Concept of the Merkabah," pp. 423–24. Farber's approach represents a significant departure from that of Dan who, in his effort to establish the autonomy of the different Pietistic circles, tends to ignore common sources and/or shared structures of thought and religious symbols. On the central role of the enthroned cherub in the mystical theosophy of the German Pietists, see Scholem, *Major Trends*, pp. 113–14, and idem, *Origins*, pp. 211, 215–16, 345–46. See also Altmann, "Eleazar of Worms' Ḥokhmath ha-ʾEgoz," p. 107 n. 28. At the time of writing the aforecited studies, Scholem did not distinguish the Kalonymide circle of Pietists from other competing groups, including most importantly the group identified by Dan as the circle of the Special Cherub. See, by contrast, Scholem, *Kabbalah*, pp. 40–41.

71. MS Paris, Bibliothéque Nationale héb. 770, fol. 33a. See J. Dan, *Ḥugge ha-Mequbbalim ha-Rishonim*, ed. I. Aggasi (Jerusalem, 1977), pp. 99–106. Compare text of Elḥanan ben Yaqar cited below in n. 73.

72. Based on Ezekiel 9:3 and 10:4.

73. *Theological Texts of German Pietism*, ed. J. Dan (Jerusalem, 1977), p. 19 (in Hebrew). See ibid., p. 16:

> "The glory of the Lord left the platform of the House and stopped above the cherubs" (Ezek. 10:18). The glory of the Lord is the holy cherub and the cherubs are the creatures. "They were the same creature that I had seen below the God of Israel" (ibid., 20), i.e., beneath the cherub that is a tabernacle for the God of Israel. The cherub and the Presence are not separated, and they are like the soul and body of a person that go together. But the glory and the chariot are separated when they shine in the Sanctuary alone only in the time of need. . . . The cherubs and the wheels and all the work of the chariot are called one creature for they all go together. And all of them had one spirit and one life force, as it says, "for the spirit of the creatures was in the wheels" (ibid., 1:20).

Both of these sources are cited by Farber, "Concept of the Merkabah," p. 424. This passage should be compared to *Sefer ha-Shem*, MS London, British Museum 737, fols. 227a–b. On the relationship of the *Shekhinah* and the cherubim see also ibid., fol. 259b.

74. See Scholem, *Origins*, pp. 108–9.

75. MS Rome, Biblioteca Angelica 46, fol. 11b.

76. In a similar vein in other passages in this text Moses ha-Darshan distinguishes the Presence and Meṭaṭron, clearly polemicizing against those who identified the two. Cf. MS Rome, Biblioteca Angelica 46, fols. 2a, 8a, 11b, (partially transcribed in G. Scholem, *Reshit ha-Qabbalah* [Tel-Aviv, 1948], pp. 201–2). I have discussed these passages in "Meṭaṭron and Shiᶜur Qomah in the Writings of Ḥaside Ashkenaz," to be published in the proceedings of the conference "Mystik, Magie und Kabbala im Aschkenasischen Judentum," Dec. 9–11, 1991, Frankfurt am Main, Germany, ed. K. E. Grözinger.

77. Text published in *Reshit ha-Qabbalah*, p. 213.

78. As Scholem points out, *Reshit ha-Qabbalah*, p. 217 n. 12, the numerical equivalence here is not precise inasmuch as the a"t ba"sh of the expression *damtah le-tamar* equals 235 and the word *ha-keruv* is 233. A"t ba"sh is an ancient technique whereby the letters of the alphabet are exchanged such that the first letter is replaced with the last and so on in sequential order.

79. That is, the expression "the one," *ᵓeḥad*, rather than simply a characteristic of the deity, is understood as a designation of the cherub who complements the deity. Scholem, *Reshit ha-Qabbalah*, p. 218 n. 9, relates this to the technical term *keruv ha-meyuḥad*.

80. Scholem, *Reshit ha-Qabbalah*, p. 218 n. 13, already remarked that this numerology is not precise, for the word *nirᵓah* equals 256 and the expression *zeh ha-keruv* is 245.

81. Scholem, op. cit., pp. 217–19.

82. MSS Rome, Biblioteca Angelica 46, fol. 7b, and Milan, Biblioteca Ambrosiana 70, fol. 214b.

83. Cf. Genesis 32:25–26.

84. There is a slight discrepancy here, for the expression *u-demut penehem pene ᵓadam* equals 826, while *u-vi-demut pene yaᶜaqov hem* is 825. In Ashkenazi numerologies, however, a discrepancy of one is quite common and functionally negligible.

85. MS Paris, Bibliothéque Nationale héb. 850, fol. 57a. Cf. *Perush Rabbenu ᵓEfrayim ᶜal ha-Torah* 1:272, ad Exod. 24:11: " 'Each of them had a human face,' *u-demut penehem pene ᵓadam* (Ezek. 1:10), the final letters spell *tamim*. And this is 'you will see My back,' *we-raᵓita ᵓet ᵓaḥorai* (Exod. 33:23), which is numerically equal to *bi-demut yaᶜaqov she-ḥaquqah ba-kisseᵓ*." Concerning this numerology, see n. 171. On the ontic transformation of Jacob into an angel, cf. *Sefer ha-Shem*, MS London, British Museum 737, fol. 362a.

86. *Sode Razzayaᵓ*, ed. Weiss, p. 148, partially corrected according to MS Oxford, Bodleian Library 1638, fol. 56a. Cf. MS Munich, Bayerische Staatsbibliothek 61, fol. 65b; and see Farber, "Concept of the Merkabah," p. 611.

87. *Shirat ha-Rokeʾah: The Poems of Rabbi Eleazar ben Yehudah of Worms*, ed. I. Meiseles (Jerusalem, 1993), p. 27 (in Hebrew).

88. See M. Idel, "The Concept of Torah in the Hekhalot and Its Metamorphosis in the Kabbalah," *Jerusalem Studies in Jewish Thought* 1 (1981): 31 n. 30 (in Hebrew); Fishbane, "'Measures' of God's Glory," pp. 62–63, and relevant notes.

89. This is precisely the intent of another poem wherein this terminology is employed. See *Shirat ha-Rokeʾah*, p. 31: *gaʾawat kevodi le-yisraʾel.*

90. See n. 139.

91. *Synopse*, § 164.

92. *Sode Razayyaʾ*, ed. Kamelhar, p. 18. Eleazar's text is copied in "Commentary on Ezekiel's Chariot," p. 48.

93. See N. A. Van Uchelen, "*Maʿaseh Merkabah* in *Sefer Ḥasidim*," *Jerusalem Studies in Jewish Thought* 6:3–4 (1987): 45–46 (English section). A similar usage is evident in *Zohar Ḥadash*, ed. R. Margaliot (Jerusalem, 1978), 31b, where the *Shekhinah* is called "*maʿaseh merkavah* when she rides upon that creature that is an eagle, an ox, a lion, or a human." See also *Zohar* 3:223b (*Raʿayaʾ Mehemnaʾ*) cited below in n. 121. It seems to me that the term *maʿaseh merkavah* is employed as a technical designation of the *Shekhinah* in *Zohar* 3:95a: "R. Abba said, This is what R. Simeon used to do. When the time to partake of the [third Sabbath] meal arrived he would set the table and occupy himself in the work of the chariot (*maʿaseh merkavah*) and he would say, 'This is the meal of the King who has come to eat with me.' " In this context the expression "to be occupied with the work of the chariot" signifies mystical communion with the divine Presence. See *Sod ha-Shabbat (The Mystery of the Sabbath) from the Tolaʿat Yaʿaqov of R. Meir ibn Gabbai*, translated with a critical commentary by E. K. Ginsburg (Albany, 1989), p. 207.

94. Van Uchelen, "*Maʿaseh Merkabah* in *Sefer Ḥasidim*," p. 45 n. 13, remarks that the words *demut yisraʾel* in Eleazar's comment seemingly refer to one of the angelic creatures that surround the throne. He does not, however, specifically mention the motif of the image of Jacob engraved upon the throne.

95. See Dan, *Esoteric Theology*, p. 49 n. 11 (in that context mention is made of the text but not the author's name); idem, "The Vicissitudes of the Esoterism of the German Ḥasidim," in *Studies in Mysticism and Religion Presented to Gershom G. Scholem* (Jerusalem, 1967), pp. 96–97 (Hebrew section); and discussion of Farber, "Commentary on Ezekiel's Chariot," pp. 9–14 of the Introduction; idem, "Concept of the Merkabah," pp. 68, 214, 217, 400, 468, 525, 612, passim. On the more general influence of German Pietism on Jacob ha-Kohen, see comments of G. Scholem, *The Kabbalah of Sefer Temunah and R. Abraham Abulafia*, ed. J. Ben-Shlomo (Jerusalem, 1987), pp. 88–89 (in Hebrew); A. Farber, "On the Sources of Rabbi Moses de Leon's Early Kabbalistic System," in *Studies in Jewish Mysticism, Philosophy and Ethical Literature Presented to Isaiah Tishby on His Seventy-Fifth Birthday*, ed. J. Dan and J. Hacker (Jerusalem, 1986), pp. 94–96 (in

Hebrew); idem, "Concept of the Merkabah," pp. 400, 410, 468, 598, 612, 626–27; and D. Abrams, "'The Book of Illumination' of R. Jacob ben Jacob ha-Kohen: A Synoptic Edition from Various Manuscripts" (Ph.D. dissertation, New York University, 1993), pp. 42–43.

96. "Commentary on Ezekiel's Chariot," p. 42. See, however, p. 46, where the author apparently distinguishes between the image of Jacob and the beast whose name is Israel: "This is 'He issued His commands to Jacob' (Ps. 147:19), the one who is engraved on the chariot, 'His statutes and rules to Israel' (ibid.), this is the creature whose name is Israel, which is underneath the firmament. This is a great secret from the secrets of the verses of Scripture." A similar distinction is discernible in Eleazar ben Moses ha-Darshan's commentary on the Torah, *Sefer ha-Gimaṭriʾot,* MS Munich, Bayerische Staatsbibliothek 221, fol. 133a:

> "Then Israel bowed at the head of the bed" (Gen. 47:31). The crownlets (*tagin*) on [the words] "Israel" and "the bed" transform the plain meaning of the verses and take them out of their literal sense. This is how they should be interpreted: the crownlets on "Israel" and "the bed" allude to that which is above. This is an allusion that above there is a countenance with the form of Jacob (*parṣuf yaʿaqov meṣuyyar*) and [the word "Israel"] alludes to this. Further, there is an angel above and its name is Israel and it stands in the middle of the firmament and says, "Bless the Lord who is blessed," and the supernal beings respond, "Blessed is the Lord who is blessed forever," as it is the Book of the Chariot (*sefer ha-merkavah*) [cf. *Synopse*, §§ 296, 406]. This is [the import of] "Then Israel bowed," that angel who is in heaven. "At the head of the bed": the bed is the supernal chariot for the Presence, as it were, rests on it and the angel bows down to there. This is "at the head of the bed."

According to this author, then, the word Israel refers to either the image of Jacob or the angel named Israel who leads the other angels in praising the glory. Obviously, the two must be distinguished.

97. G. Scholem, "The Traditions of R. Jacob and R. Isaac, sons of R. Jacob ha-Kohen," *Maddaʿe ha-Yahadut* 2 (1927): 208 (in Hebrew). See Farber, "Commentary on Ezekiel's Chariot," p. 98 n. 7, and idem, "Concept of the Merkabah," p. 546. For a later reverberation of the identification of the living creature named Israel and the heavenly image of Jacob engraved upon the moon (see n. 190), see Judah ben Solomon Campanton, *ʾArbaʿah Qinyyanim,* MS New York, Jewish Theological Seminary of America Mic. 2532, fol. 23a; see ibid., fol. 76a. See also the tradition of R. Yom Ṭov Ishbili (Ritba), the teacher of Judah Campanton, cited in ibid., fol. 22a: "The soul of Israel emanates from the form of the creature whose face is that of a human face." Underlying this passage is clearly the identification of the creature named Israel and the human face of the living creatures of the chariot.

98. Scholem, "Traditions of R. Jacob and R. Isaac," p. 210.

99. MS New York, Jewish Theological Seminary of America Mic. 1806, fol. 18b.

100. See Farber, "Commentary on Ezekiel's Chariot," p. 6 n. 6 of the introduction. In that context Farber mentions the commentary on the chariot extant in MS Jerusalem, Mussajoff 145, fols. 48a–52a, and notes the similarities between it and the compositions of Ṭodros Abulafia. See, however, "Concept of the Merkabah," p. 560, where Farber asserts that this commentary originated from the "circle of the Kohen brothers," without attributing it specifically to Ṭodros Abulafia. See, op. cit., pp. 626, 631. The matter requires a closer examination.

101. MS Jerusalem, Mussajoff 145, fol. 48b. Cf. Ṭodros Abulafia, *ʾOṣar ha-Kavod,* 3c: "The face of the anthropos [in the celestial creatures] corresponds to the merit of Jacob, peace be upon him, for the image of his icon was engraved on the throne of glory."

102. Cf. MS Jerusalem, Mussajoff 145, fol. 50a: "All of this vision is also said in reference to the four holy creatures, concerning the image of Jacob that is a head for these four."

103. See above n. 63.

104. MS Jerusalem, Mussajoff 145, fol. 51b. Cf. *Zohar* 1:18b and parallel in 3:274a.

105. Regarding the *Ḥug ha-ʿIyyun,* see Scholem *Origins,* pp. 309–62, and M. Verman, *The Books of Contemplation: Medieval Jewish Mystical Sources* (Albany, 1992).

106. On the description of the four creatures (*ḥayyot*) seen by Ezekiel as the primal elements (*yesodot*), cf. also the Iyyun text (see Scholem, *Reshit ha-Qabbalah,* p. 256 n. 5), *Sod Yediʿat ha-Meṣiʾut,* MS Munich, Bayerische Staatsbibliothek 83, fol. 165b: "'They had the figures of human beings' (Ezek. 1:5): here is an allusion to the Primal Ether together with the four elements and their decomposition, for their goal is to return to the earth, which is the fourth element, and all of the elements are equalized within it, and it is in the elements, and the Ether mediates between them." As Halperin, *Faces of the Chariot,* p. 474, has noted, the correlation between the four creatures of the divine chariot and the four primal elements is made already in formative Christian exegesis on the chariot and from there influenced Islamic exegesis.

107. Verman, *Books of Contemplation,* p. 105; Hebrew text on p. 93.

108. "Commentary on Ezekiel's Chariot," p. 96 n. 11.

109. See Hebrew text in Verman, *Books of Contemplation,* p. 92, and English translation on p. 104.

110. M. Idel, "The World of Angels in Human Form," in *Studies in Jewish Mysticism, Philosophy and Ethical Literature Presented to Isaiah Tishby on His Seventy-Fifth Birthday,* p. 30 (in Hebrew).

111. See Verman, *Books of Contemplation*, p. 227.

112. Hebrew text in Verman, *Books of Contemplation*, p. 230. See Idel, "World of Angels," p. 24, and especially the text of Meir ibn Sahula cited in n. 87 ad locum.

113. Farber, "Commentary on Ezekiel's Chariot," p. 96 n. 11; Idel, "World of Angels," p. 24.

114. G. Scholem, "R. Moses of Burgos, Disciple of R. Isaac," *Tarbiz* 5 (1934): 189 (in Hebrew).

115. That is, the last of the gradations or the *Shekhinah*, which is depicted as the lower point that is parallel to the upper point, the beginning of emanation, *Ḥokhmah*.

116. *Zohar Ḥadash*, ed. R. Margaliot (Jerusalem, 1978), 38c. The matter of the containment of all the forms of the chariot in the form of an anthropos is reiterated many times in zoharic literature. Cf. *Zohar* 1:18b–19a, 71b; 2:80b, 211b; 3:48a, 118b, 240b, 274a; and see Y. Liebes, *Sections of a Zohar Lexicon* (Jerusalem, 1976), pp. 50–51 n. 123; 53–54 n. 141 (in Hebrew). In the relevant zoharic texts the four celestial creatures are forms engraved on the throne; see, e.g., *Zohar* 3:240b. Needless to say, this notion is much older. See, e.g., *Liturgical Poems of Rabbi Yannai*, p. 217.

117. The description of Meṭaṭron as the body of the Presence and as an anthropomorphic image corresponds to the view of Joseph of Hamadan who, it seems, influenced the author of *Tiqqune Zohar*. See Idel, "World of Angels," p. 57, and Farber, "On the Sources," p. 83 n. 35. On the kabbalist Joseph of Hamadan and his relationship to zoharic literature, see Y. Liebes, *Studies in the Zohar*, trans. A. Schwartz, S. Nakache, and P. Pelli (Albany, 1993), pp. 103–26.

118. The consonants of the word *mah* are *mem* and *he*ʾ, which equal forty-five, the numerical value of the Tetragrammaton when spelled out in full as YWD HA WAW HA, 10 + 6 + 4 + 5 + 1 + 6 +1 + 6 + 5 +1.

119. Cf. *Zohar* 1:18b, 149b (*Sitre Torah*); 2:118a (*Raʿayaʾ Mehemnaʾ*); 3:274a; and *Zohar Ḥadash* 38c.

120. That is, Meṭaṭron is the secret of the chariot of the Presence designated as *mah*, the numerical equivalent of the Tetragrammaton.

121. *Tiqqune Zohar*, ed. R. Margaliot (Jerusalem, 1978), Introduction, 14b. In this passage it is said of Meṭaṭron that he is the "work of the chariot" (*maʿaseh merkavah*). See, however, *Zohar* 3:223b (*Raʿayaʾ Mehemnaʾ*): "The work of the chariot (*maʿaseh merkavah*) is *Malkhut* . . . and there is a chariot below *Zeʿeir ʾAnpin* that is Meṭaṭron." See above n. 93. On Meṭaṭron as a chariot for *Tifʾeret*, compare *Tiqqune Zohar*, Introduction, 4a: "Meṭaṭron is in the image of the Righteous, Foundation of the World [cf. ibid., 7a] . . . and he is the one 'by the Chebar Canal' (Ezek. 1:1, 3). What is [the meaning of] Chebar? This is Meṭaṭron, a chariot [*rekhev*, the same consonants as the word *kevar*] for the Middle Pillar. 'He mounted a cherub and flew' (2 Sam. 22:11; Ps. 18:11)." In this text there is a

link made between the chariot (*rekhev*), the canal Chebar (*kevar*) alongside of which Ezekiel had his chariot vision, and the cherub (*keruv*); all of these terms refer to Meṭaṭron who is also depicted in the image of *Yesod*, the divine phallus. Cf. the German Pietistic text, *Perush Hafṭarah*, MS Berlin, Staatsbibliothek Or. 942, fol. 154a, cited in my "Meṭaṭron and Shiᶜur Qomah in the Writings of Ḥaside Ashkenaz," n. 90. The phallic position accorded Meṭaṭron may be implied in *Sefer ha-Shem*, MS London, British Museum 737, fol. 290b. Immediately after a discussion on several facets of the angel Meṭaṭron derived from *Hekhalot* literature, there appears the following statement: "'Who measured the waters with the hollow of His hand' (Isa. 40:12): this is the balance (*moᵓznayim*), one scale from one side, another scale from the other side, and the tongue in the middle." (See n. 296.) The text is accompanied by a drawing of the scales. Although it is not stated explicitly that the scales are attributed to Meṭaṭron, the fact that this discussion follows the description of Meṭaṭron at least suggests this possibilty. The suggestion is strengthened by the fact that the biblical verse that introduces the discussion of the scales has obvious demiurgic connotations. On the phallic status of Meṭaṭron, cf. Joseph Gikatilla, *Ginnat ᵓEgoz* (Hanau, 1615), 44d: "Understand what they have said regarding the soul of Moses that is placed between the throne of glory and Meṭaṭron. This matter is very deep, and it is the Righteous, foundation of the world. We do not say this for everyone, and the enlightened will understand." See Farber, "On the Sources," p. 94 n. 61, who suggests that the text of Gikatilla resembles the "secret of the moon" found in Jacob ha-Kohen's *Sefer ha-ᵓOrah*; see n. 190. Cf. *Zohar* 3:230b (*Raᶜayaᵓ Mehemnaᵓ*): "The angel Meṭaṭron is a chariot for the Presence . . . the Middle Pillar is a chariot for the Cause of Causes and His Presence is a chariot for the Middle Pillar." Cf. MS New York, Jewish Theological Seminary of America Mic. 2430, fol. 70a, where Eleazar's disciple, Shem Ṭov ben Simḥah reports a tradition that he received from his teacher according to which Meṭaṭron is referred to as the unique chariot, *rekhev meyuḥad*. (On this collection of German Pietistic secrets and its editor, see Scholem, *Major Trends*, p. 376 n. 122; Dan, *Esoteric Theology*, pp. 48, 255; idem, "The Vicissitudes," p. 91; and idem, "The Intention of Prayer from the Tradition of R. Judah the Pious," *Daᶜat* 10 (1983): 47–56 [in Hebrew].) Dan, "The Vicissitudes," p. 91 n. 17, suggests to emend the text from *rkv* to *krv*, thereby seeing here a reference to the *keruv ha-meyuḥad*, the special cherub. However, if one were to accept this textual emendation, it would stand as a proof against Dan's own repeated insistence that the term *keruv ha-meyuḥad* does not appear in the writings of the Pietists from the Kalonymide circle. In "Meṭaṭron and Shiᶜur Qomah," I have suggested that the text should be left intact, the expression *rekhev meyuḥad* signifying that Meṭaṭron is a chariot upon which the divine glory dwells. See also the reference to the *keruv yaḥid* in a text of Eleazar cited below in n. 324. On the identification of the Active Intellect, also designated as the something (*yesh*) created out of nothing (*ᶜayin*) and the seventh heaven, ᶜAravot, as the special cherub (*keruv ha-meyuḥad*), see Judah Campanton, *ᵓArbaᶜah Qinyyanim*, MSS New York, Jewish Theological Seminary of America Mic. 2532, fol. 11a, Trinity College F.12.153, fol. 13b. On Meṭaṭron as the throne of glory, see Farber, "On the Sources," p. 83 n. 35, and M. Idel, "Additional Fragments from the Writings of R. Joseph of Hamadan," *Daᶜat* 21 (1988): 49, n. 16 (in Hebrew).

The critical text cited by Idel from MS New York, Jewish Theological Seminary of America Mic. 1884, fol. 18a, is also transcribed in Verman, *Books of Contemplation*, p. 94, in the critical apparatus to lines 97–99. A trace of this motif is discernible in the Pietistic commentary on the different names of Meṭaṭron where one of the names of the latter, געיטיה, is said to "numerically equal כסא יהוה (throne of the Lord) for he is engraved and standing near the throne and the throne is engraved from him, and he himself is hewn within it." Cf. MSS New York, Jewish Theological Seminary of America Mic. 1804, fol. 9b, 2026, fol. 5a; Cambridge, University Library Add. 405, fol. 313a; Moscow-Guenzberg, Russian State Library 90, fol. 132a; and Oxford, Bodleian Library 2286, fol. 164a. Cf. also the passage cited below in n. 140. Concerning this text, see Dan, *Esoteric Theology*, pp. 220–23; idem, "The Seventy Names of Meṭaṭron," *Proceedings of the Eighth World Congress of Jewish Studies—Division C* (Jerusalem, 1982), pp. 19–23; Farber, "Concept of the Merkabah," pp. 237, 300, 423; and Y. Liebes, "The Angels of the Shofar and Yeshua Sar ha-Panim," *Jerusalem Studies in Jewish Thought* 6, 1–2 (1987): 171–98 (in Hebrew), esp. nn. 7, 9, 10, 13, 20, 21, 22, 33, 42.

122. On the connection between Jacob's dream and the vision of the chariot in medieval Jewish philosophical literature, see A. Altmann, "The Ladder of Ascension," in *Studies in Mysticism and Religion Presented to Gershom G. Scholem on his Seventieth Birthday* (Jerusalem, 1967), pp. 1–32, esp. 19–26. According to another midrashic tradition, Jacob's dream of the ladder is connected with the Sinaitic theophany, based on the numerical equivalence of the words *sullam* and *sinai*, i.e., both are 130. Cf. *Genesis Rabbah* 68:12, p. 786. For a later development of this numerology in the literature of the German Pietists, cf. *Sefer ha-Ḥokhmah*, MS Oxford, Bodleian Library 1812, fol. 77b; *Sode Razayya'*, ed. Kamelhar, p. 35; and *Sefer ha-Roqeaḥ* (Jerusalem, 1967), p. 106.

123. *Synopse*, § 199; see also § 237. On the use of the ladder as a symbol for the *via mystica* in this context, see P. Schäfer, *The Hidden and Manifest God: Some Major Themes in Early Jewish Mysticism* (Albany, 1992), p. 146, and J. Dan, "The Beginnings of Ancient Jewish Mysticism," *Da'at* 29 (1992): 5–25 (in Hebrew), esp. 20–21. Dan likewise surmises that the archetype for the ladder of ascent in the passage from *Hekhalot Rabbati* was the ladder of Jacob.

124. *Synopse*, §§ 181–82.

125. MS New York, Jewish Theological Seminary of America Mic. 1806, fol. 20b.

126. *Studies in Ashkenazi Ḥasidic Literature*, pp. 134–87.

127. Literally, the Tigris, *ḥiddeqel*; cf. Gen. 2:14.

128. *Studies in Ashkenazi Ḥasidic Literature*, p. 172, corrected slightly according to MS Oxford, Bodleian Library 1567, fol. 10a.

129. See M. Idel, "On the Metamorphosis of an Ancient Technique of Prophetic Vision in the Middle Ages," *Sinai* 86 (1979): 1–7 (in Hebrew). The text under discussion is cited by Idel, op. cit., pp. 1–2.

130. *Megalleh 'Amuqot*, ed. S. Weiss (New York, 1982), p. 75.

131. *Midrash Leqaḥ Ṭov*, ed. S. Buber (Vilna, 1888), 71a.

132. The connection between Meṭaṭron and the Logos was already noted by D. Neumark, *Toledot ha-Pilosofiyah be-Yisraʾel* (New York, 1921), 1:74. On the identification of Meṭaṭron as the Demiurge, see J. Dan, "Anafiel, Meṭaṭron, and the Creator," *Tarbiz* 52 (1983): 447–57 (in Hebrew). It is relevant in this context to note that in one passage in *Hekhalot Rabbati* (cf. *Synopse*, § 190) the expressions "mighty one of Jacob" (*ʾavir yaʿaqov*), "holy one of Israel" (*qedosh yisraʾel*), and "creator" (*yoṣer bereʾshit*) are synonymous: *hater hater yoṣer bereʾshit selaḥ selaḥ ʾavir yaʿaqov meḥal meḥal qedosh yisraʾel ki ʾadir melakhim ʾatah*. The use of this passage is discernible in the poem *ʾet pene mevin we-yodeʿa din dal*, by Meir bar Isaac, in *Maḥzor la-Yamim Noraʾim*, ed. Goldschmidt, 2:673: *selaḥ ʾavir yaʿaqov yoṣer bereʾshit hater*. Eleazar of Worms cites this passage from *Hekhalot Rabbati* in his writings, but it seems that in his case the "mighty one of Jacob" is connected to the icon of Jacob engraved upon the throne of glory. Cf. *Perush ha-Merkavah*, MS Paris, Bibliothéque Nationale héb. 850, fol. 59a; "Commentary on Ezekiel's Chariot," p. 31; and *Sode Razayyaʾ*, ed. Kamelhar, p. 49. On the expression *ʾavir yaʿaqov* as a designation for the enthroned glory, see the version of *Sod ha-ʾEgoz* in MS Oxford, Bodleian Library 1960, fols. 129b–131b published by Dan, "Ḥokhmath ha-ʾEgoz," p. 80. However, *ʾavir yaʿaqov* is one of the names of Meṭaṭron according to the Pietistic commentary on the different names of this angel (see above n. 121). Cf. MS New York, Jewish Theological Seminary of America Mic. 2026, fols. 8a–b.

133. See G. Scholem, "The Secret of the Tree of Emanation by R. Isaac: A Treatise from the Kabbalistic Tradition of *Sefer ha-Temunah*," *Qoveṣ ʿal Yad* 5 (1951): 67 n. 2 (in Hebrew). I would like to take this opportunity to correct my description of this work in "Letter Symbolism and Merkavah Imagery in the Zohar," in *ʿAlei Shefer: Studies in the Literature of Jewish Thought Presented to Rabbi Dr. Alexandre Safran*, ed. M. Hallamish (Bar-Ilan, 1990), p. 100 (English section), where I neglected to mention Scholem's attribution of the text to the circle of *Sefer ha-Temunah*.

134. See, e.g., MSS Cambridge, University Library Add. 671, fols. 84b–89b; Oxford, Bodleian Library 1557, fols. 12a–26b; New York, Jewish Theological Seminary of America Mic. 1990, fols. 49a–63b, 8115, fols. 76b–81a; and Vatican, Biblioteca Apostolica ebr. 194, fols. 2a–28b. Regarding this commentary, see also G. Scholem, *Kitve Yad ba-Qabbalah* (Jerusalem, 1930), p. 7, and references supplied there. In that context Scholem concluded that the commentaries on the seventy-two-letter name derived from the school of Abraham Abulafia, even though he acknowledged as well the influence of the doctrine of cosmic cycles (*shemiṭṭot*) of *Sefer ha-Temunah*.

135. *Sefer Raziʾel*, 33b; MSS Cambridge, University Library Add. 671, fol. 89a; New York, Jewish Theological Seminary of America Mic. 8115, fol. 79b; Oxford, Bodleian Library 1557, fol. 26b.

136. For example, Abraham Abulafia, Moses de León, Joseph Gikatilla, Moses Narboni, Levi ben Gershom, and Isaac Albalag, to name a few of the better-known authors.

137. This, of course, reflects the oft-cited tradition in medieval sources to the effect that the name "Meṭaṭron" has the same numerical value as the name "Shaddai," i.e., 314.

138. *Sefer Razi ᵓel*, 33b; MSS Cambridge, University Library Add. 671, fol. 89a; New York, Jewish Theological Seminary of America Mic. 8115, fol. 79b; Vatican, Biblioteca Apostolica ebr. 194, fol. 28b.

139. See *ᶜArugat ha-Bosem*, ed. E. E. Urbach (Jerusalem, 1963), 4:36–38, and esp. 38 n. 81.

140. See *Maḥzor min Rosh ha-Shanah we-Yom ha-Kippurim ᶜim Perush Qorban ᵓAharon* (Lemberg, 1766), 13a, cited in *Maḥzor la-Yamin ha-Nora ᵓim*, ed. Goldschmidt, 1:84 n. 44 (Rosh ha-Shanah).

141. See above n. 121.

142. MSS New York, Jewish Theological Seminary of America Mic. 2026, fol. 20a, Cambridge, University Library Heb. Add. 405, fol. 307b, Moscow-Guenzberg, Russian State Library 90, fol. 129a, Oxford, Bodleian Library 2256, fol. 160a. In this connection it is also of interest to note the following remark of Eleazar ben Moses ha-Darshan in his commentary on the Torah, *Sefer ha-Gimaṭri ᵓot*, MS Munich, Bayerische Staatsbibliothek 221, fol. 148a: "'And the angel of God now moved' (Exod. 14:19), ["angel of God," *mal ᵓakh ha-ᵓelohim*] is numerically equal to Jacob [i.e., *ya ᶜaqov* = 182 = *mal ᵓakh ha-ᵓelohim*]. This alludes to the fact that Jacob was like an angel." Cf. Isaac bar Judah ha-Levi, *Sefer Pa ᶜneaḥ Raza ᵓ* (Jerusalem, 1984), Toledot, 30b:

> "[The name] *ya ᶜaqov* is numerically equal to *mal ᵓakh ha-ᵓelohim*. This alludes to the fact that his image is engraved on the throne. And thus [with respect to] what is written, "O throne of glory, exalted from of old," *kisse ᵓ khavod marom me-ri ᵓshon* (Jer. 17:12), the final letters [of the first three words] are *ᵓadam*, as it is written, "Each of them had a human face" (Ezek. 1:10). It is alluded to there that the human face was the form of the *tam* [i.e, Jacob], for the final letters of *u-demut penehem* spell *tam*. Thus it says the face of an anthropos (*pene ᵓadam*), i.e., the image of the *tam* that is the human face upon the throne."

If one is to surmise that the angel of God mentioned in Exod. 14:19 refers to Meṭaṭron, then the tacit assumption of this comment is that Meṭaṭron is identical with the angelic Jacob. The likelihood that this explanation is implied is strengthened by a comment on Exod. 14:19 extant in a manuscript collection of Ashkenazi comments on the Torah cited in *Tosafot ha-Shalem: Commentary on the Bible*, ed. J. Gellis (Jerusalem, 1987), 7:198 (in Hebrew): "The angel of God (*mal ᵓakh ha-ᵓelohim*) numerically equals Jacob (*ya ᶜaqov*), i.e., Jacob is considered an angel for he wrestled with him (cf. Gen. 32:25), and the two of them were high priests before the Holy One, blessed be He." It is also possible that reflected here is the notion that the angel with whom Jacob struggled was Michael. See *Midrash Tanḥuma ᵓ*, ed. Buber, Vayishlaḥ § 7, 83a, and the passage from *Midrash Avkir* in *Yalqut Shim ᶜoni* to Gen. 32:25, § 132, cited as well in S. Buber, *Liqquṭim mi-Midrash ʾAvkir* (Vienna, 1883), pp. 7–8. See also the pseudo-Eleazar *Perush ha-Roqeaḥ ʿal ha-Torah*, ed. Ch. Konyevsky (Bene-Beraq, 1986), 1:249. Concerning the unreliability of this attribution, see J. Dan, "The Commentary on the Torah of Eleazar of Worms," *Kiryat Sefer* 59 (1984): 644 (in Hebrew), and idem, "The Ashkenazi Hasidic 'Gates of Wisdom,' " in *Hommage à Georges Vajda*, ed. G. Nahon and Ch. Touati (Louvain, 1980), pp. 183–89. On the tradition of Meṭaṭron (or Michael) as celestial high priest, see G. Scholem, *Jewish Gnosticism, Merkabah Mysticism, and Talmudic Tradition* (New York, 1965), p. 49. On the application of this title to Jesus in Christian exegesis, see, e.g., Origen, *Hom. in Num.* 11:9, cited in *The Teaching of Sylvanus (Nag Hammadi Codex VII, 4)*, text, trans., and commentary by J. Zandee (Leiden, 1991), p. 157. For the interpretation of the angel of God mentioned in Exod. 14:19 as a probable reference to Meṭaṭron, see Joseph Bekhor Shor, *Perush ʿal ha-Torah* (Jerusalem, 1983), p. 81.

143. Cf. *Synopse*, § 398. It should be noted as well that in these older sources, the crown upon the head of the divine glory is likewise given the name "Israel." See above, n. 40. On the association of the name "Israel" with Meṭaṭron, see Jacob ben Jacob ha-Kohen, *Sefer ha-ʾOrah*, MS Milan, Biblioteca Ambrosiana 62, fol. 108b [see the printed version of this text in Abrams, "'Book of Illumination,' " p. 274] and the passage from the same composition published by Scholem, "Traditions of R. Jacob and R. Isaac," p. 242. On the relationship of the fragmentary secrets published by Scholem and the anthology of the *Sefer ha-ʾOrah*, see Farber, "Commentary on Ezekiel's Chariot," p. 125 n. 16. On various aspects of Meṭaṭron in the writings of Jacob ha-Kohen, see my study, "Meṭaṭron and Shiʿur Qomah in the Writings of Ḥaside Ashkenaz," nn. 36, 73, 86, 87, 116, 118 , and see now the discussion in Abrams, op. cit., pp. 65–89.

144. *Perush ʿal ha-Torah*, ed. A. Weiser (Jerusalem, 1977), 3:309, ad Deut. 32:8.

145. Cf., e.g., the commentary of Abraham ibn Ezra to Isa. 66:1; the introduction to the commentary on Daniel; *The Religious Poems of Abraham Ibn Ezra*, ed. I. Levin (Jerusalem, 1975; in Hebrew), 1:160 (poem no. 86); 288 (poem no. 154); 431 (poem no. 225); and 438 (poem no. 228).

146. Cf., e.g., *Perush ʿal ha-Torah*, ed. Weiser, 2:27, ad Exod. 3:15; commentary to Ps. 8:4; *Religious Poems of Abraham Ibn Ezra* 1: 164 (poem no. 89); 515 (poem no. 258); and D. Rosin, "Die Religionsphilosophie Abraham Ibn Esra's," *Monatsschrift für Geschichte und Wissenschaft des Judentums* 42 (1898): 243–54.

147. Cf. Farber, "Commentary on Ezekiel's Chariot," p. 31: "Concerning that which is written, 'He cast down from heaven to earth the majesty of Israel' (Lam. 2:1), i.e., the level of the four supernal creatures, who are fixed in the supernal, encompassing sphere and in whom the image of Jacob is engraved, was cast down to the floor of the lowest sphere of the moon that is called earth."

148. E. R. Wolfson, "God, the Demiurge, and the Intellect: On the Usage of the Word *Kol* in Abraham ibn Ezra," *Revue des ètudes juives* 149 (1990): 77–111.

See also relevant discussion in Rosin, "Die Religionsphilosophie," p. 202; A. Altmann, "Moses Narboni's 'Epistle on Shiᶜur Qomah,' " in *Jewish Medieval and Renaissance Studies*, ed. A. Altmann (Cambridge, Mass., 1967), p. 267 n. 21; G. Vajda, *Juda ben Nissim ibn Malka: Philosophe Juif Marocain* (Paris, 1954), p. 79; and idem, "Pour le Dossier de Meṭaṭron," in *Studies in Jewish Religious and Intellectual History Presented to Alexander Altmann on the Occasion of His Seventieth Birthday*, ed. S. Stein and R. Loewe (University, Alabama, 1979), pp. 345–54.

149. The interpretation of ibn Ezra's secret that I have offered is confirmed in several supercommentaries on his commentary. See, e.g., Joseph ben Eliezer Ṭov Elem, *Ṣofnat Paᶜneaḥ* (Berlin, 1930), 2:88–89:

> The explanation of "[He fixed the boundaries of peoples] in relation to Israel's numbers" (Deut. 32:8): the sages, blessed be their memory, said that the form of Jacob, our patriarch, is engraved on the throne of glory, and this is a great secret. . . . Understand that when it is the proper noun it alludes to the awesome and glorious name and when it is an adjective, i.e., a name of an attribute, it alludes to the Active Intellect [needless to say, here the Active Intellect is the first or universal intellect and not the tenth of the separate intellects as we find, e.g., in the case of Maimonides] and this is the angel that advises and guides Israel . . . and Israel is the lot of this holy angel just as the nations are all the lot of the stars that guide them. . . . Since the universal form of each and every nation, i.e., the name of every nation, is engraved upon its star so that its group would be guarded, they thus said that the form of Jacob is engraved upon the throne of glory for he is the one that guards the class of Israelites and guides them. . . . All of this is in order to remove them from under the dominion of the stars so that there is no archon over them except for the archon of the world who is Michael, the angel of the countenance who is the Active Intellect.

Cf. MS Paris, Bibliothéque Nationale héb. 188, fol. 128a. See also Samuel ibn Moṭoṭ, *Megillat Setarim* (Venice, 1554), 51b: "This is the reason that the sages, blessed be their memory, said that the form of Jacob, our patriarch, is engraved on the throne of glory, and this is a great secret. The explanation refers to the order of Jacob, our patriarch, peace be upon him, and the matter of this image and this number is that the ninth [sphere] is the throne. . . . Remember the view of the sage, may his memory be for a blessing, with respect to the matter of the throne and the glorious name that sits upon it." It may be inferred from this that the image of Jacob is the glorious name that sits upon the throne, a symbolic depiction of the intellect that moves the ninth sphere. Cf. the words of ibn Moṭoṭ, ibid., 11a: "The explanation for what they said, 'He rides upon His swift cherub' (*keruv qal*), is in accordance with the view of those who say that He is the one who moves the ninth [sphere], the one who moves everything, for he is in truth His swift cherub." From here it follows that the swift cherub is the intellect that moves the ninth sphere. The manner in which the cherub is described in this second passage is identical with the manner in which the image of Jacob is described in the first passage. Can one conclude that implied here is some older esoteric tradition according to which the image of Jacob engraved on the throne was identified as a cherub? See my comments in "God, the Demiurge, and the Intellect," pp. 92–93 n. 61. A tradition such as this does appear in the literature of the German Pietists, as will be made clear. On the identification of the Active Intellect as Meṭaṭron designated by the names "angel," "cherub," and "Elohim," see Abraham Abulafia, *Sitre Torah*, MS Paris, Bibliothéque Nationale héb. 774, fol. 129b.

150. The reference is to the *sheti wa-ᶜerev*, the warp and woof, an expression employed on any number of occasions in Abulafia's extensive corpus to refer to opposites or polarities. See, e.g., *Perush Sefer Yeṣirah ᵓAlmoni mi-Yesodo shel Rabbi ᵓAvraham ᵓAbulᶜafiya*, ed. I Weinstock (Jerusalem, 1984), pp. 28 n. 12, 29 n. 16. In the second reference the connection to Meṭaṭron is obvious. See also M. Idel, *The Mystical Experience in Abraham Abulafia* (Albany, 1988) p. 217 n. 97; idem, *Studies in Ecstatic Kabbalah* (Albany, 1988), p. 41 n. 16.

151. In MS Munich, Bayerische Staatsbibliothek 92 (see following note) the reading is *ᶜaqevo*, "his heel," but I have corrected this obvious scribal error according to MS Vatican, Biblioteca Apostolica ebr. 233, fol. 97b, for the letters of *ᶜaqevi* are those of *yaᶜaqov*.

152. MS Munich, Bayerische Staatsbibliothek 92, fol. 59b (my thanks to Moshe Idel who discussed this text with me and made some important remarks that helped me decode Abulafia's somewhat obtuse style). Cf. *Sefer ha-Melammed*, MS Oxford, Bodleian Library 1649, fol. 204b.

153. See Scholem, *Major Trends*, p. 140; idem, *Kabbalah of Sefer ha-Temunah*, pp. 156–57; Idel, *Mystical Experience*, pp. 27, 117–19; and *Perush Sefer Yeṣirah*, ed. Weinstock, p. 24 n. 27.

154. See Farber, "On the Sources," pp. 84–87, and Idel, *Mystical Experience*, p. 165 n. 208.

155. On Israel as a designation of the Active Intellect in Abulafia, see M. Idel, *Language, Torah, and Hermeneutics in Abraham Abulafia* (Albany, 1989), pp. 36, 38, 40, 109, 119, and Farber, "On the Sources," p. 84 n. 36.

156. It is possible that the twofold aspect of Meṭaṭron related to the double image of Jacob, i.e., the earthly patriarch and his celestial icon engraved upon the throne, underlies the complicated exegesis of Jacob's dream in Abulafia's epistle, *Shevaᶜ Netivot Torah*, in A. Jellinek, *Philosophie und Kabbala* (Leipzig, 1854), Erstes Heft, p. 10:

> They have alluded to the secret in their saying that the ladder that Jacob saw was Sinai, and this secret was revealed by way of numerology [see above, n. 122] . . . It is known by us that the secret of Sinai is double and that is *qof-lamed* [i.e., Sinai = 130 = *qof-lamed*] and it emerges from the two holy names, Adonai Adonai

> [each name = 65 x 2= 130], and [the sum] emerges from the five occurrences of the unique name [YHWH] for each one of them is the secret of *kaf waw* [i.e., 26; I have here followed the suggested emendation of Jellinek, p. 38 n. 10], and there are five [times 26] in *qof-lamed* (130). The five movements [of the voice represented in the letters *qof-lamed* that spell *qol* in a defective form] instruct about the first five essences (*hawwayot*) by way of the right and five by way of the left. This is [alluded to in *Sefer Yeṣirah* 1:3] "Ten *sefirot belimah,* the number of the ten fingers, five corresponding to five." Thus the name of God [YHWH] begins with a Y (*yod*) in general, and then HWH, the secret of it is *he*ʾ and the *waw* connecting it to another *he*ʾ, to divide the [ten] essences into two *he*ʾ*in,* five corresponding to five. . . . It is known that the attribute of the hands signifies the reality of the attribute of judgment, and the ten toes signifies the attribute of mercy.

Compare this passage to *Ḥayye Nefesh,* MS Munich, Bayerische Staatsbibliothek 408, fols. 18b–19a; *ʾOṣar ʿEden Ganuz,* MS Oxford, Bodleian Library 1580, fol. 10a. See also *Sitre Torah,* MS Paris, Bibliothéque Nationale héb. 774, fols. 148b and 172a. On the notion of *hawwayot* in Abulafia, see Idel, "*Sefirot* above the *Sefirot,*" pp. 260–62 and idem, *Kabbalah: New Perspectives,* p. 147.

157. See Idel, *Mystical Experience,* pp. 117–18, and relevant notes, esp. p. 165 n. 206. The dialectical nature of the Active Intellect as the first and last of the separate intellects is emphasized, for example, by Abulafia in *ʾOr ha-Sekhel,* MS Vatican, Biblioteca Apostolica ebr. 233, fol. 33a. See also Abulafia's description of the tenth *sefirah* in *Gan Naʿul,* MS Munich, Bayerische Staatsbibliothek 58, fol. 319b. Cf. the anonymous work influenced by Abulafia, *Ner ʾElohim,* MS Munich, Bayerische Staatsbibliothek 10, fol. 145b. On the dual character of Meṭaṭron as the elder and the youth, see the work printed under the name of David ben Aryeh Leib of Lida, *Sefer Migdal David* (Amsterdam, 1680), 60a (according to some scholars this work is a forgery based on the *Torat Ḥesed* of Ḥayyim ben Abraham ha-Kohen of Aleppo): "First he was called Jacob and afterwards he was called Israel . . . so too Meṭaṭron was a servant in the secret of *naʿar,* and now he is a *zaqen.*" See also *Zohar* 3:215a (*Raʿayaʾ Mehemnaʾ*) where the scriptural expression, "senior servant of his household," *ʿavdo zeqan beito* (Gen. 24:2), is applied to Meṭaṭron.

158. Cf. Abulafia, *Sefer ha-Mafteḥot,* MS New York, Jewish Theological Seminary of America Mic. 1686, fol. 127a; *Gan Naʿul,* MS Munich, Bayerische Staatsbibliothek 58, fol. 324b; and *Ner ʾElohim,* MS Munich, Bayerische Staatsbibliothek 10, fol. 133b. See also the passage from *ʾOṣar ʿEden Ganuz* referred to below in n. 167, and the text from *ʾImre Shefer* cited by Idel, *Kabbalah: New Perspectives,* p. 206; and ibid., p. 377 n. 18. See as well the passage from Isaiah ben Joseph's *ʾOṣar ha-Ḥokhmah* cited by Idel, *Mystical Experience,* p. 197.

159. On the relationship of this part of the text to the secret of the seventy-two-letter name of the Iyyun corpus, see Scholem, *Reshit ha-Qabbalah,* pp. 256–

57, n. 6, and idem, *Origins*, p. 323 n. 256. On the authorship of the introduction to *Sefer ha-ʾOrah*, see G. Scholem's review of *Codices hebraici Bybliothecae Ambrosianae descripti a Carolo Bernheimer*, in *Kiryat Sefer* 11 (1934/35):189. Scholem already suggested that it was written either by R. Jacob ha-Kohen himself or by one of his students. See, by contrast, Scholem's description in *Origins*, p. 323 n. 256. The latter possibility has now been argued in more detail by Abrams, "'Book of Illumination,' " pp. 57–61. Unfortunately, in the Hebrew version of this study, I did not take note of Scholem's comment and simply assumed that the introduction was written by Jacob.

160. It is possible that this term, *sekhel ṣaḥ*, betrays the particular influence of the expression *ʾor ṣaḥ* as it is employed in the literature of the Iyyun circle (see below, n. 165). On this usage, see Verman, *Books of Contemplation*, pp. 59, 118, and 163, where the author suggests that this term reflects the influence of the writings of Eleazar of Worms upon the Iyyun material.

161. On the conjunction of Jacob and the Active Intellect, see Elnathan ben Moses Kalkish, *ʾEven Sappir*, MS Vatican, Biblioteca Apostolica ebr. 284, fols. 6b–7a. On the image of the ladder, see ibid., fol. 49b. The influence of Abulafia on this author has been noted by Idel, *Mystical Experience*, pp. 94–95, and idem, *Kabbalah: New Perspectives*, pp. 351–52 n. 358. See also Simeon bar Samuel, *ʾAdam Sikhli* (Thiengen, 1560), 9b–10a (pagination supplied by me), where the aggadic motif of the image of Jacob engraved upon the throne is cited in the context of a discussion about Jacob's conjunction (*devequt*) with the supernal, spiritual world. On the intellectual background of this author, see J. M. Davis, "Philosophy, Dogma, and Exegesis in Medieval Ashkenazic Judaism: The Evidence of *Sefer Hadrat Qodesh*," *AJS Review* 18 (1993): 195–222.

162. See midrashic reference cited above in n. 41.

163. I have rendered the verse in accordance with the meaning assumed by the author rather than in line with its plain sense.

164. MS Milan, Biblioteca Ambrosiana 62, fol. 86a.

165. Ibid. Cf. fol. 105b: "The light of this rainbow (*qeshet*) is great for it derived [from] the light of the intellect and that is the level of Meṭaṭron, for the intellect is fixed in him like the holy spirit in the body. Therefore it says, 'That was the appearance of the semblance of the Presence of the Lord' (Ezek. 1:28), i.e., the derived intellect (*sekhel ha-nigzar*), for his name is like the name of his Master [cf. B. Sanhedrin 38b], as it says, 'since My name is in him' (Exod. 23:21)." (Cf. *Zohar* 3:215a [*Raʿayaʾ Mehemnaʾ*]: "Certainly this rainbow (*qeshet*) that is revealed in the exile is none other than Meṭaṭron who is called Shaddai.") Cf. the language of the standard recension of *Sefer ha-ʿIyyun* in Verman, *Books of Contemplation*, p. 106: "The breath is the intellect that is fixed in the heart (*ha-sekhel ha-qavuʿa ba-lev*)" (Hebrew text on p. 93). See Verman's suggestion, p. 106 n. 227, that a possible source for this expression may have been the *Moʾzne Ṣedeq*, the thirteenth-century Hebrew translation of the treatise by al-Ghazali. See also the

language of the long recension of *Sefer ha-ʿIyyun* in Verman, p. 78: "the Marvellous Light that is fixed in the Unity" (Hebrew text on p. 68). The term *sekhel qavuʿa* appears as the name of the first path in the commentary on the thirty-two paths of Wisdom that is also included in the list of works composed by this circle (see Scholem, *Reshit ha-Qabbalah*, p. 257 n. 8). See, e.g., MS Vatican, Biblioteca Apostolica ebr. 291, fol. 11b, and another Iyyun commentary on the thirty-two paths of Wisdom included in Joseph ben Shalom Ashkenazi's commentary on *Sefer Yeṣirah* (falsely attributed to Rabad), in *Sefer Yeṣirah* (Jerusalem, 1962), 10b, wherein the fourth path is called the "fixed intellect" (*sekhel qavuʿa*). The use of this terminology is evident in a third work that belongs to the literature of the Iyyun circle, *Sod wi-Yesod ha-Qadmoni* (see Scholem, *Reshit ha-Qabbalah*, pp. 259–60 n. 19), MS Munich, Bayerische Staatsbibliothek 54, fol. 285b: "The shining light, i.e., the branches of Wisdom increase above until [they reach] *Keter* to the point that it is not recognizable at all except from the intellect that is fixed in the ponderings of a man's heart." Ibid., fol. 288a: "Know that the paths of the intellect are twenty-six corresponding to the numerical value of the name [YHWH]. The first path is called the aspect of the fixed intellect." The last passage is printed with slight variations in *Sefer ha-Peliʾah* (Przemysl, 1884), pt. 2, 72c. Finally, mention should be made of the commentary on ten *sefirot* from the Iyyun circle published by G. Scholem, *Kitve Yad ba-Qabbalah*, p. 204, where the term *sekhel qavuʿa* is applied to the second of the *sefirot*. For discussion of this term in Iyyun material, see M. Kallus, "Two mid-13th Century Kabbalistic Texts from the 'Iyun Circle" (M.A. thesis, Hebrew University, 1992), second part, pp. 14–18 n. 3. (The work of Kallus, needless to say, was not available to me when I wrote the Hebrew version of this study in the fall of 1989. The last reference to the commentary on the ten *sefirot* has been added on the basis of Kallus's extensive note.) The influence of the Iyyun material on Jacob ha-Kohen and other members of his circle in Castile has been noted by various scholars. See Scholem, "Traditions of R. Jacob and R. Isaac," pp. 191–92; idem, *Reshit ha-Qabbalah*, pp. 256–57 n. 6; idem, *Origins*, pp. 310, 321, 323 n. 256, 325 n. 261; Farber, "Commentary on Ezekiel's Chariot," p. 14 of the introduction and pp. 77 n. 6, 79 n. 15, 80 n. 4; and Verman, *Books of Contemplation*, pp. 183–84.

166. *Genesis Rabbah* 68:9, p. 778.

167. *Books of Contemplation*, p. 109 (original Hebrew text on pp. 95–96). I have slightly modified Verman's translation. Cf. the anonymous kabbalistic explanation of Prov. 8:30 in MS New York, Jewish Theological Seminary of America Mic. 1855, fol. 3b, and Abulafia, *ʾOṣar ʿEden Ganuz*, MS Oxford, Bodleian Library 1580, fol. 11a.

168. Printed in the pseudo-Eleazar *Perush ha-Roqeaḥ ʿal ha-Torah*, 1:35 (see above, n. 142). This source was already noted by Verman, *Books of Contemplation*, p. 109 n. 249. It is possible that this tradition influenced the view expressed in *Sod wi-Yesod ha-Qadmoni*, MS Munich, Bayerische Staatsbibliothek 54, fol. 288b (*Sefer ha-Peliʾah*, pt. 2, 72c) with respect to *Keter* that it is "the first

path in which His splendor is revealed and the glory of the Holy One, blessed be He, is seen . . . and it divides into four squared parts."

169. On the identification in older sources of the image of Jacob and the celestial creature named "Israel," see Ginzberg, *Legends*, 5:307n. 253.

170. That is, both expressions equal 1237.

171. "Commentary on Ezekiel's Chariot," p. 8. The numerical equivalence of the expressions *we-raʾita ʾet ʾaḥorai* and *bi-demut yaʿaqov she-ḥaquq ba-kisseʾ* has its origin in Eleazar of Worms' commentary on the chariot, MS Paris, Bibliothéque Nationale héb. 850, fol. 57a. See also *Perush Sodot ha-Tefillah*, MS Oxford, Bodleian Library 1204, fol. 97a, and *Sode Razayyaʾ*, ed. Weiss, p. 148. See also the citation from Ephraim ben Shimshon above in n. 85.

172. See *Aruch Completum*, ed. A. Kohut (Jerusalem, 1969), s.v., ספקלר, 6: 110.

173. "Commentary on Ezekiel's Chariot," p. 9.

174. Ibid., p. 28. It is of interest to note that in the version of this text extant in MS New York, Jewish Theological Seminary of America 8118, fol. 16b (the manuscript dates from the fourteenth century and is written in an Ashkenazi script) there is a drawing of a human form (head and neck) to accompany the catchword *bi-demut yaʿaqov*, "in the image of Jacob." The figure is that of a young male with what appears to me to be a definite effeminate quality, perhaps related to the description of Jacob in Gen. 27:11. This graphic depiction has also been noted by Abrams, "'Book of Illumination,' " p. 83 n. 1, but he did not relate to the issue of the gender of the anthropomorphic form. Cf. Moses of Burgos, *Sefer ha-ʾOrah*, MS New York, Jewish Theological Seminary of America Mic. 1806, fol. 14a (MS Jerusalem, Mussajoff 145, fol. 60a): "Sandalphon binds [a crown] to the glory that is engraved upon the chariot." And in MS Jerusalem, Mussajoff 145, fol. 71a: "'You cannot see My face' (Exod. 33:20) . . . i.e., the image of the human face engraved upon the chariot." Noteworthy as well is the following passage from the *seder ha-merkavah* attributed to Eliezer (!) of Worms, extant in MS New York, Jewish Theological Seminary of America Mic. 9005, fol. 182a: "The upper glory [consists of] ten supernal *sefirot* that are in *Tifʾeret*, the supernal Jacob . . . and underneath him is the throne, and upon the throne is a second glory, and that is the face of the lower Jacob." A different explanation may be found in Isaac ha-Kohen's treatise on the left emanations in Scholem, "Traditions of R. Jacob and R. Isaac," p. 262. According to what is said there, corresponding to the creature in the domain of the chariot whose name is Israel in the sefirotic pleroma is the "crown of royalty whose name is Israel," i.e., the tenth emanation, *Malkhut*, rather than the sixth emanation, *Tifʾeret*.

175. See Farber, "Commentary on Ezekiel's Chariot," pp. 86 n. 10, and 98 n. 7. The influence of this tradition is discernible in a number of other kabbalistic sources of which I will here mention a small representative sampling. Cf. the passage in the treatise *ʾOr ha-Sekhel*, composed by R. Jonathan (see Scholem, *Kitve Yad ba-Qabbalah*, pp. 52–54), MS New York, Jewish Theological Seminary

of America Mic. 1831, fol. 21b: "Thus the sages, blessed be their memory, said that there is one creature in heaven whose name is Israel and engraved on its forehead is [the word] *be-yisraʾel*. The secret of Israel is the Active Intellect and it is the tenth angel, for in truth it is Meṭaṭron . . . and he is called Israel the Elder (*yisraʾel sabbaʾ*)." See Nathan Naṭa ben Solomon Spira, *Megalleh ʿAmuqot: Reish-nun-bet ʾOfanim ʿal Wa-ʾetḥanan* (Bene-Beraq, 1992), 113, 90b: "At the time of the destruction [it is written] 'He cast down from heaven to earth the majesty of Israel' (Lam. 2:1). It is found in the midrash [see above n. 39] that the king said, Are you becoming haughty on account of the diadem that you gave Me? Behold I will cast the diadem below, as it says, 'He cast down from heaven to earth the majesty of Israel.' This is the one creature whose name is Israel, for the Holy One, blessed be He, took it and threw it to the earth. The secret of the matter is as it is found in the *Pirqe Hekhalot* concerning the diadem that the Holy One, blessed be He, places on the head of Meṭaṭron, which is called Israel. And this is the secret of 'Israel in whom I glory' (Isa. 49:3)." On the identification of Meṭaṭron and the celestial creature whose name is Israel, cf. the text in MS Paris, Bibliothéque Nationale héb. 793, fol. 246b.

176. According to MSS Vatican, Biblioteca Apostolica ebr. 228 and Budapest-Kaufmann, Rabbinerseminar 238. MSS Munich, Bayerische Staatsbibliothek 40 and Philadelphia, Dropsie University 436 preserve two readings: "Bear witness to him," and "to them." MSS New York, Jewish Theological Seminary of America Mic. 8128 and Oxford, Bodleian Library 1531 read: "Bear witness to me." MS Munich, Bayerische Staatsbibliothek 22 has: "Establish for them."

177. Five of the manuscripts here employ the third person feminine pronoun, שהיא. One manuscript (Munich, Bayerische Staatsbibliothek 22) uses the third person masculine, שהוא. MS Vatican, Biblioteca Apostolica ebr. 228 has no pronoun here. The perplexing grammatical point is that the subject of the sentence, *qelaster panav*, requires a masculine form. See the following two notes.

178. Again the feminine form (*ḥaquqah*) is employed.

179. Here too the feminine form is employed, עליה, which should be translated "over her."

180. Following the reading of MSS Vatican, Biblioteca Apostolica ebr. 228 and Munich, Bayerische Staatsbibliothek 22, presumably referring to the throne upon which is engraved the visage of Jacob. See Schäfer, *The Hidden and Manifest God*, pp. 46, 119. According to MSS New York, Jewish Theological Seminary of America Mic. 8128, Oxford, Bodleian Library 1531, Munich, Bayerische Staatsbibliothek 40, Philadelphia, Dropsie University 436, and Kaufmann-Budapest, Rabbinerseminar 238, the reading is "on My arms," thus conveying the image of God's full embrace of the throne with His hands wrapped around His own arms. This reading is attested in the passage from Judah ben Yaqar cited below in n. 196 and the passage of Eleazar cited below in n. 373.

181. *Synopse*, § 164.

182. Similar imagery is used in another passage in *Hekhalot Rabbati* to describe the relationship of the celestial creatures to the enthroned glory (see *Synopse*, § 189). Parenthetically, it is worth noting that in some talmudic contexts the words *gippef* and *nishsheq*, to embrace and to kiss, appear together in the context of describing an act of idolatrous worship; see, e.g., B. Yoma 66b and Sanhedrin 60b. My thanks to Prof. David Weiss Halivni for drawing my attention to this fact. See, however, *Seder Eliahu Zuṭa*, ed. M. Friedmann (Vienna, 1904), 13, pp. 194–95, where a more positive use is attested for the words *megappef*, *meḥabbeq*, and *menashsheq*. See also the Ashkenazi commentary on the forty-two-letter name of God extant in MS Moscow-Guenzberg, Russian State Library 366, fol. 40b, where God is described as fondling (*meḥabbeq*) and kissing (*menashsheq*) the feminine Torah.

183. Cf. *Synopse*, §§ 94, 99, 154, 159, 687, and *Geniza-Fragmente zur Hekhalot-Literature*, ed. P. Schäfer (Tübingen, 1984), pp. 105, 185. See Scholem, *Jewish Gnosticism*, pp. 25–26; M. Idel, "Metaphores et pratiques sexuelles dans la cabale," in *Lettre sur la sainteté, le secret de la relation entre l'homme et la femme dans la cabale*, étude préliminaire, traduction de 'l'hébreu et commentaires par Ch. Mopsik (Paris, 1986), p. 340 n. 35; idem, "Additional Fragments," p. 49 n. 16; and E. R. Wolfson, "Female Imaging of the Torah: From Literary Metaphor to Religious Symbol," in *From Ancient Israel to Modern Judaism Intellect in Quest of Understanding: Essays in Honor of Marvin Fox*, ed. J. Neusner, E. S. Frerichs, and N. M. Sarna (Atlanta, 1989), 2:283 n. 43. On the development of this motif in the writings of the German Pietists, see E. R. Wolfson, "Circumcision and the Divine Name: A Study in the Transmission of Esoteric Doctrine," *Jewish Quarterly Review* 78 (1987): 95 n. 53; and see especially reference to Farber cited below in n. 209. To the sources that I mentioned there that posit a correlation between circumcision and the Tetragrammaton one should add an important text in a composition that Dan has attributed to Judah the Pious (see above n. 126), MS Oxford, Bodleian Library 1566, fol. 113b:

> "Who among us can go up to the heavens," *mi ya*ᶜ*aleh lanu ha-shamaymah* (Deut. 30:12). [The word] *milah* [circumcision] is alluded to in the first letters of the words and the name [YHWH] in the last letters . . . for with respect to circumcision it is written "to be God to you" (Gen. 17:7), to indicate that those who are circumcised cleave to the throne of glory. The souls of the Jews who are circumcised ascend for the word of Torah (*millah shel torah*) is on his tongue, as it says, "No, the thing is very close to you, in your mouth and in your heart, to observe it" (Deut. 30:14), and it is written, "The utterance of a man set on high" (2 Sam. 23:1), above everything in the Garden of Eden, and it is written, "His word is on my tongue" (ibid., 2).

This passage is based on *Sefer Yeṣirah* 1:3, according to which the covenant of the one (*berit yaḥid*) is said to be "set in the middle in the circumcision of the tongue (*milat ha-lashon*) and the circumcision of the foreskin (*milat ha-ma ᶜor*)." I have followed the version of the text in I. Gruenwald, "A Preliminary Critical Edition of Sefer Yezira," *Israel Oriental Studies* 1 (1971): 141. It should be evident that the cleaving to the throne, awarded to male Jews by virtue of circumcision, entails an erotic element that is based on the feminine nature of the throne. The sweeping generalization of Dan that in the writings of the German Pietists there is no parallel to the kabbalistic literature with respect to the bisexual nature of the divine realm (see above n. 9) totally neglects those passages in the relevant Pietistic material that unambiguously affirm the feminine character of the throne. Even if my conjecture regarding the icon of Jacob is rejected, one would still have to deal with the texts that ascribe feminine images to the throne itself. The feminine nature of the throne of glory (related to the ark of the covenant) is implied in the Pietistic text published by Dan, *Studies in Ashkenazi Ḥasidic Literature*, pp. 186–87. The mystical secret derived from the correlation of the ark (or the throne) and circumcision is linked to a visionary experience of the divine splendor. On the feminization of the throne as a hypostatic power, see also the passage from the *Sefer ha-Yiḥud ha-ʾAmiti* in Kallus, "Two Mid-13th Century Kabbalistic Texts," p. 3: "Throne is called in this way (i.e., *kisseʾ*) because within her (!) are hidden (*mitkassin*) all the potencies. And she sits and is silent." See ibid., p. 7: "And the Primordial Aether, which is emanated from the Power of the Exalted Cause of all causes, is made into a circle and becomes the Throne of Majesty, which becomes bright and shouts and says: 'Adiriron Yah Lord of Hosts, be glorified, for upon me sits the Magnificent King.' " (This text is copied and elaborated upon in "Commentary on Ezekiel's Chariot," p. 50; and see Farber's remarks on pp. 191–92 nn. 4, 5.) In the second passage the verbs that refer to the throne are all in feminine form. Here the grammar reflects ontology, for the presumption clearly is that the throne is a female potency. This is conveyed as well in the circular shape that is attributed to the throne (see above n. 65). Paraphrasing the text from *Hekhalot Rabbati* (see *Synopse* § 99 [see n. 352], already noted by Farber, "Commentary on Ezekiel's Chariot," p. 152 n. 6; Kallus, p. 74 n. 159) the author of the Iyyun text describes the enthronement as a sacred union of the masculine glory and the feminine throne. It is also evident from other works belonging to the Iyyun corpus that the Primordial Ether represents a feminine potency vis-à-vis the masculine Godhead; see discussion in my study, "Erasing the Erasure/Gender and the Writing of God's Body in Kabbalistic Symbolism," in *Circle in the Square: Studies in the Use of Gender in Kabbalistic Symbolism* (Albany, 1995), pp. 64–65. On the circularity and femininity of the throne, see also the Iyyun commentary on the thirty-two paths of Wisdom, MS Vatican, Biblioteca Apostolica ebr. 291, fol. 12b, transcribed in Kallus, pt. 2, p. 3, and English translation on p. 9. According to that text, the fourteenth of the thirty-two paths is called the "glorious throne," *kisseʾ nogah*, because the various powers coalesce to form a circle in the likeness of the throne that constitutes the unification of the Presence (*yiḥud la-shekhinah*). The latter is described in explicit female imagery.

184. This is precisely how the passage from *Hekhalot Rabbati* was understood by several traditional rabbinic commentators. See, e.g., Ṣedeqiah

ben Abraham, *Shibbole ha-Leqeṭ ha-Shalem*, ed. S. Buber (Vilna, 1886), § 20, p. 19, cited by Joseph Karo in *Bet Yosef* on Jacob ben Asher, *Ṭur, ʾOraḥ Ḥayyim*, 125; and Zevi Hirsch Kaidanover, *Qav ha-Yashar ha-Shalem* (Jerusalem, 1993), ch. 41, p. 192. Some early critics of my hypothesis concerning the feminization of the image of Jacob called attention to the obvious fact that the biblical persona of Jacob is a male and thus challenged my suggestion that it can symbolically represent a feminine potency. This criticism reflects a very narrow and naive conception of the use of gender symbolism in religious contexts. The issue here is not one of biological sex but rather gender, which is a sociocultural category. One that is biologically male can function as a symbol for the feminine just as a biological woman can be portrayed as masculine. The same reversal of gender symbolism is evident in the theosophic kabbalah where, for instance, the biblical figure of King David became a standard symbol for the feminine divine Presence. See my study, "Crossing Gender Boundaries in Kabbalistic Ritual and Myth," in *Circle in the Square: Studies in the Use of Gender in Kabbalistic Symbolism*. A classical study of such gender reversal is C. Bynum Walker, *Jesus as Mother: Studies in the Spirituality of the High Middle Ages* (Berkeley, 1982).

185. See, e.g., the description of God's relationship to the letters in *Midrash ʾOtiyyot de-R. ʿAqivaʾ*, in *Batte Midrashot* 1:289: "What does the Holy One, blessed be He, do at that time? He takes hold of all the letters on the chariot, embraces and kisses them, and binds crowns on them." Cf. *Sode Razayyaʾ*, ed. Kamelhar, p. 25. In this connection it is worthwhile to recall the words of Augustine, *De Trinitate*, Bk. 6, ch. 10, sec. 1: "Illa igitur ineffabilis quidam complexus Patris et imaginis non est sine perfruitione, sine charitate, sine gaudio." Cf. the passage from *Hekhalot Zuṭarti*, in *Synopse* § 411: "R. Akiva said: Thus the light of the face of Jacob, our patriarch, shined before Adiriyon, YHWH, the God of Israel." The connection between this text and the passage from *Hekhalot Rabbati* about the visage of Jacob (*Synopse* § 164) has already been noted by R. Elior, *Hekhalot Zuṭarti, Jerusalem Studies in Jewish Thought*, Supplement 1 (1982): 73 n. 317 (in Hebrew). I contend that the shining of the face has a sexual connotation.

186. Cf. the description of Jacob in the poem *ʾayom temim deʿim*, by Benjamin bar Samuel, in *Maḥzor la-Yamim Noraʾim*, ed. Goldschmidt, 1:183: *ḥalaq ha-rashum be-khes setarim*. See also the language in *Shir ha-Yiḥud* from the circle of the Ashkenazi Pietists, in *Shire ha-Yiḥud we-ha-Kavod*, ed. A. M. Habermann (Jerusalem, 1948), p. 30: *ḥeleq yaʿaqov yoṣer ha-kol*, based on Deut. 32:9 and Jer. 51:19. Is there an allusion in the expression *ḥeleq yaʿaqov*, the portion of Jacob, to the motif of the image of Jacob, as we have seen in other sources where there is a wordplay between *ḥeleq*, portion, and *ḥalaq*, smooth-skinned? If we assume this to be the case, then there is a tacit assertion here that the image of Jacob is the demiurge! The wordplay between *ḥalaq* and *ḥeleq* as applied to Jacob is evident, for example, in the anonymous commentary on the *sefirot* extant in MS Oxford, Bodleian Library 1943, fol. 48b: "[*Tifʾeret*] is called Jacob . . . and there are two pipes that overflow to *Tifʾeret*, one from the right and the other from the left. This is the secret of 'and I am smooth-skinned (*ḥalaq*)' (Gen. 27:11), for he takes a portion (*ḥeleq*) from one side and the other side."

187. *Batte Midrashot* 2:415. Cf. the version in MS New York, Jewish Theological Seminary of America Mic. 1804, fol. 86a.

188. MS Vatican, Biblioteca Apostolica ebr. 228, fol. 36b.

189. See, e.g., *Zohar* 1:210b; 2:2b; 3:210b. See esp. *Zohar* 1:266b (*Ra ᶜaya ᵓ Mehemna ᵓ*) where the formulation reflects the Ashkenazi traditions: "He is called Jacob and he is called Israel. Jacob is the language of heel (*ᶜuqva*) and that is feminine. . . . And he is called Israel for there is a head (*ro ᵓsh*), the masculine, the head of the feminine that is the heel." Cf. the fragment from the circle of *Sefer ha-Temunah* in MS Vatican, Biblioteca Apostolica ebr. 194, fol. 17a: "And Jacob is called small (*qaṭan*) before Esau because he alludes to *ᶜAṭarah* [i.e., the Presence], which is called the lesser light (*ma ᵓor qaṭan*)." On this codex and the relationship of the material it contains to *Sefer ha-Temunah*, see Scholem, "Secret of the Tree of Emanation," p. 67. See also Isaac of Acre, *Sefer Me ᵓirat ᶜEinayim*, ed. A. Goldreich (Jerusalem, 1981), p. 154 (cited already by Scholem, "R. Moses of Burgos, the Disciple of R. Isaac," *Tarbiz* 3 [1932], p. 281 n. 1 [in Hebrew]): "The expression [used in conjunction with Jacob] smooth-skinned, *ḥalaq* (Gen. 27:11) alludes to the fact that he is the place of the middle line that is called the portion of Jacob (*ḥeleq ya ᶜaqov*; cf. Jer. 51:19). The portion of Jacob (*ḥeleq ya ᶜaqov*) is that which is called in most cases *Shekhinah*, for it is the God of Israel." See ibid., p. 155, where Isaac of Acre criticizes this view on the grounds that *ḥeleq ya ᶜaqov* symbolically corresponds to the *Ṣaddiq*, i.e., the *sefirah* of *Yesod*, also called the "God of Israel," whereas the *Shekhinah* is the God of Jacob and the portion of David. The feminine valence of the symbol Jacob may also underlie the philosophical interpretation that associates Jacob with matter and Israel with form. Cf., e.g., Simeon ben Ṣemaḥ Duran, *Tif ᵓeret Yisra ᵓel* (Venice, 1600), 37b.

190. This motif is fairly common in theosophic kabbalistic sources. Cf. Ṭodros Abulafia, *ᵓOṣar ha-Kavod*, 32a: "Thus they have said that the image of the icon of Jacob is engraved in the sphere of the sun, and there are those who say in the sphere of the moon, and it is all true." (On the significance of the moon in the kabbalistic writings of Ṭodros Abulafia, see the material collected and analyzed by M. Oron in her edition of *Sha ᶜar ha-Razim*, p. 49 n. 19.) Cf. *Tiqqune Zohar*, 18, 36b: "Because of Jacob whose icon is engraved upon the moon." Cf. the commentary on the ten *sefirot* in MS Oxford, Bodleian Library 1598 (See G. Scholem, "Index of the Commentaries on the Ten *Sefirot*," *Kiryat Sefer* 10 [1934]: 508 n. 93 [in Hebrew]), fol. 112a: "The sixth is *Tif ᵓeret*, the third letter of the letters of the [divine] name, Jacob the mild man . . . and his image is engraved upon the moon." Cf. also the anonymous kabbalistic text in MS Vatican, Biblioteca Apostolica ebr. 228, fol. 19a:

> That which the rabbis, may their memory be for a blessing, said concerning the image of Jacob engraved upon the moon bears two explanations, but it all amounts to one thing. The rabbis, may their memory be for a blessing, suggested to us in this statement that the efflux that comes to the world from *ᶜAṭarah* [the Pres-

> ence] derives from *Tif'eret*. Therefore they said that the form of Jacob is engraved upon the moon, for *Tif'eret* is called Jacob inasmuch as it took his portion and the moon is called *ʿAṭarah* inasmuch as she is the power of the moon. Or you can say that the light that comes from the moon is from the sun, for the splendor of the sun enters the moon and the moon shines. Therefore they speak of the form of Jacob insofar as it is the power of the moon. Or you can say that the light that comes from the moon is from the sun, for the splendor of the sun enters the moon and the moon shines. Therefore they speak of the form of Jacob insofar as the sun receives from *Tif'eret* who is called Jacob.

Cf. Judah Campanton, *'Arbaʿah Qinyyanim*, MS New York, Jewish Theological Seminary of America Mic. 2532, fols. 22b–23a, where the ophan is described as the ontic source of all souls (hence identified as the *guf* in accordance with the aggadic statement in B. Yevamot 62a) as well as the "creature about whom the sages, may their memory be for a blessing, said that there is one creature suspended in the middle of the firmament and its name is Israel, and it is that of which they said that the form of Jacob is engraved upon the moon." The two traditions—the image of Jacob being engraved on the throne or on the moon—are combined in Abraham Abulafia, *'Oṣar ʿEden Ganuz*, MS Oxford, Bodleian Library 1580, fol. 9b: "The secret of His throne (*kiss'o*) is the moon (*levanah*) [i.e., *kiss'o* and *levanah* both equal 87]. Thus the sages said that the form of Jacob is engraved on the throne of glory and it is engraved upon the moon." It is likely that underlying Abulafia's remark is the identification of the form of Jacob with the Active Intellect and the moon with the human intellect. On the relationship of the moon and the throne of glory, see *Perush Sefer Yeṣirah 'Almoni mi-Yesodo shel Rabbi 'Avraham 'Abulʿafiya'*, pp. 30–31. For additional comments of Abulafia regarding the moon, see op. cit., pp. 41–43. For discussion of thirteenth-century kabbalistic texts in which the sun represents the Active Intellect and the moon represents the human intellect, see M. Idel, "Jerusalem in Thirteenth-Century Jewish Thought," in *The History of Jerusalem: Crusades and Ayyubids, 1099–1250* (Jerusalem, 1991), p. 280 n. 87 (in Hebrew). Along similar lines, one finds the following tradition in Jacob ha-Kohen, *Sefer ha-'Orah*, MS Milan, Biblioteca Ambrosiana 62, fol. 79b (cf. MSS Paris, Bibliothéque Nationale héb. 835, fols. 1a–b and Vatican, Biblioteca Apostolica ebr. 428, fols. 28a–b; Scholem, "Traditions of R. Jacob and R. Isaac," p. 240) interpreting the reference to the northern wind (*ruaḥ ṣefonit*):

> This is the holy spirit of Moses our master, may peace be upon him, that is hidden (*ṣefunah*) and concealed (*genuzah*) underneath the throne of glory. The spirit of Moses our master, may peace be upon him, emanated and the holy spirt of Moses was placed in the moon, for the moon (*levanah*) is derived (*gezurah*) from the white firmament (*ha-raqiʿa ha-lavan*) that Ezekiel the prophet saw. And on account of the merit of Moses the light of the intellect of Meṭaṭron is in the moon together with Moses. . . . and from where (do we know) that the spirit of Moses was placed in the moon? As

> it says, "She saw that he was good and hid him" (Exod. 2:2). After his death he was (placed) underneath the throne of glory, the first place whence he was taken. The three months here allude to the moon.

For a published version of the text, see Abrams, "'Book of Illumination,' " pp. 331–32. See esp. the version in MS Vatican, Biblioteca Apostolica ebr. 428, fol. 28b (and parallels in MSS Jerusalem, Sassoon Collection 396–97; Rome, Biblioteca Angelica 3086, fol. 62b; and Paris, Bibliothéque Nationale héb. 806, fols. 201a–b transcribed in Abrams, op. cit., pp. 335–36): "And from where (do we know) that the spirit of Moses was placed in the moon? As it says, 'She saw that he was good and hid him' (Exod. 2:2). That is, the Presence saw that he was good in order to comprehend the level of the intellect. 'She hid him,' after his death underneath the throne of glory, the first place whence he was taken." Compare the related numerology in MS Paris, Bibliothéque Nationale héb. 840, fol. 173b: "*Levanah* is numerically equal to *ba-kisse*ʾ" [in fact the former word equals 87 and the latter 83], cited by Abrams, op. cit., p. 330 n. 1. In a similar vein cf. Abraham Saba, *Ṣeror ha-Mor* (Jerusalem, 1985), p. 129: "They said that the form of Jacob is engraved on the throne of glory and it is engraved upon the moon." The last source was already noted by Ginzberg, *Legends* 5:291 n. 134. See also Knorr Von Rosenroth, *Kabbalah Denudata* (Hildesheim, 1974), p. 647: "Facies Jacob est luna." See Naftali Herz Treves, *Siddur Malʾah ha-ʾAreṣ Deʿah* (Thiengen, 1560), *yoṣer shel shabbat*, on the hymn *ʾel ʾadon ʿal kol ha-maʿasim*: "The form of the moon is in the throne and that is the form of Jacob . . . 'and He diminished," *we-hiqṭin*, the form of Jacob the small one (*ha-qaṭan*) who is called according to her name." On the attribution of the word *qaṭan* to Jacob, see n. 192. See ibid., *birkat ha-levanah*: "The form of Jacob is in the moon, and it alludes to the Community of Israel [i.e., the *Shekhinah*], which is under the throne of glory." See *Siddur of R. Solomon ben Samson of Garmaise*, p. 196, and the marginal note on the blessing for the new moon in Eleazar's commentary on the secrets of prayer, MS Paris, Bibliothéque Nationale héb. 772, fol. 144b: "*Barukh yoṣrekha, barukh ʿosekha, barukh qonekha, barukh borʾekha*, and the sign [made of the first letter of these four words] is *yaʿaqov*, for his form is engraved upon the throne and the moon." See Jacob ben Asher, *Ṭur, ʾOraḥ Ḥayyim*, 426: "There are those who say [the blessing on the new moon] in this order, *Barukh yoṣrekha, barukh ʿosekha, barukh qonekha, barukh borʾekha*, and the sign is *yaʿaqov*, for she symbolizes him." On the allusion to the name "Jacob" in the form of the blessing for the moon, see also *Kol Bo*, sec. 43, and *Sefer Abudarham ha-Shalem* (Jerusalem, 1963), p. 344: "*Barukh yoṣrekha, barukh ʿosekha, barukh qonekha, barukh borʾekha*, the first letters are *yaʿaqov* for he is compared to the moon." See the remark of Joel Sirkes in his commentary, *Beit Ḥadash*, to the *Ṭur, ʾOraḥ Ḥayyim*, 281, s.v., *qaraʾ la-shemesh*: "It must be explained, moreover, that the form of Jacob is seen in the moon. Therefore, they established in the blessing of the moon, *Barukh yoṣrekha* [*barukh ʿosekha, barukh qonekha, barukh borʾekha*], the first letters are *yaʿaqov*. . . . Thus, according to this it is said [in the liturgical poem recited on Sabbath, *ʾel ʾadon ʿal kol ha-maʿasim*] *qaraʾ la-shemesh wa-yizraḥ ʾor* [He called to the sun and it shone forth in light], for the light of the *Shekhinah* dwells on the splendor of the icon of Jacob whose name is sun (*shemesh*). *Ra᾿ah we-hitqin ṣurat ha-levanah* [He saw and established the form of the moon] in order that the light of the sun will strike and illuminate the moon, so that by means of this the form of Jacob will take shape in the moon, for the moon receives its light from the sun, which is verily the form of Jacob." See also Jacob Emden, *Siddur ᶜAmude Shamayim* (Altona, 1547), 2:13b–14a: "[In the blessing *Barukh*] *yoṣrekha* the name *yaᶜaqov* is alluded to in the first letters, for he was called small (*qaṭan*) on account of the lesser light (*ha-ma᾿or ha-qaṭan*)." It is interesting to note that according to this tradition Jacob is linked to all the epithets that describe God as creator. It is worth noting as well a change in the order of the blessing, attributed to Menaḥem Ṣiyyoni in MS Oxford, Bodleian Library 1651, fol. 23a, with the purpose of alluding to the hierarchy of the four worlds from below to above: "*Barukh ᶜosekha* corresponds to *ᶜAsiyyah, barukh yoṣrekha* corresponds to *Yeṣirah, barukh bor᾿ekha* corresponds to *Beri᾿ah, barukh qonekha* corresponds to *᾿Aṣilut*. One should say this three times and jump each time in order to elevate the three worlds, *Beri᾿ah, Yeṣirah*, and *ᶜAsiyyah*, to [the world of] *᾿Aṣilut*." In Ḥayyim Vital, *Peri ᶜEṣ Ḥayyim* (Jerusalem, 1980), 19:3, p. 463, this order appears as part of the blessing of the moon attributed to the *ḥaverim*, i.e., the fraternity of Lurianic kabbalists. This change in the version of the prayer is found in several kabbalistic prayerbooks and sometimes in the name of Isaac Luria. Cf. *Siddur ha-᾿Ari* (Zolkiew, 1781), 136b, and Moses Cordovero, *Tefillah le-Mosheh* (Przemysl, 1892), 285b: "This is the order [*yoṣrekha, ᶜosekha, qonekha*, and *bor᾿ekha*] and it is a sign of *yaᶜaqov*; however, according to the Ari, may his memory be for a blessing, one should say *ᶜosekha, yoṣrekha, bor᾿ekha*, and *qonekha*." Cf. Isaiah Horowitz, *Siddur Shaᶜar ha-Shamayim*, 220b–21a:

> "Jacob then got fresh shoots of poplar" (Gen. 30:37), [the expression *maqqal livneh*] alludes to the moon (*levanah*), for the two faces (*du-parṣufin*) are joined as one. Then the face of Jacob is engraved in the moon. Thus [the blessing is fixed] *Barukh yoṣrekha, barukh ᶜosekha, barukh qonekha, barukh bor᾿ekha*, according to the first letters, *yaᶜaqov*. These four allude to the chain of [the four worlds] *᾿Aṣilut, Beri᾿ah, Yeṣirah*, and *ᶜAsiyyah*. . . . Thus *ᶜosekha* alludes to the world of *ᶜAsiyyah, yoṣrekha* to the world of *Yeṣirah, bor᾿ekha* to the world of *Beri᾿ah*, and *qonekha* to the world of *᾿Aṣilut*. The reason that it is not mentioned according to order is so that it could allude to the name of Jacob.

See Jacob Koppel Lipschitz, *Siddur Qol Yaᶜaqov* (Slavuta, 1804), *kawwanat ḥiddush ha-ḥodesh*, 53b: "One says [the prayer] *Barukh ᶜosekha* corresponding to the four worlds, *᾿Aṣilut, Beri᾿ah, Yeṣirah*, and *ᶜAsiyyah*, and one jumps three times to elevate *Beri᾿ah* in *᾿Aṣilut, Yeṣirah* in *Beri᾿ah*, and *ᶜAsiyyah* in *Yeṣirah*. *Yoṣrekha, ᶜosekha, qonekha*, and *bor᾿ekha* contain the initials of *yaᶜaqov*, since Jacob was small." See also Moses Zacuto, *᾿Iggerot ha-ReMeZ* (Livorno, 1780), 6b–7a; Ḥayyim Joseph David Azulai, *Maḥaziq Berakhah* (Livorno, 1785), 426:3; and Shalom Sharabi, *Sefer ᾿Or Levanah* (Jerusalem, 1925), pp. 33–35.

191. Gen. 1:16.

192. Cf. B. Ḥullin 60b; *ʾAvot de Rabbi Natan,* ed. S. Schechter (Vienna, 1887), version A, ch. 36, p. 107; and commentary of Rashi to Isa. 44:5. See also the commentary on the forty-two-letter name of God in *Sefer Raziʾel,* 45b: "The [holy creatures] mention the merit of Jacob who is called small, as it says, 'How will Jacob survive? He is so small' (Amos 7:2, 5)." On the relationship of this commentary to the literature of the German Pietists, see Farber, "Concept of the Merkabah," p. 236.

193. *Synopse,* §§ 296, 406; see above n. 96.

194. Deut. 6:4.

195. That is, in *Hekhalot Rabbati;* for reference see n. 181.

196. *Perush ha-Tefillot we-ha-Berakhot,* ed. S. Yerushalmi, 2nd ed. (Jerusalem, 1979), pt. 1, pp. 97–98. This passage has also been discussed by E. Ginsburg in an unpublished study of the motif of *hieros gamos* in Judah ben Yaqar.

197. See Ginsburg, *The Sabbath in the Classical Kabbalah,* p. 169 n. 189.

198. Cf. commentary of Naḥmanides to Gen. 33:20 and Deut. 32:7. See E. R. Wolfson, "'By Way of Truth': Aspects of Naḥmanides' Kabbalistic Hermeneutics," *AJS Review* 14 (1989): 149–50. A parallel to the words of Naḥmanides is found in the *Yalquṭ Ḥakham Maskil* extant in MS Oxford, Bodleian Library 1945, fols. 48b–49a (and cf. MS Oxford, Bodleian Library 2456, fol. 8b, as well as the version in Isaac of Acre, *Sefer Meʾirat ʿEinayim,* p. 55):

> The image of Jacob upon the throne is *Tifʾeret,* a throne for *Teshuvah.* There are those who say that it is *Yesod,* and a proof for their words is the word 'truth' that signifies the Covenant, as it is said that his icon is engraved on the throne of glory. It is said that *Yesod* is the throne for *Tifʾeret* . . . the attribute of mercy, God of Israel . . . *Yesod* is the attribute of Jacob. To this alludes their statement that the icon of Jacob is engraved on the throne of glory, and the intention is that the *Shekhinah* dwells in the land of Israel, i.e., the icon of Jacob is engraved upon the throne of glory. The throne of glory is *Yesod,* which is the throne for the master of mercy. . . . The intention [of the claim] that the *Shekhinah* dwells in the land of Israel is that *Yesod* dwells in the land of Israel.

See Ezra's commentary on Song of Songs, in *Kitve Ramban,* ed. C. D. Chavel (Jerusalem, 1964), 2:477; *Maʿarekhet ha-ʾElohut* (Mantua, 1558; rpt. Jerusalem, 1963), 161a; and MS Jerusalem, Mussajoff 145, fol. 52a: "This is the statement of the [sages], may their memory be for a blessing, that the patriarchs are the chariot, and when they mentioned the face of an anthropos this alludes to all the patriarchs. Jacob is mentioned by the sages, may their memory be for a blessing, in their speaking about the icon of Jacob, for he draws from both of them." On the identification of the image of Jacob as *Yesod,* cf. also the kabbalistic secret on the fingernails (*sod ha-ṣippornayim*) by Moses de León, extant in MSS

Vatican, Biblioteca Apostolica ebr. 428, fol. 44b and Jerusalem, Schocken Library 14, fol. 91a. See E. Ginsburg, "The Havdalah Ceremony in Zoharic Kabbalah," *Jerusalem Studies in Jewish Thought* 8 (1989): 205–7 (in Hebrew).

199. Cf. MS New York, Jewish Theological Seminary of America Mic. 2430, fol. 68b: "Thus the intent of the verse, 'The beginning of Your word is truth' (Ps. 119:160), the 'beginning' refers to *Keter*, and 'Your word is truth' to *Tif*ʾ*eret*, the Written Torah. The rabbis, may their memory be for a blessing, said that the patriarchs are the chariot. Therefore it says 'and the God of Jacob' (cf. Exod. 3:15, 4:5), the [letter] *waw* [in the expression *we*ʾ*lohe ya*ʿ*aqov*] adds to the first matter, and the form of Jacob is under the throne of glory. The verse, 'Am I under God' (Gen. 30:2),' is proof of this." The prooftext is based on the fact that the word ʾ*anokhi*, "I," is numerically equal to *kisse*ʾ, "throne" (see above n. 66). On the image of the form of Jacob engraved underneath the throne, see the formulation in the commentary attributed to Eleazar of Worms on Song of Songs 2:6 cited in *Tosafot ha-Shalem: Commentary on the Bible*, ed. J. Gellis (Jerusalem, 1989), 8:121 (in Hebrew): "The verse says, 'His left hand was under my head, his right hand embraced me,' for the glory embraced the image of Jacob upon the throne of glory that is engraved beneath the throne of glory. And this is [the import of] 'under my head,' *taḥat le-ro*ʾ*shi* [the word *le-ro*ʾ*shi*] has the letters *yisra*ʾ*el*." For another version of this text see *Perush ha-Roqeaḥ* ʿ*al Ḥamesh Megillot*, ed. Ch. Konyevsky (Bene-Beraq, 1985), p. 115 (see n. 364). In that version (based on MS Oxford, Bodleian Library 1576 with variants from MS Oxford, Bodleian Library 757) the critical words, "that is engraved beneath the throne of glory," are lacking. On the unreliability of the attribution of this text to Eleazar of Worms, see I. G. Marcus, "The Song of Songs in German Ḥasidism and the School of Rashi: A Preliminary Comparison," in *The Frank Talmage Memorial Volume*, ed. B. Walfish (Haifa, 1993), 1:188 n. 21. Marcus applies the conclusion that Dan reached with respect to the *Perush ha-Roqeaḥ* ʿ*al ha-Torah* published by Konyevsky (see above n. 142) to this collection of sources. See also the article in the same volume by B. Walfish, "An Annotated Bibliography of Medieval Jewish Commentaries on the Book of Ruth in Print and in Manuscript," p. 262, item B.5. For some later attestations to the tradition that the form of Jacob was engraved underneath the throne of glory, see Abraham Lask, ʿ*Ayin Panim ba-Torah*, 13a, and Levi Yiṣḥaq of Berditchev, *Qedushat Levi* (Brooklyn, 1978), 15a.

200. Cf. *Keter Shem Ṭov* (Amsterdam, 1593), 5b: "*Tif*ʾ*eret* is the attribute of Jacob . . . and he is called the throne of glory . . . so too Jacob chose truth, which is called the throne of glory. Thus they said that the form of Jacob, our patriarch, is engraved on the throne of glory."

201. See *Studies in Ashkenazi Ḥasidic Literature*, p. 138.

202. MS Oxford, Bodleian Library 1566, fol. 31a. Cf. the passage in the poem ʾ*azkir gevurot* ʾ*eloha* in *Piyyuṭe Yosse ben Yosse*, ed. A. Mirsky, 2nd ed. (Jerusalem, 1991), p. 144: *yordim we-*ʿ*olim qedoshim la-ma*ʿ*anehu le-hakir to*ʾ*aro ḥaquq ba-meromim*. Cf. the formulation in the *qerovah* for Rosh

ha-Shanah, *ʾadon ʾim maʿasim ʾein banu*, in *Piyyuṭe R. Shimʿon bar Yiṣḥaq*, ed. A. M. Habermann (Berlin and Jerusalem, 1938), p. 117 (cf. *Maḥzor la-Yamim Noraʾim*, ed. Goldschmidt, 1:102): *naʿim ʾasher ṭovu ʾohalav/ we-toʾaro ḥaquq be-khes zevulav we-hinneh yhwh niṣṣav ʿalav*. On the divine status of Jacob, cf. the passage in an anonymous Ashkenazi commentary on Psalms in MS Oxford, Bodleian Library 1551, fol. 204a: "[The expression] *wa-teḥasserehu meʿaṭ me-ʾelohim*, 'You have made me a little less than divine' (Ps. 8:6) is numerically equal to *yaʿaqov ʾish tam*, 'Jacob was a mild man' (Gen. 25:27) with a deficiency of three [i.e., the former expression has a numerical sum of 930 and the latter 933] in the merit of the [three parts of Scripture] Pentateuch, Prophets, and Writings."

203. MS Oxford, Bodleian Library 1566, fol. 87a. See the passage from *Tanḥumaʾ* cited above, n. 35. Cf. the Ashkenazi text in MS Paris, Bibliothéque Nationale héb. 767, fol. 31b, that begins with citations from Jer. 51:19 and Deut. 6:4. In this connection it is worthwhile to mention a passage in an Ashkenazi commentary on the forty-two-letter name of God (see above n. 192), in *Sefer Raziʾel*, 45b: "Then [the angels] receive permission from Jacob, our patriarch, may peace be upon him, and they utter a song, as it says, 'no one can find a trace of it,' *we-loʾ yeʿaqqevem* (Job. 37:4) . . . *ye-ʿaqqevem* has the letters *mi-yaʿaqov*, from Jacob." In my opinion, in this case too there is an allusion that Jacob symbolizes a divine power in the world of the chariot. See the poem of Simeon bar Isaac Abun, *ʾaluf mesubbal be-hod ʾefodim*, in *Maḥzor* (Venice, 1599), 272a.

204. Cf. Eleazar of Worms, *Perush Sodot ha-Tefillah*, MS Paris, Bibliothéque Nationale héb. 772, fol. 156a: "Jacob is [written] in the plene form with a *waw* in five places [in Scripture], for it says with respect to Jacob, 'I will go down with you to Egypt and I will go up with you,' to include all the other exiles. He thus went down from the land of Israel to the exile in Egypt and the four other exiles, making a total of five." (For the printed version of this text, see *Perushe Siddur ha-Tefillah la-Roqeaḥ*, p. 669.) It appears that in this context the name "Jacob" written in the plene form alludes to the condition of the Presence in exile. The plene form of "Jacob" is interpreted in many kabbalistic sources as a symbolic reference to *Tifʾeret*, for that emanation is said to comprise within itself the six central emanations. Cf., e.g., *Zohar* 1:168a: " 'Then I will remember My covenant with Jacob' (Lev. 26:42). Jacob [*yaʿaqov*] is here written with a *waw*. Why with a *waw*? For he is verily the icon of Jacob." See Abraham ben Solomon Adrutiel, *Sefer Avne Zikkaron*, MS New York, Jewish Theological Seminary of America Mic. 2089, fol. 180a: "Jacob is written in the plene form with a *waw* to indicate that he bears the six extremities." Needless to say, the textual examples could be greatly multiplied. Another tradition, which may also be related to German Pietistic sources, is found in Jacob ha-Kohen's *Sefer ha-ʾOrah*, wherein the letter *waw* is associated with Meṭaṭron. On the simplest level this association is linked to the fact that the name "Meṭaṭron" itself, in one of its spellings, consists of six letters. Thus see *Sefer ha-ʾOrah*, MSS Bar-Ilan, University Library 747, fol. 15b, Jerusalem, Schocken Library 14, fol. 54b [see also Abrams,

"'Book of Illumination,' " p. 259, who utilized the aforementioned manuscripts as well as MS Guenzberg-Moscow, Russian State Library 302, fol. 136a, which was not available to me]. The letter *waw* may also have phallic connotations in this context.

205. Cf. the pseudo-Eleazar commentary on the Torah (see above n. 142), 3:184: "*Shema*ᶜ *yisra*ʾ*el* teaches [cf. B. Pesaḥim 56a] that when Jacob was dying he said, Perhaps defilement came out from me, and the tribes responded, *Shema*ᶜ *yisra*ʾ*el*, which consists of six words, and Jacob replied silently the six words, *barukh shem kevod malkhuto le-*ᶜ*olam va*ᶜ*ed*. Thus there were twelve words corresponding to the twelve tribes that parallel the twelve zodiac signs and the twelve months."

206. On the literary structure of *Sefer ha-Ḥokhmah*, see Dan, *Studies in Ashkenazi Ḥasidic Literature*, pp. 44–57. I do not accept the view of Dan (see *Esoteric Theology*, pp. 122–27) that Eleazar of Worms copied the pseudo-Hai commentary without understanding its protokabbalistic intent and never used it in his own works. See idem, *Ḥugge ha-Mequbbalim ha-Rishonim*, p. 161, and, most recently, "Jewish Mysticism in Medieval Germany," p. 79, where the same view is categorically repeated: "Rabbi Eleazar, however, copied this commentary, but never used its symbols or ideas in any way in his extensive works." The tenability of this position is hardly defensible in light of the overwhelming evidence to the contrary: Eleazar's own writings are saturated with the protokabbalistic symbols and ideas expressed in the pseudo-Hai material incorporated in the introduction to his first work. I am in agreement, therefore, with the assumption of Farber that the commentary reflects an authentic Ashkenazi orientation that influenced Eleazar in his own writings, including the parts of *Sefer ha-Ḥokhmah* authentically written by him. See "Concept of the Merkabah," pp. 236–37 [see n. 268], 256–57, 627; see also p. 142 where Farber rejects Dan's view that Eleazar is the author of the commentary to the pseudo-Hai text called *Sefer Yirqaḥ*. See also Idel, *Kabbalah: New Perspectives*, p. 195. To be sure, Eleazar did not commit to writing in his other works these esoteric matters except by means of limited and concealed allusions. Scholem, *Origins*, p. 184 n. 206, suggests that the pseudo-Hai text included in *Sefer ha-Ḥokhmah* "may have been composed by an earlier mystic of the Hasidic group—certainly earlier than Eleazar." But see ibid., p. 311 n. 229, where Scholem surmises that the mystical interpretations of the divine names attributed to Hai Gaon in *Sefer ha-Ḥokhmah* and *Sefer ha-Shem* "probably reached the German Hasidim via Italy."

207. Cf. Moses Zacuto, *Sefer ha-Shemot* (Jerusalem, 1987), 12b: "*PZQ* is numerically equal to ᶜ*al kiss*ʾ*o*, and he is engraved upon the throne of glory." See the commentary of Joseph ben Shalom Ashkenazi to *Sefer Yeṣirah*, attributed to Rabad in the standard editions of the work, 1:12, 34a.

208. MS Oxford, Bodleian Library 1812, fol. 59a. The passage is cited in *Merkavah Shelemah* (Jerusalem, 1971), 30a. See Farber, "Concept of the Merkabah," p. 406.

209. See above n. 190. Cf. *ʾOr ha-Sekhel* (concerning this text and its author, see above n. 175), MS New York, Jewish Theological Seminary of America Mic. 1831, fol. 15a: "This is what [the sages], may their memory be for a blessing, said concerning [the biblical expression] '[angels of God] were going up and down on it' (Gen. 28:12). They ascended and gazed upon his icon above for his form was engraved upon the moon." See ibid., fols. 22a–b, and the passage from Judah Campanton referred to in n. 97. On the connection between the divine Presence, the moon, and the image of the throne, cf. *Perush Sodot ha-Tefillah* of Eleazar of Worms, MS Paris, Bibliothéque Nationale héb. 772, fol. 144b (as my colleague and friend, Elliot Ginsburg, reminded me): "It is said in Sanhedrin [42a]: He who sanctifies the moon it is as if he received the face of the Presence. Therefore we dance as [it is written] 'the creatures ran to and fro like the appearance of lightning' (Ezek. 1:14). Therefore we bless the moon until midnight when her blemish is filled [cf. B. Sanhedrin 41b] and the rainbow is formed. The throne is [in the form of the letter] *kaf*, thus is 'the appearance of the splendor like the appearance of the image of the throne,' 'the secret of the Lord is with those who fear Him' (Ps. 25:14)." For a slightly different, and in my opinion inferior, version of this text, see *Perushe Siddur ha-Tefillah la-Roqeaḥ*, p. 605. See also *Sode Razayyaʾ*, ed. Weiss, p. 68. On the connection of the throne and the image of the *kaf*, cf. *Midrash ʾOtiyyot de-R. ʿAqivaʾ*, version B, in *Batte Midrashot*, 2:406; Eleazar's *Perush ha-Merkavah*, MS Paris, Bibliothéque Nationale héb. 850, fol. 67a; *Sode Razayyaʾ*, ed. Kamelhar, p. 23; and *Perush Sodot ha-Tefillah*, MS Paris, Bibliothéque Nationale héb. 772, fols. 90b (see n. 353), 123a. On the reworking of this aggadic tradition in the Pietistic sources, see Farber, "Concept of the Merkabah," pp. 116, 581, 618–19. As Farber suggests, the symbolization of the throne by the letter *kaf* assumes a decidedly gender character in the Pietistic sources, i.e., the throne is treated as a feminine entity. See op. cit., pp. 571–74, 620–27; and see above n. 183. See especially the diagram of the throne in "Commentary on the Chariot," p. 53. The Pietistic elaboration of the aggadic tradition influenced as well Baḥya ben Asher. Cf. *Rabbenu Baḥya ʿal ha-Torah*, ed. Chavel, 2:274, ad Exod. 25:18: "The reason for the addition is that the letter *kaf* signifies the throne (*kisseʾ*), for the throne is established on the letter *kaf* [which alludes] to a hidden matter, and it also signifies the glory (*kavod*)." Cf. *Rabbenu Baḥya ʿal ha-Torah*, ed. Chavel, 2:583, ad Lev. 27:2. I intend to elaborate on the influence of the Ashkenazi esoteric traditions upon Baḥya in a separate study, focusing particularly on how these traditions shaped his conception of kabbalah. In the meantime, see Dan, *Esoteric Theology*, p. 261; Idel, *Kabbalah: New Perspectives*, p. 162; idem, *Language, Torah, and Hermeneutics*, p. 168 n. 77; idem, "Defining Kabbalah: The Kabbalah of the Divine Names," in *Mystics of the Book*, pp. 102–4, 118 n. 62; and Wolfson, "Circumcision and the Divine Name," pp. 106–7. See below, nn. 224 and 353. See also *Zohar* 3:248b (*Raʿayaʾ Mehemnaʾ*) where the form of the moon is described as a letter *kaf*. In light of the text of Eleazar cited above, as well as the other Ashkenazi material discussed in the body of this study, I cannot agree with the conclusion of Y. Liebes, *Studies in Jewish Myth and Jewish Messianism*, trans. B. Stein (Albany, 1992), p. 51, that a major difference between the symbolism of the moon in a passage from the German Pietistic

work *Sefer Ḥasidim* and the sefirotic kabbalah is that only in the latter case does the moon symbolize the *Shekhinah* as a divine entity. The evidence of my research suggests quite convincingly that some such theosophic implication underlies the use of the symbol of the moon in the German Pietistic source.

210. See R. Elior, "The Concept of God in Hekhalot Mysticism," in *Binah: Studies in Jewish Thought*, ed. J. Dan (New York, 1989), pp. 106–8. See also S. Leiter, "Worthiness, Acclamation and Appointment: Some Rabbinic Terms," *Proceedings of the American Academy of Jewish Research* 41–42 (1973–74): 137–68, esp. 143–45.

211. The text actually paraphrases two passages from *Hekhalot Rabbati*; cf. *Synopse* §§ 163–64.

212. For this rendering of the technical term, *yorde merkavah*, see E. R. Wolfson, "Yeridah la-Merkavah: Typology of Ecstasy and Enthronement in Ancient Jewish Mysticism," in *Mystics of the Book*, pp. 13–44.

213. Concerning this parenthetical notation in the introduction to Eleazar's *Sefer ha-Ḥokhmah*, see Dan, *Esoteric Theology*, pp. 126–28.

214. MS Oxford, Bodleian Library 1812, fol. 59b (corrected according to MS Oxford, Bodleian Library 1568, fol. 4b).

215. The actual numerology is slightly off here insofar as the expression *we-raʾita ʾet ʾaḥorai* equals 1243 and the expression *ki-demut yaʿaqov ḥaquqah ba-kisseʾ* equals 1254.

216. MS Paris, Bibliothéque Nationale héb. 850, fols. 56b–57a. Cf. "Commentary on Ezekiel's Chariot," p. 25.

217. Cf. *Sefer ha-Shem*, MS London, British Museum 737, fol. 208a.

218. MS Jerusalem, Mussajoff 145, fol. 35b. Cf. *Perush Rabbenu ʾEfrayim ʿal ha-Torah*, 1:272: "'And under His feet,' this indicates that the image of Jacob is engraved on the throne. Therefore Jacob said to Rachel, 'Am I under God?' (Gen. 30:2), [the word *ʾanokhi*] numerically equals *kisseʾ*."

219. See, however, the interpretation of Exod. 33:23 attributed to Eleazar in *ʿArugat ha-Bosem*, 1:198, that parallels MS New York, Jewish Theological Seminary of America Mic. 2430, fol. 74a: " 'You will see My back,' the angels that are behind Me [reading in MS New York, Jewish Theological Seminary of America: those angels of My back], as it is rendered in the Targum, 'that which is behind Me,' the angels, i.e., the images (*demuyot*) that are behind Me." It is possible that there is an allusion here to a motif that Eleazar mentions in other places in his writings: the glory is revealed through nine images or appearances (*maḥazot*) that are above the image of Jacob. Cf. *Sode Razayyaʾ*, ed. Kamelhar, p. 29: "The image of Jacob is on the throne. Therefore in Scripture there are nine occurences of [the expression] *ʿavdi yaʿaqov*

(My servant, Jacob) that correspond to the nine kinds of splendor. . . . Thus there are nine images (*maḥazot*) of the glory and they appear upon the image of Jacob." See parallel to this passage in Eleazar's commentary on the liturgy, MS Paris, Bibliothéque Nationale héb. 772, fol. 134a (and printed version in *Perushe Siddur ha-Tefillah la-Roqeaḥ*, p. 540). Interestingly, in that context the passage ends with the warning, "It is the glory of God to conceal a matter" (Prov. 25:2), suggesting that the subject of the image of Jacob visualized through the nine appearances is an esoteric matter that needs to be hidden. See also MS Paris, Bibliothéque Nationale héb. 772, fol. 76a (printed text in *Perushe Siddur ha-Tefillah la-Roqeaḥ*, pp. 325–26) where mention is made as well of the nine theophanic appearances (*mar*ʾ*ot*) connected with the image of Jacob engraved upon the throne. Cf. the passage from MS Munich, Bayerische Staatsbibliothek 232, fol. 7b cited below at n. 355, and *Sefer ha-Shem*, MS London, British Museum 737, fol. 361a. An allusion to this matter is found in the "Secret of the Nut"; see, e.g., the version of the text cited by Altmann, "Eleazar of Worms' Ḥokhmath Ha-ʾEgoz," p. 113: "Nine images (*mar*ʾ*ot*) of the glory, nine leaves for every branch of the nut." See Farber, "Concept of the Merkabah," p. 412. It seems to me that there is an allusion to this matter as well in MS Oxford, Bodleian Library 1566, fol. 37b:

> "The name of Your splendor" (*le-shem tif*ʾ*artekha*) is numerically equivalent to [the expression] "the four-letter name" (*le-shem ben ha-*ʾ*arba*ᶜ ʾ*otiyyot*) [the two phrases as they appear in the manuscripts are not equivalent, for the former equals 1471 and the latter 1523. The obvious correction consists of erasing the word *ben* in the second phrase (thus rendering it as *le-shem ha-*ʾ*arba*ᶜ ʾ*otiyyot*) which equals 52; if that sum is removed from 1523 one gets the desired 1471]. The nine times [in Scripture] that [the expressions] "to place His name," *lasum shemo*, and "to cause His name to dwell," *leshaken shemo*, correspond to the nine visions (*mar*ʾ*ot*) that He skips over the righteous.

See ibid., fol. 41b: "Therefore Ezekiel saw nine visions (*mar*ʾ*ot*) of the Presence. Hence, it is written nine times in the Torah, 'to place His name,' *lasum shemo*, and 'to cause His name to dwell,' *leshaken shemo*." See Eleazar of Worms, *Perush Sodot ha-Tefillah*, MS Paris, Bibliothéque Nationale héb. 772, fol. 48b: "Nine times [it is written in the Torah] 'to place His name,' *lasum shemo*, and 'to cause His name to dwell,' *leshaken shemo*" (see printed text in *Perushe Siddur ha-Tefillah la-Roqeaḥ*, p. 193). Cf. *Sefer Tagi*, MS Oxford, Bodleian Library 1566, fol. 226b; Eleazar ben Moses ha-Darshan, *Sefer ha-Gimaṭri*ʾ*ot*, MS Munich, Bayerische Staatsbibliothek 221, fol. 161b; Scholem, "Traditions of R. Jacob and R. Isaac," p. 211; and Abraham Abulafia, *Sefer ha-Melammed*, MS Oxford, Bodleian Library 1649, fol. 206a: "It is appropriate to complete everything with a *yod* for everything is in it. From *yod* and above is the ʾ*alef* [that corresponds to the] throne of glory. The ones who comprehend the cause are the prophets, for they see from behind the nine images that are the truth; the ʾ*alef* rises upward for the effect is from the cause and so the cause is from the effect." See idem, *Sheva ᶜ Netivot ha-Torah*, p. 20. The source for this notion of the nine visions (*maḥazot*) or images (*mar ᵓot*) of the glory is in the words attributed to R. Judah in *Leviticus Rabbah* 1:14, p. 31: "all the prophets saw through nine images (*ᵓispaqlariyot*)." Cf. the Ashkenazi text extant in MS London, British Museum Or. 10855 printed in *Perush Rabbenu ᵓEfrayim ᶜal ha-Torah*, 1:22.

220. MS Paris, Bibliothéque Nationale héb. 772, fols. 103a–b (printed text in *Perushe Siddur ha-Tefillah la-Roqeaḥ*, p. 432).

221. See S. Lieberman, *Shkiin* (Jerusalem, 1970), pp. 13–14 (in Hebrew), and Cohen, *Shi ᶜur Qomah*, pp. 36 n. 38, 128, 149.

222. See above n. 40.

223. Cf. MS Oxford, Bodleian Library 1566, fols. 37b, 58a–b, 118a.

224. Cf. MS Jerusalem, Mussajoff 145, fol. 50a: "'And a cherub stretched out his hand' (Ezek. 10:7), this is the cherub about whom we said that it emanated from the Splendor, 'among the cherubs,' these are the eight cherubim and their troops that surround the face of Jacob." It should be noted that on occasion Eleazar designates all the patriarchs, not just Jacob, by the name "cherub." Cf. *Sode Razayya ᵓ*, ed. Weiss, p. 121, and parallel in the *Perush ha-Merkavah*, MS Paris, Bibliothéque Nationale héb. 850, fol. 59b. This matter is obviously related to the aggadic notion that the patriarchs were the chariot (cf. *Genesis Rabbah* 47:8). Cf. *Sode Razayya ᵓ*, ed. Kamelhar, p. 13. The influence of the German Pietists is clearly discernible in *Rabbenu Baḥya ᶜal ha-Torah*, ed. Chavel, 1:245–46, ad Gen. 28:13:

> "And behold the Lord stood above him". . . . By way of tradition (*qabbalah*) the expression "upon him" refers to Jacob. Scripture compares him to a cherub concerning which it is written, "He rode upon a cherub and flew" (2 Sam. 22:11; Ps. 18:11), for the patriarchs are verily the chariot in the pattern of the cherubim above. You already know that Jacob is called small, and the masters of truth have said with respect to the matter of the cherubim, large faces and small faces. . . . I am illuminating the eyes of your heart with respect to the fact that the form of Jacob is engraved upon the throne of glory. Thus, the verse said, "a dweller of tents" (Gen. 25:27), the tents above and below [cf. *Sode Razayya ᵓ*, ed. Weiss, p. 147]. This is found explicitly in the revelation of Torah [at Sinai], "They saw the God of Israel and under His feet." This alludes to Israel who is below His feet. This is why it is said in this section, "Am I under God" (Gen. 30:2), which is not to be understood as a question. Understand this.

Cf. also *Rabbenu Baḥya ᶜal ha-Torah*, ed. Chavel, 1:260–61, ad Gen. 30:2, and 3:178, ad Num. 24:5. Finally, it is worth mentioning in this context the view expressed by Idel (*Kabbalah: New Perspectives*, pp. 134–35) and Liebes (*Studies in the Zohar*, pp. 105–7) regarding the interpretation of *ʾappe zuṭre* (or *zeʿeir ʾanpin* following the new locution of the zoharic literature), as a symbol for the feminine potency in thirteenth-century kabbalistic sources. It would be valuable to examine this kabbalistic symbol in light of the Ashkenazi traditions on the cherub that I have discussed in this study, but such a project must await a future publication.

225. See above n. 192. Cf. *Sefer ha-Shem*, MS London, British Museum 737, fols. 199a–b; and see also *Piyyuṭe Rashi*, ed. A. M. Habermann (Jerusalem, 1941), p. 8.

226. Cf. Farber, "Commentary on Ezekiel's Chariot," p. 126 n. 8. See especially the formulation in *Ḥokhmat ha-Nefesh*, § 61, p. 69: "Cherub is numerically like a small child" (the numerology does not work insofar as the word *keruv* is 228 and the expression *ke-yeled qaṭan* is 223). See also the *Perush Sodot ha-Tefillah*, MS Paris, Bibliothéque Nationale héb. 772, fol. 170b (printed text in *Perushe Siddur ha-Tefillah la-Roqeaḥ*, p. 708): "The cherubim [consist of] the face of the human, Jacob the small one. This is the appearance of the glory," i.e., the expression *marʾeh ha-kavod*, "the appearance of the glory," has the same numerical value, 278, as the word *keruvim*. Cf. the tradition cited by Shem Ṭov ben Simḥah ha-Kohen, MS New York, Jewish Theological Seminary of America Mic. 2430, fol. 66a:

> The intention of the [prayer] *barekhu*: the cantor should intend when he says the word *barekhu* that the congregation should intend in their hearts that the cherub, who is called the lesser Lord (*ʾadonai ha-qaṭan*), is blessed from above, from the Cause of Causes through the attribute of *Tifʾeret* . . . "above" [according to the wording of the *qaddish* prayer], i.e., the cherub is above all blessings. The songs, praises, and comforts we expect that the cherub will bring us so that we will be comforted through him. Concerning the exodus from Egypt it is said, "He mounted a cherub etc." (2 Sam. 22:11, Ps. 18:11). The intention of the saying of *barekhu* should be to the cherub so that it will be blessed from the highest level, i.e., the cherub who is called the lesser Lord.

See ibid.: "I have also received [a tradition regarding] the saying of *Shemaʿ* from the great kabbalist, Rabbi Judah the Pious: one must unify the power of the many in the power of the one. *Shemaʿ yisraʾel*, i.e., the name of the diadem is Israel, and this is the cherub that is called the lesser Lord." Underlying the former intention is the fact that the consonants of the word *keruv* are those of the word *barekhu*; cf. *Siddur Malʾah ha-ʾAreṣ Deʿah, shaḥarit*, s.v., *barekhu*; op. cit., *yoṣer shel shabbat*, s.v., *qedushah*; *ʿArugat ha-Bosem*, 4:104, n. 96; and Eleazar's *Perush Sodot ha-Tefillah*, MS Paris, Bibliothéque Nationale héb. 772, fol. 133b: "Know that the letters of *barukh* are those of *keruv*" (see printed version in *Perushe Siddur ha-Tefillah la-Roqeaḥ*, p. 539). See also the Ashkenazi commentary on Psalms in MS Oxford, Bodleian Library 1551, fol. 209a. On the direction of intention in prayer to the Special Cherub according to this author, see text cited by Scholem, *Reshit ha-Qabbalah*, p. 78 n. 1 (based on MS New York, Jewish Theological Seminary of America Mic. 2430, fol. 65b); see also discussion of the thematically related *Pesaq ha-Yir'ah we-ha-'Emunah* in Dan, "The Emergence of Mystical Prayer," pp. 93–102, and idem, "Pesaq Ha-Yirah veha-Emunah," pp. 200–2.

227. The identification of the cherubim with the throne is an ancient motif that can be found in Scripture, and especially in the technical epithet for God, *yoshev ha-keruvim*, the "one enthroned upon the cherubim." See M. Haran, "The Ark and the Cherubim," *Israel Exploration Journal* 9 (1959): 30–38, 89–94. See also the passage in *Re'uyot Yeḥezqel*, ed. I. Gruenwald, in *Temirin: Texts and Studies in Kabbala and Ḥasidism*, ed. I. Weinstock (Jerusalem, 1972), 1:134–35: "And what is the name of the chariot? [It is named] *rekhev*, on account of the cherub that is in it, and it goes down to the [sea]. 'He mounted a cherub and flew' (2 Sam. 22:11, Ps. 18:11)." For a different suggestion regarding the emendation of this text, see Gruenwald, p. 135 n. 92. Cf. passage in *3 Enoch* in *Synopse* § 37: "How many chariots does the Holy One, blessed be He, have? He has chariots of the cherub, as it says, 'He mounted a cherub and flew.' " Cf. ibid., §§ 588, 748. See also the poem *melekh ʿelyon*, in *Maḥzor la-Yamim Nora'im*, vol. 1: Rosh ha-Shanah, p. 107: *rekhuvo keruvim*. See "Commentary on Ezekiel's Chariot," p. 39: "The cherubim instruct about the upper glory that is above them. Therefore the [word] *keruvim* numerically equals *mar'eh kavod* (the appearance of the glory; the printed text reads *mar'eh 'adam*, the appearance of a human, but I have corrected it according to the suggestion of Farber, p. 39 n. 6)." See ibid., p. 54: "The Presence comes . . . and sits upon the throne of glory, on the holy cherubim who are made in the image of the glory that is above. Therefore, [the word] *keruvim* [cherubs] is numerically equal to *mar'eh kavod* [the appearance of the glory]." This numerology already appears in the works of Judah the Pious and recurs in the writings of Eleazar of Worms. See J. Dan, "The Book of Angels of R. Judah the Pious," *Daʿat* 2–3 (1978/79): 116 (in Hebrew); *Sefer ha-Roqeaḥ*, p. 22; *Perush ha-Merkavah*, MS Paris, Bibliothéque Nationale héb. 850, fols. 61b, 76b; MS New York, Jewish Theological Seminary of America Mic. 2430, fol. 71a: "The cherubs are the essence of the apperance of the glory of the Presence; therefore *mar'eh ha-kavod* numerically equals *keruvim*."

228. On the identification of Jacob with the throne, see the passage from *Midrash ha-Neʿelam* in *Zohar* 1:97a–b: "Jacob our patriarch is the throne of glory, and thus it has been taught in the school of Elijah, Jacob our patriarch is a throne in and of himself . . . as it is written, 'granting them seats of honor,' *we-khisse' khavod yanḥilem* (1 Sam 2:8). What is [the implication of] 'granting them seats of honor'? This refers to Jacob our patriarch for whom alone a throne of glory was made in order to receive the instructions of the souls of the righteous." Cf. ibid., 173b: "Jacob is the upper holy chariot that exists in order to illuminate the moon, and he alone is the chariot." In the second passage it is obvious that Jacob symbolizes the emanation of *Tif'eret* and the moon, the *Shekhinah*. Cf. also *Zohar* 2:242a: "The throne beneath the God of Israel

[*Binah*] is the icon of Jacob [*Tif*ʾ*eret*] and the throne beneath the icon of David [*Shekhinah*] is the fourfold that divides into the four dimensions of the world." J. Wijnhoven, "Sefer ha-Mishkal: Text and Study" (Ph.D. dissertation, Brandeis University, 1964), p. 109: "Jacob is the elite of the patriarchs . . . thus he is the secret of the chariot." *The Book of the Pomegranate: Moses de León's Sefer ha-Rimmon*, ed. E. R. Wolfson (Atlanta, 1988), p. 318 (Hebrew section): "The [sages], may their memory be for a blessing, said, the image of the icon of Jacob [is] the image of the throne of glory and the foundation of the gradations in the upper and lower realms . . . and the essence of the foundation of the patriarchs is the pattern of the icon of the throne of glory." It is clear that in this context as well the aggadic motif of the iconic image of Jacob is explained as a symbol of the sixth emanation, *Tif*ʾ*eret*, that corresponds to Jacob in the sefirotic world. Moses de León has reworked an ancient tradition according to which the image of Jacob was identified as the throne.

229. On the esoteric significance of the foot in the thought of the German Pietists, cf. MS Oxford, Bodleian Library 1566, fol. 106a, discussed in E. R. Wolfson, "Images of God's Feet: Some Observations on the Divine Body in Judaism," in *People of the Body: Jews and Judaism from an Embodied Perspective*, ed. H. Eilberg-Schwartz (Albany, 1992), pp. 156–57.

230. MS Oxford, Bodleian Library 1204, fol. 160b; cf. MS Paris, Bibliothéque Nationale héb. 772, fol. 134a.

231. D. Castelli, *Il Commento di Sabbatai Donnolo sul Libro Della Creazione* (Firenze, 1880), pp. 7–8. The passage is cited in the compilation of Ashkenazi secrets in MS New York, Jewish Theological Seminary of America 2430, fol. 75a.

232. *Sode Razayya*ʾ, ed. Weiss, pp. 147–48 (with slight emendations according to the reading in MS Oxford, Bodleian Library 1638, fol. 56a). This passage is paraphrased by Nathan Naṭa ben Solomon Spira, *Megalleh* ʿ*Amuqot: Reish-nun-bet* ʾ*Ofanim* ʿ*al Wa-*ʾ*etḥanan*, 92, 68a. See also *Yalquṭ Re*ʾ*uveni* (Warsaw, 1884), 87b, ad Exod. 33:23, in the name of the "one wise in mysteries," *ḥakham ha-razim*.

233. See *Genesis Rabbah* 68:11, p. 784, and the other sources cited there in n. 3.

234. Cf. the Ashkenazi tradition in *Sefer ha-Ḥokhmah*, MS Oxford, Bodleian Library 1812, fol. 60a: "The crown is called Israel [see above n. 40] . . . it rises above . . . numerically it is ʾ*elef* [the Hebrew consonants can also be read ʾ*alef*] for there are one thousand camps of angels who make a crown from prayer, and from the crown phylacteries. There are twelve stones in the crown and upon each crown is engraved the name of a tribe." For the conceptual background of this motif, see M. Bar-Ilan, "The Idea of Crowning God in Hekhalot Mysticism and Karaitic Polemic," *Jerusalem Studies in Jewish Thought* 6, 1–2 (1987): 221–33 (in Hebrew). It should be noted that in *Sefer ha-Bahir* § 37 the throne is identified with the phylacteries. Moreover,

it is clear from that passage that the throne, symbolized by the open *mem* (cf. § 84; on the connection between the letter *mem* and the throne, cf. *Midrash ʾOtiyyot de.-R. ʿAqivaʾ*, in *Batte Midrashot*, 1:387–89), is described in imagery associated with the female. See Scholem, *Origins*, p. 60, and Stern, *Parables in Midrash*, p, 221. (For a different interpretation of this symbolism, see E. R. Wolfson, "The Tree That Is All: Jewish-Christian Roots of a Kabbalistic Symbol in *Sefer ha-Bahir*," *Journal of Jewish Thought and Philosophy* 3 [1993]: 71–72 [above, pp. 85–86].) On the interchange of the crown and the throne, see also *Sefer ha-Bahir*, § 152. See further discussion in Wolfson, "Images of God's Feet," pp. 161–62. On the feminine character of the throne in Jewish esotericism, see above nn. 65 and 209, and below n. 353. On the correspondence between five occurrences in Scripture where God's sitting on a throne is mentioned and the five compartments of the head and arm phylacteries, cf. *Sefer ha-Shem*, MS London, British Museum 737, fols. 362a–b. On the symbolic nexus between the throne, the head phylacteries, and Jerusalem—the connecting link being their exalted height—see Eleazar's commentary on the liturgy, MS Paris, Bibliothéque Nationale héb. 772, fol. 126b (printed text in *Perushe Siddur ha-Tefillah la-Roqeaḥ*, p. 512). And see op. cit., fol. 152a (*Perushe Siddur ha-Tefillah la-Roqeaḥ*, p. 658), where a connection is made between the throne, the head phylacteries, and the temple. See also op. cit., fol. 170b (*Perushe Siddur ha-Tefillah la-Roqeaḥ*, p. 708), where a comparison is made between the throne, Jerusalem, and the head of a person, the latter associated especially with the phylacteries:

> The throne is one, and concerning what is written, "Thrones were set in place" (Dan. 7:9), one is for judgment and the other for righteousness. The throne is one and it is divided. How [the throne] stands should not be revealed except to the humble of the generation, but in the head of a person, when he binds the phylacteries on his head, they reveal and speak by allusion. "The secret of the Lord is with those who fear Him" (Ps. 25:14). The throne, Jerusalem, and the head of a person are equivalent.

(The phallic position accorded Jerusalem seems to be implied in *Sefer ha-Shem*, MS London, British Museum 737, fol. 290b; see above n. 121.) On the divided throne in the theosophy of the Ḥaside Ashkenaz, see nn. 289 and 319. On the symbolic correlation of the throne and the brain, see MS Paris, Bibliothéque Nationale héb. 772, fol. 123a (printed text in *Perush Siddur ha-Tefillah la-Roqeaḥ*, pp. 503–4). On the identification of the head and the throne, see the third explanation of Abraham ibn Ezra on the verse, "His head is finest gold" (Song of Songs 5:11): "This is the throne of glory." The influence of ibn Ezra's comment is discernible in the standard recension of *Sefer ha-ʿIyyun* as noted by Idel, "World of Angels," p. 21. See also Verman, *Books of Contemplation*, p. 110 n. 255. On the nexus of the throne and Jerusalem depicted as a bride, cf. Eleazar ben Moses ha-Darshan's interpretation of Exod. 24:10 in *Sefer ha-Gimaṭriʾot*, MS Munich, Bayerische Staatsbibliothek 221, fol. 153b.

235. The full force of Eleazar's rhetoric can only be gathered if one heeds the double signification of the word *pe'er* as "glory" and "diadem" or "head ornament."

236. *Sefer Yeṣirah* 3:8. See Gruenwald, "Preliminary Critical Edition," p. 155. I have emended the passage according to the received text.

237. That is, the scriptural verses that are written on the pieces of parchment contained in the compartments of the head phylacteries. The four biblical sections include Exod. 13:2 and 5, Deut. 6:4, and 11:13. See *Mekhilta' de-Rabbi Ishmael*, ed. H. S. Horowitz and I. A. Rabin, 2nd ed. (Jerusalem, 1970), Pisḥa 17, p. 66, and B. Menaḥot 37b.

238. Compare the passage from *Re'uyot Yeḥezqel* cited above in n. 227. See also *Mekhilta' de-Rabbi Ishmael*, Shirah 4, p. 129: "He revealed Himself to them [at the sea] like a horseman, as it says, 'He rode upon a cherub and flew.' " See also *Mekhilta' de-Rabbi Simeon bar Yoḥai*, ed. J. N. Epstein and E. Z. Melamed (Jerusalem, 1955), pp. 68, 87. On the female imagery of the cherub, see the exegetical tradition in *'Avot de-Rabbi Natan*, version A, ch. 27, p. 83: "R. Joshua ben Qorḥah said that when Pharaoh came to the sea he came on a male horse and was revealed upon it, and the Holy One, blessed be He, came upon a female horse, as it says, 'I have likened you, my darling, to a mare in Pharaoh's chariots' (Song of Songs 1:9). Yet, did He not ride only upon a cherub, as it says, 'He rode upon a cherub and flew; he was seen on the wings of the wind' (2 Sam. 22:11; Ps. 18:11)? Rather, the cherub resembled the horse of Pharaoh that was female, and all of them entered the sea." Cf. the Ashkenazi commentary on Psalms, MS Oxford, Bodleian Library 1551, fol. 209a.

239. Cf. *Commentary on the Passover Haggadah by Eleazar of Worms*, p. 94: "'And when Israel saw' (Exod. 14:31), Israel the elder, for he descended to Egypt." See ibid., p. 161: "'He made Israel pass through it' (Ps. 136:14), that refers to Israel the elder. Therefore in the [song] 'Then [Moses and the Israelites] sang [this song to the Lord]' (Exod. 15 :1) there are 182 [the numerical value of the consonants of the name "Jacob"] words, on account of [the verse] 'I Myself will also bring you back' (Gen. 46:4)." See also the pseudo-Eleazar *Perush Roqeaḥ ʿal ha-Torah* 1:220. Exodus 14:31 is interpreted in a similar manner in the written works of Samuel the Pious and Judah the Pious, but it is clear that for Eleazar this interpretation takes on an entirely different signification. Cf. *Sefer Ḥasidim*, ed. J. Wistinetzki and J. Freimann (Frankfurt am Main, 1924), 33, p. 34, and the commentary of Samuel the Pious to the prayer, "Rock of Israel" (*ṣur yisra'el*), cited in Urbach, *ʿArugat ha-Bosem*, 4:85. See the commentary attributed to Rashi in B. Taʿanit 5b, s.v., *'af hu' ba-ḥayyim*: "'And when Israel saw' (Exod. 14:31), there are those who interpret this as Israel the elder." Urbach, op. cit., n. 77, calls attention in this context to *Genesis Rabbah* 92:2 as the source of this interpretation: "The Holy One, blessed be He, took the feet of Jacob, our patriarch, and placed them in the sea. He said to him, See the miracles that I perform for your descendants, as it is written, 'When Israel went forth from Egypt' (Ps. 114:1), Israel the elder." Urbach also noted the version of Targum Yerushalmi to Exod. 14:31

cited by M. M. Kasher, *Torah Shelemah* 14:87: "'And when Israel saw,' Israel the elder." Cf. *Zohar* 2:33a.

240. *Sode Razayya*ʾ, ed. Weiss, pp. 4–5. Compare the version with slight variants in *Sefer Raziʾel,* 8a–b. See also *Ḥokhmat ha-Nefesh* 46, pp. 76–77, and MS Paris, Bibliothéque Nationale héb. 772, fol. 67b (printed text in *Perushe Siddur ha-Tefillah la-Roqeaḥ,* p. 287). The influence of Eleazar is discernible in a commentary on the name "Shaddai" (in which are mentioned "the sage R. Eliezer of Germaiza" and "R. Jacob ha-Kohen of Segovia") in MS Guenzberg-Moscow, Russian State Library 366, fol. 49b: "The *shin* of Jacob for thus it is written on the head phylacteries, 'Israel in whom I glory' (Isa. 49:3). Moreover, it is written that the icon of Jacob, our patriarch, peace be upon him, is fixed on the throne of glory . . . and this is the *bet* from the name Jacob that interchanges with the *shin* according [to the technique of] a"t ba"sh, and this is the *shin* of Shaddai." See n. 291. Cf. *Megalleh ʿAmuqot* (Lemberg, 1882), 8d.

241. *Perush ha-Roqeaḥ ʿal Ḥamesh ha-Megillot* (Bene-Beraq, 1985), p. 23.

242. See above n. 199.

243. Cf. *Sefer ha-Ḥokhmah,* MS Oxford, Bodleian Library 1812, fol. 77b: "Thus is the numerical value of *yhwh ha-ʾelohim ʾeḥad* [= 130], and this is the numerical value of *zeh yhwh ʾeḥad ha-ʾel gadol* [= 130] and the numerical value of *ḥasid ha-gadol* [= 130], and the numerical value of *ʾani ha-din* [=130] . . . and the numerical value of *u-veʿavim* [=130], for the Holy One, blessed be He, rode upon a swift cherub at the sea, as it says, 'He rode upon a cherub and flew,' when He was revealed upon the sea in His unity and power."

244. MS London, British Museum 737, fol. 100b. Cf. the pseudo-Eleazar commentary on Song of Songs 3:11. It should be noted that in this particular verse there are twelve words corresponding to "twelve angels that surround the glory and the twelve tribes."

245. MS Paris, Bibliothéque Nationale héb. 772, fol. 127a (*Perushe Siddur ha-Tefillah la-Roqeaḥ,* p. 514). Cf. MS New York, Jewish Theological Seminary of America Mic. 2430, fol. 75b in the name of Eleazar as he "received from the Pious one who received from his father, and his teacher from his teacher, a law given to Moses at Sinai": "Outside the throne there are twelve [angels] appointed to every side . . . before Him, blessed be His name . . . who sits in the middle and manifests His glory like a *ḥashmalah.*" See n. 353. The image of the twelve tribes above surrounding the glory appears also in theosophic kabbalistic literature. See, e.g., *Sefer ha-Bahir,* § 113; *Zohar Ḥadash* on Ruth, 76d (see n. 366); *Zohar* 1:159b; 2:229b; and 3:134b (*ʾIdraʾ Rabbaʾ*).

246. MS Oxford, Bodleian Library 1812, fol. 62a. Cf. *Sefer ha-Shem,* MS London, British Museum 737, fol. 339a. "The name of the Lord is proclaimed over you" (Deut. 28:10) was interpreted as a reference to phylacteries in much older

sources. See, e.g., Targum Pseudo-Jonathan to the verse and B. Berakhot 6a. What the Ashkenazi source has done is to combine this exegesis with the tradition concerning the *shin* of the phylacteries in such a way that the letter *shin* is derived from the initial letters of the expression *shem yhwh niqra*ʾ, *shin*, *yod*, and *nun* that spells *shin*. This tradition is quoted in the name of Eleazar of Worms by Jacob ben Sheshet, *Sefer ha-ʾEmunah we-ha-Biṭṭaḥon*, ch. 22, in *Kitve Ramban* 2:430. Cf. the words of Menaḥem Ṣiyyoni, *Sefer Ṣiyyoni* (Jerusalem, 1924), 28c, based on *Sode Razayya*ʾ of Eleazar, called by the name *rav sodi*, the master of secrets (see Dan, *Esoteric Theology*, p. 259, and I. J. Yuval, *Scholars in Their Time: The Religious Leadership of German Jewry in the Late Middle Ages* [Jerusalem, 1988], p. 288 [in Hebrew]):

> It is appropriate for a *shin* to be on the head phylacteries and from it they will see their king upon their heads alluded to by the *shin*, for YHWH equals *shin* through [the technique of] a"t ba"sh. And this is the pattern of what is above as it is in the work of the chariot, for Sandalphon binds phylacteries to the head of the Creator, the Lord, God of Israel. What is written in them? "And who is like Your people Israel?" (1 Chron. 17:21), "Or what great nation [has laws and rules as perfect as all this Teaching that I set before you this day?]" (Deut. 4:8). . . . And when He wants to adjure by means of the phylacteries, He takes the phylacteries from His head and annuls the decrees from the earth. When the crown ascends to the head of the Creator the face of Jacob shines before Adiriron, the Lord, God of Israel. . . . Understand well this secret that I have brought from the source of the master of secrets.

See n. 363.

247. MS Paris, Bibliothéque Nationale héb. 850, fol. 69a. See ibid., fol. 74a. On the connection between the glory and the eyes, see ibid., fol. 70a. Cf. the tradition regarding the letters of the phylacteries attributed to "R. Judah the Pious the son of R. Samuel the Pious the son of R. Qalonymus the Elder," extant in MS Parma, Biblioteca Palatina 2486, fol. 56a: "*Shin* is described as the cherubim between the wings." For another interpretation of the name MṢP"Ṣ, see the words of Eleazar in *Shaʿare ha-Sod ha-Yiḥud we-ha-ʾEmunah*, ed. J. Dan, in *Temirin: Texts and Studies in Kabbala and Hasidism*, ed. I. Weinstock (Jerusalem, 1972), 1:153: "MṢP"Ṣ: *yhwh* in a"t ba"sh is *mṣp"ṣ*. This is numerically equal to *be-raḥamim* [with mercy]." Cf. the similar statement in the pseudo-Hai commentary in *Sefer ha-Ḥokhmah*, MS Oxford, Bodleian Library 1812, fol. 66a: "Thus the numerical value of [the expression] *wa-yhwh ʾeḥad be-raḥamim* is *we-mṣp"ṣ yhwh ʾeḥad*." See MSS Munich, Bayerische Staatsbibliothek 92, fol. 12a; New York, Jewish Theological Seminary of America Mic. 2430, fol. 74a; and *Keter Shem Ṭov*, 5b. See also passage from the commentary on *Sefer Yeṣirah* discussed in n. 291.

248. MS Paris, Bibliothéque Nationale héb. 850, fol. 74b. It stands to reason that Eleazar influenced the following formulation of *Sefer Ṣiyyoni*, 28c: "There remains for me to explain what the sages, may their memory be blessed, said

with respect to the *shin* of the phylacteries that it is a law given to Moses from Sinai, as it says, 'And all the peoples of the earth shall see that the Lord's name is proclaimed over you' (Deut. 28:10), for they see those who wear phylacteries and they direct their intention to her commandments for the Presence dwells upon them and speaks from the top of his head like from between the two cherubim, as is says, '[the Ark of God] to which the Name was attached, the name Lord of Hosts Enthroned on the Cherubim' (2 Sam. 6:2)."

249. Cf. Num. 6:25; Ps. 4:7, 31:17; 44:4; 67:2; 80:4, 8, 20; 89:16; 119:135; Prov. 16:15; Job 29:24; and Dan. 9:17.

250. In fact, the numerical values of the two expressions are not equal: the former equals 524 and the latter 278.

251. Both expressions equal 278.

252. MS New York, Jewish Theological Seminary of America Mic. 2430, fols. 74a–b. Cf. the passage in the pseudo-Hai commentary included in *Sefer ha-Ḥokhmah*, MS Oxford, Bodleian Library 1812, fol. 5b: "ABG"Y—a father of Israel from thirteen years of age [this is alluded to in the divine name ABG"Y, i.e., AB spells ᵓ*av*, father, and the remaining letters G"Y reversed allude to *yod-gimmel*, which equals thirteen] . . . and similarly a father must support his son until thirteen years of age. . . . Thus [the name is] ABG"Y, the father opens thirteen windows above through which the prayer ascends corresponding to the twelve tribes and Jacob their father, which makes thirteen. Therefore, the sons of Jacob said, 'Hear O, Israel, the Lord is our God, the Lord is one' (Deut. 6:4), [the word ᵓ*eḥad*] is numerically thirteen. Thus the Father remembers the thirteen attributes of mercy on behalf of Israel. 'The Lord, the Lord, a God compasionate and gracious' (Exod. 34:6)." See the passage from the commentary on the forty-two-letter name in MS Florence, Biblioteca Medicea-Laurenziana 44:14, fol. 221b cited by G. Scholem, "R. Moses of Burgos, the Disciple of R. Isaac," *Tarbiz* 5 (1934): 320–22 (in Hebrew). Scholem notes the likely provenance of this text in either German or French Pietists (see p. 320 n. 1). See also Scholem's comment in *Tarbiz* 4 (1933): 60 that the commentary of Moses of Burgos on the forty-two-letter name was based on a similar commentary that originated amongst the German Pietists. Cf. MS Oxford, Bodleian Library 1565, fol. 97a, printed in *Liqquṭim mi-Rav Hai Gaon* (Warsaw, 1798), 5a. Compare the formulation in a commentary on the forty-two-letter name of God in MS Oxford, Bodleian Library 1960, fol. 154a: AB"G . . . a father for Israel who is the third of the patriarchs. Therefore, his icon is engraved upon the throne of glory. Another interpretation: AB"G, a father for the three patriarchs who comprise thirteen letters [i.e., the letters of their three names combined] . . . and the son is the responsibility of the father until the thirteenth year. Corresponding to this there are thirteen windows in heaven through which the prayer ascends, corresponding to Jacob and the twelve tribes, and corresponding to the thirteen attributes of the Holy One, blessed be He." Cf. MS Oxford, Bodleian Library 1816, fol. 74a.

253. Since I wrote the Hebrew version of this study I have continued to reflect on the role of gender symbolism in the various forms of Jewish esotericism,

including German Pietism and theosophic kabbalah. In my present view, the image of Jacob still functions as a feminine symbol in the esoteric teaching of the Pietists, but I would qualify my original argument by noting that it is the feminine aspect of the masculine. (See, however, n. 329.) In brief, it seems to me that the image of Jacob engraved on the throne represents the corona of the male organ, which is feminized in the Jewish sources. The contextualization of the feminine as part of the phallus, rather than existing as an autonomous potency, is consistent with other expressions of gender symbolism in Jewish esotericism, including, most importantly, theosophic kabbalah. See E. R. Wolfson, "Woman—The Feminine as Other in Theosophic Kabbalah: Some Philosophic Reflections on the Divine Androgyne," in *The Other in Jewish Thought and History: Constructions of Jewish Culture and Identity*, ed. L. Silberstein and R. Cohn (New York, 1994).

254. On the pseudo-Hai provenance of the text, see Dan, *Esoteric Theology*, pp. 122–27.

255. See Scholem, *Origins*, pp. 184–85; Dan, *Esoteric Theology*, pp. 119–22; Farber, "Concept of the Merkabah," pp. 142–43, 231–44; Idel, *Kabbalah: New Perspectives*, pp. 193–96; and Ch. Mopsik, *Les Grands Textes de la Cabale: Les rites qui font Dieu* (Paris, 1993), pp. 612–14.

256. According to the traditional liturgical formulation for the *qedushah*, based on Ezek. 2:12, which is essentially a recounting of the angelic hymning of the glory.

257. That is, both expressions equal 662. This numerology appears frequently in Ashkenazi sources. See, e.g., *Merkavah Shelemah*, 23b (on the attribution of this text to Eleazar, see Farber, "Concept of the Merkabah," p. 237); and Eleazar's commentary on the liturgical poem *ha-ʾoḥez be-yad middat mishpaṭ* (see Scholem, *Origins*, p. 125 n. 129), extant in several manuscripts, e.g., MS Munich, Bayerische Staatsbibliothek 92, fol. 26b; and MS New York, Jewish Theological Seminary of America Mic. 1786, fol. 43b, cited and discussed by Idel, *Kabbalah: New Perspectives*, pp. 195–96, 374 n. 196.

258. That is, "let us dwell in the prayer of Shaddai." It is evident, as has been noted by various scholars (see references in n. 255), that in this context the term "prayer" assumes a hypostatic connotation. The midrashic exegesis of Ps. 91:1 is based in part on *Numbers Rabbah* 12:3 (the reference in Dan, *Ḥugge Mequbbalim ha-Rishonim*, p. 159, to 2:3 should be corrected accordingly).

259. That is, "he has this prayer."

260. MS Oxford, Bodleian Library 1812, fols. 60b–61a; text is printed in Dan, *Esoteric Theology*, p. 120, on the basis of MS Oxford, Bodleian Library 1568, fols. 5a–b.

261. Scholem, *Origins*, pp. 185–86.

262. Ibid., p. 185. This qualifying comment is lacking in the original German edition, *Ursprung und Anfänge der Kabbala* (Berlin, 1962), p. 164, and

in the French translation by J. Loewenson, *Les origines de la kabbale* (Paris, 1966), p. 199. Without having access to Scholem's private copy of the *Ursprung*, it is difficult to determine if this parenthetical remark reflects an annotation of Scholem or the editor (Werblowsky). Concerning the additions in general to this version of Scholem's text, see the editor's Preface, p. xiii.

263. MS Oxford, Bodleian Library 1568, fol. 25b; the text is printed in the *Perush ha-Roqeaḥ ʿal ha-Torah* 1:15. Regarding this text, see also Farber, "Concept of the Merkabah," p. 609. This text alone renders questionable Dan's opinion that the protokabbalistic material was simply copied by Eleazar and had no impact on his own writings. See above n. 205.

264. *Origins*, p. 98.

265. Ibid., p. 125 n. 129.

266. MS Oxford, Bodleian Library 1812, fol. 63a.

267. See Scholem, *Origins*, pp. 98, 184; Idel, *Kabbalah: New Perspectives*, p. 195; and the extensive discussion in Farber, "Concept of the Merkabah," pp. 231–44.

268. See Farber, "Concept of the Merkabah," pp. 236–37: "In my opinion, the possibility should be considered that the protokabbalistic texts in *Sefer ha-Ḥokhmah* faithfully reflect a radical Ashkenazi theological doctrine . . . that which R. Eleazar brought to light in his first composition. . . . The material of the protokabbalistic type recurs in additional texts from *Sefer ha-Ḥokhmah* . . . and amongst them authentic discussions of R. Eleazar." See ibid., pp. 142–43, 254. Needless to say, the position of Farber is in diametric opposition to that of Dan who has consistently maintained that the protokabbalistic texts in the introduction to *Sefer ha-Ḥokhmah* had no impact upon Eleazar's own writings. See previous references in n. 206. My own work supports the view of Farber who has persuasively shown the untenableness of Dan's position.

269. The full force of Eleazar's exegesis can only be grasped from the Hebrew insofar as the expression in Prov. 8:30, *ʾeṣlo*, "with Him," is related to the word *ʾaṣilut*, emanation. The point of the comment, then, is that the Torah, personified as primordial Wisdom, is the feminine Presence that emanates from the Creator. A similiar wordplay is evident in the pseudo-Hai commentary included in the introduction to *Sefer ha-Ḥokhmah*. See Scholem, *Origins*, p. 185. Cf. *Perush ha-Ramban ʿal ha-Torah*, ed. C. D. Chavel (Jerusalem, 1960), 2: 234–35, ad Num. 11:17.

270. Scholem, *Origins*, p. 185 n. 213, suggests that the reference may be to the Targum to Num. 11:17, although he also notes that no precise Targum is found that matches what is mentioned in the text. The reading accepted by Scholem differs from the one that I have followed: instead of *mitravyah* the Aramaic is *mitrabeit* that is transposed into *bat mareih*, rendered by Scholem as "daughter of his master" (pp. 185–86). See, however, *Perush ha-Roqeaḥ ʿal ha-Torah*, 1:15 n. 14, where the editor mentions the Targum to Esther 2:20 (mistakenly cited as 3:20). In that context the biblical expression *ve-ʾomnah ʾitto*, "under his tutelage," is translated as *mitravyah ʿimeih*. The exegetical linkage

of Esther 2:20 to Prov. 8:30 is related, of course, to the appearance of the word *ʾamon*, "confidant," in the latter.

271. That is, both expressions equal 620.

272. *Perush ha-Roqeaḥ ʿal ha-Torah*, 1:15–6, corrected according to MS Oxford, Bodleian Library 1568, fols. 25a–b. On the feminization of the Torah in the esoteric teaching of the German Pietists, see Farber, "Concept of the Merkabah," pp. 242, 609, and my study referred to above in n. 13.

273. *Perush ha-Roqeaḥ ʿal ha-Torah*, 1:25.

274. *Kabbalah: New Perspectives*, pp. 193, 372–73 n. 158.

275. Cf. Ezek. 1:25.

276. That is, "prayer of one father." Both expressions have the numerical value of 541.

277. MS New York, Jewish Theological Seminary of America Mic. 1786, fol. 43a. I have slightly modified the English rendering in Idel, *Kabbalah: New Perspectives*, p. 193.

278. Cf. "Book of Angels," p. 115, where mention is made of Sariel who is before the glory and "from whose mouth fire goes forth." The angel Sariel is known from ancient Jewish literature, such as the Qumran scrolls, the Aramaic fragments of the Book of Enoch, and the Targum Neophiti. See G. Vermes, "The Archangel Sariel: A Targumic Parallel to the Dead Sea Scrolls," in *Christianity, Judaism, and Other Greco-Roman Cults*, ed. J. Neusner (Leiden, 1975), 3:159–66; *The Books of Enoch: Aramaic Fragments of Qumrân Cave 4*, ed. J. T. Millik with M. Black (Oxford, 1978), pp. 170–74; and M. A. Knibb, *The Ethiopic Book of Enoch* (Oxford, 1978), 2:84 n. 9. Finally, it is noteworthy that according to a passage in the magical treatise *Shimmushe Torah*, MS New York, Jewish Theological Seminary of America Mic. 2026, fol. 11b, the name that is derived from the section of Genesis that begins with Jacob's dream of the ladder is Sariel.

279. See "Commentary on Ezekiel's Chariot ," p. 62, where the *ḥasmalah*, the last of the divine gradations, is said to "rise to the head of them all and envelop them like a crown and like a throne." A similar convergence of symbols, specifically the throne, the crown, and the phylacteries, is found in different sections of the *Bahir*. See Farber, "Concept of the Merkabah," p. 247, and my analysis in "Images of God's Feet," p. 161.

280. B. Yoma 54a; Baba Batra 99a.

281. *Sefer Yeṣirah* (Jerusalem, 1961), 21a. In the fuller version of this commentary, *Perush ha-Rav ʾEleʿazar Mi-Garmaiza ʿal Sefer Yeṣirah* (Przemysl, 1883), 3b, the words, "for they were in the Temple to increase the procreation of Israel," are missing. Idel, *Kabbalah: New Perspectives*, p. 338 n. 162, already noted this textual discrepancy. See ibid., p. 130. The sexual nature of the cherubim is also specified in *Sefer ha-Shem*, MS London, British Museum 737, fols. 297a and 322a.

282. Cf. A. Epstein, *Mi-Qadmoniyot ha-Yehudim* (Jerusalem, 1957), p. 144: "The two cherubim on the ark of testimony correspond to the two holy names, YHWH Elohim."

283. *Perush ha-Rav ᵓEleᶜazar Mi-Garmaiza ᶜal Sefer Yeṣirah*, 22a.

284. This represents the consonants of the name of God, YHWH, and the appellation, Adonai (which means Lord), spelled out in full.

285. Both expressions equal 733.

286. Both expressions equal 86.

287. There is a discrepancy of one: the former expression equals 102 and the latter 101.

288. *Sefer ha-Roqeaḥ*, p. 22, slightly corrected according to the parallel in *ᶜArugat ha-Bosem*, 1:183–84. Cf. *Sefer ha-Shem*, MS London, British Museum 737, fol. 358a: "YHWH in a"t ba"sh [MṢP"Ṣ] is [numerically] equivalent to *be-raḥamim*. Elohenu is numerically *ha-dan yeḥidi*. Know that 'the Lord is one' (Deut. 6:4)." Cf. ibid., fol. 363a. On the association of the cherubim and the attributes of judgment and mercy, cf. *Sefer ha-Shem*, MS London, British Museum 737, fol. 263b. Needless to say, the correlation between the cherubim and the attributes of God from one side and the masculine and feminine powers from the other is a much older Jewish tradition. See G. G. Stroumsa, "Le Couple de l'ange et de l'espirit," *Revue Biblique* 88 (1981): 46–47, 53–55; Idel, "Métaphores et pratiques sexuelles," pp. 337–41; and idem, *Kabbalah: New Perspectives*, pp. 128–33.

289. Cf. *Sefer ha-Ḥokhmah*, MS Oxford, Bodleian Library 1812, fol. 61b:

> The *Shekhinah* has two thrones, two crowns, and two ophanim, one below and one above. . . . Michael is the archon of mercy and Gabriel the archon of judgment, and when the *Shekhinah* sits in the attribute of judgment then the crowns and ophanim mention the name of forty-two letters . . . and the attribute of judgment is transformed into the attribute of mercy. Concerning this Isaiah said, "For lo! The Lord shall come forth from His place," *hinneh yhwh yoṣeᵓ mi-meqomo* (Isa. 26:21). The word *yoṣeᵓ* [comes forth] has the numerical value of Michael [i.e., both expressions equal 101]. [The expression] *hinneh yhwh yoṣeᵓ mi-meqomo* has the numerical value of [the expression] *yhwh u-mṣp"ṣ kissoᵓ* [i.e., both expressions equal 419] *be-raḥamim* [in mercy]. Therefore we say, *yhwh ᵓel raḥum we-ḥannun*, "the Lord, a God compassionate and gracious" (Exod. 34:6) for they are ten letters. Similarly, [the expression] *yhwh yhwh ᵓel*, "the Lord, the Lord, a God" (ibid.). . . . The throne of judgment is transformed into a throne of mercy. Therefore, we say in the *qedushah*, *huᵓ yifen be-raḥamim* ("He looks with mercy"), these are the letters [of the expression] *ha-ᵓofanim be-raḥamim* ("the ophanim in mercy") [in fact, one letter,

the *mem,* is extra] for the ophanim transform the throne of judgment into a throne of mercy and a crown of mercy.

On the double throne and the double crown in this Ashkenazi proto-kabbalistic text and its resemblance to motifs expressed in the *Bahir,* see Farber, "Concept of the Merkabah," p. 247. See above n. 234, and below nn. 318–19.

290. See, e.g., "Book of Angels," p. 116.

291. Cf. MS Rome, Biblioteca Angelica 46, fol. 2b (concerning this manuscript see Scholem, *Reshit ha-Qabbalah,* p. 196), and Moses Zacuto, *Sefer ha-Shemot,* 10b. See the commentary on the name "Shaddai" in MS Vatican, Biblioteca Apostolica ebr. 236, fols. 79a: "The *shin* has a great secret and this is the name (*shem*) of the Holy One, blessed be He, and this is the first letter through which the world was created. This is *shin* [which refers to] YHWH, for the *shin* in a"t ba"sh is MṢP"Ṣ [i.e, the transposition of YHWH through a"t ba"sh], which has the numerical value of *shin.*" Similar language is found in the commentary on *Sefer Yeṣirah* extant in several manuscripts including MS Paris, Bibliothéque Nationale héb. 680, fol. 201b (the text is printed in *Shoshan Sodot* [Korets, 1784], 3b): "The three mothers, *ʾalef, mem,* and *shin,* correspond to the name Shaddai, for in the letter *shin* there is a great mystery . . . in it is [an allusion to] the name of the Creator, blessed be He, for the name YHWH through transposition of letters by a"t ba"sh is MṢP"Ṣ, which has the numerical value of *shin,* and this is the *shin* of the phylacteries, and it is the attribute of mercy." It has been argued by Abrams, "'Book of Illumination,' " pp. 4, 105, that this commentary was written by Jacob ha-Kohen. In an unpublished study Abrams has prepared a critical edition of the text and presents his arguments for attributing it to R. Jacob.

292. That is, the name Elohim when written out in full = *be-raḥamim* = 300, which is also the numerical value of MṢP"Ṣ, the Tetragrammaton written out in a"t ba"sh form.

293. *Perush ha-Roqeaḥ ʿal ha-Torah,* 1:24.

294. See above n. 126.

295. That is, the hidden (*neʿelam*) letters that make up the name Adonai, i.e., the letters necessary for the vocalization of any letter that are nevertheless not graphically visible.

296. The relevance of this verse exegetically can only be understood if one bears in mind the phallic implication of the expression skilled tongue, *leshon limmudim.* More precisely, the tongue here is probably related to the image of scales that symbolically represent the union of male and female. This unity is represented as well by the two names, Adonai and YHWH, that appear in the beginning of the verse. On the sexual symbolism of the scales, see references to work of Liebes in Wolfson, "Erasing the Erasure," p. 180 n. 122. See above n. 121.

297. A view frequently expressed in Pietistic writings based on B. Shabbat 152b and its parallels. For references to primary and secondary literature

relevant to this theme, see Wolfson, "Circumcision and the Divine Name," pp. 91–92 n. 41.

298. MS Oxford 1566, fol. 38a. Cf. ibid., fols. 74a, 87b, 89b. On the placing of the Torah scroll in the throne, see the comment of Eleazar in *Sode Razayya*ᵓ, ed. Kamelhar, p. 38: "The Torah is in His throne as it is in the ark. From the side of the ark is the Torah scroll, a testimony for Israel who fulfill the Torah." See ibid., p. 19, and the text from *Sefer ha-Kavod* cited in Abraham bar Azriel, *ᶜArugat ha-Bosem,* 1:161. Cf. *Sefer Tagi,* MS Oxford, Bodleian Library 1566, fol. 224b: "The Torah and the throne of glory are one pair, for the tablets were taken from the throne of glory [for references to this aggadic motif, see Ginzberg, *Legends,* 6: 49–50 n. 258 and 59 nn. 305–6]. . . . Just as the *Shekhinah* is upon the throne so [it is] upon the Torah and upon the ark. The Torah and the tablets are found there. Thus the Torah is His throne." On the correlation of the Torah scroll and the tablets in the ark see as well in *Sefer Ḥasidim,* §§ 695–96, 698. On the relation of the two cherubim and the study of Torah, see ibid., § 780. It is worthwhile noting here a passage in MS New York, Jewish Theological Seminary of America Mic. 1892, fol. 66b: "Therefore [God] chose [Jacob], raised and exalted him to be His Torah engraved upon His throne." This may be related to another motif based on a depiction of Jacob as the incarnate Torah, viz., the 172 words of the Decalogue together with the ten commadments themselves equals 182, the numerical value of the consonants of the word *yaᶜaqov.* Cf. MSS Oxford, Bodleian Library 1566, fol. 168a; Paris, Bibliothéque Nationale héb. 772, fols. 28a–b, 84a; and Cambridge, University Library Add. 644, fol. 19a. See n. 330.

299. The other two letters of the Tetragrammaton are accounted for inasmuch as the *he*ᵓ is doubled and the *yod* of Adonai has already been counted.

300. On the mystical conception in the writings of the German Pietists of the Torah being composed of divine names, see Dan, *Esoteric Theology,* p. 124 n. 45; Idel, "Concept of the Torah," p. 54 n. 102; and idem, "We Have No Kabbalistic Tradition on This," in *Rabbi Moses Naḥmanides (Ramban): Explorations in His Literary and Religious Virtuosity,* ed. I. Twersky (Cambridge, Mass., 1983), p. 54 n. 10. See further my study cited above in n. 13. On the development of these motifs in kabbalistic literature, see G. Scholem, *On the Kabbalah and Its Symbolism,* trans. R. Manheim (New York, 1965), pp. 37–44, and Idel, "Concept of the Torah," pp. 49–84.

301. Cf. *Baraita of Joseph ben Uziel,* MS Paris, Bibliothéque Nationale héb. 770, fol. 33a, quoted in Dan, *Ḥugge ha-Mequbbalim ha-Rishonim,* p. 101. According to this text, the divine name is said to be written on the crown of the enthroned cherub just as the words *qodesh la-shem* are inscribed on the forehead of Aaron.

302. MS Oxford, Bodleian Library 1566, fol. 42a.

303. Cf. *Sefer ha-Shem,* MS London, British Museum 737, fols. 213a–b, 227a, 363a. And in *Siddur Malᵓah ha-ᵓAreṣ Deᶜah,* 14a (pagination lacking in the

original): "God of Israel, *ʾelohe yisraʾel,* has the numerical value of 613, for the name of the Holy One, blessed be He, is unique to those occupied with the commandments."

304. MS Oxford, Bodleian Library 1566, fol. 118a. Cf. Eleazar's comments in his *Perush Sodot ha-Tefillah,* MS Paris, Bibliothéque Nationale héb. 772, fol. 49a: "'God of Israel,' *ʾelohe yisraʾel* (1 Chron. 29:10) is the glory that Israel the elder (*yisraʾel sabbaʾ*) saw and all the prophets. It is a glorious appearance, a bright fire, that has no image except in the imaginative vision of a person." For a slightly different text, see *Perushe Siddur ha-Tefillah la-Roqeaḥ,* p. 195. See also the passage from MS Paris, Bibliothéque Nationale héb. 772, fol. 77a noted below in n. 348. Cf. "The First Commentary of R. Elḥanan Isaac ben Yaqar of London to *Sefer Yeṣirah,*" ed. G. Vajda, *Qoveṣ ʿal Yad* 6 (1966): 156, where the expression "God of Israel" signifies the "archons above who are called *ʾel,* like Michael and Gabriel, and the rest of the holy ministering angels." It would be instructive to compare the use of this technical term in the Pietistic literature to its use in the writings of Judah Halevi. See E. R. Wolfson, "Merkavah Traditions in Philosophical Garb: Judah Halevi Reconsidered," *Proceedings of the American Academy for Jewish Research* 57 (1990–91): 206–7.

305. This expression occurs several times in Scripture. Cf. Exod. 5:1, 32:27, and Joshua 7:13, 24:2.

306. MS Oxford, Bodleian Library 1566, fol. 100b. Cf. the tradition recorded in MS Paris, Bibliothéque Nationale héb. 1408, fol. 44a: "The ten commandments are the beginning of all the words that God spoke, all the commandments. This is an allusion that He unified His name and His divinity, the [expression] God of Israel, *yhwh ʾelohe yisraʾel,* has the numerical value of 613." For a detailed description of this codex, see C. Sirat, "Le manuscrit hébreu n° 1408 de la bibliothèque nationale de Paris," *Revue des études juives* 123 (1964): 335–58.

307. *Sode Razayyaʾ,* ed. Kamelhar, p. 41: "When Israel utter a blessing then the glory is increased." Cf. *Sode Razayyaʾ,* ed. Weiss, p. 92: "The glory and the splendor increase by [means of] the blessing." And *Perush Sodot ha-Tefillah,* MS Paris, Bibliothéque Nationale héb. 772, fol. 38b: "'The glorious majesty of Your splendor' (Ps. 145:5) when 'they declare Your mighty acts' (ibid., 4), then the glory is increased." Ibid., fol. 30a: "When the pious bless His name then the glory and the kingship increase." Ibid., fol. 110a: "When Israel bless His glorious name the glory is increased." (This passage is cited already by Idel, *Kabbalah: New Perspectives,* p. 160, as an illustration of the theurgical element in Eleazar's thinking.) Cf. the corresponding versions in MS Oxford, Bodleian Library 1204, fol. 111b (this version is printed in *Perushe Siddur ha-Tefillah la-Roqeaḥ,* p. 145): "'The glorious majesty of Your splendor': when one mentions 'they declare Your mighty acts,' one immediately says 'the glorious majesty.' This indicates that when the righteous declare His wonders and mighty acts the glory is increased." Ibid., fol. 112b (*Perushe Siddur ha-Tefillah la-Roqeaḥ,* p. 148): "'And your mighty acts' that You show to human beings, 'all Your works shall speak of You and Your faithful ones shall bless You' (based on Ps. 145:10 with some variations) the glory. This indicates that

the glory is increased by the blessings of Israel for it appears as if He were crowned in their crowns." Cf. MS Paris, Bibliothèque Nationale héb. 850, fol. 122a: "When a person makes a blessing with the intention of the heart . . . the glory increases in efflugence and splendor. In the future one will merit that light, 'upon you the Lord will shine [and His Presence be seen over you]' (Isa. 60:2), for the glory and splendor increase through the blessing, as it is written, 'Your faithful ones shall bless You, they shall talk of the majesty of Your kingship, and the majestic glory of His kingship' (Ps. 145: 10–12)." Cf. *Commentary on the Passover Haggadah by Eleazar of Worms*, p. 165: "When Israel glorify the praise [of God] the throne and the glory are exalted and enlarged." On the elevation and enlargement of the throne, see *Sode Razayya*ʾ, ed. Kamelhar, p. 27: "When Israel exalt [God] in praise the throne, as it were, is exalted." Ibid., p. 36: "As the glory ascends so too the throne ascends, and as the glory expands so too the throne expands." See also the passage of Eleazar quoted by Naftali Herz Treves in his commentary on the prayer book, discussed in Idel, "Concept of Torah," p. 24 n. 2, and a second passage from the same work cited by Idel, *Kabbalah: New Perspectives*, pp. 160 and 357 n. 40. Cf. *Sefer ha-Shem*, MS London, British Museum 737, fol. 267b, where the motif of the augmented glory is connected with the name "Shaddai" traditionally associated with male virility (cf. *Sode Razayya*ʾ, ed. Weiss, p. 3): "Since this name is found in relation to procreation [the divine] appeared to the prophets in the name Shaddai; they saw the glory increase and expand" (*roʾim ha-kavod mitrabbeh we-holekh*). In the continuation of this passage the expanding glory is compared to the voice that increases and expands. (On the hypostatic nature of the voice, perhaps related to older speculations on the Logos, cf. ibid., fols. 306a–7b.) It is of interest to note that in *Perush Sodot ha-Tefillah*, MS Paris, Bibliothèque Nationale héb. 772, fol. 171b (cf. *Perushe Siddur ha-Tefillah la-Roqeaḥ*, p. 711) Eleazar discusses the epiphany of the glory through the appearance or vision of Shaddai (cf. Num. 24:16) immediately after his reflections on the process of procreation. These examples, and many others that could have been cited, greatly support Idel's theurgical interpretation of the German Pietistic use of the image of the ascending crown. See *Kabbalah: New Perspectives*, pp. 160–61, 193–97. See as well idem, "In the Light of Life," pp. 205–7. For possible influences on Eleazar with respect to the expression *kavod ha-mitrabbeh*, cf. Judah ben Barzillai, *Perush Sefer Yeṣirah*, p. 37, where the expression *ha-kavod ha-merubbeh* occurs. See also *Numbers Rabbah* 14:22, and especially the *yoṣer* for Rosh ha-Shanah in *Piyyuṭe R. Shimʿon bar Yiṣḥaq*, p. 48, wherein those who observe the commandments are said to increase God's glory, *leharbot kevodekha* (cf. Goldschmidt, *Maḥzor la-Yamim ha-Noraʾim*, 1:47).

308. The manuscript reads *ha-keruv*, but the masoretic text has *ha-keruvim*.

309. MS Oxford, Bodleian Library 1566, fol. 119a.

310. Cf. the *qerovah* for Passover, *ʾomeṣ gevurotekha mi yemalel*, by Moses bar Qalonymus, appendix to *Piyyuṭe R. Shimʿon bar Yiṣḥaq*, p. 217, where the theophany of the "glory of the God of Israel" is depicted in terms of the image of enthronement upon a cherub.

311. Naturally, in the theosophic kabbalistic symbolism as well the unity of the two names symbolizes the union between the masculine and the feminine potencies in the divine realm. See M. Verman, "The Development of Yiḥudim in Spanish Kabbalah," *Jerusalem Studies in Jewish Thought* 8 (1989): 25–41 (English section).

312. On the sexual connotation of the image of riding upon the cherub, see the commentary on the *Shema*ᶜ from the circle of the *Sefer ha-Temunah*, printed in *Sefer ha-Temunah* (Lemberg, 1892), 73a (cf. MS Oxford, Bodleian Library 1557, fol. 29b): "When the sun stands in an erect posture (*qomah zequfah*) upon the moon, as it says, 'He rode upon a cherub,' then 'His wisdom is beyond reckoning' (Ps. 147:5)." See in slightly different terms another version of this text in MS Vatican, Biblioteca Apostolica ebr. 194, fol. 70b: "The crown of majesty, as it says, 'He rode upon a cherub,' to be one form, the sun upon the moon." It is relevant to note in this context the view expressed by Maimonides in the *Guide of the Perplexed* I.70, on the nature of the act of riding (*rekhivah*) and the allegorical significance of the one who rides as the one who controls and rules over that which one rides. See especially Abraham Abulafia's discussion of this motif in a fragment from *Sefer ha-Melammed*, MS Paris, Bibliothéque Nationale héb. 680, fols. 301a–b. (Concerning the identification of this text, see M. Idel, "The Writings of Abraham Abulafia and His Teaching" [Ph.D. dissertation, Hebrew University, 1976], pp. 15–16 [in Hebrew]). Although there is no explicit sexual connotation in the case of Maimonides' philosophical explanation, it is not difficult to imagine the imposition of such imagery given the accepted medieval mindset with respect to such matters as the typical posture of man and woman during sexual intercourse. Cf. the anonymous text of prophetic kabbalah, *Sefer ha-Ṣeruf*, MS Munich, Bayerische Staatsbibliothek 22, fol. 205b–207a: "All the gradations are in accordance with their level one atop the other, the lower one is always called female and the one above her male in relation to her, for he rides upon her and this one is ridden upon, even though this is not actual riding but a matter of level and great dominion. . . . You must contemplate the secret of the account of the chariot, and the chariot of which we spoke of the four creatures that bear the throne. Contemplate the secret of the throne. . . . Understand well that I do not have permission to reveal more explicitly, but everything is intimated to the one who sees with the eye of the intellect. Understand this and then great matters concerning the secret of the throne and chariot, the simple and the compounded, and the secret of which we spoke before, which is the secret of the male and female, will be clarified for you." Also instructive in this context is the wording of Judah Alḥarizi cited in *Hebrew Poetry in Spain and Provence*, ed. J. Schirmann (Jerusalem and Tel-Aviv, 1957), 2:118 (in Hebrew): "Fortunate is the man who rides upon her chariot (*be-merkavttah rakhav*), 'at her feet he sank, laying outstretched' (Judges 5:27)." It is obvious that in this poem the image of riding upon a chariot is a metaphor for coitus.

313. The manuscript (see reference in following note) here repeats the notation for the Tetragrammaton, but according to the masorertic text the correct

reading is Adonai YHWH. The force of the Pietistic exegesis is only understood in light of the received biblical text; i.e., there is a unity of the two names symbolized by the two cherubim.

314. MS Oxford, Bodleian Library 1566, fol. 87b.

315. *Ḥokhmat ha-Nefesh*, ch. 73, p. 126. Cf. ibid., ch. 68, p. 118: "With respect to all the commandments He alludes to the fact that He unifies His name and His divinity upon Israel. [The title] 'Lord, God of Israel' (*yhwh ʾelohe yisraʾel*) has the numerical value of 613." Cf. *Commentary on the Passover Haggadah by Eleazar of Worms*, p. 72: "He said to them, 'Thus says the Lord, God of Israel,' to indicate that we must observe the 613 commandments and then He is called Lord, God of Israel." It is reasonable to assume that Eleazar's formulation, *le-maʿalah demut*, reflects the expression *demut le-maʿalah*, "the image above," which signifies the anthropomorphic form of the glory of the Dynamis. Cf. *ʾAvot de-Rabbi Natan*, ch. 33, 58b, and *Pesiqta de Rav Kahana*, ed. B. Mandelbaum (New York, 1962) p. 65. On the doctrine of the *demut* in rabbinic literature, see A. J. Heschel, *Theology of Ancient Judaism* (London and New York, 1962), 1:220–23 (in Hebrew); S. Lieberman, "How Much Greek in Jewish Palestine?" in *Biblical and Other Studies*, ed. A. Altmann (Cambridge, Mass., 1966), pp. 140–41; and M. Fishbane, "Some Forms of Divine Appearance in Ancient Jewish Thought," in *From Ancient Israel to Modern Judaism Intellect in Quest of Understanding: Essays in Honor of Marvin Fox*, ed. J. Neusner, E. S. Frerichs, and N. M. Sarna (Atlanta, 1989), 2:265–68.

316. MS London, British Museum 737, fol. 212b.

317. Cf. *Sefer ha-Shem*, MS Oxford, Bodleian Library 1569, fol. 116a. The version there matches that of MS London, British Museum 737, fol. 221b, as well as that of MS Munich, Bayerische Staatsbibliothek 81, fol. 140b, but the picture found there in the margin matches the view expressed in the theosophic text attributed to Judah the Pious: ADNYHW L"F L"T W"N W"D A"W.

318. *Sode Razayyaʾ*, ed. Kamelhar, p. 58.

319. On the motif of the double throne in Haside Ashkenaz, see reference to Farber cited above in n. 289. See also the passage from Eleazar's commentary on the liturgy cited above in n. 234. In that text in particular the esoteric nature of the singular throne that is divided into two is emphasized. It seems to me, as Farber too has suggested, that the secret of the throne is decidedly sexual. I would suggest that the deep secret here, as in the theosophic kabbalistic symbolism, is related to the androgynous phallus. See n. 329.

320. It is possible that the move from the plural cherubim to the singular cherub is based on Ezek. 10:3–4, a point already made by Scholem, *Major Trends*, p. 113, although in that context he was speaking about material from the *Ḥug ha-Keruv ha-Meyuḥad*, without however identifying it as such. Cf. the commentary on Song of Songs 3:11 attributed to Eleazar, printed in *Perush ha-Roqeaḥ ʿal ha-Megillot*, p. 127: *merkavo mi-keruv keruvim*.

321. MS London, British Museum 737, fol. 184a. Cf. ibid., fols. 339a, 352b, and Abraham Abulafia, *Ḥayye ha-ʿOlam ha-Baʾ*, MS Oxford, Bodleian Library 1582, fol. 20b.

322. The manuscript that I examined (see n. 325) reads, *ʿal ha-ʾareṣ kevodo*, in place of the correct wording of the *qedushah* prayer, *kol ha-ʾareṣ kevodo* (based on Isa. 6:3). In my translation, however, I have followed the reading in *Perushe Siddur ha-Tefillah la-Roqeaḥ*, p. 327, which conforms to the traditional prayer.

323. On the motif of "faces" signifying attributes of God's actions vis-à-vis the world, cf. *Sefer ha-Shem*, MS London, British Museum 737, fol. 305a: "And there are also faces, faces of the glory (*pene ha-kavod*) . . . and the prophet who sees the faces knows the supernal mind (*daʿat ʿelyon*) that turns from the side of the speech that is made known to the prophet." In the continuation of that passage Eleazar explicitly contrasts the faces of anger, *pene ha-zaʿam*, with the faces of goodness, *panim ṭovim*, or light, *panim shel ʾorah*. (An important parallel to Eleazar's text is found in the *Sefer ha-Kavod* extant in MS Oxford, Bodleian Library 1566, fols. 42b–43b.) It is evident from this context that the *pene ha-kavod* are ontically akin to the angels in whose image Adam was created, a motif that Eleazar repeats in many of his writings. See Scholem, *Major Trends*, pp. 117–18; idem, *Origins*, p. 112 n. 114; Dan, *Esoteric Theology*, pp. 218, 224–29; and Ch. Mopsik, *Le Livre hébreu d'Hénoch ou Livre des palais* (Paris, 1989), p. 53. For a docetic interpretation of the traditional idiom *pene ha-shekhinah*, cf. *Sefer ha-Shem*, MS London, British Museum 737, fol. 378a.

324. In MS Oxford, Bodleian Library 1204, fol. 79a: "the glory near the glory," *ha-kavod ʾeṣel ha-kavod*, and in a parallel in MS Munich, Bayerische Staatsbibliothek 232, fol. 7b: "the glory near the special cherub," *kavod ʾeṣel keruv yaḥid*.

325. MS Paris, Bibliothéque Nationale héb. 772, fol. 76b.

326. According to Ezek. 1:27. Cf. *Pirqe Rabbi ʾEliʿezer*, ch. 4: "The Presence of the Holy One, blessed be He, is in the middle, and He sits on a high and exalted throne. . . . He manifests His glory in the likeness of the *ḥashmal*."

327. That is, 182. Cf. the pseudo-Eleazar *Perush ha-Roqeaḥ ʿal ha-Torah* 3:38: "[The word] *bi-nesoʿa* has the numerical value of *yaʿaqov* for he is upon the throne."

328. *Perush ha-Merkavah*, MS Paris, Bibliothéque Nationale héb. 850, fol. 68b, and precise parallel in *Sode Razayyaʾ*, ed. Kamelhar, p. 13. Cf. *Perush ha-Merkavah*, MS Paris, Bibliothéque Nationale héb. 850, fols. 67a–b:

> It is said, "in the likeness of a *ḥashmal*" (Ezek. 1:4, 27), for when Ezekiel saw the effulgence of the glory he could endure it until He showed him the *ḥashmal* in the likeness of the splendor of the glory. "When the Ark was to set out," *wa-yehi bi-nesoʿa ha-ʾaron* (Num. 10:35). The *bet* and *samekh* [of the word *bi-nesoʿa*] through the permutation of letters [by means of the technique of] a"t ba"sh

> are *ḥet* and *shin*, and the *ʿayin* [of the word *bi-nesoʿa* exchanges with the letters *mem* and *lamed* insofar as *ʿayin* = 70, which is the sum of *mem* and *lamed*, 40 + 30]. Thus [one derives from the word] *ḥashmal*. And the inverted *nun* [according to the masoretic text] is to indicate that he guides the chariot (*molikh ha-merkavah*). *Ḥashmal* has the numerical value of *molikh ha-merkavah* [i.e., 378].

See ibid., fol. 74b; MS New York, Jewish Theological Seminary of America Mic. 2430, fol. 71a: "R. Eliezer (!) wrote that the *ḥashmal* stands surrounding the throne of glory. He has three appearances, and he is the most important of the angels for he guides the chariot. Therefore, *ḥashmal* has the numerical value of *molikh ha-merkavah*." See Farber, "Concept of the Merkabah," pp. 42, 328. Cf. *Rabbenu Baḥya ʿal ha-Torah*, ed. Chavel, 2:276, ad Exod. 25:18: "The reality of the *ḥashmal* is from the splendors of the throne of glory. You should know that he surrounds the throne, and he leads (*molikh*) the word of the glory to the holy creatures."

329. While I did not articulate fully the implications of my own thinking in the original Hebrew version of this study, I did consider the image of Jacob to be an androgynous symbol. However, what is more clear to me now is that the phallus assumes the androgynous character inasmuch as both masculinity and femininity are localized in the male organ. See above nn. 253 and 319, and below n. 376. The bisexual element of the glory may also be implied in the following statement of Eleazar in *Sefer ha-Shem*, MS London, British Museum 737, fol. 288a: "If you say, 'how did Ezekiel see the "semblance of a human form" (1:26)'? It is like a person who sees in a large mirror a large face (*parṣuf gadol*) and in a small mirror a small face (*parṣuf qaṭan*)." The symbolism underlying this metaphor may involve the masculine and feminine hypostases referred to respectively as the large and the small faces. If my interpretation is correct, then this is another striking resemblance of Pietistic theosophy to the symbolism of kabbalah.

330. That is, 172 + 10 = 182, the sum of the Hebrew letters in the name Jacob. See above n. 298.

331. The reference is to Qallir's poem, *we-ḥayyot ʾasher henah merubbaʿot kisseʾ*. See above n. 56.

332. The continuation of the verse is "under my head," *taḥat le-roʾshi*. The letters of the last word can be transposed into *yisraʾel*.

333. The continuation of the verse in Exod. 24:10 is *ke-maʿaseh livnat ha-sappir*, "the likeness of a pavement of sapphire." It is possible that Eleazar is drawing an analogy between these words and the expression describing the throne in Ezek. 1:26, *ke-marʾeh ʾeven sappir*, "in appearance like sapphire." On the other hand, it is possible that the word *ke-marʾeh* is an allusion to the expression *ke-marʾeh ʾadam* in the same verse from Ezekiel. The "semblance of the human form" upon the throne is to be identified as Israel or the image of Jacob. Cf. the passage from the *Perush Sodot ha-Tefillah* cited below in n. 373.

334. This refrain is part of the traditional liturgy.

335. If "Jacob" is written in the plene form with a *waw*, then the numerical value of *mi-ya*ʿ*aqov* is 228, which is the same as that of the word *keruv*. See above n. 203.

336. MS Paris, Bibliothéque Nationale héb. 772, fols. 159a–b. See printed version, based on MS Oxford, Bodleian Library 1204, in *Perushe Siddur ha-Tefillah la-Roqeaḥ*, pp. 678–80.

337. See, e.g., *Pesiqta de-Rav Kahana*, 23, pp. 376–77; *Pesiqta Rabbati*, ed. M. Friedmann (Vienna, 1880), 40, 168b; *Leviticus Rabbah* 29:3, p. 674; and *Midrash Tehillim* 47:2, ed. S. Buber (Vilna, 1891), 137b.

338. Quoted in E. Fleischer, *Hebrew Liturgical Poetry in the Middle Ages* (Jerusalem, 1975), p. 435 (in Hebrew).

339. According to the description of Jacob in Gen. 25:27.

340. Goldschmidt, *Maḥzor la-Yamim ha-Nora*ʾ*im*, 1:83. In the continuation of the poem it says: *u-va-*ʿ*aṭarah* ʾ*asher be-ro*ʾ*shekha zequqah/ u-ve-shem yisra*ʾ*el be-khinnuy meḥuzzaqah* (and the diadem that is bound to Your head, that which is called by the name Israel). See, however, the version in MS Oxford, Bodleian Library 1038, fol. 6b: *histakkel ba-tavnit* ʾ*asher be-kisse*ʾ *ḥaquqah . . . u-va-*ʿ*aṭarah* ʾ*asher be-ro*ʾ*sho zequqah/ be-shem yisra*ʾ*el be-khinnuy meḥuzzaqah*. According to this version, the diadem whose name is Israel is bound to the head of the image of Jacob engraved upon the throne. Cf. Goldschmidt, *Maḥzor la-Yamim ha-Nora*ʾ*im*, 1:178: *yewwada*ʿ *ḥesed ḥaquq be-khes shiv*ʿ*ah*. And in *Maḥzor la-Yamim ha-Nora*ʾ*im*, 2:120: *ḥotmam me-reḥem yoshev* ʾ*ohalim/ ṣurato be-khis*ʾ*akha ḥaqttah behillim*. In another liturgical poem for Yom Kippur (op. cit., p. 402) reference is made to the image of the patriarchs (designated the "ancient mountains," *harere qedem*; cf. *Sifre on Deuteronomy*, pisqa 353, p. 414) upon the throne rather than the image of Jacob alone: *we-tavnit harere qedem ba-kisse*ʾ*/ meḥannenim be*ʿ*ad* ʿ*am zu mi-taḥat la-kisse*ʾ. Cf. the Ashkenazi *Perush Hafṭarah*, MS Berlin, Staatsbibliothek Or. 945, fol. 154b. It is possible that there is an allusion to this very matter in the poem published in M. Zulay, *The Liturgical Poetry of Sa*ʿ*adya Gaon and His School* (Jerusalem, 1964), p. 141 (in Hebrew): *yizzakher lefanekha ṣedeq hamamshilim be-*ʾ*arba*ʿ*ah fanim* ʾ*asher ba-kes ḥarutim/ shahas we-shor we-*ʿ*ayiṭ we-reshem to*ʾ*ar mefasel ba-rehatim*.

341. Based on Naḥum 2:11.

342. *Maḥzor la-Yamim ha-Nora*ʾ*im*, 1:217.

343. Cf. 1 Kings 7:7.

344. See, e.g., Eleazar's *ma*ʿ*arivim* for Rosh ha-Shanah, in *Shirat ha-Roke*ʾ*aḥ*, ed. Meiseles, p. 77: *sod tam* ʾ*ezkkor ba-kesse*ʾ*/* ʿ*atiratkhem* ʾ*eshma*ʿ *ba-kesse*ʾ*/ we-*ʾ*et qol ha-shofar* (the secret of the innocent one I recall upon the throne/ your prayers I hear upon the throne/ and the voice of the ram's horn.)

It should be noted that in this poem Eleazar mentions the merit of the three patriarchs, not solely that of Jacob whose image is engraved upon the throne. Eleazar's dependence upon the *piyyuṭ* literature has been well noted by other scholars. See Urbach, *ʿArugat ha-Bosem,* 4:100–11, and H. Soloveitchik, "Three Themes in Sefer Ḥasidim," *ASJ Review* 1 (1976): 352.

345. MS London, British Museum 737, fol. 184b. Cf. *Sode Razayyaʾ*, ed. Weiss, p. 150: "The glory immediately looks at the human countenance, the image of Jacob, and he has pity upon them." On the ocular gaze of God as an expression of mercy or the transformation of the attribute of judgment into the attribute of mercy, see Eleazar ben Moses ha-Darshan, *Sefer ha-Gimaṭriʾot,* MS Munich, Bayerische Staatsbibliothek 221, fol. 160a. There is little question in my mind that the gaze in the Ashkenazi sources, as in theosophic kabbalistic symbolism, has an implicit erotic connotation. See my extended discussion of this theme in *Through a Speculum That Shines: Vision and Imagination in Medieval Jewish Mysticism* (Princeton, 1994). On the erotic implication of the gaze in kabbalistic texts, see also Liebes, *Studies in the Zohar,* pp. 68–69.

346. *Sefer ha-Roqeaḥ,* p. 105.

347. MS Paris, Bibliothéque Nationale héb. 850, fol. 59a. See "The Commentary on Ezekiel's Chariot by R. Jacob," p. 29. The influence of this motif is discernible in the passage from *Midrash ha-Neʿelam* published by G. Scholem, "A New Section from the *Midrash ha-Neʿelam* of the *Zohar,*" *Festschrift in Honor of Louis Ginzberg* (New York, 1946), p. 431 (in Hebrew):

> R. Abbahu said: He made the icon [of Jacob] in heaven and when Israel sin and the attribute of judgment is upon them, the Holy One, blessed be He, looks at his icon and has mercy on them as it is written, "God said, Let there be lights in the expanse of the sky" (Gen. 1:14). . . . Therefore, Joseph saw in his dream "the sun and the moon" (ibid. 37:9), for this referred to Jacob. . . . The Holy One, blessed be He, engraved Jacob near His throne . . . and when the Holy One, blessed be He, wants to have mercy on Israel He looks at the icon of Jacob and has mercy on them.

Cf. the metamorphosis of this motif in *Zohar* 1:168a: "In times of distress for the children of Jacob the Holy one, blessed be He, looks at the icon of Jacob that is before Him and has pity upon the world." The influence of this motif, perhaps reflecting more specifically the zoharic passages, is discernible in the following statement of Abner of Burgos, "Therefore they say, the Holy One, blessed be He said, They would anger Me were it not for the image of their father, Jacob, that is engraved on the throne." See Hecht, "The Polemical Exchange between Isaac Pollegar and Abner of Burgos," pp. 184 and 372. See above n. 36. On Jacob as a symbol for the attribute of lovingkindness or mercy, cf. the passage of Eleazar of Worms in MS Munich, Bayerische Staatsbibliothek 232, fol. 5a.

348. Cf. *Perush Sodot ha-Tefillah,* MS Paris, Bibliothéque Nationale héb. 772, fol. 65a (printed text in *Perushe Siddur ha-Tefillah la-Roqeaḥ,* p. 264):

> The three times that the word *qadosh* appears [in the Trisagion based on Isa. 6:3] correspond to . . . [the three scriptural expressions] (1) *yoshev ha-keruvim,* "enthroned on the cherubim" (1 Sam. 4:4, 2 Sam. 6:2, 2 Kings 19:15, Isa. 37:16, Ps. 80:2, 1 Chron. 13:6; see also Ps. 99:1); (2) *wa-ya*ᶜ*amod* ᶜ*al ha-keruvim,* "and stood above the cherubim" (Ezek. 10:18); (3) *wa-yirkav* ᶜ*al keruv,* "He mounted a cherub" (2 Sam. 22:11, Ps. 18:11). Thus there are three [postures]: sitting (*yeshivah*), standing (ᶜ*amidah*), and riding (*rekhivah*). Therefore [it says] "Holy, holy, holy, the Lord of Hosts" (Isa. 6:3).

Is there here an allusion to the fact that these different postures are symbolic characterizations of the *hieros gamos* between the glory and the cherub? This interpretation would appear to be enhanced by the exegetical context in which this comment appears, viz., an explication of the Trisagion. The erotic element of this liturgical refrain is underscored by the critical passage in *Hekhalot Rabbati* (see above n. 181) that alludes to the dynamic between the enthroned glory and the iconic image of Jacob engraved upon the throne. Eleazar cites this very text when he comments on the *qedushah de-*ᶜ*amidah,* i.e., the Trisagion of the Eighteen Benedictions. Cf. MS Paris, Bibliothéque Nationale héb. 772, fol. 76a (printed text in *Perushe Siddur ha-Tefillah la-Roqeaḥ,* pp. 325–26). See n. 352. Cf., however, MS Paris, Bibliothéque Nationale héb. 772, fol. 77a (*Perushe Siddur ha-Tefillah la-Roqeaḥ,* p. 329) where the custom to rise on one's feet when the Trisagion is recited is related to the need to stand before God when one of the divine names is mentioned. In that context a spurious talmudic passage (the exact reference given is the Yerushalmi, the ninth chapter of Berakhot called *ha-ro*ʾ*eh*; cf. ᶜ*Arugat ha-Bosem,* 1:215, where Abraham bar Azriel cites a similiar source in the name of the Yerushalmi but in that context the narrative is about Eleazar ben Azariah; see E. Zimmer, "Poses and Postures During Prayer," *Sidra* 5 [1989]: 128 n. 219 [in Hebrew], who suggests that Abraham bar Azriel considered the *Hekhalot* literature to be part of the talmudic corpus of the Palestinian sages) is cited that is in fact based on the passage from *Hekhalot Rabbati* referred to above: "When Eleazar ben Arakh ascended to heaven, the Holy One, blessed be He, said to him: Eleazar, My son, don't you know how beloved are My children before Me? When they say 'Holy, holy, holy,' and cast their eyes to Mine, and lift their bodies by their heels, I embrace and kiss the visage of Jacob, their patriarch, that is engraved upon My throne of glory. Whoever is seated must stand. Similarly, R. Simeon would stand when they said 'Lord, God of Israel.' " (Here again we note parenthetically that the title, "Lord, God of Israel," indicates in a technical sense the enthronement of the glory; see above n. 304.) The standing posture of the worshipper both sets into motion and reflects the status of the glory vis-à-vis the image of Jacob engraved upon the throne. More specifically, the erotic dynamic of the glory embracing and kissing the iconic visage of Jacob is related to the standing of the worshipper. There is thus a reverse correlation of what occurs above and below: as the worshipper stands and lifts his body the glory stoops down and sits upon the throne. On the custom to leap during the recitation of the Trisagion in the *qedushah* and its linkage to the passage in *Hekhalot Rabbati* in medieval Provençal and Ashkenazi halakhic figures, see sources discussed by Zimmer, "Poses and Postures During Prayer," pp. 128–29. Zimmer surmises that the custom began in France and from there disseminated to Germany and Italy as well as Provence and Spain. The passage from Eleazar's *Perush Sodot ha-Tefillah,* according to MS Paris, Bibliothéque Nationale héb. 772, is not discussed by Zimmer. See also passage from the Ashkenazi prayer book extant in MS Rome, Biblioteca Angelica 324, cited in the *Siddur of R. Solomon ben Samson of Garmaise,* p. 87 n. 63 (as noted in *Perushe Siddur ha-Tefillah la-Roqeaḥ,* p. 329 n. 100): "The reason that we stand on our toes when we say 'Holy, holy, holy' is on account of the [image of] Jacob on the throne of glory. When Israel stand on their toes, the Holy One, blessed be He, takes him and kisses him."

349. See Dan, *Studies,* p. 137.

350. MS Oxford, Bodleian Library 1566, fol. 278b.

351. To be sure, in other places in his writings Eleazar cites the passage of Nathan ben Yeḥiel without any indication that he has imputed sexual meaning to it. See *Sod ha-Yiḥud* of Eleazar published by Dan, *Studies,* p. 86; *Sha*ᶜ*are ha-Sod ha-Yiḥud we-ha-*ᵓ*Emunah,* p. 148; and ᶜ*Arugat ha-Bosem,* 1:200. See Verman, *Books of Contemplation,* p. 141. Support for my interpretation of Eleazar's use of the saying "glory above the glory" to refer to masculine and feminine potencies of the divine may be found in the text in MS New York, Jewish Theological Seminary of America Mic. 1884, fol. 20b, transcribed and translated in Verman, op. cit., pp. 202–3. In that text the Primal Ether, described as an androgynous female (see my discussion in "Erasing the Erasure," n. 145), is identified by R. Meir of Germany as the Primal Light and by R. Peres of France as the Tenth Level as well as the cherub. (Concerning the possible identity of the aforementioned rabbinic figures as, respectively, R. Meir of Rothenburg and R. Peres ben Elijah of Corbeil, see Kanarfogel, "Rabbinic Figures in Castilian Kabbalistic Pseudepigraphy," pp. 100–2.) The last identification is predicated on the fact that just as the cherub was both male and female (following the talmudic tradition; see above, n. 280), so too this potency is androgynous. I will cite the most relevant part of the text according to Verman's translation: "There is in this the secret of the Cherubs: an allusion to one who understands what is written in Scripture—'male and female He created them . . . and He called their name Adam, on the day He created them' (Gen. 5:2), so it is. Similarly, the proponents of interior religion called its name, the glory above the glory." There can be no question that the esoteric masters referred to as "proponents of interior religion" (ᵓ*anshe ha-dat ha-penimit*) understood the statement of Nathan ben Yeḥiel in terms of a male-female polarity, precisely the way that I have interpreted the comment of Eleazar cited in the body of this study. It is evident as well that this text preserves authentic German Pietistic traditions; see Verman, op. cit., p. 200. It is noteworthy that the androgynous nature of the cherub is emphasized in

another text that betrays the influence of the German Pietists, and particularly of Eleazar of Worms, viz., the kabbalah of Meshullam the Zadokite, extant in MS Milan, Biblioteca Ambrosiana 62, fol. 109b, transcribed and translated in Verman, op. cit., pp. 207–10 (see esp. 208). See Farber, "Concept of the Merkabah," pp. 560, 633–38. Finally, it is of interest to recall that M. Idel, "On the Concept of Ẓimẓum in Kabbalah and Its Research," *Jerusalem Studies in Jewish Thought* 10 (1992): 66 n. 46 (in Hebrew), observed that an expression similiar to that of Nathan ben Yeḥiel's remark concerning the "glory above the glory" is found in the Gnostic work, the *Gospel of Phillip* 85, trans. W. W. Isenberg in *The Nag Hammadi Library in English*, ed. J. Robinson, revised edition (San Francisco, 1988), p. 159: "There is glory which surpasses glory. There is power which surpasses power." It is evident from the context that this remark signifies the union of the upper spiritual powers and the lower spiritual powers. Thus the text continues: "Therefore the perfect things have opened up to us, together with the hidden things of truth. The holies of the holies were revealed, and the bridal chamber invited us in." The reference to the bridal chamber suggests that the reunification of the upper and the lower spiritual powers is a reunification of the masculine and the feminine. If my reading is correct, then it can be concluded that already in this Gnostic source the locution of the glory above the glory has a sexual connotation. The affinity of this Gnostic text and esoteric Jewish motifs has been well noted in the scholarly literature; for references see "The Tree That Is All," p. 73 n. 168 [below p. 221 n. 172].

352. The sitting of the glory upon the throne assumes a sexual nuance already in one of the main macroforms of *Hekhalot* literature, *Hekhalot Rabbati*, § 94: "Beginning of praise and the first song, beginning of rejoicing and the first exultation, the archons, who serve each day, sing before YHWH, the God of Israel, they exalt the wheel of His throne of glory, (singing): Rejoice, rejoice, throne of glory! Exult, exult, supernal dwelling! Shout, shout for joy, precious vessel. . . . Gladden the king who (sits) upon you, as the joy of the bridegroom in his nuptial chamber." See ibid., § 99 in which the throne of glory is described as prostrating itself thrice daily before the glory and uttering: "Zoharariel, YHWH, God of Israel, glorify Yourself, and sit down upon me, magnificient King, for Your burden is dear to me, and it is not heavy." On the feminine quality of the throne, see above n. 183. It seems to me that the sexual implication of enthronement underlies the following comment in *Sefer ha-Shem*, MS London, British Museum 737, fol. 280a, on the passage in *Sefer Yeṣirah* 1:8 (Gruenwald, "Preliminary Critical Edition," p. 142), "If your heart runs, return to the place whence you came": "If the heart begins to contemplate he should rush and quickly place his heart as if the throne of glory above were facing him and the supernal God sitting on it, and he should bow down to Him, and he will remember the One (*we-yizkor ha-yiḥud*)." The realization of divine oneness is here connected to the enthronement of God, which is actualized only through imaginative visualization since the One is not a body that occupies a throne. Cf. ibid., fol. 288b: "The One has no limit (*ha-yiḥud ʾein lo sof*) for He is everything, and if not for the fact that 'through the prophets [God] was imaged' (Hosea 12:11) as a king sitting upon a throne, they would not have known to whom to pray. . . . This is what is said in

Sefer Yeṣirah (1:8) 'and set the Creator on His place.'" The imaginative visualization of God, which provides the iconic representation necessary for prayer, is expressed particularly in terms of the structure of enthronement. For a more extensive discussion of the process of visualization in the writings of Ḥaside Ashkenaz, see chapter 5 of my *Through a Speculum That Shines*. Needless to say, in theosophic kabbalistic symbolism as well the sitting of God upon the throne symbolizes the unity between the masculine and the feminine potencies in the divine realm, i.e., the union of *Tif*ʾ*eret* and *Malkhut*, the Holy One, blessed be He, and the Presence. See, e.g., the well-known passage in *Zohar* 2:135a–b (recited liturgically by certain communities under the title *raza*ʾ *de-shabbat*, "the mystery of Sabbath"): "The Holy One, blessed be He, is one above, and He does not sit upon His throne of glory until she is unified in the secret of the one as He is, so that they will be one together with one. . . . The prayer of Sabbath evening: the holy throne of glory is unified in the secret of the one and she is prepared for the supernal holy King to rest upon her." See Ginsburg, *Sabbath in the Classical Kabbalah*, pp. 167 n. 176, 168 n. 183. Cf. *Zohar* 3:48a: "When is there said to be perfection above? When the Holy One, blessed be He, sits upon the throne, and prior to His sitting upon the throne there is no perfection, as it is written, 'and on top, upon this semblance of a throne, there was the semblance of a human form' (Ezek. 1:26). From the fact that it is written human it may be inferred that it is the containment and perfection of everything." Concerning this text and its possible relation to the Idrot sections of zoharic literature, see Liebes, *Studies in the Zohar*, p. 113. Liebes also noted the sexual nuance of the image of sitting upon a throne. The words of the *Zohar* are based on the rabbinic view that a person is not called "Adam," i.e., a human, unless there is a pairing of male and female. Cf. B. Yevamot 63a; *Sefer ha-Bahir*, § 172; *Zohar* 1:55b; and 3:141b (ʾ*Idra*ʾ *Rabba*ʾ). For other sources, see Liebes, *Sections of the Zohar Lexicon*, p. 33 n. 26. On the perfection (or completion) of a person in terms of the union of masculine and feminine, see *Zohar* 1:239a, and 3:7a. This image is supported in zoharic literature by another rabbinic idea, based on a much older myth, regarding the androgynous nature of Adam. Cf. *Genesis Rabbah* 8:1; B. Berakhot 61a; ʿEruvin 18a; and many places in the *Zohar*, e.g., 1:2b, 34b–35a, 37b, 165a; 2:55a, 70b, 231a–b; and 3:10b, 19a, 44b, 117a; *Zohar Ḥadash* 16c (*Midrash ha-Ne*ʿ*elam*), 55c, 66c. See Ginzberg, *Legends*, 5:88–89 n. 42; Tishby, *Wisdom of the Zohar*, pp. 1355–56; D. C. Matt, *Zohar: The Book of Enlightenment* (New York, 1983), p. 217; and Liebes, *Studies in the Zohar*, pp. 70–71.

353. Cf. *Perush Sodot ha-Tefillah*, MS Paris, Bibliothéque Nationale héb. 772, fol. 90b: "'The secret of the Lord is with those who fear Him' (Ps. 25:14). There are three secrets and they are: 'The secret of the Lord is with those who fear Him,' 'But His secret is with the straightforward' (Prov. 3:32), 'For He revealed His secret to His servants the prophets' (Amos 3:7), corresponding to the three patriarchs and the three sides of the throne above. Your sign for this is [the letter] *kaf*. This cannot be explained further except to those who are fearers [of God]." See printed text in *Perushe Siddur ha-Tefillah la-Roqeaḥ*, p. 402. The reference in that version to the letter *samekh* should be corrected because the throne is symbolized by the letter *kaf*, which also makes sense in this context in light of

the reference to three sides of the throne, the letter *kaf* being closed on three out of four sides. On the depiction of the throne in terms of the letter *kaf* in the Pietistic writings, reflecting an earlier aggadic motif, see above n. 209. It is evident that the secret in this case involves some sexual element connected particularly with the feminine nature of the three-pronged throne. See also above nn. 65 and 183. See also the passage concerning the divided throne in *Perush Sodot ha-Tefillah,* MS Paris, Bibliothéque Nationale héb. 772, fol. 170b cited above, n. 234. Cf. op. cit., fol. 49a (printed text in *Perushe Siddur ha-Tefillah la-Roqeaḥ,* p. 195): "The glory surrounds the prophet with a cloud the whole time that it speaks with him. This cannot be transmitted in writing but only orally." It is likely that the image of the prophet being surrounded by the glory also carries a sexual connotation. See, e.g., op. cit., fol. 152a (printed text in *Perushe Siddur ha-Tefillah la-Roqeaḥ,* p. 658): "The *ḥashmalah* is surrounded by the *ḥashmal.*" According to this passage, the enveloping reality is masculine (*ḥashmal*), and that which is enveloped is the female (*ḥashmalah*). If my interpretation is correct, then we have another piece of textual evidence that Eleazar emphasizes the esoteric nature of a doctrine and the need to transmit it orally in a context where the divine entity is described in terms of an erotic element. On the masculine valence accorded the image of enveloping, see the view of Joseph of Hamadan discussed in Liebes, *Studies in the Zohar,* pp. 105 and 208, n. 128. I note, parenthetically, that the image of the female enveloping the male can be found in certain texts, reflecting the locution of Jer. 31:21, "a woman shall encircle a man." Cf. the comment attributed to Samuel ben Naḥman in *Midrash Tehillim* 73:4, p. 335: "In this world the male surrounds the female but in the future the female will surround the male, as it says, 'a woman shall encircle the male.' " Cf. the kabbalistic text cited in "Erasing the Erasure," n. 145; *Book of the Pomegranate,* pp. 24, 89, 143, 327; and *Rabbenu Baḥya ᶜal ha-Torah* 2: 276, ad Exod. 25:18. On the role of the female encompassing the male, cf. the kabbalistic explication of *sukkah* included in Moses de León, *Nefesh ha-Ḥakhamah*: "The *sukkah* alludes to Wisdom, and Wisdom is feminine . . . she is a house for all the emanations for she encompasses everything." Cf. MS Paris, Bibliothéque Nationale héb. 772, fol. 171b (printed text in *Perushe Siddur ha-Tefillah la-Roqeaḥ,* p. 711) where a discussion about prophetic vision, and particularly the manifestation of the glory through the different divine names, that leads to an explication of the thirteen attributes of mercy is prefaced with the following remark: "This is the whole of the person to know the essence in order to praise Him that He is one. Therefore, David commanded his son, Solomon, 'Know the God of your father and serve Him' (1 Chron. 28:9). God does not grant that this is understood except by those who are straightforward in their hearts. I will write a little for one should not transmit everything in writing but only the main elements orally." The issue of esotericism is also linked to eroticism in Eleazar's *Perush ha-Merkavah,* MS Paris, Bibliothéque Nationale héb. 850, fols. 77b–78a:

> Ezekiel wanted to see the glory first but he could not. He saw the *ḥashmal* in order to know matters pertaining to the glory. Thus it is written, "Above the expanse over their heads was the sem-

blance of a throne, in appearance like sapphire; and on top, upon this semblance of a throne, there was the semblance of a human form. From what appeared as his loins up, I saw a gleam of amber—what looked like fire encased in a frame" (Ezek. 1:26–27). It did not say what it appeared like from his loins up, but it says in another place, "From his loins up, his appearance was resplendent and had the color of amber" (Ezek. 8:2). He did not want to explain what the splendor is. From here [it is deduced that] only the chapter headings are transmitted. . . . He linked the visions to the likeness of the *ḥashmal* and the likeness of the *ḥashmalah*, for there are strange visions of which the mouth is not permitted to speak.

354. The reference is to the nine occurrences of the word *marʾeh* in Ezek. 1:26–28.

355. MS Munich, Bayerische Staatsbibliothek 232, fol. 7b.

356. Based on a passage in B. ʿAvodah Zarah 3b. The motif is employed in *3 Enoch* and *Seder Rabbah di-Bereshit*, works related to the *Hekhalot* corpus. Cf. *Synopse* §§ 38, 441, 442, 746, 747, 837. Cf. *Sefer ha-Shem*, MS London, British Museum 737, fol. 361a: "He alone sees the 18,000 worlds." Cf. *Zohar* 1:24a; 3:226b (*Raʿayaʾ Mehemnaʾ*); *Zohar Ḥadash* 49b.

357. MS London, British Museum 737, fol. 316a.

358. In the continuation of this passage Eleazar extends the ontic angelification to anyone who dies with "proper teaching in his mouth and nothing perverse on his lips" (Mal. 2:6). In my chapter on Ḥaside Ashkenaz in *Through a Speculum That Shines* I have discussed the mimetic transformation of human beings into angels through the mystical praxis of mentioning the divine name. It is evident that other, more normative rituals were understood by Eleazar in precisely this vein. See above n. 348. Cf. Eleazar's description of the ritual of the fringe garment in *Sefer ha-Shem*, MS London, British Museum 737, fols. 261b–62a and *Ḥokhmat ha-Nefesh*, ch. 58, p. 101, and the text of Eleazar Seligman of Bingen, *Ḥiddushim Beʾurim u-Fesaqim* (Jerusalem, 1985), pp. 110–11 and *ʿArugat ha-Bosem*, 3:207, 234, 245. On the ritualistic application of the ancient mythic motif of God's sitting upon the throne of glory on Sabbath (cf. *Synopse*, § 849; *Bereshit Rabbati*, pp. 35–36; Ginzberg, *Legends*, 5: 110, n. 101; and Ginsburg, *Sabbath in the Classical Kabbalah*, pp. 103–4), cf. *Sefer Tagi*, MS Oxford, Bodleian Library 1566, fol. 247a: "Concerning all that which is said with respect to the matter of [the Sabbath hymn] 'For God who rested from all the acts [of creation],' so a person is obligated to rest. 'He ascended and sat [on the throne] in the highest heaven,' so too a person should sit in a palace in order to comfort his mind (*leharḥiv daʿato*; cf. B. Berakhot 57b)." Cf. *Sefer Ḥasidim*, § 628; *Perush Sodot ha-Tefillah*, MS Paris, Bibliothéque Nationale héb. 772, fol. 128b (printed text in *Perushe Siddur ha-Tefillah la-Roqeaḥ*, p. 526); and *ʿArugat ha-Bosem*, 4:125 n. 96.

359. The erotic implications of the entry of the high priest into the Holy of Holies on Yom Kippur are explicitly drawn in kabbalistic sources where the sexual myth of *hieros gamos* is blatant. See Liebes, *Studies in the Zohar*, pp. 65–66. On the special distinction of Yom Kippur as the propitious hour for mentioning the divine name, cf. *Sefer ha-Shem*, MS London, British Museum 737, fols. 308a, 334b–35a.

360. On the theurgical effect of the priest's utterance of the name on Yom Kippur, cf. *Sode Razayya*ʾ, ed. Kamelhar, p. 8, and MS New York, Jewish Theological Seminary of America Mic. 2430, fol. 67a. On other occasions the theurgical effect of mentioning the name in the Temple is assigned to Israel more generally. Cf. *Sefer ha-Shem*, MS London, British Museum 737, fol. 169a, and *Perush Sodot ha-Tefillah*, MS Paris, Bibliothéque Nationale héb. 772, fol. 110a (printed text in *Perushe Siddur ha-Tefillah la-Roqeaḥ*, p. 464). On the transforation of the high priest into an angel, cf. *Sefer ha-Shem*, MS London, British Museum 737, fol. 362a: "When the high priest entered the innermost [Holy of Holies] he was in the image of God."

361. The same verses from Song of Songs are employed by Eleazar to depict the union of the prophet and his celestial counterpart in the angelic realm that results from gnosis of the supernal mind of the glory. Cf. *Sefer ha-Shem*, MS London, British Museum 737, fol. 281a: "It is said, 'Let us make man in our image, after our likeness . . . in the image of God' (Gen. 1:26–27). . . . The angels are called *ʾelohim*. With regard to what is written, 'the semblance of a human form' (Ezek. 1:26), this is so that the prophet will know the supernal mind. 'I am my beloved's and my beloved is mine' (Song of Songs 6:3). 'My beloved is mine and I am his' (ibid. 2:16)." Cf. ibid., fols. 314b–15a where Song of Songs 6:3 and 7:11 are applied to the one who knows and mentions the seventy-two-letter name of God. Cf. ibid., fol. 367a. But cf. *Sefer ha-Shem*, MS London, British Museum 737, fol. 290b, where Eleazar cites Song of Songs 2:16 to depict the relationship of Meṭaṭron and God.

362. See, e.g., the *Sod ha-Yiḥud* of Eleazar published by Dan, *Studies*, pp. 86–87; *Shaʿare ha-Sod ha-Yiḥud we-ha-ʾEmunah*, pp. 147–48; and *ʿArugat ha-Bosem*, 1:200. This terminology is not unique to Eleazar, and its roots can be found in older sources. Cf. Nathan ben Yeḥiel, *Aruch Completum*, s.v., ספקלר, 6: 110: "The splendor (*ha-hod*) and the great glory (*ha-kavod ha-gadol*) refer to the glory of the Presence (*kevod ha-shekhinah*) concerning which permission has not been granted to any creature to see." Cf. the words of Ḥananel ben Ḥushiel cited in B. M. Lewin, *Otzar ha-Geonim to the Tractate Yebamot* (Jerusalem, 1984), pp. 123, 314. And cf. Judah ben Barzillai, *Perush Sefer Yeṣirah*, p. 12: "There is a glory above the glory, and the glory that is the great splendor (*ha-hod ha-gadol*) that is close to the Presence cannot be seen by man." See ibid., p. 22: "Many of the geonim, may their memory be for a blessing, explained that Akatriel . . . is from the light of the glory, blessed be he, and from the great splendor from which R. Ishmael saw a form." See G. Vajda, "Or ha-Sekhina: Compléments et Autocritique," *Revue des études juives* 134 (1975): 134. Cf. MS Oxford, Bodleian Library 1567, fol. 42a: "The glorious splendor (*hod kavod*) of the cherubim." Cf. MS

Jerusalem, Mussajoff 145, fols. 49b–50a: "The glory of the God of Israel by way of tradition: this glory is the splendor (*hod*) that is the glory of the Presence (*kevod ha-shekhinah*) and from it there emanates an angel whose name is Keruv, and some say Keruviel, and he participates with Gabriel, and the two of them are comprised of the attribute of power (*middat ha-gevurah*) and the attribute of loving kindness (*middat ha-ḥesed*)." In the *Baraita of Jonathan ben Uziel* the word *hod* designates the lower potency, the special cherub (*keruv ha-meyuḥad*), that emanates from the *nogah*, the glory of the Presence (*kevod ha-shekhinah*). See Dan, *Ḥugge ha-Mequbbalim ha-Rishonim*, pp. 101–2. Finally, let me note that in the *Hekhalot* literature the word *hod* is synonymous with *hadar*, and its signification is the luminous splendor of the glory. See, e.g., *Synopse*, §§ 33, 73, 252, 592.

363. Cf. *Perush ha-ʾAderet we-ha-ʾEmunah*, MS Vatican, Biblioteca Apostolica ebr. 228, fol. 107b: "On every heaven that the crown is glorified it expands more and more, and when it reaches the image of Jacob, our patriarch, which is engraved upon the throne of glory, then it expands according to the glory, and it is entirely glorified on account of the merit of Jacob, our patriarch." On this commentary and its relationship to Eleazar, see J. Dan, "Ashkenazi Hasidic Commentaries on the Hymn *Ha-ʾAderet we-ha-ʾEmunah*," *Tarbiz* 50 (1981): 396–404 (in Hebrew). It seems that underlying this text is the motif discussed in the body of this chapter, i.e., the erotic dynamic of the image of Jacob in relation to the glory is expressed here in terms of the expansion of the crown. While the expansion and glorification of the crown, woven from the prayers of Israel, occurs in each heaven, the process reaches its fullest expression when the crown arrives at the image of Jacob engraved upon the throne. Cf. the language cited by Ṣiyyoni (above in n. 248): "When the crown ascends to the head of the Creator the face of Jacob shines before Adiriron, the Lord, God of Israel." Here too the sexual nuance is obvious, especially the image of the shining face of Jacob, an image that is reminiscent of the passage from *Hekhalot Zuṭarti* cited above in n. 185. Cf. *Sefer ha-Shem*, MS London, British Museum 737, fol. 365b, and the German Pietistic text extant in MS New York, Jewish Theological Seminary of America Mic. 1878, fol. 44a. The latter text describes the ascent of the crown made from the prayers of Israel from Sandalphon to Meṭaṭron and from the latter to the image of Jacob engraved upon the throne. I translate at the point of the text when the crown has reached Jacob's image: "Then the crown is clothed in a shining fire upon which no eye can gaze on account of the abundant brightness. Immediately, all the creatures, ophanim, electrums, seraphim, and the throne of glory give splendid praise to the glorious king. Then the crown expands infinitely."

364. *Perush ha-Roqeaḥ ʿal Ḥamesh ha-Megillot*, p. 115 (cf. the version that I cited above in n. 199). Cf. the commentary to Song of Songs 1:2, op. cit., p. 101: " 'Oh give me of the kisses of your mouth,' in the Book of Hekhalot [it says that the glory] embraces and kisses the image of Jacob." Both of these passages from the pseudo-Eleazar commentary on Song of Songs are noted by Marcus, "The Song of Songs in German Hasidism and the School of Rashi," p. 188 n. 22. Despite the fact that the published commentary on Song of Songs attributed to Eleazar of Worms was not written by him, it is evident, as Marcus has noted (p. 185), that

there is much congruence between the commentary and the exegetical techniques delineated in Eleazar's *Sefer ha-Ḥokhmah*. From a thematic perspective as well the ideas expressed in the pseudo-Eleazar commentary share much with motifs found in Eleazar's own writings in general and specifically related to the Song of Songs. This is certainly the case with respect to the motif of the glory's embracing and kissing the image of Jacob derived from *Hekhalot Rabbati*, a motif that Eleazar too connects with the relevant verse from Song of Songs. See references cited in nn. 218, 230, 232, 336, 367. Finally, it is important to emphasize that a true appreciation of the Song of Songs in the esoteric theosophy of the German Ḥasidim requires a thorough examination of a significant number of printed pages and manuscript folios in which are scattered exegetical references to verses in this biblical text. The prominent place that Song of Songs occupied in their theological ruminations cannot be denied. A study limited to the literary genre of biblical commentary is necessary but hardly sufficient.

365. See above n. 181.

366. Cf. *Perush Sodot ha-Tefillah*, MS Paris, Bibliothéque Nationale héb. 772, fols. 76a, 77a, 127a, 132b (see *Persuhe Siddur ha-Tefillah la-Roqeaḥ*, pp. 325–26, 329, 514, 535); *Sode Razayya*ʾ, ed. Kamelhar, p. 29; and *Sode Razayya*ʾ, ed. Weiss, p. 43. It is worthwhile comparing the last mentioned source of Eleazar to the passage in *Zohar Ḥadash* 76c–d (*Midrash ha-Ne*ʿ*elam*).

367. *Sode Razayya*ʾ, ed. Kamelhar, p. 29.

368. *Ḥokhmat ha-Nefesh*, ch. 76, p. 129.

369. See above n. 87.

370. See above n. 92.

371. *Synopse*, §§ 163–64.

372. See above n. 180.

373. MS Paris, Bibliothéque Nationale héb. 772, fol. 132b, and with slight variations in MS Oxford, Bodleian Library 1204, fols. 157a–b (printed in *Perushe Siddur ha-Tefillah la-Roqeaḥ*, pp. 535–36).

374. *Sode Razayya*ʾ, ed. Kamelhar, p. 27.

375. MS Paris, Bibliothéque Nationale héb. 772, fol. 170b (printed text in *Perushe Siddur ha-Tefillah la-Roqeaḥ*, p. 708).

376. As I have explained (see nn. 253, 319, and 329), the feminine potency symbolized by the image of Jacob is located in the masculine potency, and, more specifically, in the phallus. That is to say, just as in the standard theosophic symbolism the feminine potency is the corona of the phallus, so too in the esoteric doctrine preserved and cultivated by the German Pietists.

377. See Scholem, *Major Trends*, p. 211, and M. Idel, *Golem: Jewish Magical and Mystical Traditions on the Artificial Anthropoid* (Albany, 1990), pp. 81–95.

378. See above n. 70.

379. *Major Trends*, p. 113.

380. Ibid., pp. 113–15; *Origins*, pp. 211, 215–16, 345–46. See also Altmann, "Eleazar of Worms' Ḥokhmath Ha-ʾEgoz," p. 107 n. 28. See above n. 70.

381. "Concept of the Merkabah," p. 309.

382. Ibid., pp. 312–13. The relevant text is cited above in n. 240.

383. See "Concept of the Merkabah," pp. 623–24: "There is no doubt that the description of the *ḥashmal* that appears in the circle of R. Judah the Pious . . . reveals a closeness to the description of the '*ḥashmal-pargod*' in the writings of the circle of the Special Cherub." See ibid., pp. 553–54 (see above nn. 67–68).

384. Cf. *Synopse*, §§ 33, 557; *Merkavah Shelemah*, 27b (see Elior, *Hekhalot Zuṭarti*, p. 70 n. 231–39); and *Sode Razayya*ʾ, ed, Kamelhar, p. 29. On the identification of Meṭaṭron and the cherub in the teaching of Isaac ben Yedaiah, see M. Saperstein, *Decoding the Rabbis: A Thirteenth-Century Commentary on the Aggadah* (Cambridge, Mass., 1980), p. 84.

385. "Concept of the Merkabah," pp. 310–11. See ibid., p. 560.

386. See above nn. 74–82.

2. The Tree That Is All: Jewish-Christian Roots of a Kabbalistic Symbol in *Sefer ha-Bahir*

* An earlier version of this study was published in the *Journal of Jewish Thought and Philosophy* 3 (1993): 31–76, and is here reprinted with the permission of the publishers.

1. See G. Scholem, *Origins of the Kabbalah*, trans. A. Arkush and ed. R. J. Zwi Werblowsky (Princeton, 1987), pp. 49–198, and H. Pedaya, "The Provençal Stratum in the Redaction of *Sefer ha-Bahir*," *Jerusalem Studies in Jewish Thought* 9:2 (1990):139–64 (in Hebrew). See also O. H. Lehmann, "The Theology of the Mystical Book Bahir and Its Sources," *Studia Patristica* 1 (1957):477–83. For a survey on the different opinions regarding the time of composition of *Sefer ha-Bahir*, see I. Weinstock, *Studies in Jewish Philosophy and Mysticism* (Jerusalem, 1969), pp. 15–50 (in Hebrew). I thank Moshe Idel for reminding me of this work. For a challenge to the conventional scholarly view regarding a twelfth-century Provençal setting for the redaction of *Sefer ha-Bahir*, see M. Verman, *The Books of Contemplation: Medieval Jewish Mystical Sources* (Albany, 1992), pp. 166–69, who suggests that the *Bahir* assumed its redactional form as a kabbalistic work in thirteenth-century Catalonia, perhaps in the circle of Ezra and Azriel of Gerona, the first authors to cite the *Bahir*. See n. 28. Steven Wasserstrom has graciously

shared with me his hitherto unpublished study of the *Bahir* in relation to the anonymous Shīʿi work *Umm al-kitāb*, which also incorporates a cosmology based on a Gnostic myth and the doctrine of metempsychosis. Concerning this work in general, see E. F. Tijdens, *Der mythologisch-gnostische Hintergrund des 'Umm al-Kitab'* (Leiden, 1977), and F. Daftary, *The Ismaʿilis: Their History and Doctrines* (Cambridge and New York, 1992), pp. 100–2. On the relation of this work to another source of Jewish esotericism, *Sefer Yeṣirah*, see the evidence adduced by S. Wasserstrom, "*Sefer Yeṣirah* and Early Islam: A Reappraisal," *Journal of Jewish Thought and Philosophy* 3 (1993): 1-30.

2. M. Idel, "The Problem of the Sources of the *Bahir*," *Jerusalem Studies in Jewish Thought* 6:3–4 (1987): 55–72 (in Hebrew); idem, *Kabbalah: New Perspectives* (New Haven, 1988), pp. 122–28.

3. See *Origins*, pp. 86–97, esp. 96, and 234, where the Gnostic character is said to have entered the *Bahir* "through an internal Jewish tradition," by which Scholem meant that the Gnostic motifs were transformed by aggadic modes of discourse or, as he puts it elsewhere, they were Judaized. See G. Scholem, *On the Mystical Shape of the Godhead*, trans. J. Neugroschel and ed. J. Chipman (New York, 1991), p. 158, where the *Bahir* is described as a "collection of short fragments, remnants, and reworkings of ancient fragments originating in Oriental gnosis, as well as fragments of theosophic aggadah." Even though in this context Scholem contrasts gnosis and aggadah, it is significant that he speaks of a theosophic aggadah by which he intended, I submit, internal Jewish traditions that parallel in some measure the mythic teachings of Gnosticism. See ibid., pp. 170–71, where Scholem observed that the images of the relationship of the *Shekhinah* to the masculine God in the *Bahir* "appear in all their original freshness, whether they were taken from the legacy of Gnostic speculation in late antiquity or whether they took shape in the course of the creative reflection of anonymous Jewish God-seekers of the twelfth century upon the meaning of the images of their own tradition." See following note.

4. *Origins*, p. 238. See the remark of B. A. Pearson, *Gnosticism, Judaism, and Egyptian Christianity* (Minneapolis, 1990), p. 28 n. 51: "In a letter to me (Jan. 28, 1973), Scholem stated his belief that the Gnostic revolt did indeed arise from within Judaism." See ibid., p. 125 n. 6: "It should be added, however, that Scholem has (orally) expressed his essential agreement with my (and others') arguments for the Jewish origins of Gnosticism (in the technical sense of the word used here)." See Scholem's own assessment in the lecture "Judaism and Gnosticism" delivered at Dartmouth College in 1965 and published in Hebrew translation in *Explications and Implications: Writings on Jewish Heritage and Renaissance*, vol. 2, ed. A. Shapira (Tel-Aviv, 1989), pp. 176–86.

5. See, e.g., *Origins*, pp. 82, 86, 123, 197, and *On the Mystical Shape*, pp. 158 (see n. 3), 170–71.

6. For discussion of the Bogomil heresy in the Bulgarian Empire, see H. C. Puech and A. Vaillant, *Le Traité contre les Bogomiles de Cosmas le Prêtre* (Paris, 1945); D. Obolensky, *The Bogomils* (Cambridge, 1948); M. Loos, *Dualist Heresy in the Middle Ages* (Prague, 1974), pp. 41–102; and the useful summary in M. Lambert, *Medieval Heresy: Popular Movements from Bogomil to Hus* (New York, 1976), pp. 12–23. For discussion of the Cathar doctrines, see S. Runciman, *The Medieval Manichee* (Cambridge, 1947); H. Söderberg, *La Religion des Cathares, Étude sur le gnosticisme de la basse antiquité et du Moyen Age* (Uppsala, 1949); A. Borst, *Die Katharer* (Stuttgart, 1953), pp. 143–222; Loos, *Dualist Heresy*, pp. 127–61; J. H. Duvernoy, *Le Catharisme, La religion des Les Cathares* (Toulouse, 1976); and Lambert, *Medieval Heresy*, pp. 108–50.

7. See *Origins*, pp. 14–16, 234–38, and references to the work of E. Werner and S. Shahar (see following note) cited on p. 234 n. 72. S. W. Baron, *A Social and Religious History of the Jews*, 8 (Philadelphia, 1958), p. 32, notes that the factors that led to the rise of the Albigensian and Catharist heresy in Western Christianity, particularly in Provence, may have been the same as those that led to the development of mystical theosophies amongst elite circles of Provençal Jewry; but see his more cautious remark on p. 288, n. 35. See also the passing comment of W. L. Wakefield, *Heresy, Crusade and Inquisition in Southern France, 1100–1250* (Berkeley and Los Angeles, 1974), p. 61. On the general attitude of Jews to the Catharist heresy, see J. Shatzmiller, "The Albigensian Heresy as Reflected in the Eyes of Contemporary Jewry," in *Culture and Society in Medieval Jewry: Studies Dedicated to the Memory of Haim Hillel Ben-Sasson*, ed. M. Ben-Sasson, R. Bonfil, and J. R. Hacker (Jerusalem, 1989), pp. 333–52 (in Hebrew). Shahar has also discussed the influence of Catharism on the thirteenth-century Jewish mystic Abraham Abulafia; "Ecrits Cathares et commentaires d'Abraham Abulafia sur le 'Livre de la creation,' images et idées communes," *Cahiers de Fanjeaux* 12 (1977): 345–62. For a critique of this thesis, see M. Idel, *Studies in the Ecstatic Kabbalah* (Albany, 1988), pp. 33–44.

8. See S. Shahar, "Catharism and the Beginnings of the Kabbalah in Languedoc: Elements Common to the Catharic Scriptures and the Book *Bahir*," *Tarbiz* 40 (1971): 483–507 (in Hebrew), and idem, "Le Catharisme et le début de la Cabale," *Annales* 29 (1974): 1185–1210. See also Wakefield, *Heresy, Crusade and Inquisition*, pp. 34–35, and R. I. Moore, *The Origin of European Dissent* (New York, 1977), pp. 139–67.

9. The material discussed by Shahar, "Catharism and the Beginnings of Kabbalah," pp. 488–91, deals with the image of the Tree of Life and/or the Tree of Knowledge but from a different vantage point than my discussion in this study.

10. See references to Scholem and Pedaya in n. 1, especially the latter who has also shown how attention to the redactional process can highlight the preservation of older traditions in the *Bahir*. On the laconic and fragmentary nature of esoteric traditions incorporated in the *Bahir* see the recent comments

of Ch. Mopsik, *Les Grands textes de la cabale: les rites qui font Dieu* (Paris, 1993), p. 109 n. 2.

11. Scholem, *Origins,* pp. 49–50; see idem, *On the Kabbalah and Its Symbolism,* trans. R. Manheim (New York, 1969), p. 90, where the *Bahir* is characterized as a "wretchedly written and poorly organized collection of theosophical sayings in the form of Bible commentaries, for the most part imputed to imaginary authorities supposedly living in the Talmudic period." See also Baron, *A Social and Religious History of the Jews,* 8, p. 32, who characterizes the *Bahir* as "essentially a combination of disjointed homilies, obviously stemming from different periods and different environments." See as well Baron's observations on p. 33: "Nor were the *illuminati* readers particularly interested in the sequence of the sayings, which from the very outset had almost never been arranged in any systematic or logical order." And p. 35: "For this reason even the order in which such speculations were arranged seemed immaterial. The sequence of the passages in the *Bahir* was probably from the beginning quite haphazard; its planlessness increased further as a result of constant accretions and deletions." See also Weinstock, *Studies,* pp. 51–76.

12. Scholem, *Origins,* pp. 71–72. See the description of Scholem's view in J. Dan, *Gershom Scholem and the Mystical Dimension of Jewish History* (New York and London, 1987), p. 135: "Scholem felt that the picture of the divine tree and its ten branches attested to the reliance of the sources of the *Bahir* on an ancient gnostic mythology and theology." See n. 55. For a slightly different characterization of the bahiric symbol, one that is in some measure closer to my own, see Scholem, *On the Kabbalah,* pp. 91–92.

13. On the demiurgic usage of the term *kol,* see E. R. Wolfson, "God, the Demiruge, and the Intellect: On the Use of the Word *Kol* in Abraham ibn Ezra," *Revue des ètudes juives* 149 (1990): 77–111. In that study I did not discuss the *Bahir* at all, but it seems to me that certain conclusions drawn from my analysis there could be applied to the relevant bahiric passages. It should also be noted that my comments here do not directly challenge Scholem's observation (*Origins,* pp. 69–70) that the word *male*ᵓ in *Sefer ha-Bahir,* § 4, corresponds philologically and conceptually to the pleroma in the Gnostic sources, although I do not think it necessary to assume, as Scholem does, that the "old gnostic terminology" is here subjected to reinterpretation and applied to the Torah. It is plausible that the *Bahir* preserves an ancient Jewish speculation on the pleroma that is identified with Torah or Wisdom. See E. R. Wolfson, "Female Imaging of the Torah: From Literary Metaphor to Religious Symbol," in *From Ancient Israel to Modern Judaism Intellect in Quest of Understanding: Essays in Honor of Marvin Fox,* ed. J. Neusner, E. S. Frerichs, and N. M. Sarna (Atlanta, 1989), 2: 285–91. Idel, "Problems of the Sources of the *Bahir,*" pp. 67–70, suggested several alternatives to Scholem's explanation of a Gnostic background to the term *male*ᵓ, including the use of the expression *pleroma* in the New Testament. Scholem, *Origins,* pp. 94–95, discussed the imagery

of the *Bahir* in light of the wedding hymn of the ancient apocryphal text, *Acts of Thomas,* whose relationship to Jewish Wisdom speculation has long been noted by scholars. See J. M. LaFargue, *Language and Gnosis: The Opening Scenes of the Acts of Thomas* (Philadelphia, 1985), pp. 98–99. On the Jewish-Christian rather than the Gnostic character of this work, and priority given to the Syriac over the Greek version, see A. F. J. Klijn, *The Acts of Thomas,* Supplement to *Novum Testamentum* 5 (Leiden, 1962), and idem, "The Influence of Jewish Theology on the Odes of Solomon and the Acts of Thomas," in *Aspects du Judéo-Christianisme, Colloque de Strassbourg, 23–25 avril 1964* (Paris, 1965), pp. 167–79. Moreover, it is evident from the parable that appears in *Sefer ha-Bahir* § 9 that the expression *kol* is used in a context that describes the totality of divine potencies. And see § 47 where the expression *kol temunah* (based on Deut. 4:12) is contrasted with *temunah,* i.e., the Israelites at Sinai were capable of visually apprehending the latter and not the former. It would seem from that context that *kol temunah* corresponds either to the upper six voices (which represent the divine hypostases) or the sixth of them. In either case in this context *kol* signifies the totality of divine potencies. I am concerned exclusively with the image of the tree that is designated *kol.* In the reworking in § 78 of the aggadic interpretation of Gen. 24:1 in B. Baba Batra 16b the word *ba-kol* refers to the *Shekhinah* who is identified as the daughter granted to Abraham. See G. Scholem, *Das Buch Bahir* (Leipzig, 1923), p. 54 n. 4, and *Origins,* pp. 87–89.

14. See Scholem, *Origins,* pp. 314, 422–23, 440; G. Sed-Rajna, "L'influence de Jean Scot sur la doctrine du kabbaliste Azriel de Gérone," in *Jean Scot Érigène et l'histoire de la philosophie* (Paris, 1977), pp. 453–63; M. Idel, "The *Sefirot* above the *Sefirot,*" *Tarbiz* 51 (1982): 242 n. 17, 243 n. 20, 267–68, and nn. 145-153 (in Hebrew); and Mopsik, *Les Grands textes de la cabale,* pp. 627–28.

15. See G. Scholem, *Major Trends in Jewish Mysticism* (New York, 1954), p. 109, and G. Vajda, "De quelques vestiges du néoplatonisme dans la kabbale archaïque et mystique juive franco-germanique," in *Le Néoplatonisme, colloques internationaux du CNRS, Royaumont 9–13 juin 1969,* ed. du CNRS, 1971, reprinted in idem, *Sages et penseurs sépharades de Bagdad à Cordoue,* ed. J. Jolivet and M. R. Hayoun (Paris, 1989), p. 166, and see Scholem's comment published at end of article, p. 170. See also Idel, "*Sefirot* above the *Sefirot,*" pp. 246 n. 41, 261 n. 110, 268. On the parphrase in general, see R. C. Kiener, "The Hebrew Paraphrase of Saadiah Gaon's *Kitāb al-Amānāt wa᾿l-Iʿtiqādāt,*" *AJS Review* 11 (1986): 1–25, and esp. 16–20, where the influence of the paraphrase on one of the early German Pietistic compositions, the *Shir ha-Yiḥud* (Hymn of Unity), is discussed.

16. The Jewish-Christian context makes sense for some of the essential features of ancient Jewish esotericism that continued to have a major impact in medieval theosophic kabbalah, to wit, anthropomorphic conceptions of God as well as the specific use of letter symbolism to characterize the divine body. See Scholem, *On the Mystical Shape,* pp. 25–35; M. Idel, "The Concept of Torah in

the Hekhalot Literature and Its Metamorphosis in the Kabbalah," *Jerusalem Studies in Jewish Thought* 1 (1981): 42 n. 53 (in Hebrew); idem, "The Image of Adam above the *Sefirot*," *Da*ᶜ*at* 4 (1980): 46–47 (in Hebrew); idem, "*Sefirot* above the *Sefirot*," pp. 274–77; idem, *Kabbalah: New Perspectives*, pp. 116–18; and the opinion of Idel cited by Y. Liebes, *Studies in the Zohar*, trans. A. Schwartz, S. Nakache, and P. Peli (Albany, 1993), pp. 240–41 n. 73. See also Y. Liebes, "The Angels of the Shofar and Yeshua Sar ha-Panim," *Jerusalem Studies in Jewish Thought* 6, 1–2 (1987): 194 n. 86 (in Hebrew). On the relation of Christian speculation on the anthropomorphic dimensions of Jesus and early Jewish conceptions concerning the measurable demiurgical angel, see G. G. Stroumsa, "Form(s) of God: Some Notes on Metatron and Christ," *Harvard Theological Review* 76 (1983): 269–88; M. Fishbane, "The 'Measures' of God's Glory in the Ancient Midrash," in *Messiah and Christos: Studies in the Jewish Origins of Christianity Presented to David Flusser on the Occasion of His Seventy-Fifth Birthday*, ed. I. Gruenwald, S. Shaked, and G. G. Stroumsa (Tübingen, 1992), pp. 53–74, esp. 70–72; and Ch. Mopsik, "La Datation du Chiʾour Qomah d'après un texte néotestamentaire," *Revue des sciences religieuses* 68 (1994): 131–44. See also study of J. Fossum cited below in n. 46. Mention here should be made of the influence of Jewish esotericism on the Elkesaite movement, which may have represented a particular form of Jewish Christianity as a variety of scholars have argued. See G. P. Luttikhuzien, *The Revelation of Elchasai* (Tübingen, 1985), pp. 4–37, 64–65, 212–13, and J. M. Baumgarten, "The Book of Elkesai and Merkabah Mysticism," *Journal for the Study of Judaism* 17 (1986): 212–23. For the influence of esoteric Jewish traditions on St. Ephrem the Syrian, see N. Séd, "Les Hymnes sur le paradis de Saint Ephrem et les traditions juives," *Le Muséon* 81 (1968): 455–501, and the more general influence noted by S. Brock, "Jewish Traditions in Syriac Sources," *Journal of Jewish Studies* 30 (1979): 212–32. On the relation between the early Syrian church and Jewish Christianity, see A. Vööbus, *A History of Asceticism in the Syrian Orient* 1 [*Corpus Scriptorum Christianorum Orientalium* 184, subs. 14] (Louvain, 1958), pp. 3–108, and G. Quispel, "The Discussion of Judaic Christianity," *Vigiliae Christianae* 22 (1968): 81–93. H. J. W. Drijvers, "Edessa und das jüdische Christentum," *Vigiliae Christianae* 24 (1970): 4–33, reiterates the view of W. Bauer, *Orthodoxy and Heresy in Earliest Christianity*, trans. from second German edition, ed. R. A. Kraft and G. Krodel (Philadelphia, 1971), that the earliest Syriac Church subscribed to a Gnostic form of Christianity. On the possible Syriac Christian milieu for the redaction of *Sefer Yeṣirah* in the sixth or seventh century, see S. Pines, "Points of Similarity between the Exposition of the Doctrine of the *Sefirot* in the *Sefer Yeẓira* and a Text of the Pseudo-Clementine Homilies," *Proceedings of the Israeli Academy of Sciences and Humanities* 7 (1989): 63–142. The importance of Christian doctrines on the formulation of later kabbalistic motifs from late-thirteenth- and early-fourteenth-century Castile has been discussed by some scholars; see Y. Baer, "The Historical Background of the Raᶜayaʾ Mehemnaʾ," *Zion* 5 (1940): 1–44 (in Hebrew), and Liebes, *Studies in the Zohar*, pp. 139–61.

17. Scholem, *Origins*, pp. 71–74; *On the Mystical Shape*, pp. 72–74; see A. Farber, "The Concept of the Merkabah in Thirteenth-Century Jewish

Esotericism—Sod ha-ʾEgoz and Its Development" (Ph.D. dissertation, Hebrew University, 1986), p. 616 (in Hebrew). See also Scholem's earlier explanation of the symbol of the All-Tree in *Das Buch Bahir*, p. 18 n. 3. Curiously, in the Valentinian Gnostic sources that Scholem cites in his later work, *Gospel of Truth* and *Gospel of Thomas*, the image of the tree is not mentioned; at best, in both sources the pleroma is designated as the All, and in the later case Jesus is characterized as the All whence everything proceeds. Cf. *Pistis Sophia*, ed. C. Schmidt and trans. V. Macdermot (Leiden, 1978), pp. 9–10, where Jesus reports that he has come from the All; see ibid., p. 185 where Jesus is described as the only one who knows the All and who is complete in the All; and see p. 328 where Jesus is characterized, on the basis of Rev. 3:7, which is an eschatological reworking of Isa. 22:22, as the key that opens and closes the door of the All. It should also be noted that in several passages in *Pistis Sophia* there is mention of the "dissolution of the All," which designates the completion of the number of perfected souls and, in some contexts, the ascent and reintegration of these souls in the pleroma; see pp. 36, 90, 198, 231, 244. Also significant is the identification of the All with the *iota* of the divine name ἰάω, i.e, YHW; see p. 353. If we assume that the letter *iota* should be understood in terms of its Hebrew equivalent *yod*, and thus is numerically equivalent to ten, then the All is here identified with the number ten in a way comparable to the Jewish mystical tradition. Noteworthy as well is the Jewish esoteric speculation on the "tittle of the *iota*" reported by the second-century Arab gnostic Monoimus, quoted by Hippolytus, *Refutation of All Heresies* 8: 7. See Idel, "*Sefirot* above the *Sefirot*," pp. 274–77, and idem, *Kabbalah: New Perspectives*, pp. 114–17. See also the speculation on the letter *yod* as the first letter of the Hebrew name of Jesus in St. Ephrem the Syrian, *Hymns on the Nativity* 27, in *Ephrem the Syrian: Hymns*, trans. and intro. K. E. McVey and Preface by J. Meyendorff (New York and Mahwah, 1989), pp. 211–13. See especially the following passage (p. 212): "Just as enumeration has only ten levels, there are six sides to the creation: the height and depth and four directions filled by You. The letter 'yodh' of Jesus, our King, is the Queen of all numbers. On her perfection depend all reckoning as in Jesus all meanings are mixed." This text bears a striking resemblance to *Sefer Yeṣirah* 1:13, where the lower six of the ten *sefirot* are delineated as the six extremities, which include height, depth, and the four cardinal points or directions. In the context of *Sefer Yeṣirah*, moreover, each cosmic dimension is associated with a different permutation of the divine name, YHW. Some similarities between Ephrem's thought and *Sefer Yeṣirah* have been drawn by Séd, "Hymnes sur le paradis," pp. 496–99, but he did not mention the passage that I have cited above. For an echo of this Jewish-Christian tradition in a later Ethiopian text regarding the *iota* as the first letter of the name Jesus and signifying the Decalogue, thought of as the heart of all the Torah, see E. Isaac, *A New Text: Critical Introduction to Mashafa Berhan* (Leiden, 1973), pp. 49–50, 115–18. However, the third source mentioned by Scholem, the report of the system of Simon Magus in Hippolytus' *The Refutation of All Heresies*, does in fact utilize the image of the Great Tree to characterize the indefinite power, also designated the elemental fire, that is the ontic source of all being. While the cosmogonic passages from the Slavonic

Book of Enoch that Scholem discussed do have some things in common with the *Bahir*, it seems to me that these similarities are largely coincidental and do not reflect precise terminological or conceptual parallels that would warrant considering this work a source (either direct or mediate) for the bahiric text. For a completely different approach to the historical background of the kabbalistic motif of the tree of divine powers, see S. Parpola, "The Assyrian Tree of Life: Tracing the Origins of Jewish Monotheism and Greek Philosophy," *Journal of Near Eastern Studies* 52 (1993): 161–208. Despite the fact that the author has raised some fascinating questions in his attempt to draw comparisons between the sefirotic tree of medieval kabbalists and the Assyrian tree in ancient Mesopotamian esoteric lore, I am not convinced that the sefirotic tree should be called "an adaptation of a Mesopotamian model" (p. 176). Moreover, the overriding assumption of Parpola's comparative analysis is that the doctrine of ten *sefirot* is the essential core of kabbalistic theosophy. The exegetical and conceptual issues that I have raised in my study on the motif of the All-Tree in *Sefer ha-Bahir* challenge this assumption.

18. See J. Danielou, *Théologie du Judéo-Christianisme*, 2nd ed. (Paris, 1991), pp. 165–99. On the thesis that Gnosticism originated out of apocalyptic Judaism, see R. M. Grant, *Gnosticism and Early Christianity* (New York, 1966), esp. pp. 27–38. On the use of the apocalyptic genre in Gnostic sources, see F. T. Fallon, "The Gnostic Apocalypses," *Semeia* 14 (1979):123–58.

19. On the phenomenon of a Jewish-Christian gnosis, see W. Bousset, *Hauptprobleme der Gnosis* (Göttingen, 1907), pp. 196ff., and idem, *Kyrios Christos*, trans. J. E. Steely (Nashville, 1970), pp. 54–56, 332–33. On the relation of different Gnostic sects and Jewish Christianity, see Daniélou, *Théologie du Judéo-Christianisme*, pp. 104–31. See also O. Cullmann, *Le probléme littéraire et historique du Roman Pseudo-Clémentin: étude sur le rapport entre le gnosticisme et le judéo-christianisme* (Paris, 1930), pp. 170–220; H. J. Schoeps, *Theologie und Geschichte des Judenchristentums* (Tübingen, 1949), pp. 305–15, 323–34; and the brief remarks of K. Rudolph, *Gnosis: The Nature and History of Gnosticism*, trans. R. McL. Wilson (San Francisco, 1983), p. 307. See I. P. Couliano, *The Tree of Gnosis: Gnostic Mythology from Early Christianity to Modern Nihilism* (New York, 1992), p. 127: "Jewish Christians were certainly more ready to step into a gnostic type of exegesis than Jews steeped in the hermeneutical subtleties of their own tradition." Couliano is not reducing Gnosticism to Jewish-Christianity in particular or Christianity in general, but rather argues that the Platonic biblical exegesis characteristic of Gnostic sources is best explained against a Christian background that was likewise based on a similar exegetical strategy. See ibid., p. 143 n. 233. Given that hermeneutical framework, the possible involvement of Judeo-Christians is greatly enhanced. On the centrality of exegesis in the formulation of heterodox views, see the remarks of R. Gershenzon and E. Slomovic, "A Second Century Jewish-Gnostic Debate: Rabbi Jose ben Halafta and the Matrona," *Journal for the Study of Judaism* 16 (1985): 1–41, esp. p. 10: "Since Jews, Christians, Samaritans and some Gnostics all considered the whole, or at least some portion of the Jewish

Scriptures to be canonical, it is not surprising that the most complex theological and philosophical issues should have been expressed in exegetical form." It follows, moreover, that the polemical approach to refute heretical doctrines would be primarily exegetical; see ibid., p. 3.

20. See J. Daniélou, "Judéo-Christianisme et Gnose," in *Aspects du Judéo-Christianisme*, pp. 139–66; R. McL. Wilson, "Jewish Christianity and Gnosticism," *Judéo-Christianisme: Recherches historiques et théologiques offertes en hommage au Cardinal Jean Danielou* (Paris, 1972), pp. 261–72; R. M. Grant, "Jewish Christianity at Antioch," *Recherches de sciences religieuses* 60 (1972): 98–99; and G. Filoramo, *A History of Gnosticism*, trans. A. Alcock (Oxford, 1990), p. 158. On the linkage of the study of Jewish Christianity and Gnosticism in nineteenth-century scholarship, see G. G. Stroumsa, "Gnosis and Judaism in Nineteenth Century Christian Thought," *Journal of Jewish Thought and Philosophy* 2 (1992): 59. I am here deliberately avoiding the related, although distinct, thesis regarding Judaism as the origin of Gnosticism, which has been discussed by various scholars, including G. Quispel, H. Jonas, R. McL. Wilson, R. M. Grant, G. Macrae, B. A. Pearson, I. P. Couliano, G. G. Stroumsa, and F. T. Fallon, to name but a few.

21. See S. Pétrement, *A Separate God: The Christian Origins of Gnosticism*, trans. C. Harrison (New York, 1990), pp. 468–76.

22. This is not to say that the symbol of the tree is entirely lacking in the corpus of Gnostic writings. On the contrary, it is found in several contexts usually reflecting a Christian background. See, e.g., *Gospel of Truth*, 18, 24–25, where it is said of Jesus: "He was nailed to a tree (and) he became a fruit of the knowledge of the Father" (*The Nag Hammadi Library in English* [New York, 1988], p. 41; henceforth *NHLE*). As a means of rectification for the fruit of the Tree of Knowledge eaten by Adam and Eve, those who partake of the fruit of Jesus are gladdened and gain gnosis. Cf. *Apocryphon of John* 21:16–22:9 (*NHLE*, p. 117); *Gospel of Philip* 74:3–10 (*NHLE*, p. 153); and *Hypostasis of the Archons* 88:25–89:2 (*NHLE*, p. 164). On the tree as a symbol for the cross, see also *Gospel of Philip* 73:8–17 (*NHLE*, p. 153); Clement of Alexandria, *Stromateis* 5: 11, 72:3. Cf. the testimony of Epiphanius, cited in B. Layton, *The Gnostic Scriptures* (New York, 1987), p. 207, regarding the gnostic interpretation of the Tree of Life that bears twelve crops a year as referring to a woman's monthly menstrual emissions. In none of these examples does the tree symbolize the pleroma. See, however, *Trimorphic Protennoia* 44:20 (*NHLE*, p. 518) where it seems that the tree signifies the pleromatic source of the souls, although even in that case the negative characterization of the tree prevails. See the account of Irenaeus regarding the tree of gnosis that sprouted forth from the anthropos cited in Layton, *Gnostic Scriptures*, p. 168.

23. See B. Bagatti, *The Church from the Circumcision: History and Archaeology of the Judaeo-Christians* (Jerusalem, 1971), pp. 224–28. On the symbolic identification of the Tree of Life in the thought of St. Ephrem the Syrian as the sun of Paradise, the glory of God, the Word, the first-born, the Son of

God, and the soul (or living breath) of this world, see Séd, "Hymnes sur le paradis," pp. 462, 468, 482–84, 487–88, 496. Note as well the figure on p. 462 (see also p. 460) where the Tree of Life is iconically portrayed as the center of the circle that depicts Paradise. It should be noted, however, that St. Ephrem also reflects the more conventional symbolism according to which the Tree of Life is related to the Cross; see ibid., p. 489 n. 79. See n. 117.

24. In other forms of Jewish-Christian theological speculation, as one finds for example in the "Gospel according to the Hebrews," wisdom is decidely feminine, identified as the Holy Spirit and the Mother, no doubt reflecting a Jewish Hellenistic milieu, most likely in Egypt. See A. F. J. Klijn, *Jewish-Christian Gospel Tradition* (Leiden, 1992), pp. 39–40, 54–55, 98–100. On the identification of the male Jesus and Wisdom, see n. 113.

25. It is well known that within the historical phenomenon of Jewish Christianity differing views with respect to the question of the divine vs. the human nature of Jesus were articulated, the Ebionites portrayed as rejecting the divinity of Jesus and the Nazarenes accepting it like orthodox Christians. This distinction is already reflected in Justin's *Dialogue with Trypho* and Origen's *Contra Celsum*, not to mention later authors. See R. A. Pritz, *Nazarene Jewish Christianity* (Jerusalem-Leiden, 1988), pp. 19–23. The mythologoumenon that I have attempted to reconstruct obviously would have been expressed in a Jewish-Christian group that accepted some form of incarnational doctrine of the demiurgical Logos/Sophia in the person of Jesus.

26. In response to my hypothesis regarding the polemic reworking of the Judeo-Christian tradition in the *Bahir*, Moshe Idel proposed an interesting alternative that should be seriously considered: perhaps there were traditions that circulated amongst Jews before the crystallization of Judeo-Christianity, and precisely these traditions influenced not only Jewish Christians but kabbalists in the Middle Ages. The advantage of this approach, as Idel remarked to me in a private letter, lies in the fact that it does not assume the need to neutralize Christological motifs. I have no methodological problem with the counter thesis that there may have been older Jewish esoteric traditions that preceded Judeo-Christianity. It seems to me, however, that the manner in which the particular motif of the androgynous phallus is employed in the bahiric contexts suggests a polemical tone against Christianity, reflecting thereby a specific moment in the redactional process. See n. 172.

27. For recent bibliography on this work, see R. Chazan, *Daggers of Faith: Thirteenth-Century Christian Missionizing and Jewish Response* (Berkeley, 1989), pp. 187–88 n. 3.

28. I have followed Scholem's suggestion, *(Origins*, p. 43 n. 74), that the key word *ḥbr* should be vocalized as *ḥubbar*, "was composed for," rather than *ḥibber*, "was composed by." The latter reading is accepted by Verman, *Books of Contemplation*, pp. 168–69, who uses this passage in support of his contention that the bahiric text was in fact composed in the circle of Geronese

kabbalists; see n. 1. For a different explanation of this expression, see Weinstock, *Studies*, pp. 33, 43–44.

29. Based on the expression, *ʾimre shafer*, in Gen. 49:21, where it has an entirely different meaning.

30. MS Parma, Biblioteca Palatina 2749 (De Rossi 155), fol. 232a. The text was published and translated in A. Neubauer, "The Bahir and the Zohar," *Jewish Quarterly Review* 4 (1892): 358–59. See also G. Scholem, "A New Document on the History of the Beginning of Kabbalah," in *Sefer Bialik*, ed. J. Fichman (Jerusalem, 1934), pp. 148–50 (in Hebrew), and Baron, *A Social and Religious History of the Jews*, 8, p. 37.

31. *Origins*, p. 43. See *On the Kabbalah*, pp. 90–91.

32. On the midrashic quality of the *Bahir*, see J. Dan, "Midrash and the Dawn of Kabbalah," in *Midrash and Literature*, ed. G. H. Hartman and S. Budick (New Haven, 1986), pp. 127–39, and the more nuanced analysis in D. Stern, *Parables in Midrash: Narrative and Exegesis in Rabbinic Literature* (Cambridge and London, 1991), pp. 216–24.

33. The effort to combat Christian misinterpretation of talmudic aggadot fits in with Meir ben Simeon's larger strategy to offset the impact of the augmented missionizing on the part of the Church directed at Jews in Western Christendom. See R. Chazan, "Polemical Themes in the *Milḥemet Miẓvah*," in *Les Juifs au regard de l'histoire: Mélanges en l'honneur de Bernhard Blumenkranz*, ed. G. Dahan (Paris, 1985), pp. 169–84. From another passage in *Milḥemet Miṣwah* it can be concluded with certainty that Meir ben Simeon was familiar with Christian heresies such as Catharist dualism. See Scholem, "A New Document," p. 152; idem, *Origins*, p. 237 n. 83; J. E. Rembaum, "Reevaluation of a Medieval Polemical Manuscript," *AJS Review* 5 (1978): 98 n. 64; and Shatzmiller, "Albigensian Heresy," pp. 341–43. It is evident from internal sources as well—e.g., an epistle of Asher ben David, the nephew and disciple of Isaac the Blind—that the kabbalists were viewed from the outside as espousing heretical and Christological doctrines. See Scholem, "A New Document," p. 151, and Shatzmiller, "Albigensian Heresy," pp. 351–52.

34. It should be borne in mind that rabbinic literature itself can be considered a conduit that preserved traces or echoes of Jewish-Christian doctrines and/or practices. Moshe Idel reminded me of the aggadic tradition regarding the souls of the righteous being dependent upon the soul of Adam, a motif that is found in Judeo-Christian sources and subsequent kabbalistic literature, traces of which may be detected in the *Bahir* itself (see §§ 57, 157). See L. Ginzberg, *The Legends of the Jews* (Philadelphia, 1968), 5:75 n. 19. The Jewish Christians are usually referenced in the talmudic and midrashic sources as *minim*, heretics, although that term can be used for a variety of other groups as well, including Samaritans, Sadducees, and Gnostics. See R. Trevors Herford, *Christianity in Talmud and Midrash* (London, 1903), pp. 97-341, and esp. p. 122: "A Min, as such, was not necessarily a Christian; but, as a matter of fact,

most of the heretics who came into strained relations with Jews were Christians, and more particularly Jewish Christians. . . . And thus it often happens that 'Jewish-Christian' is a correct equivalent of 'Min,' while yet it remains true that Min does not properly signify 'Jewish-Christian,' but only 'heretic.'" See n. 142. For a more recent discussion of the term *min* in rabbinic literature, see A. F. Segal, *Two Powers in Heaven: Early Rabbinic Reports about Christianity and Gnosticism* (Leiden, 1977), pp. 5–7, and other bibliography cited in the relevant notes. On the beliefs of Jewish-Christian groups regarding a multiplicity of angelic powers, to be distinguished from related cosmological schemes of the Gnostics, alluded to in rabbinic polemics, see the pertinent remarks of Segal, op. cit., pp. 115, 134, 188 n. 16, 200, 218, 226, 249 n. 17. But see pp. 257–58 where Segal suggests on the basis of passages in the Pseudo-Clementine literature that the Jewish–Christians and rabbis were attacking the same traditions concerning the multiplicity of divine powers.

35. See A. Schlatter, "Die Entwicklung des jüdischen Christentums zum Islam," *Evangelisches Missionsmagazin* 62 (1918): 251–64; Schoeps, *Theologie*, pp. 334–42; and the work of Pines cited in the following note.

36. See S. Pines, "The Jewish Christians of the Early Centuries of Christianity according to a New Source," *Proceedings of the Israeli Academy of Sciences and Humanities* 2 (1966): 1–74, esp. 44–50. See also S. Wasserstrom, "The 'Isawiyya Revisted," *Studia Islamica* 75 (1992): 57–80 (my thanks to the author who kindly called my attention to his study).

37. I note here a few representative examples of studies that have charted the historical development and spread of Jewish Christianity: H. J. Schonfield, *The History of Jewish Christianity* (London, 1939); M. Simon, *Verus Israel: Étude sur les rélations entre Chrétiens et Juifs dans l'Empire Romain* (Paris, 1948); G. Strecker, "On the Problem of Jewish Christianity," in Bauer, *Orthodoxy and Heresy in Earliest Christianity*, pp. 241–85; Bagatti, *Church from the Circumcision*; M. Simon, "Réflexions sur le judéo-christianisme," in *Christianity, Judaism and Other Greco-Roman Cults: Studies for Morton Smith*, ed. J. Neusner (Leiden, 1975), 2:53–76. See also references to work of Schoeps and Daniélou cited above, n. 19, and the study of Pritz cited in n. 25. Mention should also be made of Christian groups in Byzantium who practiced Jewish observances, such as circumcision and dietary laws. See G. Dagron, "Judaïser," *Travaux et Mémoires* 11 (1991): 359–80, cited in N. R. M. de Lange, "Jews and Christians in the Byzantine Empire: Problems and Prospects," in *Christianity and Judaism*, ed. D. Wood (Oxford, 1992), p. 21 n. 9. In general, the Byzantine context may be much more important for charting the development of Jewish esotericism than has hitherto been acknowledged in scholarly literature; see my study cited, below, n. 56.

38. See n. 172. A similiar claim has been made with respect to older Gnostic sources and their impact on medieval heresies. See, e.g., Lambert, *Medieval Heresy*, p. 23: "The living context of Gnosticism had long vanished, and the writings were used harmlessly as vehicles for a fairytale literature. In the hands of the Bogomils they were made to yield poison: through them

ancient material, going back to late Judaic apocalyptic as well as to Gnosticism, was used to body out heretical doctrine."

39. See Bagatti, *Church from the Circumcision*, pp. 40–49; Pritz, *Nazarene Jewish Christianity*, pp. 19–94; and Klijn, *Jewish-Christian Gospel Tradition*, pp. 27–39. Some of the other relevant texts include the *Didascalia, Odes of Solomon, Books of the Secret Enoch, Sibylline Oracles, Ascension of Isaiah, Testament of Solomon, Shepherd of Hermas, Gospel of Thomas*, and Pseudo-Clementine *Homilies* and *Recognitions*, to name a few. See W. D. Davies, "Paul and Jewish Christianity according to Cardinal Daniélou: A Suggestion," in *Judéo-Christianisme*, pp. 71–62. It is also possible that medieval Jewish sources were influenced indirectly by Jewish-Christian motifs transmitted through Arabic translations of earlier Syriac sources; see below, n. 41.

40. See S. Lieberman, *Greek in Jewish Palestine* (New York, 1942), pp. 185–91, and Liebes, *Studies in the Zohar*, pp. 150–52, 235–37 n. 56.

41. See the study of Pines cited above, n. 36, and idem, "'Israel, My Firstborn' and the Sonship of Jesus: A Theme of Moslem Anti-Christian Polemics," in *Studies in Mysticism and Religion Presented to Gershom G. Scholem* (Jerusalem, 1967), pp. 177–90.

42. See Pines, "Jewish Christians," pp. 70–73; preface of H. Corbin, "Harmonia Abrahamica," in L. Cirillo, *Évangile de Barnabé: Recherches sur la composition et l'origine*, text and translation by L. Cirrilo and M. Frémaux (Paris, 1977), pp. 5–17.

43. Liebes, *Studies in the Zohar*, pp. 156, 240–41 n. 73.

44. Liebes, "Angels of the Shofar," pp. 171–96. See also idem, "Who Makes the Horn of Jesus to Flourish," *Jerusalem Studies in Jewish Thought* 3 (1984): 313–48 (in Hebrew), and English summary by J. Chipman in *Immanuel* 21 (1987): 55–67. In the latter study Liebes argues that the formulation *maṣmiaḥ qeren yeshuᶜah* in the traditional prayer of eighteen benedictions, *ᵓet ṣemaḥ david*, reflects a Jewish-Christian alteration of the original language, *maṣmiaḥ qeren le-David*, expressing thereby the belief in Jesus (alluded to in the word *yeshuᶜah*, salvation, which would be related to the Hebrew name of Jesus, *yeshuᶜa*) as the Messiah and the hope for the Second Coming. For criticism of this article by I. Ta-Shema, M. Kister, and S. Morag, see *Jerusalem Studies in Jewish Thought* 4 (1985): 181–89, 191–207, and 345–51 (in Hebrew), and Liebes' responses, 209–14, 215–17, 353–54; see also the supplement of Liebes, op. cit., 341–44. Also relevant in this context is my own study, "The Image of Jacob Engraved on the Throne: Further Speculation on the Esoteric Doctrine of the German Pietists," in *Massuᵓot: Studies in Kabbalistic Literature and Jewish Philosophy in Memory of Prof. Ephraim Gottlieb*, ed. M. Oron and A. Goldreich (Jerusalem, 1994), pp. 131–85 (in Hebrew), and expanded English translation in this volume. The tradition that I reconstructed in the Kalonymide circle of German Pietists draws upon earlier traditions concerning the hypostatic image of Jacob, a tradition that has affinity with the idea of the glorified demiurgic angel cultivated by Judeo-Christians. See also E. R. Wolfson, "Meṭaṭron and Shiᶜur Qomah in the Writings of the Ḥaside

Ashkenaz," to appear in the proceedings of the conference on "Mystik, Magie, und Kabbala im Aschkenasischen Judentum," held at the Johann Wolfgang Goethe-Universität, Frankfurt, West Germany, Dec. 9–11, 1991.

45. See J. Dan, *The Esoteric Theology of German Pietism* (Jerusalem, 1968), pp. 220–21 (in Hebrew), and idem, "The Seventy Names of Meṭaṭron," *Proceedings of the Eighth World Congress of Jewish Studies—Division C* (Jerusalem, 1982), pp. 19–23.

46. See J. Daniélou, "Trinité et angélologie dans la théologue judéo-chrétienne," *Recherches science religieuse* 45 (1957): 5–41; idem, *The Origins of Latin Christianity* (London, 1977), pp. 149–52; C. Rowland, "The Vision of the Risen Christ in Rev. 1:13ff.: The Debt of Early Christology to an Aspect of Jewish Angelology," *Journal of Theological Studies* 31 (1980): 1–11; W. Carr, *Angels and Principalities* (Cambridge, 1981), pp. 143–47; J. E. Fossum, "Jewish Christian Christology and Jewish Mysticism," *Vigiliae Christianae* 37 (1983): 260–87; and idem, *The Name of God and the Angel of the Lord* (Tübingen, 1985), pp. 317–19. In this connection it is important to note that early Christian authors transferred functions or characteristics from Michael or Meṭaṭron to Jesus. See Ginzberg, *Legends of the Jews*, 5:305 n. 248.

47. My method, therefore, is congruent with that used most recently by Moshe Idel and Yehuda Liebes, who in a number of studies have looked to ancient Gnostic or pagan works to uncover older Jewish myths that are expressed as well in the kabbalistic literature. See M. Idel, "The Evil Thought of the Deity," *Tarbiz* 49 (1980): 356–64 (in Hebrew); idem, "*Sefirot* above the *Sefirot*," pp. 239–80; idem, "Image of Adam above the *Sefirot*," pp. 41–55; see also reference to Idel's work cited above in n. 2; and Y. Liebes, *Studies in Jewish Myth and Jewish Messianism*, trans. B. Stein (Albany, 1992), pp. 65–92.

48. A. Goldreich, "The Theology of the *Iyyun* Circle and a Possible Source of the Term '*Ahdut Shava*,' " *Jerusalem Studies in Jewish Thought* 6, 3–4 (1987): 141–56 (in Hebrew); M. Idel, "Franz Rosenzweig and the Kabbalah," in *The Philosophy of Franz Rosenzweig*, ed. P. Mendes-Flohr (Hanover and London, 1988), p. 167, and references given on p. 244 n. 24; idem, "Jewish Kabbalah and Platonism in the Middle Ages and the Renaissance," in *Neoplatonism and Jewish Thought*, ed. L. E. Goodman (Albany, 1992), pp. 343–44; and Liebes, *Studies in Jewish Myth and Jewish Messianism*, pp. 152–53 n. 3. See also reference to forthcoming work of Wasserstrom mentioned above in n. 1. The gnostic character of Ismāᶜīlism has been the focus of several studies by H. Corbin some of which follow. See "De la gnose antique à la gnose Ismaélienne," in *Oriente ed Occidente nel medio evo: Atti del XII convegno Volta* (Rome, 1957), pp. 105–43; "Épiphanie divine et naissance spirituelle dans la gnose Ismaélienne," *Eranos Jahrbuch* 23 (1954): 141–249 (English translation, "Divine Epiphany and Spiritual Birth in Ismailian Gnosis," in *Man and Transformation*, ed. J. Campbell [Princeton, 1964], pp. 69–160); "Herméneutique spirituelle comparée (I. Swedenborg-II. Gnose Ismaélienne)," *Eranos Jahrbuch* 33 (1964): 71–176; *En Islam Iranien: aspects spirituels et*

philosophiques (Paris, 1971), 2: 258–334; *Cyclical Time and Ismā*ʿ*īli Gnosis*, trans. R. Manheim and J. W. Morris (London, 1983); and *Temple and Contemplation*, trans. P. Sherrard with L. Sherrard (London, 1986). Locating proto-kabbalistic Judaism within an Ismāʿīli milieu does not preclude Jewish-Christian origins. On the contrary, it is plausible that doctrines expounded by Ismāʿīli authors reflect in part Jewish-Christian sources that may have been part of the literary heritage translated from Syriac into Arabic. See H. Corbin, *Face de Dieu, face de l'homme: herméneutique et soufisme* (Paris, 1983), pp. 156–57. On the general Jewish and Christian background of some ideas expressed in Ismāʿīli texts, cf. S. M. Stern, *Studies in Early Ismā*ʿ*īlism* (Jerusalem and Leiden, 1983), pp. 26–29.

49. For sources that deal with the relationship of German Pietism and theosophic kabbalah in Provence and Spain in the twelfth and thirteenth centuries, see E. R. Wolfson, "Merkavah Traditions in Philosophical Garb: Judah Halevi Reconsidered," *Proceedings of the American Academy for Jewish Research* 57 (1991):180 n. 3. To the sources cited there one should add M. Idel, "Intention in Prayer in the Beginning of Kabbalah: Between Germany and Provence," *Ben Porat Yosef: Studies Presented to Rabbi Dr. Joseph Safran*, ed. B. and E. Safran (Hoboken, 1992), pp. 5–14 (in Hebrew), and idem, "In the Light of Life: An Examination of Kabbalistic Eschatology," in *Sanctity of Life and Martyrdom: Studies in Memory of Amir Yequtiel*, ed. I. Gafni and A. Ravitsky (Jerusalem, 1992), pp. 191–211, esp. 205–7 (in Hebrew). See also I. Ta-Shema, "Ashkenazi Ḥasidism in Spain: R. Jonah Gerondi—the Man and His Work," in *Exile and Diaspora: Studies in the History of the Jewish People Presented to Professor Haim Beinart on the Occasion of His Seventieth Birthday*, ed. A. Mirsky, A. Grossman, and Y. Kaplan (Jerusalem, 1988), pp. 165–94 (in Hebrew), and E. Kanarfogel, "Rabbinic Figures in Castilian Kabbalistic Pseudepigraphy: R. Yehudah He-Ḥasid and R. Elḥanan of Corbeil," *Journal of Jewish Thought and Philosophy* 3 (1993): 77–109.

50. Scholem, *Origins*, pp. 39–41. See also J. Dan, "Pesaq ha-Yirah veha-Emunah and the Intention of Prayer in Ashkenazi Ḥasidic Esotericism," *Frankfurter Judaistische Beiträge* 19 (1991–92): 196, who suggests that the use of the term *malkhut* as a designation of the visible and anthropomorphic cherub in the writings of the pietistic circle of the Special Cherub is the source for the kabbalistic usage. In Dan's own language: "Despite many doubts and difficulties, it seems to me that the textual evidence does not leave any choice but to view the literature of this circle concerning the Special Cherub as the source of the kabbalistic usage, especially as there is a possibility that the Cherub is indicated even in the Book Bahir." The bahiric passage referred to by Dan, § 128, (see op. cit., n. 41), makes no explicit or implicit (as far as I can tell) mention of the cherub even though the technical term *meyuḥad* does appear in that context. See further Dan's remark in *The Early Kabbalah*, ed. and intro. by J. Dan, texts trans. by R. C. Kiener, preface by M. Idel (New York, 1986), p. 62 n. 4.

51. *Origins*, pp. 97–123.

52. See E. R. Wolfson, "Images of God's Feet: Some Observations on the Divine Body in Judaism," in *People of the Body: Jews and Judaism from an Embodied Perspective*, ed. H. Eilberg-Schwartz (Albany, 1992), pp. 155–62.

53. See esp. *Origins*, pp. 49–68.

54. Ibid, pp. 143–44; see also pp. 56–57, 147.

55. See ibid., p. 309: "We do not know into whose hands in the various Provençal groups the Book *Bahir* first fell. Nor do we know exactly where it underwent its final redaction. It is equally difficult for us to ascertain exactly where firsthand Oriental traditions concerning the archons and the aeons of the celestial world first found their way into these regions and where they were elaborated further in conjunction with the new doctrine of the sefiroth." See as well the summary account given by Dan in *Early Kabbalah*, p. 28: "One of the earliest and most important discoveries of Gershom Scholem . . . was the identification of the *Sefer ha-Bahir* . . . as the earliest disseminated text of Kabbalistic thought, the first to utilize the symbolism of the dynamic emanated *sefirot*." See idem, *Gershom Scholem and the Mystical Dimension*, p. 136: "The most important gnostic element in the *Bahir* is the list of the ten *ma᾿amarot*, or *logoi*, which constitute the divine pleroma in the *Bahir*, which is similar in many respects to the gnostic myth of the *aeons*." See above n. 11.

56. See Scholem, *Origins*, p. 81, and idem, *Kabbalah*, p. 314. For a challenge to Scholem's view see E. R. Wolfson, "The Theosophy of Shabbetai Donnolo, with Special Emphasis on the Doctrine of *Sefirot* in His *Sefer Ḥakhmoni*," *Jewish History* 6 (1992): 281–316.

57. An important exception is the work of Idel, which has demonstrated a more nuanced reading of the *Bahir*. See reference above, n. 2.

58. Given this tendency to level out the multiple and complex theosophies incorporated in the *Bahir* in light of a single doctrine of the ten *sefirot*, I have my doubts regarding Verman's conjecture that the bahiric text was redacted in Gerona; see above n. 1. It seems more likely that the Geronese kabbalists received the text and cast it in light of their sefirotic theosophy.

59. *Sefer ha-Bahir*, ed. R. Margaliot (Jerusalem, 1978), §§ 124–25.

60. A typical expression of this one-sided way of reading the *Bahir* is found in the following statement of Dan, *Early Kabbalah*, pp. 30–31: "The most important new element in the *Bahir* is the system of ten divine powers, arranged in a specified sequence and studied in great detail. . . . There are important and puzzling differences in the order, symbolism, and function of the *sefirot* as presented in the *Bahir* and among other thirteenth-century Kabbalists, but there is not a single Kabbalist who does not reflect—at least to some extent—the basic symbolism of the *Bahir*." In support of his contention that the doctrine of the ten *sefirot* is the "most important new element" in the *Bahir*, Dan mentions the section of the text that reflects on the ten utterances by means of which the world was created. This older aggadic motif is cer-

tainly developed in different parts of the *Bahir*, and other sections of the text affirm a system of ten powers. Nevertheless, from a quantitative and analytical perspective, the doctrine of ten potencies is not the most significant one in this text. It receives that centrality only in the hands of the first kabbalistic interpreters of the book whose lead has been followed by most contemporary scholars.

61. This search for origins is evident throughout Scholem's *ouevre*, especially the various books and articles he published dealing with the so-called beginning of kabbalah (*re᾿shit ha-qabbalah*), culminating in the *Ursprung und Anfänge der Kabbala* published in 1962 (French translation in 1966 and English translation in 1987). S. Handelman, *Fragments of Redemption: Jewish Thought and Literary Theory in Benjamin, Scholem, and Levinas* (Indiana, 1991), p. 8, has observed that Scholem and Benjamin "were passionately concerned with the problem of origins, the origins of religious, literary, and historical phenomena, and this concern reflected their troubled relation to the historical past."

62. Even the question of origins as it applies to textuality is an issue that has been called into question. See, e.g., V. M. Fóti, *Heidegger and the Poets: Poiesis, Sophia, Techne* (New Jersey and London, 1992), pp. 44–59.

63. See Filoramo, *A History of Gnosticism*, pp. 144–45, who similarly remarks that despite the claim of scholars that the "origins of Gnosticism cannot be located," one may still "seek to recover the structure, the internal patterns in the Gnostic system."

64. My methodological assumption, therefore, is in basic agreement with that of Moshe Idel, who has articulated a similiar approach in any number of his studies, including *Kabbalah: New Perspectives*; *Golem: Jewish Magical and Mystical Traditions on the Artificial Anthropoid* (Albany, 1990); and, most recently, *Ḥasidism: Between Ecstasy and Magic* (Albany, 1994).

65. See reference to Idel cited above, n. 2, and idem, "In the Light of Life," p. 211 n. 110.

66. *Genesis Rabbah* 1:3, ed. J. Theodor and Ch. Albeck (Jerusalem, 1965), p. 5; and repeated in 3:8, p. 24. For discussion of this passage and its original polemical context, see Segal, *Two Powers*, p. 137.

67. This is the first explicit example of a hermeneutical strategy employed in later kabbalistic sources as well to read the contextual sense (*peshaṭ*) as the esoteric (*sod*), or to see the latter within the former. Concerning this orientation in Naḥmanides, see E. R. Wolfson, " 'By Way of Truth': Aspects of Naḥmanides' Kabbalistic Hermeneutic," *AJS Review* 14 (1989): 129–53, and idem, "Beautiful Maiden without Eyes: *Peshaṭ* and *Sod* in Zoharic Hermeneutics," in *The Midrashic Imagination*, ed. M. Fishbane (Albany, 1993), pp. 155–203, where I develop further the ramifications of this principle, especially as it relates to select zoharic texts.

68. *Sefer ha-Bahir*, § 22.

69. *On the Mystical Shape*, pp. 98–101. For a different view expressed by Scholem, see *Das Buch Bahir*, p. 17 n. 1, and *Origins*, pp. 71–72.

70. *Sefer ha-Bahir*, § 102. Concerning this theme, see Scholem, *On the Mystical Shape*, pp. 88–139, and A. Green, "The Zaddiq as Axis Mundi in Later Judaism," *Journal of the American Academy of Religion* 45 (1977): 327–47.

71. Cf. the parable in *Sefer ha-Bahir* § 63 where the king is said to enter everything (*ha-kol*) in his chamber by means of the thirty-two paths. The term *ha-kol* in this context should be rendered in a technical sense as the male organ. In my opinion this semantic usage is evident in the following interpretation of Song of Songs 1:14 recorded in B. Shabbat 88b: " 'My beloved to me is a spray of henna blooms from the vineyards of En-gedi' (*ʾeshkol ha-kofer dodi li be-kharme ʿein gedi*): The one to whom all belongs forgives me for the sin of the goat that has covered me (*mi she-ha-kol shelo mekhapper li ʿal ʿavon gedi she-karamti li*)." God is thus designated the "one to whom all belongs," *mi she-ha-kol shelo*, based on a wordplay of the biblical idiom *ʾeshkol*, which in fact may have been read as *ʾish kol*, i.e., the anthropos to whom all belongs, *ʾish she-ha-kol bo*. (Cf. *Yalquṭ Shimʿoni*, par. 984, and *Midrash Rabbah Shir ha-Shirim*, ed. S. Dunasky [Tel-Aviv, 1980], 1:59, p. 47, where Ben Gezirah [or, according to an alternative reading, Nezirah] interprets *ʾeshkol* as a reference to God, the "man in whom is everything," *ʾish she-ha-kol bo*; and see p. 46, where this precise etymology is applied to the anthropological sphere; i.e., *ʾeshkol* refers to the man who possesses everything, for he has mastered the different forms of Jewish learning. See also B. Soṭah 47b where the mishnaic reference to *ʾashkolot* is rendered as *ʾish she-ha-kol bo*.) What is the meaning of this appellation? Does it simply mean rhetorically that God possesses everything or that all things derive from and hence belong to God? In my view there is encoded here a theosophic tradition, and the word *kol* designates the phallus. (For a theosophic interpretation of the midrashic gloss on *ʾeshkol* as *ʾish she-ha-kol bo*, without necessarily referring to the phallus, see *Perush Rabbenu ʾEfrayim ʿal ha-Torah*, ed. E. Korach, Z. Leitner, and Ch. Konyevsky [Jerusalem, 1992], p. 214; for more discussion on this text see n. 93.) Support for my reading may be gathered from the continuation of the passage: God, or the one to whom the All belongs, is said to have forgiven (*mekhapper*, based on the word *ha-kofer*) the sin of the goat, *ʿavon gedi*, based on the expression *ʿein gedi*. But what is the sin of the goat? Traditional talmudic commentators explain this reference in terms of the sin of the golden calf or that of idolatry more generally. The rationale for this interpretation is the fact that the goat and the calf are specified as animals used in idolatrous practices. In my opinion, however, this is not a sufficient explanation. I would suggest that the sin of the goat may have a sexual connotation. (It is plausible that one should transpose the last two letters of the word *gedi* to derive the word *gid*, which can in fact connote the male organ. The use of the goat as a symbol of sexual virility and fecundity is not uncommon in the history of religions; see B. A. Litvnskii,

"Sheeps and Goats," in *The Encyclopedia of Religion*, ed. M. Eliade [New York, 1987], pp. 233–34.) Assuming the correctness of my interpretation, one understands perfectly the exegetical strategy of the tradent of this tradition (the passage appears in the Talmud in the context of other interpretations of verses from Song of Songs explicitly attributed to Joshua ben Levi); i.e., God who has the attribute that corresponds to the phallus, designated as the all, *ha-kol*, can atone for a sin related to the penis. It is also of interest to compare this expression, *mi she-ha-kol shelo*, to another explanation regarding the appelation of God as Solomon in Song of Songs in B. Shavu^cot 35b: "Every Solomon mentioned in Song of Songs is holy [i.e., refers to God], a song to the one to whom peace belongs (*shir li-mi she-ha-shalom shelo*)." In the continuation of the passage, two views are mentioned regarding certain verses that are an exception to this hermeneutical rule, the principle of exclusion in each case being that a particular verse clearly cannot be interpreted in an erotic manner. It is generally thought that this statement removes the eroticism of the song by allegorizing its overtly sexual language. It may be the case, however, that according to certain rabbinic figures, amongst whom should be included R. Aqiva, the allegorical reading in fact eroticized the divine-human relationship. Viewed in this light, the exegetical statement, every Solomon mentioned in the Song, with one exception, refers to God who is the king to whom peace belongs, provides the hermeneutic key for the viability of the allegorical reading; i.e., God is characterized as having a phallus that is designated as *shalom*. On this usage in rabbinic literature, see esp. B. Shabbat 152a. On the designation of God and His name as *shalom*, see B. Shabbat 10b, Sanhedrin 55b. It seems to me, therefore, that underlying both of these rabbinic passages is a theosophic tradition regarding the divine phallus, in one instance referred to as *kol* and the other as *shalom*, two terms used frequently in later kabbalistic sources to designate the *membrum virile* of the macroanthropos. See n. 86. Cf. *Sefer ha-Bahir*, § 65, where the theosophic implications of the passage that Solomon is the one to whom peace belongs are made explicit. The word *shalom* elsewhere in the *Bahir* is linked particularly with the phallus or with that which occupies the position of the middle that corresponds to the phallus. See, e.g., §§ 11 (the archon of peace, *sar shalom*, is said to mediate between Gabriel on the left and Michael on the right; see the more conventional formulation of this view expressed in § 108, where Truth in the middle is linked to Uriel who mediates between Gabriel and Michael; and § 137 where Jacob is identified as the attribute of truth [*middat* ᵓ*emet*] and the attribute of peace [*middat shalom*], in this case reflecting the contemporary theosophic symbolism; see also §§ 153, 190), 58, 75. In this connection it is also of interest to consider the following statement in B. Sanhedrin 98b: "It is written, 'Ask and see: surely males do not bear young! Why then do I see every man with his hands on his loins like a woman in labor? Why have all faces turned pale?' (Jer. 30:6). What is [the meaning of] 'I see every man' (*ra*ᵓ*iti kol gever*)? Rabba bar Isaac said in the name of Rav: The one to whom all strength belongs (*mi she-kol gevurah shelo*)." One will readily acknowledge the similarity between this reading and the previous passages that espouse theosophic traditions about

God. From the context, moreover, it is evident that the expression "every man" (*kol gever*) is interpreted as a reference to God to whom all strength (*kol gevurah*) belongs. It is possible that the term *gevurah* here too functions as a technical theosophic term for the phallus, the seat of strength and generative power, which quite naturally is connected with the loins mentioned specifically in the biblical text. There is thus an interesting gender ambiguity expressed here: in virtue of a *membrum virile* God may be compared to a woman who gives birth. Liebes, *Studies in Jewish Myth and Jewish Messianism*, pp. 39–40, discusses this passage and notes its relationship to the statement regarding Solomon as the king to whom peace belongs. He does not, however, interpret either passage as a reference to a divine phallus. On the contrary, he emphasizes that God is feminized as the mother who gives birth. In my opinion the masculine God is not feminized, rather the feminine image of a woman in labor is masculinized. The divine phallus is the generative source. Finally, it seems to me that the rabbinic statement, "the seal of the Holy One, blessed be He, is truth" (B. Shabbat 55a), also relates to a theosophic tradition concerning the divine phallus, designated in this context as the *ḥotam*. On the relation of this word to the penis, or more specifically the rite of circumcision, see E. R. Wolfson, "Circumcision and the Divine Name: A Study in the Transmission of Esoteric Doctrine," *Jewish Quarterly Review* 78 (1987): 77–112, esp. 77–85, and the relevant notes. On the possibility that the aforementioned talmudic saying may have been Judeo-Christian in origin, relating to the Christian symbol of the *taw* as a cross, see Liebes, *Studies in the Zohar*, p. 236 n. 56. (For a later Christological reading of the talmudic saying, see the dream-vision of Abner of Burgos cited by Y. Baer, *A History of the Jews in Christian Spain*, trans. L. Schoffman [Philadelphia, 1961], p. 329.) See n. 105. For an alternative interpretation, relating the word *ʾemet* to a hypostatic angel, see Idel, *Golem*, pp. 308–10. Cf. *Sefer ha-Bahir*, § 75, where the head of God is identified as truth and peace. From the relevant verse that is cited, "the beginning of Your word is truth," *roʾsh devarkha ʾemet* (Ps. 119:160), it is evident, moreover, that the head refers to the Logos. See ibid., §§ 50 (see n. 85), 58. Is this another Christological allusion in the bahiric text? On the application of Ps. 119:160 to Jesus, see evidence adduced by Liebes, *Studies in the Zohar*, pp. 235–36 n. 55. See further below, n. 78. The association of Ps. 119:160 and Gen. 1:1 figures in earlier cosmological speculation of the rabbis, perhaps for polemical reasons; see Segal, *Two Powers*, pp. 135–36. On the description in Col. 1:15 of Jesus as the "first-born of all creation" and its relation to Hellenistic Jewish traditions about Sophia, see Fossum, *Name of God*, pp. 315–17.

72. By contrast, in *Sefer ha-Bahir* § 119 the tree is explicitly described as the divine powers that are stacked one atop the other. However, in that context, which in my view reflects a later stage of theosophic reflection, the term *kol* is not used. See also § 103, which seems to intimate a different usage of the world *kol* connected more specifically with *Ḥokhmah,* here understood as the first of ten potencies.

73. See reference to my study cited above in n. 13. Steven Wasserstrom called my attention to the fact that Shahrastani reported that the Maghariyya identified God as an angel who is represented in the Torah as a tree. The demiurgic connotation of the angelified tree implied by this statement provides a significant parallel to my interpretation of the bahiric material. On the identification of angels as trees, cf. the view of Justinus reported by Hippolytus, *The Refutation of All Heresies*, 5: 21.

74. See *Sefer ha-Bahir*, § 95, where mention is made of the tree of God that has twelve diagonals that correspond to the different cosmic dimensions. The core idea of that text, elaborated in a complex way in the continuation, involves the symbol of the cosmic tree with twelve aspects. The demiurgic connotation is obvious in this context as well. Is this an implicit reference to the twelve tribes of Israel that represent the most basic dimensions of the cosmic tree? Is there further some echo of the Christian motif of the twelve apostles that are related to Jesus like branches to a tree? See § 113 where God is said to possess twelve tribes parabolically compared to the twelve channels of a spring. On the special relationship between the trunk of the tree and its heart (*guf ha-ʾillan we-libbo*) and Israel, see ibid., § 98.

75. See Wolfson, "Circumcision and the Divine Name," p. 101 n. 73.

76. *Sefer ha-Bahir*, §10.

77. It is of interest to note Scholem's comment in *Das Buch Bahir*, p. 11 n. 3, to the effect that the word *kol* in this context, unlike other bahiric passages, is not a technical mystical term for a specific emanation, but rather signifies the universe in general. In my view, by contrast, in this context the word *kol* does in fact have a technical meaning, for it connotes the demiurgic entity that comprises within itself the needs of everything created.

78. A similiar play on the Hebrew word *baraʾ* and the Aramaic *beraʾ* is operative in *Zohar* 1:3b and 2:178b (*Sifraʾ di-Ṣeniʿutaʾ*), as pointed out by Liebes, *Studies in the Zohar*, pp. 53–54.

79. See *Sefer ha-Bahir*, § 53, where the word *zahav* is said to comprise three attributes, the masculine (*zakhar*) symbolized by the *zayin* (cf. § 80), the feminine soul (*neshamah*) symbolized by the leter *heʾ* insofar as there are five grades of soul, and the *bet*, which is the foundation of the other two (*qiyyumam*). It is of especial significance that the prooftext cited in conjunction with the *bet* is Gen. 1:1, the first two words *bereʾshit baraʾ*, beginning with that very letter; I suggest that the word *baraʾ* should be read in this context as *beraʾ*, the son who establishes the *zayin* and the *heʾ*, the masculine and the feminine. (For a different interpretation of this passage, see Scholem, *On the Mystical Shape*, pp. 165–66.) My reading is supported by the parable given in § 54 in which the king marries his daughter to a prince. The king continues to be joined to the princess through a window, which obviously symbolizes both separation and union. A similiar set of relationships is

implied in the parable in § 63. The term *qiyyumam,* "their foundation," may also have a particular phallic connotation. See Y. Liebes, *Sections of the Zohar Lexicon* (Jerusalem, 1976), p. 358 n. 13 (in Hebrew). For a similiar idea expressed by Ezra of Gerona, see *Commentary on Talmudic Aggadoth by Rabbi Azriel of Gerona,* ed. I. Tishby (Jerusalem, 1945), p. 20 (in Hebrew), where the letter *lamed* (in the expression *la-ḥokhmah* in Prov. 7:4) is said to refer to the All (*kol*) by means of which the efflux of Wisdom (*mesekh ha-ḥokhmah*) is drawn forth to *Binah.* It is evident that in this context the word *kol* denotes the phallic aspect of *Ḥokhmah,* which acts as the conduit to bestow the divine efflux upon *Binah.* The appropriateness of the letter *lamed* to symbolize the phallus is related to its upward extension, which is underscored by its connection to the image of the tower that reaches into the air. See commentary of Rashi to B. Sanhedrin 106b, s.v., *be-migdal ha-poreaḥ ba-ʾawir; Zohar* 2:91a; and *Zohar Ḥadash* 66b, 70a. See also *Zohar Ḥadash* 58a where the *migdal ha-poreaḥ ba-ʾawir* seems to be connected with the aspect that correponds to the phallus in the upper recesses of the Godhead where the spark begins to emanate and to produce the measure that is the anthropomorphic configuration of the divine. I have elaborated on the phallic character of this aspect of the divine in "Woman—The Feminine as Other in Theosophic Kabbalah: Some Philosophical Observations on the Divine Androgyne," in *The Other in Jewish Thought and History: Constructions of Jewish Culture and Identity,* ed. L. Silberstein and R. Cohn (New York, 1994) and "Erasing the Erasure/ Gender and the Writing of God's Body in Kabbalistic Symbolism," in *Circle in the Square: Studies in the Use of Gender in Kabbalistic Symbolism* (Albany, 1995). On the identification of *Ḥokhmah* as the All (*ha-kol*), see comment of Azriel in *Commentary on Talmudic Aggadoth,* p. 90, and see also p. 99.

80. See *Sefer ha-Bahir,* § 23. See also § 159 where the seventh potency of the divine is compared parabolically to the spring that fills up for the needs (*ṣorekh*) of the other six potencies. It seems to me that all of these sources belong to the same layer of tradition. See, by contrast, § 87, where divine Thought (*maḥshavah*) is described as the "king that everything created in the world, the upper and lower beings, needs." It is evident that this is a later reworking of the older theme found in some of the other bahiric passages discussed in the body of the paper concerning the Demiurge that is the All or the All-Tree.

81. It is worthwhile to recall here the widespread Christological interpretation of Gen. 1:1, and in particular the first word of the verse, *bereʾshit,* as an allusion to the Trinity. For references see D. Berger, *The Jewish-Christian Debate in the High Middle Ages* (Philadelphia, 1979), pp. 233–34. In light of my interpretation of the bahiric passage it is of interest to mention the system of three principles in the Gnostic heresy of the "Book of Baruch" by Justinus as reported by Hippolytus, *The Refutation of All Heresies,* 5:21. According to Justinus, there are three unbegotten principles, two male and one female. The first is the "unbegotten good," the second the "father of all begotten things" called "Elohim," and the third the female principle called "Edem" or "Israel."

Although not precisely identical to the bahiric triad of Wisdom, the All, and Elohim, the similarity is noteworthy.

82. *Sefer ha-Bahir*, §§ 17–20.

83. See ibid., § 70, where the *ʾalef* is described as being in the image of the ear or that of the mind, and hence this letter appropriately represents the attribute of Thought. This is obviously a later reworking of the letter symbolism in light of the more crystallized theosophy regarding divine Thought. See also § 79.

84. On the phallic nature of the *gimmel* in later kabbalistic sources, see Wolfson, "Circumcision and the Divine Name," p. 100 n. 72.

85. *Sefer ha-Bahir*, § 155. See also the description of the spinal cord, symbolized as the bent *nun*, in § 83. In my opinion the Galenic view also underlies the statement in § 50:

> It has been taught: "It is the glory of God to conceal a matter," *kevod ʾelohim haster davar* (Prov. 25:2). What is the [signification of the word] *davar*? As it is said, "Truth is the essence of Your word," *roʾsh devarkha ʾemet* (Ps. 119:160). "And the glory of a king is to plumb a matter," *u-khevod melakhim ḥaqor davar* (Prov. 25:2). What is [the signification of the word] *davar*? As it is written, "a phrase well turned," *davar davur ʿal ʾofnav* (ibid., 11). Do not read *ʾofnav*, but rather *ʾofanav*.

The glory of God that must be concealed is the head, and the glory of kings that is revealed are the ophanim, which represent the testicles (cf. § 178 where the *ʾofane ha-merkavah* also seem to symbolize the aspect of God that corresponds to the testicles). The seminal fluid is conceived in the brain in a hidden state and revealed through the testicles in more concrete form.

86. See B. Shabbat 104b; *Midrash ʾOtiyyot de-R. ʿAqivaʾ*, in *Batte Midrashot*, ed. S. Wertheimer (Jerusalem, 1980), 2: 345, 358; E. R. Wolfson, "Circumcision, Vision of God, and Textual Interpretation: From Midrashic Trope to Mystical Symbol," *History of Religions* 27 (1987): 213. See especially Jacob ben Jacob ha-Kohen, *Perush ha-ʾOtiyyot*, ed. G. Scholem, in *Maddaʿe ha-Yahadut* 2 (1927): 206, where *gimmel* is identified as *shalom* (see above, n. 71) and is further associated with the covenant (*berit*), i.e., the male organ. See also Moses of Burgos's commentary on the forty-two-letter name, printed in *Liqquṭim mi-Rav Hai Gaon*, together with the commentary *Ner Yisraʾel*, by Israel ben Shabbetai, the Maggid of Kozienice, 15a: "*ʾAlef-Bet* is *ʾav* (father) and the *gimmel* is peace (*shalom*); understand."

87. *Sefer ha-Bahir*, § 19.

88. See J. Daniélou, "La Typologie d'Isaac dans la Christianisme primitif," *Biblica* 28 (1947): 363–93.

89. See Baggati, *Church from the Circumcision*, pp. 190–91. On the possible phallic connotation of the term *gevurah*, see above n. 71.

90. On the symbolic import of the *bet* as Wisdom, the dwelling-place (*bayit*) of the world, see *Sefer ha-Bahir*, §§ 14–15, 55.

91. See, however, *Sefer ha-Bahir*, § 8, where it is said that the letter *he*ʾ was added to the name of Abraham so that he "would merit all the limbs of a human being," for the name Abraham is numerically equivalent to 248 in accord with the number of limbs in a person. In Abraham, therefore, "the composition [of the body], as it were, was completed" (*kivyakhol bo nishlam ha-binyan*) "for He made Adam in the image of God" (Gen. 9:6). Alluded to here is the correlation of Abraham and the phallus, the limb that not only comprehends all the other limbs, but the one that perfects or completes the whole bodily structure. The implied meaning of the bahiric text is made explicit in an anonymous kabbalistic commentary on the rite of circumcision in MS Vatican, Biblioteca Apostolica ebr. 236, fol. 78b. See Pedaya, "Provençal Stratum," pp. 148–49, who suggests that this passage from the *Bahir* reflects the kabbalah of R. Isaac the Blind. While I accept the possibility that some of the language here does indeed reflect the twelfth-century redaction, it appears to me that the tradition being reported is in fact a much older one. One of the main points that Pedaya asserts to support her contention is the semantic use of the word *binyan* to refer to the realm of emanation, a usage that she relates specifically to Isaac the Blind's theosophic interpretation of a motif in *Sefer Yeṣirah*. The fact of the matter is, however, that in the bahiric context the word *binyan* means primarily the composition of the body (*harkavat ha-guf*) in the sense that the term is used in M. ʾOhalot 2:1; T. ʾOhalot 3:4. While it is obviously the case that the body referred to in the *Bahir* carries theosophic implications, I see no reason to accept the claim that it reflects the technical terminology of Isaac the Blind, for that assumption is based on a reading of the bahiric text in light of the doctrine of the sefirotic edifice and the divine name cultivated by Isaac the Blind and other Provençal kabbalists. Those issues are not germane to the relevant passage from the *Bahir*. See also the theosophic reworking of the end of *Sefer Yeṣirah* in § 58, in which it seems that again Abraham is linked to the covenant that is the phallus, and cf. § 77. The connection of Abraham and the phallus seems to be implied as well in § 78 where there is a theosophic reworking of the aggadic interpretation of the word *ba-kol* in Gen. 24:1; see above n. 13. In that context Abraham is the third of three potencies parabolically characterized as the king, his older brother, and the servant. The third element seems to correspond to the phallus, which is complemented or fulfilled by the fourth gradation, which is the feminine potency, the daughter given to Abraham, the *ba-kol*, that is also parabolically described as the beautiful vessel with a pearl. See, by contrast, §§ 135–37 and 190–91, where Abraham is correlated with the attribute of mercy (*middat ha-ḥesed*). These passages clearly reflect a later redaction from a setting where the correlation of the three patriarchs and the three central *sefirot* had crystallized.

92. My formulation here reflects the comments of Nathaniel Deutsch who attended my seminar on the *Bahir* offered at the Jewish Theological Seminary of America in the spring semester 1993. The remarks of Deutsch were occasioned by my interpretation of the *Bahir* transmitted orally, and I think his observations have strengthened my reading.

93. It is noteworthy that, according to Scholem's interpretation of this passage, the "three consonants of the word *ʾish* indicate the three supreme powers of God" (*Origins*, p. 103), or they are "symbols of the three supreme sefiroth" (p. 104). That is, for Scholem, this text presumes the tenfold structure of the Godhead, and reference is made to the upper three of these ten potencies. See M. Idel, *Language, Torah, and Hermeneutics in Abraham Abulafia* (Albany, 1990), p. 96. Such a reading, however, is clearly based on the assumption that the text presupposes the doctrine of ten *sefirot*, an assumption that is borne out by subsequent kabbalists interpreting the *Bahir* (see, e.g., the Geronese text in MS Oxford, Bodleian Library 2456, fol. 9a, cited by Idel, op. cit., pp. 192–93 n. 63, and Menaḥem Recanaṭi, *Perush ha-Tefillot* [Basel, 1581], 34b) but not warranted by the text itself. The other passages from the *Bahir* that Scholem cites (p. 104 n. 96) also do not prove anything about the initial passage, as these texts have to be evaluated in a critical way, taking into consideration the redactional process. Scholem's citation from the thirteenth-century Ashkenazi figure Ephraim ben Shimshon seems to me to prove that the latter interpreted the text in a way that removed it from its "original" setting where the focus of the exegesis on Exod. 15:3 was the doctrine of three potencies constituting the divine pleroma (see *Das Buch Bahir*, pp. 22–23, and *Origins*, pp. 103–5). The Ashkenazi author profers a midrashic reading that relates the word *ʾish* to the different names of God revealed to the three patriarchs and the community of Israel at the Red Sea. I do not think this textual evidence indicates that there was another version of the *Bahir* circulating in Germany, but rather attests that there were midrashic, and nonkabbalistic, interpretations of the text in that cultural environment.

94. *Sefer ha-Bahir*, § 26. The Christian kabbalist Pico della Mirandola interpreted this bahiric text as a reference to the Trinity. See the thirty-third of his *Conclusiones Cabalisticae secundum opinionem propriam*, cited in Ch. Wirszubski, *Pico della Mirandola's Encounter with Jewish Mysticism* (Cambridge and London, 1989), p. 177: "Per hanc dictionem <*ʾish*> quae scribitur per Aleph, Iod, et Scin (et significat uirum) quae Deo attribuitur, cum dicitur [Exod. 15:3] Vir belli, de trinitatis mysterio per uiam Cabale perfectissime admonemur." See Wirszubski's comments on p. 178, esp. n. 19.

95. See *Sefer ha-Bahir*, § 70, where the *ʾalef* is linked to the image of the *hekhal ha-qodesh* and is further identified as divine Thought (see also § 154). Here again we have a later, Provençal adaptation of an earlier theosophic symbol. See Pedaya, "Provençal Stratum," pp. 149–53.

96. *Sefer ha-Bahir*, §§ 117–18. See also § 128 where the three occurences of the word *qadosh* in the Trisagion (Isa. 6:6:3) are related respectively to the

supernal crown, the root of the tree, and the one that cleaves and is united with the others, i.e., the aspect of the divine that is immanent in the world. Even in this context, which strikes me as being from a later redactional stratum, the root of the tree preserves a phallic and demiurgic connotation. See also § 176 where the palm branch (*lulav*) is identified as the root of the tree. In this case too there is an obvious phallic signification.

97. Ibid., § 119. Cf. MS Vatican, Biblioteca Apostolica ebr. 236, fol. 66a.

98. *Sefer ha-Bahir*, § 81. According to an alternative reading of this passage, the *reish*, or the second letter of the word *shoresh*, is described as that which is bent. See, e.g., commentary attributed to Meir ibn Sahula, *ʾOr ha-Ganuz*, ad locum. Concerning this commentary, see the different scholarly views discussed in Z. Galili, "On the Question of the Authorship of the Commentary *Or ha-Ganuz* Attributed to Rabbi Meir Ben Solomon Abi Sahula," *Jerusalem Studies in Jewish Thought* 4 (1985): 83–96 (in Hebrew). This reading serves as the basis for Scholem's translation in *Das Buch Bahir*, p. 55: "das Resch jeder Baum gekrümmt ist." However, an examination of MS Munich, Bayerische Staatsbibliothek 209, fol. 20b, the base text utilized by Scholem, does not warrant such a translation for the key words, *we-reish kol ʾillan*, are struck by a line that indicates deletion.

99. *Sefer ha-Bahir*, § 81. Pedaya, "Provençal Stratum," pp. 146–47, argues on philological and conceptual grounds that this passage reflects the redactional hand of kabbalists from the circle of Isaac the Blind. I have interpreted the text differently and thus do not see the need to relate it to the Neoplatonic idea suggested by Pedaya. Her claim that the language of the passage suggests a Provençal redaction is well taken, but this does not necessarily imply that on conceptual grounds as well this is the case. In short, I view this text as preserving a much older theosophic tradition. On the connection of the letter *shin*, the attribute of peace (*shalom*), and the element of air or spirit (*ruaḥ*) corresponding to Jacob, which occupies the central position of the phallus, see the anonymous *Shaʿare Ṣedeq* (Jerusalem, 1989), 6b.

100. *Sefer ha-Bahir*, § 80. In light of my interpretation of the bahiric symbol of the "bent" or "crooked" root of the tree, compare the discussion of M. Philonenko, "Une Arbre se courbera et se redressera (4Q385 2 9–10)," *Revue d'histoire et de philosophie religieuses* 73 (1993–1994): 401–4 (my thanks to Steven Wasserstrom for this reference). Although the specific motif that Philonenko traces from the Qumran fragment, which he assumes to be of Essene origin, to the medieval *Midrash ʾOtiyyot de-R. ʿAqivaʾ*, is not precisely identical to the cluster of images related to the symbol of the tree in the *Bahir*, it is nevertheless interesting to ponder the possibility of a similar trajectory to explain the transmission of the motifs that I have discussed.

101. On the Jewish-Christian tradition regarding the identification of Jesus as the manifestation of the divine name, see Daniélou, *Théologie du Judéo-Christianisme*, pp. 235–51. See also the comment of Pines cited by Liebes, "Angels of the Shofar," p. 192, n. 79. Concerning the image of the tree, see further in n. 118.

102. This sentence is missing from some of the manuscript witnesses of the text. See, e.g., MS Vatican, Biblioteca Apostolica ebr. 228, fol. 30a.

103. *Batte Midrashot* 2:397–98. For a later passage that incorporates this polemical stance against Christianity, embellished by the well-known kabbalistic principle that the shell precedes the fruit, see Abraham Lask, *ᶜAyin Panim ba-Torah* (Lemberg, 1865), 22a–b.

104. For a later retrieval of this letter symbolism, see the fourteenth of Pico's *Conclusiones Cabalisticae secundum opinionem propriam*, cited in Wirszubski, *Pico della Mirandola's Encounter with Jewish Mysticism*, p. 165: "Per litteram <*shin*> id est scin quae mediat in nomine Iesu significatur nobis cabalistice, quod tum perfecte quieuit tanquam in sua perfectione mundus cum Iod coniunctus est cum Vau, quod factum est in Christo qui fuit uerus dei filius et homo." See also *Epistola Ludouici Carreti ad Iudaeos* (Paris, 1554), p. 19 (no pagination in the original): "Caeterùm si multiplices tres iod he vau mutuo, Iod per he, emanabit nun. Nun per vau, prodibit sin: quod est os Domini. . . . Idcirco habet sin tria capita. Pone ergo ipsum in medio Iod vau, & prodibit Iesu, quod est nomen aptum unitioni duorum he, quod est nomé Christi." The corresponding Hebrew text reads:
אמנם אם תכפול שלשת אותיות יהו זו על זו י' בה' יצא נ' ונ' בו' יצא ש' והוא פי' יהוה. . . על כן היו
לש' שלשה ראשים שים אותה באמצע יו יצא ישו והוא השם הנאות להתאחדות שני ההין שהוא המשיח.
Elsewhere in this text special attention is given to the name יהשוה, which consists of a combination of the Tetragrammaton and the letter *shin*, the former representing the divine father, and the latter the divine son. This name, referred to as the "hidden and holy name through which miracles are accomplished," is revealed in the form of a magical key in a dream vision to the apostate author.

105. See Liebes, *Studies in the Zohar*, pp. 236–37 n. 56. Liebes mentions this passage, "deceit has no feet," but does not interpret it as an anti-Christian polemic. On the contrary, he suggests that the word truth (*ᵓemet*) in this context as well as others in rabbinic literature—e.g., "the seal of the Holy One, blessed be He, is truth" (B. Shabbat 55a)—may reflect a Jewish-Chrisitan tradition. As Liebes points out, the seal is the letter *taw*, the cross (see Bagatti, *Church from the Circumcision*, pp. 229–30), which stands metonymically for the word *ᵓemet*. See above n. 71.

106. Cf. *Genesis Rabbah* 20:5; *ᵓAvot de-Rabbi Natan*, ed. S. Schechter (Vienna, 1887), version B, ch. 42, p. 117; *Pirqe R. ᵓEliᶜezer*, ch. 14; and *Sefer ha-Bahir*, § 200. It is possible that already in some of these earlier sources there is an anti-Christian polemic, for the serpent is associated with the Messiah. See M. M. Kasher, *Torah Shelemah* (New York, 1944), 2: 269 n. 97. On the association of the letter *shin* with Satan, related more specifically to the principle of matter, see Abraham Abulafia, *ᵓOṣar ᶜEden Ganuz*, MS Oxford, Bodleian Library 1580, fol. 27b. On the relation of Satan and Jesus in Abulafia's writings, see Idel, *Studies in the Ecstatic Kabbalah*, pp. 45–61, esp. 50–54.

107. B. Shabbat 104a.

108. For discussion of this symbolism see my study referred to above n. 52.

109. This motif is developed as well in later kabbalistic literature; cf. *Zohar* 2:103a, 109a, 112a. It seems that this idea underlies the opening statement in the *Sifra*ʾ *di-Ṣeni*ʿ*uta*ʾ, *Zohar* 2:176b, concerning the Edomite kings—i.e., Christianity—who are found without their weapons. I have discussed this passage in "Woman—The Feminine as Other." See also the relevant discussion in Liebes, *Studies in the Zohar*, pp. 146–50, 156.

110. *Batte Midrashot* 2: 409.

111. M. ʾAvot 3:17.

112. *Periphyseon (The Division of Nature)*, trans. J. J. O'Meara (Montreal and Washington, 1987), Bk. 5, 823B–24A, pp. 478–79.

113. Needless to say, the identification of Jesus and divine Wisdom goes back to much earlier sources evident already in the New Testament. See Grant, *Gnosticism and Early Christianity*, p. 153; M. J. Suggs, *Wisdom, Christology, and Law in Matthew's Gospel* (Cambridge, 1970); F. Christ, *Jesus-Sophia: Die Sophia-Christologie bei den Synoptikern* (Zürich, 1970); J. S. Robinson, "Jesus as Sophos and Sophia," in *Aspects of Wisdom in Judaism and Early Christianity*, ed. R. Wilkens (Notre Dame, 1975), pp. 1–16, and in the same volume, E. S. Fiorenza, "Wisdom Mythology and Christological Hymns," pp. 29–33; C. M. Deutsch, *Hidden Wisdom and the Easy Yoke: Wisdom, Torah and Discipleship in Mt 11, 25–30* (Sheffield, 1987); and idem, "Wisdom in Matthew: Transformation of a Symbol," *Novum Testamentum* 32 (1990): 13–47 (I thank the author for providing me with a copy of this study).

114. See, by contrast, *The Books of Jeu and the Untitled Text in the Bruce Codex*, ed. C. Schmidt and trans. V. Macdermot (Leiden, 1978), p. 233, where Christ, who is said to contain the All, is described as the fruit of the All produced by the twelve aspects of Christ, also identified as the twelve depths.

115. Cf. 1 Cor. 8:6; Jn 1:3, 3:35, 13:3, 17:2; and Col. 1:15–20. See also Mt. 11:27 and Lk. 10:22; Eph. 1:22-23, 3:19; and Col. 2:9-10, 3:11. Needless to say, the association of the word *all* (πᾶς) with Jesus or the Father in the New Testament is based on similiar descriptions of God in the Old Testament as the creator of all things or the fullness thereof. See, e.g., Deut. 10:14; Isa. 44:24, 45:7; Job 41:3; and Ps. 24.1. Cf. *Theological Dictionary of the New Testament*, ed. G. Kittel and G. Friedrich, and trans. G. W. Bromiley (Grand Rapids, 1967), 5:889–96, s.v., πᾶς, ἅπας.

116. God the Father is also described by Eriugena as the plenitude of good things. See, e.g., *Periphyseon*, Bk. 4, 796A.

117. See *Theological Dictionary of the New Testament*, 4:40–41, s.v., ζύλον; R. Bauerreiss, *Arbor Vitae* (Munich, 1938); H. Rahner, "The Christian Mystery and the Pagan Mysteries," in *The Mysteries*, ed. J. Campbell (Princeton, 1955), pp. 380–87; M. Eliade, *A History of Religious Ideas* (Chicago and London, 1982), 2: 401–2; and ibid., p. 157. (Steven Wasserstrom kindly drew my attention to a recent critique of Eliade's notion of *axis mundi*, related to the motif of the World

Tree, in F. J. Korom, "Of Navels and Mountains: A Further Inquiry into the History of an Idea," *Asian Folklore Studies* 51 [1992]: 103–25.) In some Christian texts the tree of the crucifixion is said to derive from the Tree of Knowledge. See R. Nelli, "La légende médiévale du Bois de la Croix," *Folklore* 20 (1957): 3–12, cited by Shahar, "Catharism and the Beginnings of the Kabbalah," p. 490 n. 26. It is also relevant to note here another tradition that figured prominently in Christian art and literature, viz., the Tree of Jesse that represented a messianic elaboration on Isa. 11:1. See A. Watson, *Early Iconography of the Tree of Jesse* (London, 1934). For a later, elaborate development of this tradition into the idea of three trees that correspond to God's power represented in the Trinity, which is operative in three stages of history, see M. Reeves, "The *Arbores* of Joachim of Fiore," *Studies in Italian Medieval History Presented to Miss E. M. Janson—Papers of the British School at Rome*, 24 (1956): 57–81. See also B. McGinn, *The Calabrian Abbot: Joachim of Fiore in the History of Western Thought* (New York and London, 1985), pp. 109–10, and relevant notes.

118. On the identification of Christ as the Tree of Life in Ambrose, see M. Eliade, *Myths, Dreams, and Mysteries: The Encounter Between Contemporary Faiths and Archaic Realities*, trans. P. Mairet (New York, 1960), p. 67. There is no reason to assume that the Tree of Life in the celestial Paradise mentioned in Rev. (2:7, 22:2, 14, 19) is to be identified specifically with Jesus. This conception rather reflects the image of the heavenly Tree of Life found in Jewish apocalyptic sources. See H. Strack and P. Billerbeck, *Kommentar zum Neuen Testament aus Talmud und Midrasch* (Munich, 1926–1928), 3:792; 4:1123–124, 1143, 1152.

119. Bagatti, *Church from the Circumcision*, pp. 221–24.

120. See W. R. Schoedel, "'Topological' Theology and Some Monistic Tendencies in Gnosticism," in *Essays on the Nag Hammadi Texts in Honour of Alexander Böhlig* (*Nag Hammadi Studies* 3), (Leiden, 1972), pp. 88-108; in the same volume, J. Zandee, "Die Lehren des Silvanus. Stoischer Rationalismus und Christentum im Zeitalter der frühkatolischer Kirche," pp. 144–55; and idem, *The Teachings of Sylvanus (Nag Hammadi Codex 7, 4*) (Leiden, 1991), pp. 5, 462–63. As Zandee points out, even though this treatise of Silvanus is "definitely anti-gnostic," there are concepts expressed in this literature that are comparable to Gnostic sources, e.g., the negative theology. See op. cit., pp. 9, 465-67, 539-51.

121. The location of Alexandria is significant as other Judeo-Christian writings composed there have parallels to Jewish esoteric motifs and symbols. See A. F. J. Klijn, "Jewish-Christianity in Egypt," in *The Roots of Egyptian Christianity*, ed. B. A. Pearson and J. E. Goehring (Philadelphia, 1986), pp. 161–75. On the importance of Alexandria as a center for Gnostic activity, see Pearson, *Gnosticism, Judaism, and Egyptian Christianity*, pp. 10–28. The geographical location of Alexandria is also important in Liebes's reconstruction of the merging of a Jewish and Orphic myth regarding the first manifestation of God, Erikapaios, which he relates to a later myth concerning *ʾArikh ʾAnpin* expressed in the *Zohar*; see *Studies in Jewish Myth and Jewish Messianism*, pp. 72–73, 84. See idem, "The Messiah of the Zohar," in *The Messianic Idea in*

Jewish Thought: A Study Conference in Honour of the Eightieth Birthday of Gershom Scholem (Jerusalem, 1982), pp. 225–26 n. 20 (in Hebrew). I have cited the Hebrew original in this case because the relevant material has not been translated in the English version included in *Studies in the Zohar.*

122. See G. Quispel, "Review of J. Zandee: 'The Teaching of Silvanus' and Clement of Alexandria," *Vigilae Christiane* 33 (1979): 85; the detailed analysis by J. Zandee, "'The Teachings of Silvanus' (NHC 7, 4) and Jewish Christianity," in *Studies in Gnosticism and Hellenistic Religions Presented to Gilles Quispel on the Occasion of His Sixty-Fifth Birthday,* ed. R. van der Broek and M. J. Vermaseren (Leiden, 1981), pp. 498–584; and idem, *Teachings of Sylvanus,* pp. 2–3, 9–10, *passim.*

123. See *The Teachings of Silvanus (7, 4),* intro. and trans. M. L. Peel and J. Zandee, in *NHLE,* p. 379.

124. The description of Jesus as Wisdom personified, especially in the Gospel of Matthew, has been the subject of much scholarship. For references see above n. 113.

125. *The Teaching of Silvanus* 106, 21–22 (p. 390). See the lengthy exposition of this passage in Zandee, *Teachings of Sylvanus,* pp. 332–34. Zandee provides interesting parallels from Hellenistic Jewish and Judeo-Christian sources.

126. See *The Teaching of Silvanus* 101, 9–12 (p. 388).

127. Ibid. 101, 24–102, 5 (p. 388).

128. See Schoedel, "'Topological' Theology," pp. 92–99, esp. 97ff.

129. This identification of Christ may also reflect Jewish-Christian tradition as we find, e.g., in the *Gospel of Thomas,* log. 77, 46:23–28 (*NHLE,* p. 135): "Jesus said, 'It is I who am the light which is above them all. It is I who am the all. From me did the all come forth, and unto me did the all extend. Split a piece of wood, and I am there. Lift up the stone, and you will find me there." See Zandee, "Silvanus and Jewish Christianity," p. 537.

130. See Schoedel, "'Topological' Theology," pp. 104–5. On the gnostic usage of the term "All," see above n. 17, and see *Books of Jeu and the Untitled Text,* pp. 83, 226–27, 229, *passim.*

131. See Zandee, "Silvanus and Jewish Christianity," pp. 550–51. See also Daniélou, *Théologie du Judéo-Christianisme,* pp. 327–53, esp. 340ff. See the tradition of the Jewish-Christian Symmachus, preserved by Victorinus Rhetor, cited in Bousset, *Kyrios Christos,* p. 54: "dicunt enim eum ipsum Adam esse et esse animam generalem." Christ thus is the primal Adam who is the World-Soul, i.e., the Demiurge. For a convenient review of the tradition that identified Jesus as the Logos and the Demiurge, see J. Pelikan, *Jesus Through the Centuries* (New Haven and London, 1985), pp. 57–70.

132. See I. P. Sheldon-Williams, "Eriugena's Greek Sources," in *The Mind of Eriugena: Papers of a Colloquium, Dublin 14–18 July 1970,* ed. J. J. O'Meara and L. Bieler (Dublin, 1973), pp. 1–15.

133. In rabbinic literature this is one of the names of God based on Dan. 12:7. See also *Sefer ha-Bahir,* § 183.

134. Ibid., § 180. See Scholem, *On the Mystical Shape,* pp. 96, 100.

135. See *Sefer ha-Bahir,* §§ 82, 105, 171–72, 174, 178.

136. The association of Sabbath and the word "good" (*ṭov*) is already evident in Ps. 92:1. See, in particular, *Midrash ʾOtiyyot de-R. ʿAqivaʾ*, in *Batte Midrashot,* 2: 346–47.

137. *Sefer ha-Bahir,* §§ 57–58.

138. See T. Baarda, "'If You Do Not Sabbatize the Sabbath . . .': The Sabbath as God or World in Gnostic Understanding (Ev. Thom. Log. 27)," in *Knowledge of God in the Graeco-Roman World,* ed. R. Van den Broek, T. Baarda, and J. Mansfeld (Leiden, 1988), pp. 178–201. Steven Wasserstrom suggested to me that a Sabbath-Demiurge may be implied in the thought of Monoimus as related by Hippolytus in *The Refutation of All Heresies,* 8:7: "The world, then, as Moses says, was made in six days, that is, by six powers, which (are inherent) in the one tittle of the iota. (But) the seventh (day, which is) a rest and Sabbath, has been produced from the Hebdomad, which is over earth, and water, and fire, and air. And from these (elements) the world has been formed by the one tittle" (translated by J. H. Macmahon in *The Ante-Nicene Fathers,* ed. by A. Roberts and J. Donaldson [Grand Rapids, 1981], 5:121). According to my reading of this passage, it is not the seventh potency or the Sabbath that is the demiurgic power but rather the six potencies or six days, which are contained in the tittle of the iota. The iota is the monad that is comprised within the decade symbolized by the iota, and it corresponds to the Son of Man, which is the image of the invisible perfect man or the Father. Cf. *The Refutation of All Heresies,* 8:6:

> The monad, (that is) the one tittle, is therefore, he says, also a decade. For by the actual power of this one tittle, are produced duad, and triad, and tetrad, and pentad, and hexad, and heptad, and ogdoad, and ennead, up to ten . . . All things, however, have been produced, not from the entirety, but from some part of that Son of man. For . . . the Son of man is a jot in one tittle, which proceeds from above, is full, and completely replenishes all (rays flowing down from above). And it comprises in itself whatever things the man also possesses (who is) the Father of the Son of man.

Inasmuch as the tittle of the iota is equated with the six days or powers, it follows that the demiurgic potency is not the number seven but rather the number six. On the esoteric significance of the letter *waw,* whose numerical value is six, and its relation to the Son of God, see E. R. Wolfson, "Anthropomorphic Imagery and Letter Symbolism in the Zohar," *Jerusalem Studies in Jewish Thought* 8 (1989): 172 n. 112 (in Hebrew) and other sources cited ad locum. The conceptual similarity of Monoimus and later kabbalistic motifs has been noted by Idel (see studies cited above in n. 17) and in a forthcoming study of Wasserstrom (see n. 1).

139. The essentially negative character of the Demiurge in Gnostic sources, indeed a taxonomic feature of these texts, is a commonplace in the scholarly literature on Gnosticism. See, e.g., H. Jonas, *The Gnostic Religion* (Boston, 1963), pp. 57–58, 130–36, 190–94.

140. See Isaac, *A New Text-Critical Introduction to Mashafa Berhan*, p. 117: "Whosoever abolishes the first Sabbath, destroyed the name of Jesus which is called the Iota, in number ten."

141. See J. Daniélou, *The Bible and the Liturgy* (London, 1960), pp. 222–41. On the use of this motif in medieval polemical context, see Berger, *Jewish-Christian Debate*, p. 255 n. 1. The Christological identification of Sabbath as the prefiguration of the savior Jesus parallels the teaching found in rabbinic sources to the effect that Sabbath is a foretaste of the World-to-Come or, alternatively expressed, the World-to-Come is a day that is entirely Sabbath. For discussion of this rabbinic motif and its development in kabbalistic sources, see E. K. Ginsburg, *The Sabbath in the Classical Kabbalah* (Albany, 1989), pp. 65, 72, 84, 95–100, 133, 145–46 n. 46.

142. It is interesting to compare this mystery of the seven, i.e., the six extensions plus the seventh, with the inquiry of Jacob the Min, i.e., the Jewish Christian, in B. Megillah 23a concerning the six sections of the Torah-reading on the Day of Atonement. In that context as well an attempt is made to see a reference to the seventh, which completes the six in the enumeration in Neh. 8:4 of the individuals who stood to the left of Ezra when he rose to read from the Torah scroll. According to the reading proposed by the heretic (which in fact is the *sensus literalis* of the text), there are seven, not six, people to Ezra's left, and the seventh is Meshullam. R. Judah, however, interprets the verse in such a way that Meshullam is another name for Zechariah who was called that because he was complete in his ways. While the rabbinic exegesis circumvents the Jewish-Christian reading, the talmudic passage allows us to reconstruct the theological position underlying the latter, viz., the six are complemented by a seventh referred to as Meshullam, probably with the connotation of the complete or perfect one, from the root *shlm*. On the relation of the word *shalom* and the phallus, see above n. 71. Baggati, *Church from the Circumcision*, p. 97, interprets this in terms of the doctrine of Jesus and the six archangels of creation. Cf. ibid., pp. 186–87. See, however, Tosafot, Megillah 23a, s.v., *ʾamar yaʿaqov*, where doubt is expressed concerning the heresy of this figure. See Herford, *Christianity in Talmud and Midrash*, p. 332.

143. One wonders if some such conception of the eschatological Sabbath does not underlie the Jewish-Christian logion cited in Clement of Alexandria, *Stromateis* 5: 14, 96, 3: "He who seeks will not cease until he finds and having found he will marvel and having marvelled he will become king and having become king, he will rest." In *Stromateis* 2: 9, 45, 5, Clement cites a shortened version of this passage as a direct quote from the "Gospel accord-

ing to the Hebrews." See *Gospel of Thomas* 2, in *NHLE*, p. 126, and Klijn, *Jewish-Christian Gospel Tradition*, pp. 47–51.

144. This is an obvious parallel to the teaching found in rabbinic sources that associates Sabbath with the World-to-Come; see above n. 141. See especially *Midrash ʾOtiyyot de-R. ʿAqivaʾ*, in *Batte Midrashot*, 2:346, where the Sabbath is characterized as a *dugmaʾ* of the World-to-Come. Cf. *Zohar* 1:48a. In this context the word *dugmaʾ* should be rendered, like the Greek word whence it derives, παράδειγμα, as a copy, model or token. While an Aramaized form of the Greek εἴκων is not used here, as in the case of the Pseudo-Clementine *Homilies*, I think it is fair to conclude that the two terms function synonymously in these contexts.

145. *Zohar*, 2:88b, cited in I. Tishby, *The Wisdom of the Zohar*, trans. D. Goldstein (Oxford, 1989), p. 1223, and see further references given on p. 1263 n. 83. See also A. J. Heschel, *The Sabbath* (New York, 1951), p. 20, and Ginsburg, *Sabbath*, p. 277.

146. See Pines, "Sefer Yeẓira and the Pseudo-Clementines," pp. 96–97.

147. *Sefer ha-Bahir*, § 157. It may be significant that the part of the passage that describes the position of the Sabbath in relation to the other six days is in Aramaic whereas the rest of the text is in Hebrew.

148. See Ginsburg, *Sabbath*, pp. 65, 102–6. On the personification of Sabbath in a feminine form in an Ethiopian Jewish-Christian source, see Isaac, *A New Text-Critical Introduction to Mashafa Berhan*, p. 48. On the tradition of a feminine archangel called "Shabbat" transmitted in Falasha hymns, see the comment of Mospik, *Les Grands textes de la cabale*, p. 556 n. 12.

149. In other passages the *Bahir* posits an androgynous Sabbath corresponding to the male and female aspects of the Godhead, a motif that also had a profound impact on subsequent kabbalah. See Ginsburg, *Sabbath*, pp. 106–21.

150. The word *ṣefiyyah* is used in a technical sense to connote mystical vision in the literary compositions of the *Hekhalot* corpus. See Scholem, *Major Trends*, p. 358 n. 18. See also N. A. Van Uchelen, "Tosephta Megillah III, 28: A Tannaitic Text with a Mystic Connotation?" *Jerusalem Studies in Jewish Thought* 6, 1–2 (1987): 87–94 (English section), and R. Elior, "The Concept of God in Hekhalot Mysticism," in *Binah: Studies in Jewish Thought*, ed. J. Dan (New York, 1989), pp. 109–10.

151. See Scholem, *On the Mystical Shape*, p. 99.

152. *Sefer ha-Bahir*, § 45.

153. But see *Gospel of Egyptians* (Layton, *Gnostic Scriptures*, p. 106) where seven voices are the seven hypostases of the divine pleroma. Cf. statement of Eleazar of Worms in MS Oxford, Bodleian Library 1569, fol. 43a (and MSS New York, Jewish Theological Seminary of America Mic. 2411, fol. 9a and Parma, Biblioteca Palatina 2784, fol. 75b): "Therefore there are seven voices in the revelation of the Torah and seven voices before the *Shekhinah*." In that context Ps. 29 is cited as well.

154. Cf. *Sefer ha-Bahir*, § 140.

155. See Scholem, *On the Mystical Shape*, pp. 93–94. Scholem does not mention any exceptions to the claim that in *Sefer ha-Bahir* the *ṣaddiq* assumes the position of the seventh *sefirah* in the pleroma.

156. Cf. *Sefer ha-Bahir*, § 48.

157. B. Sanhedrin 98b; *Pirqe Rabbi ʾEliʿezer*, ch. 32.

158. *Sefer ha-Bahir*, § 86. Cf. the fragment extant in MS New York, Jewish Theological Seminary of America Mic. 1736, fols. 12b–14b, that deals with human history from creation until the messianic era from the vantage point of the double *nun*, which has both a pure and an impure manifestation. The world was created with the double *nun* alluded to in the expression *gan ʿeden*, which has two occurrences of the letter *nun*. However, beginning with the sin in the Garden of Eden, the double *nun* of holiness was overpowered by the double *nun* of impurity brought about by the serpent (*naḥash*). The impure state will be fully rectified only in the messianic era. That the final redemption signifies the *tiqqun ha-nunin* is alluded to in the fact that one of the traditional names of Messiah is *Yinnon* (see fol. 14b).

159. Scholem, *Origins*, p. 142. In "Woman—The Feminine as Other" I criticize Scholem's attempt to contrast the "Jewish gnosis" expressed in this bahiric passage with the "antinomian and encratist" tendencies expressed in Gnostic gospels on the basis that the former presents redemption as the conjunction of masculine and feminine principles, whereas the latter posits an overcoming of sexual differentiation through the re-establishment of an original androgynous state. I argue that the kabbalistic idea, expressed in the *Bahir* and in subsequent literature, also was predicated on a sexual union that involved a reconstitution of an original androgynous state in which the female is contained in the male. I would still maintain my critique of Scholem, but in the present context I am not concerned with exploring again the issue of gender attribution in terms of a more nuanced cultural anthropology.

160. On the identification of Messiah with the gradation of *Yesod*, the divine *ṣaddiq*, see Liebes, *Studies in the Zohar*, pp. 12–19. On the depiction of the messianic redemption in terms of *hieros gamos* in early kabbalah, see G. Scholem, *The Messianic Idea in Judaism* (New York, 1971), p. 343 n. 32; Liebes, *Studies in the Zohar*, pp. 67–71; and M. Idel, "Types of Redemptive Activity in the Middle Ages," in *Messianism and Eschatology: A Collection of Essays*, ed. Z. Baras (Jerusalem, 1983), pp. 266–75 (in Hebrew).

161. *Sefer ha-Bahir* § 61, corrected according to MS Munich, Bayerische Staatsbibliothek 209, fol. 18a.

162. See Liebes, *Studies in the Zohar*, p. 158. On the identification of the letter *ṣaddi* as Jesus, cf. *Midrash ʾOtiyyot de-R. ʿAqivaʾ*, in *Batte Midrashot*, 2: 408–9. See E. N. Adler, "Un Fragment araméen du Toldot Yéschou," *Revue des études juives* 61 (1910): 129–30; Scholem, *Das Buch Bahir*, p. 167.

163. In this context it must also be recalled that in *Sefer ha-Bahir*, § 182, Sabbath is described as androgynous; see above, n. 149.

164. Liebes, *Studies in the Zohar*, pp. 154–58.

165. See above, n. 160.

166. *Sefer ha-Bahir*, § 85, corrected according to MS Munich, Bayerische Staatsbibliothek 209, fols. 20b–21a.

167. On the symbol of the open *mem* see also *Sefer ha-Bahir*, § 37. In that context the open *mem* is associated with an aspect of the head, upon which is placed the crown or phylacteries, which also functions parabolically as the throne upon which the king sits and the phylacteries that he places upon his arm. While the language of this text is truly enigmatic, in general it seems to be depicting the *hieros gamos* in the divine world through various images, including that of coronation: the crown is the feminine potency, and the head, or more specifically the open *mem* of the head, is the masculine. See, by contrast, Scholem, *Origins*, p. 60, who interprets the open *mem* as a symbol of the feminine. See also Stern, *Parables in Midrash*, p. 221. For discussion of this bahiric parable and the other passages that utilize these images, see Wolfson, "Images of God's Feet," p. 161.

168. B. Shabbat 104a.

169. Liebes, *Studies in the Zohar*, pp. 148–50.

170. See *Commentary on Talmudic Aggadoth by Rabbi Azriel of Gerona*, pp. 49–50, noted by Liebes, *Studies in the Zohar*, p. 233 n. 45.

171. *Sefer ha-Bahir*, § 83.

172. On the centrality of the divine syzygy in the kabbalistic gnosis expressed in the *Bahir*, see Scholem, *Origins*, pp. 142–43, 158–60. Let me emphasize again that I am not denying the role of gender symbolism in earlier Judeo-Christian sources, a case in point would be the division of the cosmos into male and female syzygies found in the Pseudo-Clementine literature. See E. Hennecke, *New Testament Apocrypha*, ed. W. Schneemelcher, English trans. R. McL. Wilson (Philadelphia, 1965), 2: 545–46. (Ch. Mopsik, *Le Secret du marriage de David et Bethsabée* [Paris, 1994], pp. 20–25, has noted the affinity between a passage in Pseudo-Clementine *Homilies* 16, which interprets the plural form in Gen. 1:26 as a reference to the male God and the feminine Wisdom, and later kabbalistic discussions of the divine androgyne.) Moreover, according to the Jewish-Christian mythologem that I have reconstructed there is a male and a female aspect to the divine. It is also the case that in earlier Gnostic texts, especially the Valentinian *Gospel of Philip*, the task of the Messiah is to unite the male and the female in the bridal chamber. See especially *Gospel of Philip*, 70 (trans. in *NHLE*, p. 151): "If the woman had not separated from the man, she should not die with the man. His separation became the beginning of death. Because of this Christ came to repair the separation which was from the beginning and again unite the two, and to give life to those who died as a result of the separation and to unite them." See R. M. Grant, "The Mystery of Marriage in the Gospel of Philip," *Vigiliae Christianae* 15 (1961): 129–40, and J.-M. Sevrin, "Les Noces spirituelles dans l'Evangile selon

Philippe," *Le Muséon* 87 (1974): 143–93. On the resemblance of this passage to the orientation adopted in zoharic literature with respect to the messianic function of Simeon bar Yoḥai as one who redeems the world by uniting with the female Presence, see Liebes, "The Messiah," pp. 230–32 (I here cite the original Hebrew because the relevant material has not been translated in the English version). Liebes suggests (p. 232) that the text was written by Jews who became Christian and turned into Gnostics, the provenance of the text being third-century Syria. He even suggests that an Aramaic version of the text reached Moses de León in thirteenth-century Spain. On the affinity of this Gnostic text and Jewish motifs, see also M. Idel, "Sexual Metaphors and Praxis in the Kabbalah," in *The Jewish Family: Metaphor and Memory*, ed. D. Kraemer (Oxford, 1989), pp. 203–4, 217 nn. 33-34, and idem, "Jerusalem in Thirteenth-Century Jewish Thought," in *The History of Jerusalem: Crusades and Ayyubids, 1099–1250* (Jerusalem, 1991), pp. 266–67 (in Hebrew). While I do not disagree with the views of Liebes and Idel, I am focusing in particular on the move from a purely masculine to an androgynous phallus, which seems to me to indicate an internal undermining of the earlier Judeo-Christian tradition in light of the current doctrine that truly marked the essential turn of theosophic kabbalah. This does not negate the possibility that an earlier Judeo-Christian text advocated a concept of redemption based on the union of masculine and feminine in line with what developed in the medieval kabbalistic sources.

173. In this context it is important to note that already in the twelfth century, esoteric literature of the Jews was being used by apostates to prove the truths of Christianity. An early example of this polemical strategy is the case of Petrus Alfonsi who cites a *secreta secretorum* in his *Dialogi contra Judaeos* 6 (*Patrologia Latinae*, ed. J.-P. Migne, 157: 611) to illustrate that the Trinity is alluded to in the Tetragrammaton written as IEVE in a triangular diagram, IE at the top of the triangle, EV at the bottom left, and VE at the bottom right. A. Büchler, "A Twelfth-Century Physician's Desk Book: The *Secreta Secretorum* of Petrus Alphonsi Quondam Moses Sephardi," *Journal of Jewish Studies* 37 (1986): 206–12, suggests that the *secreta secretorum* comprised three works: the magical treatise from the talmudic period, *Sefer ha-Razim*; the ancient work of Jewish cosmology, *Sefer Yeṣirah*; and an alchemical text that may have been the pseudo-Aristotelian *Sirr al-Asrar*, originating in the eleventh or twelfth century. See esp. pp. 208–9, where Büchler discusses the passage referred to above from the *Dialogi*, which he relates to speculation on the three letter name, YHW, in *Sefer Yeṣirah*. The view that Petrus was using *Sefer Yeṣrah* in this context has recently been challenged by B. McGinn in an unpublished paper, "Cabalists and Christians: Some Reflections on the Role of Cabala in Renaissance Philosophy and Mysticism," pp. 6–8, which the author kindly placed in my hands. Most importantly, McGinn characterizes Petrus's citation from the *secreta secretorum* as an effort to "uncover a proof for the Trinity in mystical, esoteric (or should we say 'proto-kabbalistic'?) Judaism" (p. 6). Whatever the precise source referred to by Petrus as the *secreta secretorum*, it is significant, as McGinn correctly observed, that he was utilizing Jewish esoteric motifs of a protokabbalistic nature to demonstrate the

truths of Christianity. This may provide an important clue for understanding the crystallization in writing of mystical and theosophical truths on the part of Jews beginning in the twelfth century. The matter requires further study.

174. *Sefer ha-Bahir*, § 180.

175. Ibid., §§ 181–82; see above n. 149.

176. B. Yevamot 62a.

177. *Sefer ha-Bahir*, §§ 183–84. See Scholem, *On the Mystical Shape*, pp. 205–6.

3. Walking as a Sacred Duty: Theological Transformation of Social Reality in Early Hasidism

This chapter is a slightly revised version of my study to appear in *Hasidism Reappraised*, to be published by the Littman Library of Jewish Civilization, Oxford, England. I thank the publishers for permission to reprint this essay.

1. See B. Dinur, *Be-Mifneh ha-Dorot* (Jerusalem, 1955), pp. 134–47 (English translation by E. Lederhendler in *Essential Papers on Hasidism: Origins to the Present*, ed. G. D. Hundert [New York, 1991], pp. 86–208, esp. 134–43); J. Weiss, "The Beginnings of the Hasidic Way," *Zion* 16 (1951): 46–105 (in Hebrew); and idem, *Studies in Eastern European Jewish Mysticism*, ed. D. Goldstein (Oxford, 1985), pp. 3–42. For a criticism of Weiss's views, see S. Ettinger, "The Hasidic Movement: Reality and Ideals," *Journal of World History* 11 (1968): 251–66, reprinted in *Essential Papers on Hasidism*, pp. 226–43. See also Ettinger's contribution on Hasidism in *A History of the Jewish People*, ed. H. H. Ben-Sasson (Cambridge, 1976), p. 770, and M. Piekarz, *The Beginning of Hasidism: Ideological Trends in Derush and Musar Literature* (Jerusalem, 1978), pp. 22, 96–98, 136–37, 206–7 (in Hebrew). For a reformulation of Weiss's position, see S. Sharot, *Messianism, Mysticism and Magic: A Sociological Analysis of Jewish Religious Movements* (Chapel Hill, 1982), p. 148.

2. Weiss touches upon this aspect of the phenomenon from the perspective of the shift from the itinerant leader to the settled *ṣaddiq* who typically held court. See "Beginnings, " pp. 103–5 and *Studies*, pp. 17–22. Despite the usefulness of some of his remarks, he is still more concerned with the implications of this shift for the social history of the Hasidic movement than with the intrinsic theological significance of the itinerant image. The spiritualization of the physical journey is a much older motif in Jewish sources. For example, cf. the passage of Saadya Gaon on the benefit of journeys, printed in *Saadya's Commentary on Genesis*, ed. M. Zucker (New York, 1984), pp. 431–35 (my thanks to Dr. Zev Gries for calling my attention to this reference). Cf. *Rabbenu Baḥya ʿal ha-Torah*, ed. C. D. Chavel (Jerusalem, 1981), 1:142–43, ad Gen. 13:17.

3. In Hasidic sources the words for travel or journey and walking are used interchangeably, a fact that reflects two of the basic meanings of the root *halakh*, "to walk from one place to another" or "to travel by means of some vehicle." Hence, in my treatment of the motif of walking, *halikhah*, I will also discuss passages dealing with travel, *nesiᶜah*. See, e.g., Jacob Joseph, *Ketonet Passim*, ed. G. Nigal (Jerusalem, 1985), p. 75, where *halakh* is used synonymously with *nasaᶜ*. See ibid., p. 243. A notable exception to this is the famous chorus to a song of one of the Hasidim of Menaḥem Mendel of Kotsk: "To Kotsk one does not travel (*furt men nisht*). To Kotsk one may only walk (*geyt men*). . . . To Kotsk one must walk as does a pilgrim (*darf men oyleh regel zeyn*)." See A. Green, "The Zaddiq as Axis Mundi in Later Judaism," *Journal of the American Academy of Religion* 45 (1977): 329–30. In this case walking as a sacred pilgrimage (*ᶜaliyat regel*) to see the master in his court is distinguished from everyday mundane travel. On the phenomenon of the pilgrimage to the rebbe on the part of hasidim, see A. Wertheim, *Halakhot we-Halikhot ba-Ḥasidut* (Jerusalem, 1960), trans. E. Lederhendler in *Essential Papers on Hasidism*, pp. 374–78. (For a different rendering, see A. Wertheim, *Law and Custom in Hasidism*, trans. Sh. Himelstein [Hoboken, N.J., 1992], pp. 236–41.) My concern, then, is not with *halikhah* in the narrow sense of physical walking, but with the broader sense of traveling or journeying. Nevertheless, as will be seen in the course of this analysis, the essential component of movement by foot remains a critical part of the use of *halikhah* in the Hasidic sources.

4. That the act of walking was used as a metaphor for the spiritual quest in Jacob Joseph's thought can be adduced from several contexts in his literary corpus. In particular, he contrasted *halikhah*, "going," with *biʾah*, "arriving": the one who considers that he is on the way is really at the goal, whereas the one who thinks he has arrived is not only still on the way but on the wrong way. In several places he attributes the distinction to the Baᶜal Shem Ṭov based on an interpretation of Ps. 126:6: one who constantly journeys for the sake of divine worship and does not consider that he has reached the end of his journey in the end will produce seed, whereas one who is convinced that he has reached that destination and considers that he has already come to where he has to be, begins with joy but in the end will prove to be infertile. Cf. *Ben Porat Yosef* (Brooklyn, 1976), 32d; *Toledot Yaᶜaqov Yosef* (Korets, 1780, Jerusalem reprint, 1966), 194d. A similar interpretation of Ps. 126:6, without however being attributed to the Besht, is to be found in the Maggid's *ʾOr Torah* (Brooklyn, 1972), 72b–c. Cf. Meir Margulies, *Sod Yakhin u-Voᶜaz* (Ostrog, 1794), 4a–b. See also the collection of sayings of the Maggid edited by Meshullam Phoebus Heller [on this attribution, see Weiss, *Studies*, pp. 122–23 n. 57], *Liqquṭim Yeqarim* (Jerusalem, 1974), p. 14, cited in *Sefer Baᶜal Shem Ṭov*, ed. Simeon Mendel of Gavartchov (Lodz, 1938), 2:34a. See also the interpretation of Baruch of Miedzyborz, *Boṣinaʾ di-Nehoraʾ Shalem* (Jerusalem, 1985), p. 74. It is significant that Jacob Joseph connects the Besht's teaching about *biʾah* in the sense of reaching one's destination with the mishnaic ruling (cf. Qiddushin 1:1) about *biʾah* in the sense of one's conjugal

obligation. Walking in the spiritual plane thus parallels sexual intercourse in the physical. Cf. *Ketonet Passim*, p. 192, and see discussion below in the last section of this chapter. In other contexts Jacob Joseph distinguishes at least three senses of walking or going on the way: (1) to cleave to God even when involved in corporeal matters (*ᶜavodah be-gashmiyut*), (2) to progress from grade to grade, and (3) to descend from the higher level of spiritual consciousness in order to help others. Cf. *Ketonet Passim*, p. 141. Concerning the first meaning, see also *Ben Porat Yosef*, 48c, and *Toledot*, 6c: "'And Jacob lifted up his feet' (Gen. 29:1), that is to say, he lifted up his grade, which is to say himself, to cleave by means of his walking to God (*ledabbeq be-halikhato bi-devequt qono*)." Cf. the interpretation of this verse in Dov Baer of Miedzyrzec, *ᵓOr Torah*, 9d, and in Menaḥem Naḥum of Chernobyl, *Meᵓor ᶜEinayim* (Brooklyn, 1984), 23b. With respect to the second meaning, Jacob Joseph distinguishes man from the angel: the former is in the category of *holekh*, one who goes from grade to grade, ever changing like a wheel, while the latter is in the category of *ᶜomed*, standing in one permanent condition. Cf. *Toldeot*, 37a, and see *Meᵓor ᶜEinayim*, 34d–35a, and *Boṣinaᵓ di-Nehoraᵓ Shalem*, p. 73. On the status of the *ṣaddiq* as one who walks, *holekh*, in contrast to an angel who stands, *ᶜomed*, cf. Aaron ben Eizik, *Bet ᵓAharon* (Sulzbach, 1786), 11b. Shneur Zalman of Liadi often distinguishes between the status of the angels as *ᶜomdim* and that of the Jewish souls when they descend to this world as *mehalkhim*. Cf. *Liqquṭe ᵓAmarim: Tanya* (Brooklyn, 1979), 76a; *Torah ᵓOr* (Brooklyn, 1984), 30a; *Liqquṭe Torah* (Brooklyn, 1984), *Wayiqraᵓ*, 45a, *Bemidbar*, 38b, 64c; and *Maᵓamare Admur ha-Zaqen ᶜal Parshiyyot ha-Torah we-ha-Moᶜadim* (Brooklyn, 1983), 2:729. (The characterization of the angels as beings who stand is made already in classical rabbinic sources and is often repeated in kabbalistic texts; cf. P. Berakhot 1:1; B. Berakhot 10b; Ḥagigah 15b; *Zohar* 2:241b, 3:260a; and E. R. Wolfson, *The Book of the Pomegranate: Moses de León's Sefer ha-Rimmon* (Atlanta, 1988), p. 80 [Hebrew section].) Concerning the last meaning, see n. 46. Cf. *Toledot*, 194d; *Liqquṭe Moharan* (Bene-Beraq, 1972), 1:20; and *Shivḥe ha-Ran* (Brooklyn, 1972) § 33. See also Y. Liebes, *Studies in Jewish Myth and Jewish Messianism*, trans. B. Stein (Albany, 1992), p. 120.

5. Cf. *Maggid Devarav le-Yaᶜaqov*, ed. R. Schatz Uffenheimer (Jerusalem, 1976), p. 261: "If your soul inquires how one can raise in his thought everything so that it will be mitigated in its source. . . . If one wants to ascend when he stands on the lower level, he cannot reach and attain the higher level except as he traverses from level to level. If, however, he is standing on the higher [level] he can ascend from below in one moment."

6. Cf. *Meᵓ or ᶜEinayim*, 17d, 23b, 29d. And see Asher Zevi of Ostrog (d. 1817), *Maᶜayan ha-Ḥokhmah* (Jerusalem, 1971), 11b: "A person must contemplate and know that it is impossible to raise the gradations when he is standing in one place. Rather [this can be accomplished] when he is going (*holekh*) from gradation to gradation." See ibid., 77b. Cf. Abraham Ḥayyim of Zlocziew (1750-1816), *ᵓOraḥ Ḥayyim*, reprinted in *Sefarim Qedoshim mi-Talmide Baᶜal Shem Ṭov* (Brooklyn, 1985), vol. 22, p. 47: "When the *ṣaddiq* worships God,

blessed be He, he is called 'the one who is walking' (*holekh*), for he goes from gradation to gradation. But Abraham was sitting and he did not walk. Even so [it is written] 'the Lord appeared to him' for God, blessed be He, appeared to Abraham in order to arouse him . . . he was in the aspect of sitting but not that of walking." Shneur Zalman of Liadi, *Ma᾽amare᾽ Admur ha-Zaqen 5564* (Brooklyn, 1980), pp. 111–12, distinguishes, on the basis of Ps. 126:6 (see above n. 4), two kinds of *halikhah:* the first is that which characterizes the one who, like Abraham, goes from one level of comprehension to a higher one by means of love, whereas the second, the level of Jacob or the attribute of mercy, comprises traversing in the way of crying (*halikhah she-be-derekh bekhiyah*). The second way is marked by the awareness of one's lowly state that only increases the more one ascends. For a different distinction between two types of walking (*hillukh*), see Shneur Zalman, *Torah ᾽Or,* 112a. And see *Liqquṭe Torah, Wayiqra᾽*, 48a: "the aspect of walking (*halikhah*) is the aspect of love, to be contained in unity (*lehitkallel be-᾽eḥad*) . . . for the essence of the walking (*halikhah*) is [for the person] to contain his soul in the one, to cleave to Him." The image of *hitkallelut* and its relation to the ideal of *devequt* in the thought of Shneur Zalman has been recently discussed by M. Idel, "Universalization and Integration: Two Conceptions of Mystical Union in Jewish Mysticism," in *Mystical Union in the Monotheistic Faith,* ed. M. Idel and B. McGinn (New York, 1989), pp. 42–44. Cf. *Liqquṭe Torah,* Bemidbar, 20b: "The angels are called those who stand (*ʿomdim*). . . . And the matter is that 'there is no standing but silence' [cf. B. Soṭah 39a], and the explanation of silence is the negation of the essence from everything (*biṭṭul ha-ʿaṣmut mikol vekhol*), i.e., the negation of the will (*biṭṭul ha-raṣon*). . . . And the reason this aspect is called standing (*ʿamidah*) is because when the person has love and cleaves to God, this aspect is called walking (*mehalekh*) . . . but before he can attain the level of walking (*hillukh*) and this love, he must first have the aspect of standing." Shneur Zalman goes on to contrast this type of walking with God that leads to *devequt* with the walking of the evil inclination. On the concept of *biṭṭul* in Habad philosophy, see R. Elior, *The Theory of Divinity of Hasidut HaBaD* (Jerusalem, 1982), pp. 178–243 (in Hebrew), and the shorter English summary in idem, "HaBaD: The Contemplative Ascent to God," in *Jewish Spirituality from the Sixteenth-Century Revival to the Present,* ed. A. Green (New York, 1987), pp. 181–98. See idem, The *Paradoxical Ascent to God: The Kabbalistic Theosophy of Habad Hasidism,* trans. J. M. Green (Albany, 1993), pp. 143–57. On *halikhah* (or *hillukh*) as a metaphor for the process of love leading to a state of *devequt,* see also *Liqquṭe Torah,* Devarim, 19d; and *Shir ha-Shirim,* 25d. And cf. *Ma᾽amare Admur ha-Zaqen ʿal Parshiyyot ha-Torah we-ha-Moʿadim,* 2:729–30, where Shneur Zalman explains that the status of man in his descent to the world as "one who walks," as opposed to his status before descent as "one who stands," involves a "spiritual walking from comprehension to comprehension" (*halikhah ruḥanit me-hasagah le-hasagah*) rather than a "physical walking" (*halikhah gashmit*). Cf. Dov Baer Schnersohn, *Shaʿar ha-᾽Emunah,* pt. 1 of *Ner Miṣwah we-Torah ᾽Or* (Brooklyn, 1979), 105b: "the aspect of negation (*biṭṭul*) and containment (*hitkallelut*) of the lower in the upper, for example, [to ascend] from [the world of] doing (*ʿAsiyyah*) to [the world of] formation (*Yeṣirah*), and from [the world of] formation (*Yeṣirah*) to [the world of] creation (*Beri*ʾ*ah*) etc., [is a process] that is called walking (*hillukh*), like one who goes by foot (*ke-holekh ba-regel*), for he progresses and ascends from below to above, from what is low to what is high." Cf. *Ma*ʾ*amare* ʾ*Admur ha-*ʾ*Emṣa*ʿ*i* (Brooklyn, 1985), Wayiqraʾ, 2:753; Shalom Dovber of Lubavitch, *Sefer ha-Ma*ʾ*amarim 5672–5676* (Brooklyn, 1985), p. 62. On two types of *hillukh* as the worship of God, *panim* and ʾ*aḥor*, in Habad philosophy, cf. Menaḥem Mendel Schnersohn, ʾ*Or ha-Torah* (Brooklyn, 1969), 14: 640–41, and 16: 476–77. A glance at the frequent appearance of this term in Menaḥem Mendel's corpus demonstrates how central a motif it is in Habad thinking. Cf. *Sefer ha-Liqquṭim Ṣemaḥ Ṣedeq* (Brooklyn, 1982), s.v. *halikhah*, pp. 158–77. A detailed study of this image in Habad would no doubt prove instructive. See also *Sod Yakhin u-Vo*ʿ*az*, 3b, where the term *mehalekhim* is used in reference to those who perform the commandments for they go from level to level. And cf. ibid., 4a, where the term *holekh* is applied specifically to the *ṣaddiq*.

7. See M. Verman, "Aliyah and Yeridah: Journeys of the Besht and R. Nachman to Israel," in *Approaches to Medieval Judaism*, vol. 3, ed. D. R. Blumenthal (Atlanta, 1988), p. 166. Although I have availed myself of Verman's terminology, I cannot agree with his conclusion: "Moreover, although it is in the nature of a journey for space to be traversed horizontally, traveling from point A to point B, the Hasidim, in their commitment to devekut, were much more concerned with their vertical state of being, i.e., their relationship to God." In fact, Hasidic texts abound with images of the horizontal type that depict the relationship of man to God. Cf., for example, Kalonymus Kalman of Cracow, *Ma*ʾ*or wa-Shemesh* (Brooklyn, 1985), 46a: "By means of this the *ṣaddiq* should decide if the way before him is the right one: if in the way that he goes the *ṣaddiq* does not cease from cleaving to God, then he knows that this way before him is the right one. However, if he sees that the cleaving [to God] has ceased for him, then he should stand still and go no more on that way." See nn. 4 and 6.

8. Cf. the exemplary passages from *Liqquṭim Yeqarim*, *Zot Zikkaron*, of Jacob Isaac Hurwitz, the Seer of Lublin (1745–1815), and ʾ*Or Me*ʾ*ir* of Zeʾev Wolf of Zhitomir, cited by Weiss, "Beginnings, " pp. 104–5, and *Studies*, pp. 20–21.

9. Cf. the words of the Maggid in ʾ*Or Torah*, 67a–b, on Ps. 16:8: "Sometimes a person moves about (*holekh*) and speaks with people, and as a result he cannot study; yet he must cleave to God, blessed be He, and unify the unifications. Similary when a person travels in the way *(holekh ba-derekh)* and he cannot pray or study as is his wont, he must worship [God] in other manners, and he should not worry about this. For God wants the person to worship Him in all manners. . . . Therefore the opportunity arose for him to travel in the way or to speak with people so that he would worship Him in an alternative manner." Hasidic masters linked their ideal of communion (*devequt*) as a constant state of being with God even in a social context to the view of

Naḥmanides as expressed in his commentary to Deut. 11:22. See G. Scholem, *The Messianic Idea in Judaism* (New York, 1971), pp. 204–5. See also, nn. 27 and 44.

10. I am employing the word "soteriological" to denote both individual and communal redemption, the latter of course being closely associated with messianism. Although some of the early Hasidic masters do differentiate between individual redemption and that of the nation at large, in the terminology of Jacob Joseph, *ge᾿ulah peraṭit* and *ge᾿ulah kelalit* (cf. *Toledot,* 198a), I do not think that the two aspects are ever to be viewed as absolutely separate, as they are not separate in the Lurianic writings. That is to say, individual redemption is part of the national (and cosmic) redemptive process. In light of this I cannot agree with Scholem's statements in *Messianic Idea* (pp. 195–201), to the effect that Hasidism removed the "acute Messianic tension" from the Lurianic doctrine of uplifting the sparks, for while the "school of Lurianism made every Jew a protagonist in the great Messianic struggle [and] did not allegorize Messianism into a state of personal life. . . . Hasidism in its most vigorous stages took precisely this step. The one and unique great act of final redemption . . . was thrown out, i.e., was removed from the sphere of man's immediate responsibility and thrown back into God's inscrutable councils." My reasons for disagreeing with Scholem, however, differ from the classical rebuttal of I. Tishby, "The Messianic Idea and the Messianic Tendencies in the Beginnings of Hasidism," *Zion* 32 (1967): 1–45 (in Hebrew). It strikes me that there is an implicit messianic spirit in Hasidic doctrine, and it was precisely this factor that instilled—and continues to instill—in the hearts and minds of the pious an intense religious fervor. The whole question of messianism in Hasidism, I believe, should be re-examined from a phenomenological, as opposed to a historical, point of view; i.e., it should not be judged solely from the point of view of its rejection or assimilation of Sabbatianism. See n. 63. On the implicit messianic dimension of Beshtian Hasidism, connected especially with the social need to communicate esoteric truths, see N. Lowenthal, *Communicating the Infinite: The Emergence of the Habad School* (Chicago and London, 1990), pp. 6–14.

11. Cf. *Zohar* 1:49b (cf. *Ketonet Passim,* p. 195), 68b–69a, 189a; 2:163b. The zoharic idea, of course, has its source in the older aggadic motif of the exile of the *Shekhinah.* See I. Tishby, *The Wisdom of the Zohar,* trans. D. Goldstein (Oxford, 1989), pp. 382–85.

12. See R. J. Zwi Werblowsky, *Joseph Karo Lawyer and Mystic* (Philadelphia, 1977), pp. 51–54; B. Zak, "The Exile of Israel and the Exile of the Shechina in 'Or Yaqar' of Rabbi Moses Cordovero," *Jerusalem Studies in Jewish Thought* 4 (1982): 157–78 (in Hebrew).

13. The image is talmudic in origin; cf. B. Berakhot 43b, Ḥagigah 16a, Qiddushin 31a; *Synopse zur Hekhalot-Literatur,* ed. P. Schäfer, et al. (Tübingen, 1981), §§ 441, 745–46. Cf. *Toledot,* 130d, where Israel is identified as the "feet of the Presence" (*raglin di-shekhinta᾿*) for "just as feet lead a person according to his desire and will so [they] raise prayer to the place that she loves." An

earlier source for this usage is found in *Tiqqune Zohar*, ed. R. Margaliot (Jerusalem, 1976), 18, 35a.

14. See M. Piekarz, "The Messianic Idea in the Beginnings of Hasidism," in *The Messianic Idea in Jewish Thought: A Study Conference in Honour of the Eightieth Birthday of Gershom Scholem* (Jerusalem, 1982), pp. 241–42 (in Hebrew). Dinur, *Be-Mifneh ha-Dorot*, p. 81 n. 733, noted the relationship of this text to Hasidic sources with respect to the question of specific religious customs.

15. Cf. B. Pesaḥim 68a and Zevaḥim 116b. See also Yoma 3b and Sanhedrin 91b.

16. *Sha*ʿ*ar ha-Melekh* (Zolkiew, 1774), pt. 2, 3:5, 95d. In the Talmud, the priests are referred to as *sheluḥe de-raḥmana*ʾ. Cf. B. Yoma 19a and Qiddushin 23b. Jacob Joseph refers to the *ṣaddiqim* as the *sheluḥe de-maṭronita*ʾ. Cf., e.g., *Toledot*, 32d, 38c (in the name of the Besht), 137c, and *Ben Porat Yosef*, 55b. See also Moses Ḥayyim Ephraim of Sudlikov, *Degel Maḥaneh* ʾ*Efrayim* (Brooklyn, 1984), 55a.

17. According to an account in the anthology *Keter Shem Ṭov*, compiled by R. Aaron of Opatow and published in 1784 (concerning this book see G. Nigal, "An Early Source for the Literary Genre of Hasidic Stories: On the Keter Shem Ṭov and Its Sources," *Sinai* 79 (1976): 132–46 [in Hebrew]), the Maggid of Miedzyrzecz set out on a journey to visit the Besht in order to test his learning. Upon arriving at the Besht's dwelling, the Maggid expected to hear words of Torah. Instead in their first meeting the Besht reportedly told him various anecdotes about travel. The editor adds that in all of these tales there was contained "great and wondrous wisdom (*ḥokhmah rabbah we-nifla*ʾ*ah*) for the one who understands." Cf. *Keter Shem Ṭov* (Zolkiew, 1805), 30a; also cited in *Sefer Ba*ʿ*al Shem Ṭov*, 1:12 n. 8. See A. Yaari, "Two Foundational Editions of the Shivḥe ha-Besht," *Kiryat Sefer* 39 (1964): 403–7 (in Hebrew). Concerning this tale, see also G. Nigal, *The Hasidic Tale: Its History and Topics* (Jerusalem, 1981), pp. 21–22 (in Hebrew). There is no exact parallel to this tale about the Maggid's first meeting with the Besht in the Hebrew edition of *Shivḥe ha-Besht*, but there is one in the Yiddish version, ch. 23. See Nigal, op. cit., p. 91 n. 58a. However, as Nigal notes, op. cit., p. 21, there is a parallel between this tale and another in *Keter Shem Ṭov*, 21b–22a, concerning a sage who doubted the Besht's talmudic learning. There is a parallel to this later tale in *Shivḥe ha-Besht*, ed. B. Mintz (Jerusalem, 1969), p. 97.

18. In the Lurianic scheme one can speak of two kinds of sparks: those of *Shekhinah*, and those of the soul of primal Adam. It is, moreover, the task of man to seek out the sparks of his soul root so that he may uplift them and restore them to their source. The Hasidic teaching added a unique personal dimension to this idea by stressing that there are sparks in the cosmos that belong exclusively to certain individuals. See Scholem, *Messianic Idea*, pp. 186–92, and L. Jacobs, "The Uplifting of the Sparks in Later Jewish

Mysticism," in *Jewish Spirituality from the Sixteenth-Century Revival to the Present,* p. 117.

19. Cf. Menaḥem Mendel of Przemysl, *Darkhe Yesharim,* in *Torat ha-Ḥasidim ha-Rishonim* (Bene-Beraq, 1981), p. 274: "'The steps of a man are made firm by the Lord' (Ps. 37:23): Each and every step that a person takes is through [divine] providence so that he will gather the sparks of his soul from there where they are scattered; the sparks wait and anticipate his coming so that they will be joined with him [as are the] the sparks of his soul." Cf. Aaron Roth, *Shulḥan ha-Ṭahor* (Jerusalem, 1989), 127b: "Our teacher, the Besht, may his merit protect us, revealed that sometimes a person must travel a long distance and he thinks that he travels for business, but the intended purpose [of the journey] is that there is [in that place] a spark that he must elevate . . . and every holy spark must necessarily be uplifted by that very person, for it is a portion of his soul, and it cannot be uplifted by anyone else." See Scholem, *Messianic Idea,* p. 191. This theoretical position underlies a theme repeated constantly in Hasidic tales concerning a master who is propelled by an uncontrollable force to journey to distant places in order to perform a seemingly menial task that, in fact, has the power to liberate sparks of his soul root. See Jacobs, "Uplifting of the Sparks," p. 117.

20. *Ketonet Passim,* p. 75. For an entirely different explanation of Jacob's journey from Beer Sheva to Haran, which represents the departure from a state of *devequt,* cf. *Toledot,* 6a. See also *Me'or ʿEinayim,* 18d, 20b. In contrast to the interpretation of the Besht, the rebbe from Chernobyl interprets the talmudic dictum that God folded all of Israel under Jacob not to mean that Jacob could perform his duties without traveling, but rather that wherever Jacob went the aspect of holiness emanating from the land of Israel went with him. For other interpretations of this verse that emphasize a departure, see also Jacob Isaac of Lublin, *Zikkaron Zot* (Munckas, 1942), p. 19; idem, *Divre 'Emet* (Munckas, 1942), pp. 28, 30; and Ḥayyim ben Leibush Halberstam, *Divre Ḥayyim* (Jerusalem, 1988), pt. 1, 9a.

21. *Studies,* p. 20.

22. Even in those contexts where Jacob Joseph speaks in general terms about man's *halikhah,* upon examination it becomes clear that he is really speaking about the elite segment of the population, the "men of form" or "spirit," the *ṣaddiqim,* and not the masses, the "men of matter" or "body." This phenomenon in the writings of Jacob Joseph, with special reference to the ideal of *devequt,* has been noted by A. Rapoport-Albert, "God and the Zaddik as the Two Focal Points of Hasidic Worship," *History of Religions* 18 (1979): 306–9, reprinted in *Essential Papers on Hasidism,* pp. 309–10. See also R. Schatz Uffenheimer, *Hasidism as Mysticism: Quietistic Elements in Eighteenth Century Hasidic Thought,* trans. J. Chipman (Princeton, 1993), pp. 52–53. On the doctrine of matter and form in Jacob Joseph, see Weiss, "Beginnings," p. 51 n. 13, and S. Dresner, *The Zaddik* (London, 1960), pp. 136–37.

23. *Ketonet Passim,* pp. 75–76.

24. See Dinur, *Be-Mifneh ha-Dorot*, p. 106 n. 613, and Ettinger, "Hassidic Movement," p. 255.

25. *Ketonet Passim*, pp. 242–43.

26. Cf. Levi Yiṣḥaq of Berdichev, *Qedushat Levi* (Brooklyn, 1978), 5a, 15a, and the passage from Uri Feivel of Dubnekow, *ʾOr ha-Ḥokhmah*, cited in *Sefer Baʿal Shem Ṭov*, 1:110b.

27. *Ketonet Passim*, p. 244. Elsewhere in Jacob Joseph's writings Moses is depicted as the *ṣaddiq* who was able to achieve *devequt* even when he was among others and involved in physical matters. See *Ketonet Passim*, pp. 53–54, 206, 246, 276, and *Ṣofnat Paʿneaḥ*, 95b. Jacob Joseph also attributes this interpretation of Moses' status to Menaḥem ben Aaron ibn Zeraḥ's *Ṣedah la-Derekh*. See n. 44.

28. See, e.g., *Zohar* 1:21b.

29. *Ben Porat Yosef*, 18b, 20a. The passage is partially translated and discussed by Weiss, *Studies*, pp. 19–20. See also G. Nigal, *Torot Baʿal ha-Toledot* (Jerusalem, 1974), pp. 16–17.

30. Interesting in this regard is Jacob Joseph's interpretation in *Ben Porat Yosef*, 77b, of another passage in B. Ḥullin (110b), "Whoever lives inside the land of Israel is like one who has a God but whoever lives outside of Israel is like one who has no God": "I have heard from my teacher that a person is entirely in the place where his mind is concentrated [cf. *Toledot*, 20a]. If he lives outside the land of Israel and constantly thinks about and desires the land of Israel he is like one who has no God etc. But in truth he has one because his mind is constantly on Israel unlike the one who is in Israel who sets up his livelihood in the diaspora. Such a person's mind is constantly on the diaspora to bring sustenance for his household. He is like one who has [a God] but in truth he has none because his mind is outside the land of Israel." Dinur, *Be-Mifneh ha-Dorot*, p. 194, discussed the passage from Jacob Joseph in connection with a passage from *Shivḥe ha-Besht*, p. 68, concerning Jacob Joseph's desire to immigrate to Palestine. The Besht reportedly told him: 'Do not go . . . this should be as a sign in your hand: whenever the desire to travel to the holy land falls upon you, know in truth that there are judgments [hanging] upon the city . . . Satan interferes with you so that you will not pray on behalf of the city. Therefore when the desire for Palestine falls upon you, pray on behalf of the city [where you are]." On the historical phenomenon of immigration of East-European Jews to the land of Israel during the period of the flourishing of Hasidism see Y. Ḥisdai, "Early Settlement of 'Hasidim' and of 'Mithnaggdim' in Palestine—Immigration of 'Mitzva' and of Mission," *Shalem* 4 (1984): 231–69 (in Hebrew), and Y. Raphael, *ʿAl Ḥasidut wa-Ḥasidim* (Jerusalem, 1991), pp. 50–203.

31. Y. Ḥisdai, "The Emergence of Hassidim and Mitnagdim in the Light of the Homiletical Literature" (Ph.D. dissertation, Hebrew University, 1984), pp. 147–62 (in Hebrew). As Ḥisdai notes, this tension can be traced to the

teachings of the pre-Beshtian *ṣaddiqim* and *ḥasidim*. Ḥisdai has further argued, on the basis of a key passage in the *Toledot*, 124a, that Jacob Joseph's dismissal from his post as rabbi in Sharigrod was connected with this very problem; i.e., the community decided that Jacob Joseph had neglected his social responsibilities by adopting the ascetic practices of the *ḥasidim* and by separating himself with respect to matters concerning prayer and the ritual slaughter of animals. Ḥisdai is of the opinion that for Jacob Joseph the ultimate perfection indeed consists of worshipping God and not serving human society. For a discussion of the two typologies of *devequt* in Hasidic sources, contemplation that is beyond this world and contemplation within this world, see Weiss, "Beginnings," pp. 60–69.

32. *Shene Luḥot ha-Berit* (Warsaw, 1862), 1: 52b. On the influence of this work on both ethical-homiletical and Hasidic literature, see Piekarz, *Beginning of Hasidism*, pp. 209–18. The contrast between Abraham's righteousness and that of Noah has a long tradition in Jewish sources; cf. the comment of Rashi to Gen 6:9, "Noah walked with God." Cf. Moses Alshekh, *Torat Moshe* (Amsterdam, 1777), 15c, and Ephraim Solomon ben Aaron of Leczycz (Luntshits), *ʿOlelot ʾEfrayim* (Jerusalem, 1989), § 118, pp. 157–59. R. Ephraim distinguishes, on the basis of biblical terminology, three types of *halikhah* in relation to God: (1) walking behind God, which characterizes the people of Israel after they received the Torah at Sinai, being compared to a servant of a king who is completely trustworthy because he has been both tested and has signed a contract; (2) walking in front of God, which characterizes Abraham who was like the servant that was tested but did not yet sign a contract; and (3) walking with, i.e., alongside of God, which characterizes Noah, one of "little faith," who is comparable to the servant who cannot be trusted because he was neither tested nor signed a contract.

33. *Sefer Ḥaredim* (Jerusalem, 1980), ch. 66, p. 262, translated in Werblowsky, *Joseph Karo*, p. 60.

34. *Ben Porat Yosef*, 22a.

35. See Dresner, *The Zaddik*, pp. 151–72.

36. See A. Green, "Typologies of Leadership and the Hasidic Zaddiq," in *Jewish Spirituality from the Sixteenth Century Revival to the Present*, pp. 135–36. For the earlier sources of these typologies, see Piekarz, *Beginning of Hasidism*, p. 107. On the two types of *ṣaddiq* in the writings of Elimelech of Lezajsk, see R. Schatz, "The Doctrine of the *Ṣaddiq* in R. Elimelekh of Lyzhansk," *Molad* 18:144 (1960): 370–71 (in Hebrew). For a similar doctrine in the teaching of the Maggid of Kozienice, see S. Steinfeld, "The Hassidic Teachings of Rabbi Israel, the Maggid of Koznitz" (D.H.L., The Jewish Theological Seminary of America, 1981), pp. 99–141. It is essential to note that the social function of the *ṣaddiq* to pursue the wicked at all costs in order to bring them back to divine worship is emphasized in *Zohar* 2:128b. This text served as an important basis for Jacob Joseph. Cf. *Toledot*, 61d, 139c, and *Ben Porat Yosef*, 33a, 33d. See also Nigal, *Torat Ba ʿal ha-Toledot*, p. 14 n. 18.

37. *Ben Porat Yosef,* 22a; cf. *Ṣofnat Paʿneaḥ,* 95b.

38. For a study of the concept of *hitbodedut* in the history of kabbalah, particularly as it took shape in the school of Abraham Abulafia, see M. Idel, *Studies in Ecstatic Kabbalah* (Albany, 1988), pp. 103–69.

39. *Toledot,* 14b. On Jacob Joseph's use of Noah as a symbol for the secluded leader, see Dresner, *The Zaddik,* pp. 104–7.

40. See Dresner, op. cit., pp. 151–54, and references given on pp. 283–84 nn. 15–25. On the role of Abraham in Hasidic thought, particularly from the vantage point of ritualistic practice, see A. Green, *Devotion and Commandment: The Faith of Abraham in the Hasidic Imagination* (Cincinnati, 1989).

41. *Ben Porat Yosef,* 22b.

42. Cf. *Ketonet Passim,* p. 10, and references given there in n. 101, and Dresner, *The Zaddik,* p. 271 n. 25.

43. See A. Rubenstein, "The Mentor of R. Israel Baʿal Shem-Ṭov and the Sources of His Knowledge," *Tarbiz* 48 (1978–79): 151 (in Hebrew).

44. *Ṣofnat Paʿneaḥ,* 95b. Cf. ibid. 24c, and *Ketonet Passim,* pp. 53, 206, 249. Mention should be made of the statement in *Shivḥe ha-Besht,* ed. B. Mintz (Jerusalem, 1969), p. 98, to the effect that the Besht could not talk to people on account of his *devequt.* It was the Besht's celestial teacher, Ahijah the Shilonite (see n. 78), who taught him the proper wisdom, consisting in part of the recitation of verses from Psalms, by which he could communicate with people and still remain in a state of pietistic devotion. See Rubenstein, "The Mentor of R. Israel Baʿal Shem-Ṭov," pp. 150–52. The distinction in Jacob Joseph's writings between two types of *devequt* is based in several cases on Naḥmanides' commentary to Deut. 11:22; see above n. 9. He also mentions in this context Menaḥem ben Zeraḥ's *Ṣedah la-Derekh;* see above n. 27. In other places, e.g., *Ṣofnat Paʿneaḥ,* 29a, Jacob Joseph distinguishes in another way between two types of *devequt*: that of the *talmid ḥakham* who cleaves directly to God and that of the masses who cleave to God by means of cleaving to the *talmid ḥakham.* In *Ṣofnat Paʿneaḥ,* 95a–b, he brings together the two distinctions.

45. See Weiss, "Beginnings," pp. 60–61.

46. M. ʾAvot 6:9.

47. *Ketonet Passim,* p. 194. On the contrast between *halikhah* and *biʾah* in Jacob Joseph, see above n. 4.

48. *Ketonet Passim,* p. 213.

49. *Ṣofnat Paʿneaḥ,* 20d.

50. Cf. ibid., 60a. See Weiss, "Beginnings," p. 64 n. 61. The same idea is attributed by Jacob Joseph to Menaḥem Mendel of Bar. See I. Tishby and

J. Dan, "The Teaching of Hasidism and Its Literature," in *Studies in Hasidism*, ed. A. Rubenstein (Jerusalem, 1977), p. 264 (in Hebrew).

51. See Weiss, "Beginnings," pp. 69ff., and Piekarz, *Beginning of Hasidism*, pp. 86, 206, 253, 258–59, 302.

52. *Toledot*, 18c–d. According to Shneur Zalman of Liadi, foreign thoughts lifted up by the *ṣaddiq* are in truth the evil thoughts of others. Cf. *Tanya*ʾ, 35a.

53. Cf. *Ben Porat Yosef*, 54d, where there is an attempt to synthesize the two meanings. Cf. also Yiṣḥaq Isaac Safrin of Komarno, *Netiv Miṣwotekha* (Jerusalem, 1983), p. 18. The correlation of *yeridah* and *halikhah* is also assumed, from a different perspective, in the thought of Shneur Zalman of Liadi inasmuch as he claims that the Jewish soul is transformed from the status of standing to that of walking in its descent from the heavenly realms to this world. See references given above in n. 6. On the double meaning of *yeridah* as a descent from a state of *devequt* and as the acceptance of social obligation, see Scholem, *Messianic Idea*, pp. 219–22.

54. On death as a symbol for the departure of a *ṣaddiq* from a state of *devequt*, cf. *Toledot*, 6a, 34a. Elsewhere Jacob Joseph calls the wicked "dead." Cf. *Toledot*, 11b, 197b, and see Weiss, "Beginnings," p. 63 n. 57.

55. *Toledot*, 135b. Cf. ibid., 6b, 99a, 136a.

56. According to the legend of the diminished moon in B. Ḥullin 60b.

57. *Toledot*, 34a. Cf. ibid., 16b, 54a.

58. Cf. the Maggid's interpretation of this verse in *ʾOr Torah*, 14d: " 'Jacob lifted up his feet and came to the land of the Easterners' (Gen. 29:1). That is . . . he went out from his earthliness (*she-halakh me-ʾarṣiyyut shelo*), that is, his corporeality (*ha-gashmiyyut shelo*), to the worship of God, blessed be He, a portion of divinity (*ḥeleq ʾelohut*)."

59. *Ben Porat Yosef*, 80a–b.

60. *Be-Mifneh ha-Dorot*, pp. 181–88.

61. "Messianic Idea," p. 33.

62. Scholem, *Messianic Idea*, p. 191.

63. Cf. *Toledot*, 135b, 144c, and elsewhere. In light of these passages I cannot agree with Scholem's assessment of the lack of an "acute Messianism" in the writings of Jacob Joseph (*Messianic Idea*, p. 184). Moreover, I find Scholem's general characterization lacking; see p. 185: "Hasidism, without changing the outward façade of Lurianic teaching and terminology, introduced such subtle but effective changes as would eliminate the Messianic meaning of the central doctrine of tikkun or at least defer it to a remote stage,

where it became again a matter of utopianism without immediate impact." Many of the conceptual assumptions underlying Scholem's statement have been challenged in more recent scholarship. See above, n. 10.

64. *Peri ᶜEṣ Ḥayyim* (Jerusalem, 1980), Shaᶜar Qeriᵓat Shemaᶜ, ch. 3, pp. 164–65.

65. I have yet to locate an exact source in the Lurianic corpus, but the critical passage characterizing the messianic period as a time of purification of the feet is found in several places. See, e.g., *Shaᶜar ha-Gilgulim* (Jerusalem, 1912), § 15, 16b. See also reference given in the preceding note. In fact, it is probable that the text cited by Jacob Joseph is not an exact source at all, but is rather a paraphrase of some Lurianic passage blended together with Jacob Joseph's own ideas. On this quality in Jacob Joseph's writings, see Scholem, *Messianic Idea*, p. 188.

66. *Toledot,* 123c.

67. Ibid., 123d. Cf. 189d where the feet are used as a metaphor for the exile of the soul (*galut neshamah*).

68. See *Zohar* 2:258a. The same zoharic text is cited by Vital (see references in n. 64) as well as Nathan of Gaza (see n. 79). Cf. Ḥayyim ha-Kohen of Aleppo, *Ṭur Bareqet* (Amsterdam, 1655), 3d, and Yiṣḥaq Isaac Safrin of Komarno, *Zohar Ḥai ᶜal Sefer Shemot* (Prezmysl, 1878), pt. 2, 274b.

69. See I. Tishby, *The Doctrine of Evil and the 'Kelippah' in Lurianic Kabbalism* (Jerusalem, 1942), pp. 134–35 (in Hebrew).

70. Cf. *Ben Porat Yosef,* 33d: "'Bathe your feet,' to remove the pollution from the two pillars of truth [i.e., *Neṣaḥ* and *Hod*; see n. 120], for this is faith. This is the secret of washing the feet on Sabbath eve to remove the shell and the pollution from the feet of Adam of [the world of] *ᶜAsiyyah,* as it is explained in the writings of the Ari." Cf. *Peri ᶜEṣ Ḥayyim,* Shaᶜar ha-Shabbat, ch. 3, p. 384. Cf. *Ketonet Passim,* p. 319, where the *ṣaddiq* is said to descend from the head, the "aspect of king," to the feet, "the place of dominion of the shells," and *Toledot,* 189b, where the exile of the soul is described as extending to the feet. Cf. also Nathan of Nemirov, *Liqquṭe Halakhot,* ᵓOraḥ Ḥayyim, vol. 3 (Jerusalem, 1974), Hilkhot Ḥanukah, 2:6, 243d, where the rabbinic ruling that Ḥanukah candles are lit until there is no one walking about in the marketplace *(ᶜad she-tikhleh regel min ha-shuq)* (B. Shabbat 21b; *Masekhet Soferim,* 20:2), is interpreted as follows: "That is, to elevate all the lower levels, which are the feet of holiness (*ragle ha-qedushah*) clothed and bound to the outer places [i.e., demonic forces], which are the aspect of the marketplace (*shuq*). . . . The lighting of the candle of Ḥanukah is to elevate the holiness from the [demonic] other side." A similar explanation of the rabbinic dictum is found in Meir ben Natan, *Sefer Meᵓir ᶜEine Ḥakhamim: ᵓOr Ḥadash ᶜal Ḥanukah* (Brooklyn, 1985), 9:1, p. 105.

71. R. Schatz, "The Baᶜal Shem Ṭov's Commentary to Psalm 107: Myth and Ritual of the Descent to Sheᵓol," *Tarbiz* 42 (1973): 168 (in Hebrew). (An

English translation of this important text now appears as the appendix to Schatz Uffenheimer, *Hasidism as Mysticism*, pp. 342–82.) Schatz accepted the traditional attribution of the text to the Besht as authentic. Scholem, *Messianic Idea*, p. 189, suggests that the commentary was written by Menaḥem Mendel of Bar in 1760, a view discussed and rejected by Schatz, op. cit., pp. 161–62.

72. "Messianic Idea," p. 39.

73. For references, see ibid., p. 38 nn. 169–70. See also *Maʾamare ʾAdmur ha-Zaqen 5565* (Brooklyn, 1980), p. 410; *Maʾamare ʾAdmur ha-Zaqen 5566* (Brooklyn, 1979), p. 278; Dov Baer Schnersohn, *Shaʿar ha-ʾEmunah*, 101b, 104a; and Menaḥem Mendel Schnersohn, *ʾOr ha-Torah* (Brooklyn, 1969), 14:650, where the *ʿiqvot meshiḥaʾ* is characterized as a time of *halikhah* by the *baʿal teshuvah* who purifies the sparks in the feet primarily by means of charity. See ibid., p. 280, and *ʾOr ha-Torah* (Brooklyn, 1985), 25:986.

74. *Netiv Miṣwotekha*, pp. 7–8. This version of the legend concerning the Besht's attempted journey to Palestine was discussed by B. Drobitscher, "Three Versions of the Journey of the Besht to the Land of Israel," *Yeda-ʿAm* 6 (1960): 44 (in Hebrew).

75. According to another version of the legend, discussed by Drobitscher, op. cit., p. 41, the meeting of the Besht and Ḥayyim ibn Aṭṭar was to result in the redemption due to the fact that the soul of the former was from the Messiah of David and the soul of the latter from the Messiah of Ephraim. Cf. the letter of Gershon of Kuty to the Besht cited in A. J. Heschel, *The Circle of the Baal Shem Ṭov: Studies in Hasidism*, ed. S. H. Dresner (Chicago and London, 1985), pp. 84–85.

76. The Besht's confronting the soul of the Messiah in his celestial abode in a direct visual experience is a motif known from other Hasidic sources, including the Besht's own letter to Gershon of Kuty, first published by Jacob Joseph at the end of *Ben Porat Yosef*, 128a. For the various versions of this letter, see J. Mondshein, *Shivḥe ha-Besht: A Facsimile of a Unique Manuscript, Variant Versions and Appendices* (Jerusalem, 1982), p. 234 (in Hebrew). See also *Shivḥe ha-Besht*, ed. Mintz, p. 64.

77. The Yiddish version of *Shivḥe ha-Besht* likewise relates that the Besht stayed in Istanbul on his way to the land of Israel. See Yaari, "Two Foundational Editions," pp. 559–61. One tale in the Hebrew version of *Shivḥe ha-Besht* mentions the Besht's being in Istanbul, but without any connection to his journey to Israel. See *Shivḥe ha-Besht*, p. 151. According to Yaari, this is one of several examples that show that the editors of the Hebrew version of *Shivḥe ha-Besht* wanted to obscure the details connected to the Besht's aborted effort to reach Palestine. There is no parallel to this tale in the edition published by Mondshein (see previous note).

78. On this figure as the Besht's teacher, cf. *Toledot*, 156a. See also the allusion to the Besht's teacher in his letter to Gershon of Kuty, published in *Ben Porat Yosef*, 128a. There are several allusions to Ahijah the Shilonite as

well in the standard version of *Shivḥe ha-Besht*, ed. Mintz, pp. 64, 90, 98, 102. Concerning this tradition, see the study of Rubenstein referred to above in n. 43. See also L. Ginzberg, *The Legends of the Jews* (Philadelphia, 1968), 6: 305 n. 5; G. Nigal, "The Teacher of R. Israel Baʿal Shem Ṭov," *Sinai* 71 (1972): 150–59 (in Hebrew); and A. Khitrik, "On the Meeting of the Besht and Ahijah ha-Shiloni," *Sinai* 73 (1973): 189–90 (in Hebrew).

79. See G. Scholem, *Sabbatai Ṣevi: The Mystical Messiah*, trans. R. J. Zwi Werblowsky (Princeton, 1973), p. 303, and references given in n. 279 ad locum.

80. *Toledot*, 22d, 130c.

81. Ibid., 30a.

82. Ibid. 6c. Cf. *Ben Porat Yosef*, 54d. See the similar interpretation of Jacob Isaac of Lublin, *Divre ʾEmet*, p. 33: "'Jacob lifted up his feet' (Gen. 29:1). The essence of Jacob's activity was for the sake of the children of Israel. And it says in the *Zohar* that he left all the blessings and removed them until the end of the exile (*sof ha-galut*), as is known. The [period of the] 'footsteps of Messiah' (*ʿiqvot meshiḥaʾ*) is called the end of exile. And this is [the meaning of] 'Jacob lifted up his feet etc.'"

83. *Toledot*, 17b (cf. Yiṣḥaq Isaac Safrin of Komarno, *Hekhal ha-Berakhah* [Lemberg, 1869], 1:181). Scholem, *Messianic Idea*, p. 198, takes the statement concerning those who have descended without returning as an apparent reference to the Sabbatians. Cf. *Toledot*, 18d. For a similar concern see Schatz, "Baʿal Shem Ṭov's Commentary to Psalm 107," p. 179. Within the Lurianic corpus concern is expressed as well with those who ritually re-enact a descent to the demonic shells during the prayer of *nefillat ʾappayim*. Some souls cannot ascend from this descent and they thus remain trapped in the demonic realm. Cf. *Shaʿar ha-Kawwanot*, 47b; and *Peri ʿEṣ Ḥayyim*, Shaʿar Nefillat ʾAppayim, ch. 2, p. 295. It is not, however, clear that the reference to the Besht's warning in the *Toledot* about those who do not ascend is addressing the same phenomenon.

84. B. Shabbat 127a. Cf. *Toledot*, 201b, where Jacob Joseph briefly alludes to an interpretation of this talmudic passage that he heard from the Besht.

85. I have rendered the text in accordance with the meaning assumed by Menaḥem Naḥum. The literal rendering according to the new JPS translation is: "No shackle (*ʾoraḥ*, derived from an Old Aramaic root *ʾrḥ*) is placed on his feet."

86. See above n. 16.

87. Zeʾev Wolf of Zhitomir, *ʾOr ha-Meʾir* (Lemberg, 1871), 96a–c, cites a similar interpretation of Ps. 37:23 in the name of the Besht. The passage is partially translated and discussed in Weiss, *Studies*, pp. 21–22. See also Moses Shoham ben Dan of Dolina, *Divre Moshe* (Zolkiew, 1865), 14c.

88. *Me᾽or ᶜEinayim,* 42b–c.

89. Cf. *Toledot,* 198a; and see Scholem, *Messianic Idea,* pp. 195–96.

90. A similar connection between liberating the sparks and unifying the two names is found in a passage attributed to Jacob Joseph in Gedaliah of Linitz, *Teshuᶜot Ḥen* (Brooklyn, 1982), 21b. It can also be found in Elimelech of Lezajsk, *Noᶜam ᾽Elimelekh,* ed. G. Nigal (Jerusalem, 1978), 2: 617, with specific reference to food (the numerical value of *maᶜakhal* is 91, which is the numerology of the two divine names). See Jacobs, "Uplifting of the Sparks," pp. 120–21; and idem, "Eating as an Act of Worship in Hasidic Thought," in *Studies in Jewish Religious and Intellectual History Presented to Alexander Altmann on the Occasion of his Seventieth Birthday,* ed. S. Stein and R. Loewe (University, Alabama, 1979), pp. 165–66 n. 23. See, however, *᾽Iggeret ha-Qodesh* of Shneur Zalman of Liadi, *Liqquṭe ᾽Amarim: Tanya᾽,* 145a, where the two tasks are held in distinction, for the acts of unification are said to follow the completion of the purification of the sparks. The centrality of the male-female unification in the Hasidic notion of messianic redemption can be seen in the following comment of Jacob Joseph in *Toledot,* 38d: "I have heard in the name of my teacher [the Besht] what was said to him from heaven concerning the reason for the delay in the coming of the Messiah, for [the Jews] do not prolong the 'great love' (*᾽ahavah rabbah*) [i.e., the prayer recited before the *Shemaᶜ*], the secret of the kisses prior to the unification (*ziwwug*) that are intended to arouse her desire [i.e., the desire of *Shekhinah*] so that she will produce seed first and give birth to a male, which is [the attribute of] mercy." Presumably, with the proper unification the Messiah's coming would no longer be delayed. Needless to say, the mystical understanding of messianic redemption in terms of *hieros gamos* is a theme that can be traced to earlier kabbalistic sources, most significantly, the *Zohar.* See Scholem, *Messianic Idea,* p. 343 n. 32; M. Idel, "Types of Redemptive Activity in the Middle Ages," in *Messianism and Eschatology: A Collection of Essays,* ed. Z. Baras (Jerusalem, 1983), pp. 266–75 (in Hebrew); Y. Liebes, *Studies in the Zohar,* trans. A. Schwartz, S. Nakache, and P. Peli (Albany, 1993), pp. 67–71; and Ch. Mopsik, *Lettre sur la sainteté: le secret de la relation entre l'homme et la femme dans la cabale* (Paris, 1986), pp. 214–15.

91. *Degel Maḥaneh ᾽Efrayim,* 66a.

92. Ibid., 65b–c.

93. That is, the consonants of the word *pi* equal ninety; to get the sum ninety-one, the word itself, which counts as one, must be added.

94. *Degel Maḥaneh ᾽Efrayim,* 65d.

95. On the possible etymology of *halakhah* from the root *hlkh,* see A. Even-Shoshan, *Ha-Millon he-Ḥadash* (Jerusalem, 1969), 1:271, s.v. *halakhah.* The rabbis exploited this etymological connection; see references in n. 100. The connection between *halikhah* and *halakhah* is also implicit in Shneur Zalman's assertion that by means of the fulfillment of the commandments the

soul of the Jew attains the level of *halikhah* in this world. See *Liqquṭe Torah*, Bemidbar, 38d; ibid., 64c–d; and above in n. 4. And cf. *Ma᾽amare ᾽Admur ha-Zaqen ᶜal Parshiyyot ha-Torah we-ha-Moᶜadim*, 2:603, where the aspect of Torah is described as a process of *hillukh* from above to below, and, conversely, the aspect of *miṣwot* (i.e., *halakhah*) is described as the process of *hillukh* from below to above. Cf. Menaḥem Mendel Schnersohn, *᾽Or ha-Torah* (Brooklyn, 1969), 16:638, 650–51.

96. Cf. *Toledot*, 169a, and *Ketonet Passim*, p. 8. As Nigal points out, loc. cit., n. 76, a possible source for Jacob Joseph's identification of *halakhah* as *ha-kallah* may have been the *Peri ᶜEṣ Ḥayyim*; see Shaᶜar Hanhagat ha-Limmud, p. 353. On this correspondence in the writings of Vital, see L. Fine, "The Study of Torah as a Rite of Theurgical Contemplation in Lurianic Kabbalah," in *Approaches to Judaism in Medieval Times*, vol. 3, ed. D. R. Blumenthal (Atlanta, 1988), p. 38. Cf. the wording of the following kabbalistic prayer to be uttered before the study of *halakhah* found in Nathan Naṭa Hannover, *Shaᶜare Ṣiyyon* (Jerusalem, 1980), p. 601: "Behold I am learning *halakhah*, which is the letters *he᾽ kallah*, in order to adorn (*leqasheṭ*) the name Adonai, which is the supernal *halakhah*, with twenty-four adornments of the bride (*qishshuṭe kallah*) to join her with her husband." The connection between *Shekhinah* and *halakhah* was made, however, at a much earlier period. Cf., e.g., *Zohar* 3:20a (*Raᶜaya᾽ Mehemna᾽*). According to one tradition *Shekhinah* is called *halakhah* before she receives the divine influx from the masculine potency, whereas she is called *qabbalah* after she has received it. Cf. *Tiqqune Zohar* 21, 58a; J. Zwelling, "Joseph of Hamadan's *Sefer Tashak*: Critical Text Edition with Introduction" (Ph.D. dissertation, Brandeis University, 1975), pp. 11–12; and MS New York, Jewish Theological Seminary of America Mic. 1804, fol. 61a. Cf. also Moses Cordovero, *Pardes Rimmonim* (Jerusalem, 1962), 23:5, 14a: "*Halakhah* refers to the *Shekhinah*. . . . And this is [the meaning of the expression] *halakhah le-mosheh mi-sinai*, for she is the bride of Moses (*kallat mosheh*)."

97. For a discussion of the Hasidic meaning of the traditional expression, "Torah for its own sake," see Weiss, *Studies*, pp. 56–68, and Scholem, *Messianic Idea*, pp. 212–13.

98. In this context Jacob Joseph employs the older kabbalistic interpretation of *torah li-shmah*, i.e., the theurgical meaning of Torah study as a means to enhance the *Shekhinah*, rather than the novel Hasidic doctrine "Torah for the sake of the letter." Cf. *Ben Porat Yosef*, 33a, where the expression *torah lishmah* is similarly explained as Torah for the sake of the letter *he᾽*, *le-shem he᾽*, i.e., for the sake of the *Shekhinah*. An attempt to synthesize the older kabbalistic notion of *torah li-shmah* as *le-shem he᾽* and the Hasidic idea of *le-shem ha-᾽otiyyot* can be found in Yiṣḥaq Isaac Safrin of Komarno, *Hekhal ha-Berakhah*, 5:206.

99. *Zohar Ḥadash*, ed. R. Margaliot (Jerusalem, 1978), 64a. See also Tishby, *Wisdom of the Zohar*, p. 1089. The source for the zoharic view may have been *Sefer ha-Bahir*, ed. R. Margaliot (Jerusalem, 1978), § 196, where in the context of discussing the theurgical significance of Torah study as a means

to unite the upper Torah and God, the former is described parabolically as the bride who is adorned and crowned. Cf. Isaac of Acre, *Sefer Me'irat ʿEinayim,* ed. A Goldreich (Jerusalem, 1981), pp. 61–62. In *Tiqqune Zohar* 21, 46a, halakhic decisions (*pesaqot*) are described as the "garments of the Matrona" (*levushin de-maṭronita'*). Cf. *Toledot,* 140d, 190a.

100. B. Megillah 28a; Niddah 73a.

101. *Toledot,* 131b.

102. Job 24:7, 10.

103. *Toledot,* 132b. Underlying this notion is a decidedly feminine conception of the Torah, a theme that is well rooted in older aggadic and kabbalistic sources. See E. R. Wolfson, "Female Imaging of the Torah: From Literary Metaphor to Religious Symbol," in *From Ancient Israel to Modern Judaism Intellect in Quest of Understanding: Essays in Honor of Marvin Fox,* ed. J. Neusner, E. Frerichs, and N. Sarna (Atlanta, 1989), 2:271–307, esp. 302–3.

104. B. Berakhot 8a.

105. *Ṣofnat Paʿneaḥ,* 34c.

106. B. Bava Meṣiʿa 86b.

107. Cf. Shneur Zalman, *Torah 'Or,* 27a, where the word *wa-yeshev,* "and he was sitting," is interpreted as a "lowering and descent from the place of one's standing."

108. Elsewhere Jacob Joseph identifies the angel as one who stands (*ʿomed*) in contrast to men who traverse various levels; see above n. 4. In still other places he characterizes the *ṣaddiq* as the one who stands. Cf. *Ben Porat Yosef,* 31a: "There is a difference between sitting (*yeshivah*) in the world-of-the-feminine (*be-ʿalma de-nuqba'*) and standing (*ʿamidah*) in the masculine (*bi-dekhura'*). And the righteous one (*ṣaddiq*), in contrast to the wicked, is called the one who is standing (*ʿomed*)." Cf. *Toledot,* 28a–b: "Jacob, who is called *Tif'eret,* is the masculine world that is standing, and he wanted to join the feminine world [*Shekhinah*], which is sitting, by means of *Yesod,* which is called peace and tranquility." See also the citation from Abraham Ḥayyim of Zloczew above in n. 6. Jacob Joseph is here drawing upon an older kabbalistic motif expressed in zoharic literature. The world of the feminine is a standard symbol for the tenth gradation, *Shekhinah,* whereas the world of the masculine symbolizes the ninth gradation, *Yesod,* or *Binah,* the third emanation, or the totality of the upper *sefirot.* For references see G. Scholem, "On the Development of the Doctrine of the Worlds in the Early Kabbalists," *Tarbiz* 3 (1931): 66–67 (in Hebrew). Moreover, in the *Zohar* these two divine emanations are correlated with the activities of sitting and standing: sitting with the feminine, and standing with the masculine.

109. *Ben Porat Yosef,* 34a. See above nn. 7–10. The source for the expression, "to go from gradation to gradation," may have been the interpretation of Gen. 12:9 in *Zohar* 1:80a.

110. Cf. *Toledot,* 67a, where the mystical significance for walking around the pulpit (*lehaqif be-hillukh ʾet ha-teivah*) with the *lulav* is to "draw down two apsects in *Zeʿeir ʾAnpin* to *Malkhut,*" i.e., to create an overflow from the masculine to the feminine. To be sure, this is based on earlier kabbalistic explanations of the ritual of circumambulation (*haqafah*), especially in the Lurianic corpus. Cf. *Zohar* 3:24a–b; *Shaʿar ha-Kawwanot* (Jerusalem, 1963), 104d, 105c; *Peri ʿEṣ Ḥayyim,* Shaʿar Lulav, ch. 3, p. 630; Ḥayyim ha-Kohen of Aleppo, *Ṭur Bareqet,* § 660, 403a; and *Ḥemdat Yamim* (Kushta, 1735; Jerusalem reprint, 1970), 4: 82d–83a. The sexual implication of the Hasidic understanding of walking is made explicitly by Shneur Zalman, *Liqquṭe Torah,* Bemidbar, 24b: "Walking (*halikhah*) denotes the unification (*kinnui ʾel ha-ziwwug*), for one walks by way of the *Yesod* of *Nuqbaʾ* in the foot that is blessed (*regel mevorekhet*) which is *Yesod.*" On the foot as a phallic symbol, see following note. Cf. Menaḥem Mendel Schnersohn, *ʾOr ha-Torah,* 14:651, where the aspect of *ʿamidah* is applied to a state of limitation (i.e., the feminine attribute of *din*) in which the "soul is confined in a vessel," whereas the aspect of *hillukh* is applied to a state of expansion (i.e., the masculine attribute of *ḥesed*) wherein the "light emanates and is revealed without concealment." See ibid. p. 680.

111. I have treated some of the relevant sources for this symbolic usage in Jewish mystical texts in my study "Images of God's Feet: Some Observations on the Divine Body in Judaism," in *People of the Book: Jews and Judaism in Embodied Perspective,* ed. H. Eilberg-Schwartz (Albany, 1992), pp. 143–82. For a discussion of this theme in nonJewish sources, see S. Schultze-Galléra, *Fuss- und Schusymbolik und- Erotik* (Leipzig, 1909). A particularly interesting example from Hasidic literature is found in *Maʾor wa-Shemesh,* 46d:

> "[Joseph] said to them, You are spies, you have come to see the land in its nakedness" (Gen. 42:9). . . . This alludes to the essence of the rectification of the covenant (*ʿiqqar tiqqun ha-berit*) [i.e., sins connected to the phallus], and especially in these generations, for no man can escape it. The rectification of the matter is through one's joining oneself to the *ṣaddiq,* for the *ṣaddiq* is called All (*kol*). . . . And this is [the import of] what Joseph said to them, "You are spies." [The term] spies (*meraggelim*) is from the word feet (*raglayim*), for this refers to the rectification of the covenant (*tiqqun ha-berit*). "You have come to see the land in its nakedness" . . . you want to rectify the nakedness of the land, i.e., the sin of the feet.

Cf. Schatz, "Baʿal Shem Ṭov's Commentary to Psalm 107," p. 165, where the *ṣaddiq* is described as causing the sparks trapped in the demonic shells to walk (*leholikh*) on Friday evening for they did not have the power to walk by themselves during the week. In this case walking obviously has soteriological significance that is connected to the unification of masculine and feminine. That the *ṣaddiq* is empowered to cause these sparks to walk is related to his status as the mundane representative of the divine phallus. Thus in the same page the term *wa-yadrikhem*, "he led them" (Ps. 107:6), is explained as corresponding to *Yesod* "for it guides (*molikh*) the seminal drop to *Malkhut*."

112. Cf. Judges 3:24; 1 Sam. 24:3; and Ruth 3:4, 7–8, 14.

113. Cf. B. Berakhot 23a. The thematic connection between the phallus and the feet can be traced to *Sefer Yeṣirah* 6:4, where the covenant of circumcision is said to be set between the ten toes of the feet. For a particularly interesting development of this motif in Hasidic thought, cf. the words of Pineḥas of Korets cited in *Liqquṭim mi-Rav Hai Ga ʾon ʿim Perush Ner Yisra ʾel* (Warsaw, 1840), 50b–51a.

114. See B. Zak, "On the Commentaries of R. Abraham Galante: Some Notes on Their Relationship to the Writings of His Teacher," *Misgav Yerushalayim Studies in Jewish Literature* (Jerusalem, 1987), p. 78 (in Hebrew). See also the euphemistic use of the word *meṭayyalin* (literally, "they walked about") for sexual activity in *Shene Luḥot ha-Berit*, 2:30a. For discussion of this passage, see M. Idel, *Golem: Jewish Magical and Mystical Traditions on the Artificial Anthropoid* (Albany, 1990), p. 236. A sexual connotation for the word *ṭiyyul* is evident already in *Sefer ha-Bahir*, § 62 (see also § 92 where the word *halakh* assumes a sexual meaning). Cf. the description of God's strolling (*ṭiyyula ʾ di-meṭayyel*) with the souls of the righteous in *Zohar* 1:60b. Cf. *Sifra*, Beḥuqotai 1:3, ad Lev. 26:12.

115. G. Scholem, *Major Trends in Jewish Mysticism* (New York, 1956), p. 365 n. 101; idem, *On the Kabbalah and Its Symbolism*, trans. R. Manheim (New York, 1969), p. 132. Concerning this legend, see also M. Buber, *The Origin and Meaning of Hasidism* (New York, 1960), p. 126.

116. *Sefer Me ʾirat ʿEinayim*, p. 47.

117. *Pardes Rimmonim* 22:4, 108b. Cf. ibid., 16:4, 79a. For additional sources in later kabbalistic literature where this motif occurs, see R. Margaliot, *Mal ʾakhe ʿElyon* (Jerusalem, 1988), p. 76 n. 10.

118. To be sure, this symbolism is expressed in earlier kabbalistic sources. See, e.g., *Zohar Ḥadash* 72d, and *Tiqqunei Zohar* 21, 60b. See also the tradition included in Eleazar of Worms, *Sefer ha-Ḥokhmah*, MS Oxford, Bodleian Library 1812, fol. 63a, where the glory revealed to Moses, the luminous speculum (ʾispaqlariyah meṣuḥṣaḥat), is identified as both God's crown and his shoe (*pazmeqe*). See Scholem, *Origins* 125 n. 129, and my discussion in "Images of God's Feet," pp. 159–60. In other kabbalistic contexts the shoe is associated with the masculine principle, *Yesod*. Cf. *Zohar* 3:148a, 180a; *Zohar Ḥadash* 88b (*Midrash ha-Ne ʿelam*); Moses de León, *Book of the Pomegranate*, p. 253 (Hebrew section); idem, *Shushan ʿEdut*, ed. G. Scholem, *Qoveṣ ʿal Yad*, n.s. 8 (1975): 359 n. 237; idem, "Sefer ha-Mishqal: Text and Study," ed. J. Wijnhoven (Ph.D. dissertation, Brandeis University, 1964), pp. 145–46; and *Shene Luḥot ha-Berit*, 2:28d–29a. On the specific connection between feet and the *Shekhinah*, cf. *Perush ha-Ramban ʿal ha-Torah*, ed. C. D. Chavel (Jerusalem, 1978), 1:471–72, ad Exod. 28:2; *Zohar* 1:112b; "Joseph of Hamadan's *Sefer*

Tashak," p. 82; and *Pardes Rimmonim* 23:20, 39d: "*Malkhut* is called feet in the mystery of the lowest aspect [of the divine realm] that is clothed within the shell. This is the esoteric meaning of the verse, 'I have bathed my feet, was I to soil them again?' (Song of Songs 5:3), this refers to the dissemination of the sparks that are clothed in the shells." Hasidic writers also identified the feet with the divine attribute of faith. Cf., e.g., *Toledot,* 44a, and Menaḥem Mendel of Vitebsk, *Peri ha-ʾAreṣ,* printed in *Sefarim Qedoshim mi-Talmide Baʿal Shem Ṭov,* vol. 18 (Brooklyn, 1984), 25a.

119. Cf. *Shaʿar Maʾamere Rashbi* (Jerusalem, 1898), 3d.

120. *Ṣofnat Paʿneaḥ,* 118c. Cf. *Toledot,* 16c, 17b, 29b, 167b, and elsewhere, and *Ketonet Passim,* p. 54. Cf. *Maggid Devarav le-Yaʿaqov,* pp. 164–66.

121. *Ṣofnat Paʿneaḥ,* 118c. Cf. *Hekhal Berakhah,* 1:181.

122. *Keter Shem Ṭov,* 4b. Cf. *Ben Porat Yosef,* 56a, 80a, 116a–b; *Toledot,* 47a; and *Ketonet Passim,* p. 319.

123. Cf. *Toledot,* 170a, and *Ben Porat Yosef,* 17a, 33d, 56a, 116a–b.

124. Cf., e.g., *Toledot,* 16d, 32c, 66c, 138b; *Ben Porat Yosef,* 33a; and *Ṣofnat Paʿneaḥ,* 92c.

125. *Ṣofnat Paʿneaḥ,* 46a, cited in *Keter Shem Ṭov,* p. 23. See n. 127. On dancing as an expression of ecstatic joy, cf. Dov Baer Schnersohn, *Shaʿar ha-ʾEmunah,* 106a; Shalom Dovber of Lubavitch, *Sefer ha-Maʾamarim 5646–5650* (Brooklyn, 1986), p. 366; and idem, *Sefer ha-Maʾamarim 5654* (Brooklyn, 1991), pp. 337–38. The significance of dancing in Hasidism has been discussed by Wertheim, *Law and Custom in Hasidism,* pp. 162–67, although he totally neglects the erotic implications of this phenomenon. See also the emphasis on ecstatic dance in the passage from Uziel Meisels, disciple of the Maggid of Miedzyrzecz, cited in Schatz Uffenheimer, *Hasidism as Mysticism,* pp. 202–3. Particularly interesting is the dancing of the pious in a circle around the rebbe, a rite that has parallels in the sacred round dance in other religious cultures. See, e.g., M. Pulver, "Jesus' Round Dance and Crucifixion according to the Acts of St. John," trans. R. Manheim, in *The Mysteries,* ed. J. Campbell (Princeton, 1955), pp. 169–93, and A. Schimmel, *Mystical Dimensions of Islam* (Chapel Hill, N.C., 1975), pp. 179–80.

126. B. Ketuvot 16b.

127. For an alternative expression of the same theme in another passage, cf. *Shivḥe ha-Besht,* p. 75 (ed. Mondschein, p. 94). See also reference in n. 129 to the development of this motif in Naḥman of Bratslav. On a state of illumination created by dancing on Simḥat Torah, see the letter of Ḥayyim ibn Aṭṭar cited in A. Yaari, *ʾIggerot ʾEreṣ Yisraʾel* (Jerusalem, 1950), p. 269. On the Hasidic motif of dancing with the *Shekhinah* on Simḥat Torah, see Sholom Aleichem, *Ḥayye ʾAdam,* trans. J. Berkovitz (New York, 1920), bk. 2, p. 89, and English version in *From the Fair: The Autobiography of Sholom Aleichem,* trans. and ed. C. Leviant (New York, 1985), pp. 131–32.

128. *Shivḥe ha-Besht*, p. 144. I have utilized the English translation of D. Ben-Amos and J. Mintz, *In Praise of the Baal Shem Ṭov* (New York, 1984), pp. 223–24. There is no parallel to this tale in the manuscript version of *Shivḥe ha-Besht* published by Mondschein.

129. For the sexual implication of the traditional circular dance on Simḥat Torah, cf. *Ma'or wa-Shemesh*, Beshallaḥ, 119a. The Hasidic idea is based, of course, on earlier kabbalistic writings, especially those betraying a Lurianic influence, which likewise explain the *haqafot* on Simḥat Torah in a decidedly sexual manner; i.e., the circumambulation around the pulpit—which symbolizes the Presence—creates an influx from the masculine to the feminine. Cf., e.g., *Sha'ar ha-Kawwanot*, 104a; *Ṭur Bareqet*, 411a–b; Issachar Berish, *Sefer Malbush le-Shabbat we-Yom Ṭov* (Bilgoraj, 1937), 64d; and other references cited above in n. 110. The use of feet as a euphemism for sexual activity, in my opinion, also underlies Naḥman of Bratslav's teaching concerning the centrality of dance in religious worship. See, in particular, *Liqquṭe Moharan*, 10:6:

> This is the aspect of dancing and the clapping of the hands, for dancing and clapping of the hands are derived from the aspect of the spirit in the heart. . . . This is the aspect of "his heart lifted his feet," i.e., by means of the spirit in the heart the dancing is derived. That is, by means of the *ṣaddiq* who is the aspect of the spirit the pride is annuled, as it is written, "Let not the foot of the arrogant tread on me" (Ps. 36:12). And the worship of idols was nullified, as it is written, "bathe your feet" (Gen. 18:4), this refers to idol worship. When the feet are raised by means of the dancing—the aspect of his heart lifted his feet—the pride, i.e., idol worship, is nullified and the judgments are mitigated. . . . And then the feet are in the aspect of "the feet of his pious" (1 Sam. 2:9. . . . Then is established [the verse] "My feet are on level ground" (Ps. 26:12), which is the aspect of faith. For heresy is the aspect of feet that have strayed, as Asaf says, "My feet had almost strayed" (ibid. 73:2). . . . "My feet are on level ground" instructs about faith, and then is established, "His hands were steady" (Exod. 17:12).

On the significance of dance for Naḥman, see Wertheim, *Law and Custom in Hasidism*, pp. 164–65. The messianic implication of dancing in Naḥman's teaching may be alluded to in the characterization of the seventh beggar in "The Seven Beggars" as one without feet. This beggar, unlike the previous six, never arrives at the wedding to demonstrate that his seeming imperfection is in reality a perfection. One may conjecture, however, that the seventh beggar represents the ultimate rectification (*tiqqun*) and hence the coming of the Messiah. The messianic character of this tale was perceived by the traditional editors of the *Sippure Ma'asiyyot*, who added the following postscript: "The end of the story, i.e., what occurred on the seventh day concerning the beggar without feet, as well as the end of the first part of the story concerning the king, we have not merited to hear. . . . We will not hear it until the Messiah comes." On the messianic implication of this tale, especially its end, see J. Dan, *The Hasidic Story* (Jerusalem, 1975), p. 169 (in Hebrew), and Liebes, *Studies in Jewish Myth and Jewish Messianism*, pp. 139 and 190 n. 22. The possible connection of Naḥman's teaching about feet from *Liqquṭe Moharan* cited above and the tale about the seventh beggar has been noted by M. Mantel, "Rabbi Nachman of Bratzlav's Tales: A Critical Translation from the Yiddish with Annotations and Commentary" (Ph.D. dissertation, Princeton University, 1975), 2:238–39 n. 25. See, however, op. cit., p. 239 n. 26, where Mantel rejects the soteriological reading of the "The Seven Beggars." For a more general discussion of the messianic dimensions of Naḥman's life, see A. Green, *Tormented Master: A Life of Rabbi Nahman of Bratslav* (University, Alabama, 1979), pp. 182–220.

130. A convergence of the themes that I have analyzed in this paper, the messianic and the sexual implications of walking, is evident in a striking manner in the following passage from Israel Dov Baer of Weledniki, *She*ʾ*erit Yisra*ʾ*el* (Zitomir, 1868), sermon 9, 13c:

> Jacob is the aspect of the light of Messiah . . . for with Jacob the spirit of Messiah began to shine. . . . By means of the aspect of Jacob the blemish of the All [i.e., *Yesod*, which corresponds to the phallus] was rectified. . . . This is [alluded to in the name] Jacob [Yaʿaqov]: *yod* ʿ*aqev*, the perfection of the aspect of the heels (ʿ*aqevim*), i.e., the aspect of the "feet that go down to death" (Prov. 5:5). And this is [the meaning of] "Jacob lifted up his feet" (Gen. 29:1), i.e., the aspect of the blemish of *Yesod* . . . and it thus became easy (*qal*) to walk, i.e., the aspect of 130 years [130 = *ql*, the same consonants of the word *qal*] in which Adam separated [from Eve] and gave birth to [evil spirits and demons in the world; cf. B. ʻEruvin 18b; *Zohar* 1:19b, 55a; 2: 231b; and 3:76b]. By means of the aspect of Jacob there was an uplifting of these 130 years.

According to this text, Jacob is identified as a messianic figure who specifically rectifies the blemish of *Yesod*, which corresponds to the phallus, that is, sexual sin. Furthermore, the whole process is related to the feet or the heels. Hence, it is clear that feet symbolize the phallus, and the aspect of walking is the perfection of the sexual offence brought about through the feet.

◆ BIBLIOGRAPHY ◆
OF SECONDARY SOURCES

Abrams D., " 'The Book of Illumination' of R. Jacob ben Jacob ha-Kohen: A Synoptic Edition from Various Manuscripts." Ph.D. dissertation, New York University, 1993.

Altmann, A. "Eleazar of Worms' Ḥokhmath Ha-ʾEgoz." *Journal of Jewish Studies* 11 (1960): 101–13.

———. *Essays in Jewish Intellectual History*. Hanover, 1981.

———. "The Ladder of Ascension." In *Studies in Mysticism and Religion Presented to Gershom G. Scholem on his Seventieth Birthday*, 1–32. Jerusalem, 1967.

———. "Moses Narboni's 'Epistle on Shiʿur Qomah." In *Jewish Medieval and Renaissance Studies*, edited by A. Altmann, 225–88. Cambridge, Mass., 1967.

Baarda, T. "'If You Do Not Sabbatize the Sabbath . . .': The Sabbath as God or World in Gnostic Understanding (Ev. Thom. Log. 27)." In *Knowledge of God in the Graeco-Roman World*, edited by R. Van den Broek, T. Baarda, and J. Mansfeld, 178–201. Leiden, 1988.

Baer, Y. *A History of the Jews in Christian Spain*. Translated by L. Schoffman. 2 vols. Philadelphia, 1961.

———. "The Historical Background of the Raʿayaʾ Mehemnaʾ," *Zion* 5 (1940): 1–44. In Hebrew.

Bagatti, B. *The Church from the Circumcision: History and Archaeology of the Judaeo-Christians*. Jerusalem, 1971.

Bar-Ilan, M. "The Idea of Crowning God in Hekhalot Mysticism and Karaitic Polemic." *Jerusalem Studies in Jewish Thought* 6, 1–2 (1987): 221–33. In Hebrew.

Bauer, W. *Orthodoxy and Heresy in Earliest Christianity.* Translated from second German edition. Edited by R. A. Kraft and G. Krodel. Philadelphia, 1971.

Bauerreiss, R. *Arbor Vitae.* Munich, 1938.

Baumgarten, J. M. "The Book of Elkesai and Merkabah Mysticism." *Journal for the Study of Judaism* 17 (1986): 212–23.

Ben-Amos, D., and J. Mintz. *In Praise of the Baal Shem Ṭov.* New York, 1984.

Berger, D. *The Jewish-Christian Debate in the High Middle Ages.* Philadelphia, 1979.

Biale, D. *Eros and the Jews: From Biblical Israel to Contemporary America.* New York, 1992.

Böhlig, A. "Jakob als Engel in Gnostizismus und Manichäismus." *Erkenntnisse und Meinungen,* edited by G. Wiessner, 1–14. Wiesbaden, 1978. English translation in *Nag Hammadi and Gnosis,* edited by R. Mcl. Wilson, 122–30. Leiden, 1978.

Borst, A. *Die Katharer.* Stuttgart, 1953.

Bousset, W. *Hauptprobleme der Gnosis.* Göttingen, 1907.

———. *Kyrios Christos.* Translated by J. E. Steely. Nashville, 1970.

Brock, S. "Jewish Traditions in Syriac Sources," *Journal of Jewish Studies* 30 (1979): 212–32.

Buber, M. *The Origin and Meaning of Hasidism.* New York, 1960.

Büchler, A. "A Twelfth-Century Physician's Desk Book: The *Secreta Secretorum* of Petrus Alphonsi Quondam Moses Sephardi," *Journal of Jewish Studies* 37 (1986): 206–12.

Carr, W. *Angels and Principalities.* Cambridge, 1981.

Charlesworth, J. H. "The Portrayal of the Righteous as an Angel." In *Ideal Figures in Ancient Judaism: Profiles and Paradigms,* edited by J. J. Collins and G. W. E. Nickelsburg, 135–51. Chico, 1980.

Chazan, R. *Daggers of Faith: Thirteenth-Century Christian Missionizing and Jewish Response.* Berkeley, 1989.

———. "Polemical Themes in the *Milḥemet Miẓvah.*" In *Les Juifs au regard de l'histoire: Mélanges en l'honneur de Bernhard Blumenkranz,* edited by G. Dahan, 169–84. Paris, 1985.

Christ, F. *Jesus-Sophia: die Sophia-Christologie bei den Synoptikern.* Zürich, 1970.

Cohen, M. S. *The Shiʿur Qomah: Texts and Recensions.* Tübingen, 1985.

Corbin, H. *Cyclical Time and Ismaili Gnosis.* Translated by R. Manheim and J. W. Morris. London, 1983.

———. "De la gnose antique à la gnose Ismaélienne." In *Oriente ed Occidente nel medio evo: Atti del XII convegno Volta,* 105–43. Rome, 1957.

———. *En Islam Iranien: aspects spirituels et philosophiques.* 4 vols. Paris, 1971.

———. "Épiphanie divine et naissance spirituelle dans la gnose Ismaélienne," *Eranos Jahrbuch* 23 (1954): 141–249. English translation in *Man and Transformation,* edited by J. Campbell, 69–160. Princeton, 1964.

———. *Face de Dieu, face de l'homme: herméneutique et soufisme.* Paris, 1983.

———. "Harmonia Abrahamica." In L. Cirillo, *Évangile de Barnabé: Recherches sur la composition et l'origine,* text and translation by L. Cirrilo and M. Frémaux, 5–17. Paris, 1977.

———. "Herméneutique spirituelle comparée (I. Swedenborg-II. Gnose Ismaélienne)." *Eranos Jahrbuch* 33 (1964): 71–176.

———. *Temple and Contemplation.* Translated by P. Sherrard with the assistance of L. Sherrard. London, 1986.

Couliano, I. P. *The Tree of Gnosis: Gnostic Mythology from Early Christianity to Modern Nihilism.* New York, 1992.

Cullmann, O. *Le probléme littéraire et historique du Roman Pseudo-Clémentin: étude sur le rapport entre le gnosticisme et le judeó-christianisme.* Paris, 1930.

Daftary, F. *The Ismāʿīlīs: Their History and Doctrines.* Cambridge and New York, 1992.

Dan, J. "Anafiel, Meṭaṭron, and the Creator." *Tarbiz* 52 (1983): 447–57. In Hebrew.

———. "The Ashkenazi Ḥasidic 'Gates of Wisdom.' " In *Hommage à Georges Vajda,* edited by G. Nahon and Ch. Touati, 183–89. Louvain, 1980.

———. "The Beginnings of Ancient Jewish Mysticism." *Daᶜat* 29 (1992): 5–25. In Hebrew.

———. "The Book of Angels of R. Judah the Pious." *Daᶜat* 2-3 (1978/79): 99–120. In Hebrew.

———. *The Early Kabbalah.* Edited by and introduced by J. Dan, texts translated by R. C. Kiener. New York, 1986.

———. "The Emergence of Jewish Mysticism in Medieval Germany." In *Mystics of the Book: Themes, Topics and Typologies,* edited by R. A. Herrera, 57–95. New York, 1993.

———. "The Emergence of Mystical Prayer." In *Studies in Jewish Mysticism,* edited by J. Dan and F. Talmage, 85–120. Cambridge, 1982.

———. *The Esoteric Theology of German Pietism.* Jerusalem, 1968. In Hebrew.

———. *Gershom Scholem and the Mystical Dimension of Jewish History.* New York and London, 1987.

———. *The Hasidic Story.* Jerusalem, 1975. In Hebrew.

———. "Ḥokhmath Ha-ʾEgoz, Its Origins and Development." *Journal of Jewish Studies* 17 (1966): 73–83.

———. *Ḥugge ha-Mequbbalim ha-Rishonim.* Edited by I. Aggasi. Jerusalem, 1977.

———. "The Intention of Prayer from the Tradition of R. Judah the Pious." *Daᶜat* 10 (1983): 47–56. In Hebrew.

———. "Midrash and the Dawn of Kabbalah." In *Midrash and Literature,* edited by G. H. Hartman and S. Budick, 127–39. New Haven, 1986.

———. "Pesaq ha-Yirah veha-Emunah and the Intention of Prayer in Ashkenazi Hasidic Esotericism." *Frankfurter Judaistische Beiträge* 19 (1991/92): 185–215.

———. "Prayer as Text and Prayer as Mystical Experience." In *Torah and Wisdom: Essays in Honor of Arthur Hyman,* edited by R. Link-Salinger, 33–47. New York, 1992.

———. "A Re-evaluation of the 'Ashkenazi Kabbalah.' " *Jerusalem Studies in Jewish Thought* 6, 3–4 (1987): 125–39. In Hebrew.

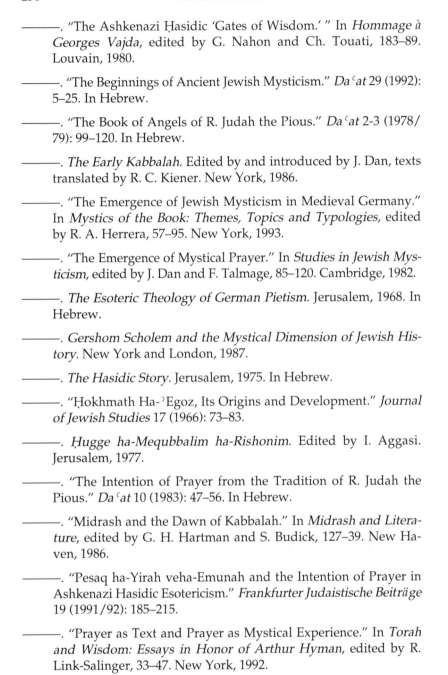

———. "The Seventy Names of Meṭaṭron." *Proceedings of the Eighth World Congress of Jewish Studies—Division C,* 19–23. Jerusalem, 1982.

———. *Studies in Ashkenazi Ḥasidic Literature.* Ramat-Gan, 1978.

———. "The Vicissitudes of the Esoterism of the German Ḥasidim." In *Studies in Mysticism and Religion Presented to Gershom G. Scholem,* 87–99. Jerusalem, 1967. Hebrew section.

Daniélou, J. *The Bible and the Liturgy.* London, 1960.

———. "Judéo-Christianisme et Gnose." In *Aspects du Judéo-Christianisme, Colloque de Strassbourg, 23–25 avril 1964,* 139–66. Paris, 1965.

———. *The Origins of Latin Christianity.* London, 1977.

———. *Théologie du Judéo-Christianisme.* 2nd edititition. Paris, 1991.

———. "Trinité et angélologie dans la théologue judéo-chrétienne." *Recherches science religieuse* 45 (1957): 5–41.

———. "La Typologie d'Isaac dans la Christianisme primitif." *Biblica* 28 (1947): 363–93.

Davies, W. D. "Paul and Jewish Christianity according to Cardinal Daniélou: A Suggestion." In *Judéo-Christianisme: Recherches historiques et theólogiques offertes en hommage au Cardinal Jean Danielou,* 71–62. Paris, 1972.

Davis, J. M. "Philosophy, Dogma, and Exegesis in Medieval Ashkenazic Judaism: The Evidence of *Sefer Hadrat Qodesh.*" *AJS Review* 18 (1993): 195–222.

Delling, G. "The 'One Who Sees God' in Philo." In *Nourished with Peace: Studies in Hellenistic Judaism in Memory of Samuel Sandmel,* edited by F. E. Greenspahn, E. Hilgert, and B. L. Mack, 27–42. Chico, Ca., 1984.

Deutsch, C. M. *Hidden Wisdom and the Easy Yoke: Wisdom, Torah and Discipleship in Mt 11, 25–30.* Sheffield, 1987.

———. "Wisdom in Matthew: Transformation of a Symbol." *Novum Testamentum* 32 (1990): 13–47.

Dinur, B. *Be-Mifneh ha-Dorot.* Jerusalem, 1955. English translation by E. Lederhendler in *Essential Papers on Hasidism: Origins to the Present,* edited by G. D. Hundert, 86–208. New York, 1991.

Dodd, C. H. *The Interpretation of the Fourth Gospel.* Cambridge, 1953.

Doresse, J. *The Secret Books of the Egyptian Gnostics*. New York, 1960.

Dresner, S. *The Zaddik*. London, 1960.

Drijvers, H. J. W. "Edessa und das jüdische Christentum." *Vigiliae Christianae* 24 (1970): 4–33.

Drummond, J. *Philo Judaeus; or, the Jewish-Alexandrian Philosophy in Its Development and Completion*. London, 1888.

Duvernoy, J. H. *Le Catharisme, La religion des Les Cathares*. Toulouse, 1976.

Eliade, M. *A History of Religious Ideas*. 3 vols. Chicago and London, 1982.

Elior, R. "The Concept of God in Hekhalot Mysticism." In *Binah: Studies in Jewish Thought*, edited by J. Dan, 97–120. New York, 1989.

———. "Ḥ̣aBaD: The Contemplative Ascent to God." In *Jewish Spirituality from the Sixteenth-Century Revival to the Present*, edited by A. Green, 181–98. New York, 1987.

———. *The Paradoxical Ascent to God: The Kabbalistic Theosophy of Habad Hasidism*. Translated by J. M. Green, Albany, 1993.

———. *The Theory of Divinity of Ḥasidut ḤaBaD*. Jerusalem, 1982. In Hebrew.

Ettinger, S. "The Hasidic Movement—Reality and Ideals." *Journal of World History* 11 (1968): 251–66. Reprinted in *Essential Papers on Hasidism: Origins to the Present*, edited by G. D. Hundert, 226–43. New York, 1991.

Fallon, F. T. "The Gnostic Apocalypses." *Semeia* 14 (1979): 123–58. In Hebrew.

Farber, A. "The Commentary on Ezekiel's Chariot by R. Jacob ben Jacob ha-Kohen of Castile." M.A. thesis, Hebrew University, 1978. In Hebrew.

———. "The Concept of the Merkabah in Thirteenth-Century Jewish Esotericism—'Sod ha-ʾEgoz' and Its Development. " Ph.D. thesis, Hebrew University, 1986. In Hebrew.

———. "On the Sources of Rabbi Moses de Leon's Early Kabbalistic System." In *Studies in Jewish Mysticism, Philosophy and Ethical Literature Presented to Isaiah Tishby On His Seventy-Fifth Birthday*, edited by J. Dan and J. Hacker, 67–96. Jerusalem, 1986. In Hebrew.

Filoramo, G. *A History of Gnosticism*. Translated by A. Alcock. Oxford, 1990.

Fine, L. "The Study of Torah as a Rite of Theurgical Contemplation in Lurianic Kabbalah." In *Approaches to Judaism in Medieval Times*, edited by D. R. Blumenthal, 3: 29–40. Atlanta, 1988.

Fiorenza, E. S. "Wisdom Mythology and Christological Hymns." In *Aspects of Wisdom in Judaism and Early Christianity*, edited by R. Wilkens, 29–33. Notre Dame, 1975.

Fishbane, M. "The 'Measures' of God's Glory in the Ancient Midrash." In *Messiah and Christos: Studies in the Jewish Origins of Christianity Presented to David Flusser on the Occasion of His Seventy-Fifth Birthday*, edited by I. Gruenwald, Sh. Shaked, and G. G. Stroumsa, 53–74. Tübingen, 1992.

———. "Some Forms of Divine Appearance in Ancient Jewish Thought." In *From Ancient Israel to Modern Judaism Intellect in Quest of Understanding: Essays in Honor of Marvin Fox*, edited by J. Neusner, E. S. Frerichs, and N. M. Sarna, 2:265–68. Atlanta, 1989.

Fleischer, E. *Hebrew Liturgical Poetry in the Middle Ages*. Jerusalem, 1975. In Hebrew.

———. *The Yoẓer: Its Emergence and Development*. Jerusalem, 1984. In Hebrew.

Fossum, J. E. "Jewish Christian Christology and Jewish Mysticism." *Vigiliae Christianae* 37 (1983): 260–87.

———. *The Name of God and the Angel of the Lord*. Tübingen, 1985.

Galili, Z. "On the Question of the Authorship of the Commentary *Or ha-Ganuz* Attributed to Rabbi Meir Ben Solomon Abi Sahula." *Jerusalem Studies in Jewish Thought* 4 (1985): 83–96. In Hebrew.

Gershenzon R., and Slomovic, E. "A Second Century Jewish-Gnostic Debate: Rabbi Jose ben Halafta and the Matrona." *Journal for the Study of Judaism* 16 (1985): 1–41.

Ginzberg, L. *The Legends of the Jews*. Philadelphia, 1968.

Ginsburg, E. "The Havdalah Ceremony in Zoharic Kabbalah." *Jerusalem Studies in Jewish Thought* 8 (1989): 183–216. In Hebrew.

———. *The Sabbath in the Classical Kabbalah*. Albany, 1989.

———. *Sod ha-Shabbat (The Mystery of the Sabbath) from the Tolaʿat Yaʿaqov of R. Meir ibn Gabbai.* Albany, 1989.

Goldreich, A. "The Theology of the *Iyyun* Circle and a Possible Source of the Term *'Ahdut Shava.'* " *Jerusalem Studies in Jewish Thought* 6, 3–4 (1987): 141–56. In Hebrew.

Goldziher, I. *Gesammelte Schriften.* Hildesheim, 1970.

Grant, R. M. *Gnosticism and Early Christianity.* New York, 1966.

———. "The Mystery of Marriage in the Gospel of Philip." *Vigiliae Christianae* 15 (1961): 129–40.

Green, A. *Devotion and Commandment: The Faith of Abraham in the Hasidic Imagination.* Cincinnati, 1989.

———. *Tormented Master: A Life of Rabbi Nahman of Bratslav.* University, Alabama, 1979.

———. "Typologies of Leadership and the Hasidic Zaddiq." In *Jewish Spirituality from the Sixteenth Century Revival to the Present,* edited by A. Green, 127–56. New York, 1987.

———. "The Zaddiq as Axis Mundi in Later Judaism." *Journal of the American Academy of Religion* 45 (1977): 327–47.

Gruenwald, I. "The Poetry of Yannai and the Literature of the Yorde Merkavah." *Tarbiz* 36 (1967): 257–77. In Hebrew.

Halperin, D. J. *The Faces of the Chariot.* Tübingen, 1988.

Handelman, S. *Fragments of Redemption: Jewish Thought and Literary Theory in Benjamin, Scholem, and Levinas.* Indiana, 1991.

Haran, M. "The Ark and the Cherubim." *Israel Exploration Journal* 9 (1959): 30–38, 89–94.

Harris, M. "The Concept of Love in Sepher Ḥassidim." *Jewish Quarterly Review* 50 (1959): 13–44.

Hecht, J. "The Polemical Exchange between Isaac Pollegar and Abner of Burgos/Alfonso of Valladolid According to Parma MS 2440: *Iggeret Teshuvot Apikoros* and *Teshuvat la-Meḥaref.*" Ph.D. dissertation, New York University, 1993.

Herford, R. T. *Christianity in Talmud and Midrash.* London, 1903.

Heschel, A. J. *The Circle of the Baal Shem Ṭov: Studies in Hasidism.* Edited by S. H. Dresner. Chicago and London, 1985.

———. *The Sabbath.* New York, 1951.

———. *Theology of Ancient Judaism.* 2 vols. London and New York, 1962.

Ḥisdai, Y. "Early Settlement of 'Hasidim' and of 'Mithnaggdim' in Palestine—Immigration of 'Mitzva' and of Mission." *Shalem* 4 (1984): 231–69. In Hebrew.

———. "The Emergence of Hassidim and Mitnagdim in the Light of the Homiletical Literature." Ph.D. dissertation, Hebrew University, 1984. In Hebrew.

Horst, P. W. van der. *Essays on the Jewish World of Early Christianity.* Göttingen, 1990.

Idel, M. "Additional Fragments from the Writings of R. Joseph of Hamadan." *Daᶜat* 21 (1988): 47–55. In Hebrew.

———. "The Concept of Torah in the Hekhalot and Its Metamorphosis in the Kabbalah." *Jerusalem Studies in Jewish Thought* 1 (1981): 23–84. In Hebrew.

———. "Defining Kabbalah: The Kabbalah of the Divine Names." In *Mystics of the Book: Topics, Themes, and Typologies,* edited by R. A. Herrera, 97–122. New York, 1993.

———. "The Evil Thought of the Deity." *Tarbiz* 49 (1980): 356–64. In Hebrew.

———. "Franz Rosenzweig and the Kabbalah." In *The Philosophy of Franz Rosenzweig,* edited by P. Mendes-Flohr, 162–71. Hanover and London, 1988.

———. *Golem: Jewish Magical and Mystical Traditions on the Artificial Anthropoid.* Albany, 1990.

———. "The Image of Adam above the *Sefirot.*" *Daᶜat* 4 (1980): 41–55. In Hebrew.

———. "Intention in Prayer in the Beginning of Kabbalah: Between Germany and Provence." In *Ben Porat Yosef: Studies Presented to Rabbi Dr. Joseph Safran,* edited by B. and E. Safran, 5–14. Hoboken, 1992. In Hebrew.

———. "In the Light of Life: An Examination of Kabbalistic Eschatology." In *Sanctity of Life and Martyrdom: Studies in Memory of Amir Yequtiel,* edited by I. Gafni and A. Ravitsky, 191–211. Jerusalem, 1992. In Hebrew.

———. "Jerusalem in Thirteenth-Century Jewish Thought." In *The History of Jerusalem: Crusades and Ayyubids, 1099–1250,* 264–86. Jerusalem, 1991. In Hebrew.

———. "Jewish Kabbalah and Platonism in the Middle Ages and the Renaissance." In *Neoplatonism and Jewish Thought,* edited by L. E. Goodman, 319–51. Albany, 1992.

———. *Kabbalah: New Perspectives.* New Haven, 1988.

———. *Language, Torah, and Hermeneutics in Abraham Abulafia.* Albany, 1989.

———. "Metaphores et pratiques sexuelles dans la cabale." In *Lettre sur la sainteté, le secret de la relation entre l'homme et la femme dans la cabale,* étude préliminaire, traduction de 'l'hébreu et commentaires par Ch. Mopsik, 329–58. Paris, 1986. English version in *The Jewish Family: Metaphor and Memory,* edited by D. Kraemer, 197–224. Oxford, 1989.

———. *The Mystical Experience in Abraham Abulafia.* Albany, 1988.

———. "On the Concept of Ẓimẓum in Kabbalah and Its Research." *Jerusalem Studies in Jewish Thought* 10 (1992): 59–112. In Hebrew.

———. "On the Metamorphosis of an Ancient Technique of Prophetic Vision in the Middle Ages." *Sinai* 86 (1979): 1–7. In Hebrew.

———. "The Problem of the Sources of the *Bahir.*" *Jerusalem Studies in Jewish Thought* 6, 3–4 (1987): 55–72. In Hebrew.

———. "The *Sefirot* above the *Sefirot.*" *Tarbiz* 51 (1982): 239–80. In Hebrew.

———. *Studies in Ecstatic Kabbalah.* Albany, 1988.

———. "Types of Redemptive Activity in the Middle Ages." In *Messianism and Eschatology: A Collection of Essays,* edited by Z. Baras, 253–79. Jerusalem, 1983. In Hebrew.

———. "Universalization and Integration: Two Conceptions of Mystical Union in Jewish Mysticism." In *Mystical Union in the Monotheistic Faith,* edited by M. Idel and B. McGinn, 27–57. New York, 1989.

———. "We Have No Kabbalistic Tradition on This." In *Rabbi Moses Naḥmanides (Ramban): Explorations in His Literary and Religious Virtuosity,* edited by I. Twersky, 51–73. Cambridge, Mass., 1983.

———. "The World of Angels in Human Form." In *Studies in Jewish Mysticism, Philosophy and Ethical Literature Presented to Isaiah Tishby On His Seventy-Fifth Birthday,* edited by J. Dan and J. Hacker, 1–66. Jerusalem, 1986. In Hebrew.

———. "The Writings of Abraham Abulafia and His Teaching." Ph.D. dissertation, Hebrew University, 1976. In Hebrew.

Isaac, E. *A New Text-Critical Introduction to Mashafa Berhan*. Leiden, 1973.

Jacobs, L. "Eating as an Act of Worship in Hasidic Thought." In *Studies in Jewish Religious and Intellectual History Presented to Alexander Altmann on the Occasion of His Seventieth Birthday*, edited by S. Stein and R. Loewe, 157–66. University, Alabama, 1979.

———. "The Uplifting of the Sparks in Later Jewish Mysticism." In *Jewish Spirituality from the Sixteenth-Century Revival to the Present*, edited by A. Green, 99–126. New York, 1987.

Jonas, H. *The Gnostic Religion*. Boston, 1963.

Kallus, M. "Two mid-13th Century Kabbalistic Texts from the ʿIyun Circle." M.A. thesis, Hebrew University, 1992.

Kanarfogel, E. "Rabbinic Figures in Castilian Kabbalistic Pseudepigraphy: R. Yehudah He-Ḥasid and R. Elḥanan of Corbeil." *Journal of Jewish Thought and Philosophy* 3 (1993): 77–109.

Khitrik, A. "On the Meeting of the Besht and Ahijah ha-Shiloni." *Sinai* 73 (1973): 189–90. In Hebrew.

Kiener, R. C. "The Hebrew Paraphrase of Saadiah Gaon's *Kitāb al-Amānāt wa ʾl-Iʿtiqādāt*." *AJS Review* 11 (1986): 1–25.

Klijn, A. F. J. *The Acts of Thomas*. Supplement to *Novum Testamentum* 5. Leiden, 1962.

———. "The Influence of Jewish Theology on the Odes of Solomon and the Acts of Thomas." In *Aspects du Judéo-Christianisme, Colloque de Strassbourg, 23–25 avril 1964*, 167–79. Paris, 1965.

———. *Jewish-Christian Gospel Tradition*. Leiden, 1992.

———. "Jewish-Christianity in Egypt." In *The Roots of Egyptian Christianity*, edited by B. A. Pearson and J. E. Goehring, 161–75. Philadelphia, 1986.

Korom, F. J. "Of Navels and Mountains: A Further Inquiry into the History of an Idea." *Asian Folklore Studies* 51 (1992): 103–25.

Kugel, J. L. *In Potiphar's House: The Interpretive Life of Biblical Texts*. San Francisco, 1990.

LaFargue, M. *Language and Gnosis: The Opening Scenes of the Acts of Thomas*. Philadelphia, 1985.

Lambert, M. *Medieval Heresy: Popular Movements from Bogomil to Hus*. New York, 1976.

Lehmann, O. H. "The Theology of the Mystical Book Bahir and Its Sources." *Studia Patristica* 1 (1957): 477–83.

Leiter, S. "Worthiness, Acclamation and Appointment: Some Rabbinic Terms." *Proceedings of the American Academy of Jewish Research* 41–42 (1973–74): 137–68.

Lieberman, S. *Greek in Jewish Palestine*. New York, 1942.

———. "How Much Greek in Jewish Palestine?" In *Biblical and Other Studies*, edited by A. Altmann, 123–41. Cambridge, Mass., 1966.

Liebes, Y. "The Angels of the Shofar and Yeshua Sar ha-Panim." *Jerusalem Studies in Jewish Thought* 6, 1–2 (1987): 171–98. In Hebrew.

———. "The Messiah of the Zohar." In *The Messianic Idea in Jewish Thought: A Study Conference in Honour of the Eightieth Birthday of Gershom Scholem*, 87–236. Jerusalem, 1982. In Hebrew.

———. *Sections of a Zohar Lexicon*. Jerusalem, 1976. In Hebrew.

———. *Studies in Jewish Myth and Jewish Messianism*. Translated by B. Stein. Albany, 1992.

———. *Studies in the Zohar*. Translated by A. Schwartz, S. Nakache, and P. Pelli. Albany, 1993.

———. "Who Makes the Horn of Jesus to Flourish." *Jerusalem Studies in Jewish Thought* 3 (1984): 313–48. In Hebrew. English summary by J. Chipman in *Immanuel* 21 (1987): 55–67.

Loos, M. *Dualist Heresy in the Middle Ages*. Prague, 1974.

Lowenthal, N. *Communicating the Infinite: The Emergence of the Habad School*. Chicago and London, 1990.

Luttikhuzien, G. P. *The Revelation of Elchasai*. Tübingen, 1985.

Mach, M. *Entwicklungsstadien des jüdischen Engelglaubens in vorrabbinischer Zeit*. Tübingen, 1992.

Mantel, M. "Rabbi Nachman of Bratzlav's Tales: A Critical Translation from the Yiddish with Annotations and Commentary." Ph.D. dissertation, Princeton University, 1975.

Marcus, I. G. *Piety and Society: The Jewish Pietists of Medieval Germany*. Leiden, 1981.

———. "The Song of Songs in German Ḥasidism and the School of Rashi: A Preliminary Comparison." In *The Frank Talmage Memorial Volume*, edited by B. Walfish, 1: 181–89. Haifa, 1993.

Matt, D. C. *Zohar: The Book of Enlightenment*. New York, 1983.

McGinn, B. "Cabalists and Christians: Some Reflections on the Role of Cabala in Renaissance Philosophy and Mysticism." Unpublished paper.

———. *The Calabrian Abbot: Joachim of Fiore in the History of Western Thought*. New York and London, 1985.

Moke, D. F. *Eroticism in the Greek Magical Papyri: Selected Studies*. Ph.D. dissertation, University of Minnesota, 1975.

Moore, R. I. *The Origin of European Dissent* . New York, 1977.

Mopsik, Ch. "La Datation du Chiʾour Qomah d'après un texte néotestamentaire." *Revue des sciences religieuses* 68 (1994): 131–44.

———. *Les Grands Textes de la Cabale: Les rites qui font Dieu*. Paris, 1993.

———. *Lettre sur la sainteté: le secret de la relation entre l'homme et la femme dans la cabale*. Paris, 1986.

———. *Le Livre hébreu d'Hénoch ou Livre des palais*. Paris, 1989.

———. *Le Secret du marriage de David et Bethsabée*. Paris, 1994.

Neubauer, A. "The Bahir and the Zohar." *Jewish Quarterly Review* 4 (1892): 357–68.

Nigal, G. "An Early Source for the Literary Genre of Hasidic Stories: On the Keter Shem Ṭov and Its Sources." *Sinai* 79 (1976): 132–46. In Hebrew.

———. *The Hasidic Tale: Its History and Topics*. Jerusalem, 1981. In Hebrew.

———. "The Teacher of R. Israel Baʿal Shem Ṭov." *Sinai* 71 (1972): 150–59. In Hebrew.

———. *Torot Baʿal ha-Toledot*. Jerusalem, 1974.

Obolensky, D. *The Bogomils*. Cambridge, 1948.

Parpola, S. "The Assyrian Tree of Life: Tracing the Origins of Jewish Monotheism and Greek Philosophy." *Journal of Near Eastern Studies* 52 (1993): 161–208.

Pearson, B. A. *Gnosticism, Judaism, and Egyptian Christianity*. Minneapolis, 1990.

Pedaya, H. " 'Flaw' and 'Correction' in the Concept of the Godhead in the Teachings of Rabbi Isaac the Blind." *Jerusalem Studies in Jewish Thought* 6, 3–4 (1987): 157–220. In Hebrew.

———. "The Provençal Stratum in the Redaction of *Sefer ha-Bahir*." *Jerusalem Studies in Jewish Thought* 9, 2 (1990): 139–64. In Hebrew.

Pétrement, S. *A Separate God: The Christian Origins of Gnosticism*. Translated by C. Harrison. New York, 1990.

Philonenko, M. "Une Arbre se courbera et se redressera (4Q385 2 9–10)." *Revue d'histoire et de philosophie religieuses* 73 (1993–1994): 401–4.

Piekarz, M. *The Beginning of Hasidism: Ideological Trends in Derush and Musar Literature*. Jerusalem, 1978. In Hebrew.

———. "The Messianic Idea in the Beginnings of Hasidism." In *The Messianic Idea in Jewish Thought: A Study Conference in Honour of the Eightieth Birthday of Gershom Scholem*, 237–53. Jerusalem, 1982. In Hebrew.

Pines, S. " 'Israel, My Firstborn' and the Sonship of Jesus: A Theme of Moslem Anti-Christian Polemics." In *Studies in Mysticism and Religion Presented to Gershom G. Scholem*, 177–90. Jerusalem, 1967.

———. "The Jewish Chrisitans of the Early Centuries of Christianity according to a New Source." *Proceedings of the Israeli Academy of Sciences and Humanities* 2 (1966): 1–74.

———. "Points of Similarity between the Exposition of the Doctrine of the *Sefirot* in the *Sefer Yeẓira* and a Text of the Pseudo-Clementine Homilies." *Proceedings of the Israeli Academy of Sciences and Humanities* 7 (1989): 63–142.

Pritz, R. A. *Nazarene Jewish Christianity*. Jerusalem-Leiden, 1988.

Puech H. C., and A. Vaillant. *Le Traité contre les Bogomiles de Cosmas le Prêtre*. Paris, 1945.

Pulver, M. "Jesus' Round Dance and Crucifixion according to the Acts of St. John." Translated by R. Manheim. In *The Mysteries*, edited by J. Campbell, 169–93. Princeton, 1955.

Quispel, G. "The Discussion of Judaic Christianity." *Vigiliae Christianae* 22 (1968): 81–93.

Rabinovitz, Z. M. *Halakhah and Aggadah in the Liturgical Poems of Yannai. The Sources of the Poet, His Language and His Period.* Tel-Aviv, 1965. In Hebrew.

Rahner, H. "The Christian Mystery and the Pagan Mysteries." Translated by R. Manheim. In *The Mysteries*, edited by J. Campbell, 337–401. Princeton, 1955.

Raphael, Y. *ᶜAl Ḥasidut wa-Ḥasidim.* Jerusalem, 1991.

Rapoport-Albert, Ada. "God and the Zaddik as the Two Focal Points of Hasidic Worship." *History of Religions* 18 (1979): 296–325. Reprinted in *Essential Papers on Hasidism: Origins to the Present*, edited by G. D. Hundert, 299–329. New York, 1991.

Reeves, M. "The *Arbores* of Joachim of Fiore." *Studies in Italian Medieval History Presented to Miss E. M. Janson—Papers of the British School at Rome*, 24 (1956): 57–81.

Robinson, J. S. "Jesus as Sophos and Sophia." In *Aspects of Wisdom in Judaism and Early Christianity*, edited by R. Wilkens, 1–16. Notre Dame, 1975.

Rosin, D. "Die Religionsphilosophie Abraham Ibn Esra's." *Monatsschrift für Geschichte und Wissenschaft des Judentums* 42 (1898): 243–54.

Rowland, C. "The Vision of the Risen Christ in Rev. 1:13ff.: The Debt of Early Christology to an Aspect of Jewish Angelology." *Journal of Theological Studies* 31 (1980): 1–11.

Rubenstein, A. "The Mentor of R. Israel Baᶜal Shem Ṭov and the Sources of His Knowledge." *Tarbiz* 48 (1978–79): 146–58. In Hebrew.

Rudolph, K. *Gnosis: The Nature and History of Gnosticism.* Translated by R. McL. Wilson. San Francisco, 1983.

Runciman, S. *The Medieval Manichee.* Cambridge, 1947.

Saperstein, M. *Decoding the Rabbis: A Thirteenth-Century Commentary on the Aggadah.* Cambridge, Mass., 1980.

Schachter, S. J. "The Liturgical Commentary of Mahzor Ashkenazi (JTSA MS # 4466)." DHL., Jewish Theological Seminary of America, 1986.

Schäfer, P. *The Hidden and Manifest God: Some Major Themes in Early Jewish Mysticism.* Albany, 1992.

———, ed. *Geniza-Fragmente zur Hekhalot-Literature.* Tübingen, 1984.

———. *Rivalität zwischen Engeln und Menschen.* Berlin, 1975.

———, ed. *Synopse zur Hekhalot-Literatur.* Tübingen, 1982.

Schlatter, A. "Die Entwicklung des jüdischen Christentums zum Islam." *Evangelisches Missionsmagazin* 62 (1918): 251–64.

Schatz, R. "The Baʿal Shem Ṭov's Commentary to Psalm 107: Myth and Ritual of the Descent to Sheʾol." *Tarbiz* 42 (1973):154–84. In Hebrew.

———. "The Doctrine of the *Ṣaddiq* in R. Elimelekh of Lyzhansk." *Molad* 18:144 (1960): 365–78. In Hebrew.

Schatz, Uffenheimer. *Hasidism as Mysticism: Quietistic Elements in Eighteenth Century Hasidic Thought.* Translated by J. Chipman. Princeton, 1993.

Schimmel, A. *Mystical Dimensions of Islam.* Chapel Hill, N.C., 1975.

Schmelzer, M. H. "Perush Alfabetin by Rabbi Benjamin ben Abraham min Ha-Anavim." In *Texts and Studies: Analecta Judaica,* edited by H. Z. Dmiitrovsky, 167–274. New York, 1977. In Hebrew.

Schoedel, W. R. "'Topological' Theology and Some Monistic Tendencies in Gnosticism." In *Essays on the Nag Hammadi Texts in Honour of Alexander Böhlig,* 88–108. Leiden, 1972.

Schoeps, J. *Theologie und Geschichte des Judenchristentums.* Tübingen, 1949.

Scholem, G. *Das Buch Bahir.* Leipzig, 1923.

———. "Eine unbekannte mystische Schrift des Mose de Leon." *Monatsschrift für Geschichte und Wissenschaft des Judentums* 71 (1927): 109–23.

———. *Explications and Implications: Writings on Jewish Heritage and Renaissance.* edited by A. Shapira. 2 vols. Tel-Aviv, 1989. In Hebrew.

———. *Kabbalah.* Jerusalem, 1974.

———. *The Kabbalah of Sefer Temunah and R. Abraham Abulafia.* Edited by J. Ben-Shlomo. Jerusalem, 1987. In Hebrew.

———. *Kitve Yad ba-Qabbalah.* Jerusalem, 1930.

———. *Major Trends in Jewish Mysticism.* New York, 1956.

———. *The Messianic Idea in Judaism.* New York, 1971.

———. "R. Moses of Burgos: the Disciple of R. Isaac." *Tarbiz* 3 (1932): 258–86; 5 (1934): 180–98, 305–23. In Hebrew.

———. "A New Document on the History of the Beginning of Kabbalah." In *Sefer Bialik,* edited by J. Fichman, 141–62. Jerusalem, 1934. In Hebrew.

———. "On the Development of the Doctrine of the Worlds in the Early Kabbalists." *Tarbiz* 3 (1931): 33–66. In Hebrew.

———. *On the Kabbalah and Its Symbolism.* Translated by R. Manheim. New York, 1965.

———. *On the Mystical Shape of the Godhead.* Translated by J. Neugroschel and edited by J. Chipman. New York, 1991.

———. *Origins of the Kabbalah.* Translated by A. Arkush and edited by R. J. Zwi Werblowsky. Princeton, 1987.

———. *Reshit ha-Qabbalah.* Tel-Aviv, 1948.

———. *Sabbatai Ṣevi: The Mystical Messiah.* Translated by R. J. Zwi Werblowsky. Princeton, 1973.

———. "The Secret of the Tree of Emanation by R. Isaac: A Treatise from the Kabbalistic Tradition of *Sefer ha-Temunah.*" *Qoveṣ ᶜal Yad* 5 (1951): 64–102. In Hebrew.

———. "The Traditions of R. Jacob and R. Isaac, Sons of R. Jacob ha-Kohen." *Maddaᶜe ha-Yahadut* 2 (1927): 165–293. In Hebrew.

Schonfield, H. J. *The History of Jewish Christianity.* London, 1939.

Schultze-Galléra, S. *Fuss- und Schusymbolik und- Erotik.* Leipzig, 1909.

Séd, N. "Les Hymnes sur le paradis de Saint Ephrem et les traditions juives." *Le Muséon* 81 (1968): 455–501.

Sed-Rajna, G. "L'influence de Jean Scot sur la doctrine du kabbaliste Azriel de Gérone." In *Jean Scot Érigène et l'histoire de la philosophie,* 453-–63. Paris, 1977.

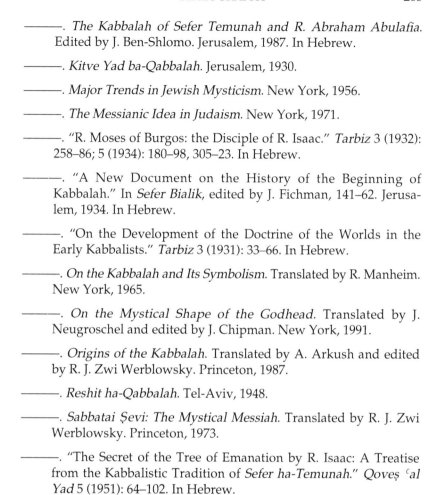

Segal, A. F. *Two Powers in Heaven: Early Rabbinic Reports about Christianity and Gnosticism.* Leiden, 1977.

Sevrin, J.-M. "Les Noces spirituelles dans l'Evangile selon Philippe." *Le Muséon* 87 (1974): 143–93.

Shahar. S. "Catharism and the Beginnings of the Kabbalah in Languedoc: Elements Common to the Catharic Scriptures and the Book *Bahir.*" *Tarbiz* 40 (1971): 483–507. In Hebrew.

———. "Le Catharisme et le début de la Cabale." *Annales* 29 (1974): 1185–1210.

———. "Ecrits Cathares et commentaires d'Abraham Abulafia sur le 'Livre de la creation,' images et idées communes." *Cahiers de Fanjeaux* 12 (1977): 345–62.

Sharot, S. *Messianism, Mysticism and Magic: A Sociological Analysis of Jewish Religious Movements.* Chapel Hill, 1982.

Shatzmiller, J. "The Albigensian Heresy as Reflected in the Eyes of Contemporary Jewry." In *Culture and Society in Medieval Jewry: Studies Dedicated to the Memory of Haim Hillel Ben-Sasson,* edited by M. Ben-Sasson, R. Bonfil, and J. R. Hacker, 333–52. Jerusalem, 1989. In Hebrew.

Sheldon-Williams, I. P. "Eriugena's Greek Sources." In *The Mind of Eriugena: Papers of a Colloquium Dublin 14–18 July 1970,* edited by J. J. O'Meara and L. Bieler, 1–15. Dublin, 1973.

Simon, M. "Réflexions sur le judéo-christianisme." In *Christianity, Judaism and Other Greco-Roman Cults: Studies for Morton Smith,* edited by J. Neusner, 2: 53–76. Leiden, 1975.

———. *Verus Israel: Étude sur les rélations entre Chrétiens et Juifs dans l'Empire Romain.* Paris, 1948.

Smith, J. Z. "The Prayer of Joseph." In *Religions in Antiquity: Essays in Memory of Erwin Ramsdell Goodenough,* edited by J. Neusner, 254–94. Leiden, 1970.

Söderberg, H. *La Religion des Cathares, Étude sur le gnosticisme de la basse antiquité et du Moyen Age.* Uppsala, 1949.

Soloveitchik, H. "Three Themes in Sefer Ḥasidim." *ASJ Review* 1 (1976): 311–57.

Steinfeld, S. "The Hassidic Teachings of Rabbi Israel, the Maggid of Koznitz." D.H.L., The Jewish Theological Seminary of America, 1981.

Stern, D. M. *Parables in Midrash: Narrative and Exegesis in Rabbinic Literature.* Cambridge and London, 1991.

Stern, S. M. *Studies in Early Ismā ʿīlism.* Jerusalem and Leiden, 1983.

Strecker, G. "On the Problem of Jewish Christianity." In Bauer, *Orthodoxy and Heresy in Earliest Christianity,* 241–85.

Stroumsa, G. G. "Le Couple de l'ange et de l'espirit." *Revue Biblique* 88 (1981): 42–61.

———. "Form(s) of God: Some Notes on Meṭaṭron and Christ." *Harvard Theological Review* 76 (1983): 269–88.

———. "Gnosis and Judaism in Nineteenth Century Christian Thought." *Journal of Jewish Thought and Philosophy* 2 (1992): 45–62.

Suggs, M. J. *Wisdom, Christology, and Law in Matthew's Gospel.* Cambridge, 1970.

Tal (Rosenthal), A. "The Aramaic Piyyuṭim for Shavuot: Their Dialectal Aspect and Their Contribution to an Aramaic Lexicon." M.A. thesis, Hebrew University, 1966. In Hebrew.

Ta-Shema, I. "Ashkenazi Ḥasidism in Spain: R. Jonah Gerondi—the Man and His Work." In *Exile and Diaspora: Studies in the History of the Jewish People Presented to Professor Haim Beinart on the Occasion of His Seventieth Birthday,* edited by A. Mirsky, A. Grossman, and Y. Kaplan, 165–94. Jerusalem, 1988. In Hebrew.

———. "The Library of the Ashkenazi Sages of the Eleventh and Twelfth Centuries." *Tarbiz* 40 (1985): 298–309. In Hebrew.

Tijdens, E. F. *Der mythologisch-gnostische Hintergrund des 'Umm al-Kitab'.* Leiden, 1977.

Tishby, I. *The Doctrine of Evil and the "Kelippah" in Lurianic Kabbalism.* Jerusalem, 1942. In Hebrew.

———. "The Messianic Idea and the Messianic Tendencies in the Beginnings of Hasidism." *Zion* 32 (1967): 1–45. In Hebrew.

———. *The Wisdom of the Zohar.* Translated by D. Goldstein. Oxford, 1989.

Tishby, I., and J. Dan. "The Teaching of Hasidism and Its Literature." In *Studies in Hasidism,* edited by A. Rubenstein, 250–312. Jerusalem, 1977.

Uchelen, N. A. van. "*Ma^caseh Merkabah* in *Sefer Ḥasidim*." *Jerusalem Studies in Jewish Thought* 6:3–4 (1987): 43–52. English section.

———. "Tosephta Megillah III, 28: A Tannaitic Text with a Mystic Connotation?" *Jerusalem Studies in Jewish Thought* 6, 1–2 (1987): 87–94. English section.

Vajda, G. *L'Amour de dieu dans la théologie juive du moyen age.* Paris, 1957.

———. *Juda ben Nissim ibn Malka: Philosophe Juif Marocain.* Paris, 1954.

———. "Pour le Dossier de Meṭaṭron." In *Studies in Jewish Religious and Intellectual History Presented to Alexander Altmann on the Occasion of his Seventieth Birthday,* edited by S. Stein and R. Loewe, 345–54. University, Alabama, 1979.

———. *Sages et penseurs sépharades de Bagdad à Cordoue.* Edited by J. Jolivet and M. R. Hayoun. Paris, 1989.

Verman, M. "Aliyah and Yeridah: Journeys of the Besht and R. Nachman to Israel." In *Approaches to Medieval Judaism,* edited by D. R. Blumenthal, 3: 159–71. Atlanta, 1988.

———. *The Books of Contemplation: Medieval Jewish Mystical Sources.* Albany, 1992.

———. "The Development of Yiḥudim in Spanish Kabbalah." *Jerusalem Studies in Jewish Thought* 8 (1989): 25–41. English section.

Vermes, G. "The Archangel Sariel: A Targumic Parallel to the Dead Sea Scrolls." In *Christianity, Judaism, and Other Greco-Roman Cults,* edited by J. Neusner, 3:159–66. Leiden, 1975.

Vööbus, A. *A History of Asceticism in the Syrian Orient.* Louvain, 1958.

Wakefield, W. L. *Heresy, Crusade and Inquisition in Southern France, 1100–1250.* Berkeley and Los Angeles, 1974.

Walker, C. Bynum. *Jesus as Mother: Studies in the Spirituality of the High Middle Ages.* Berkeley, 1982.

Wasserstrom, S. "The ^cIsawiyya Revisted." *Studia Islamica* 75 (1992): 57–80.

———. "*Sefer Yeṣirah* and Early Islam: A Reappraisal." *Journal of Jewish Thought and Philosophy* 3 (1993): 1–30.

Watson, A. *Early Iconography of the Tree of Jesse.* London, 1934.

Weinstock, I. *Studies in Jewish Philosophy and Mysticism*. Jerusalem, 1969. In Hebrew.

Weiss, J. "The Beginnings of the Hasidic Way." *Zion* 16 (1951): 46–105. In Hebrew.

———. *Studies in Eastern European Jewish Mysticism*. Edited by D. Goldstein. Oxford, 1985.

Werblowsky, R. J. Zwi. *Joseph Karo Lawyer and Mystic*. Philadelphia, 1977.

Wertheim, A. *Law and Custom in Hasidism*. Translated by Sh. Himelstein. Hoboken, N.J., 1992.

Wilson, R. McL. "Jewish Christianity and Gnosticism." *Judéo-Christianisme: Recherches historiques et theólogiques offertes en hommage au Cardinal Jean Danielou*, 261–72. Paris, 1972.

Wirszubski, Ch. *Pico della Mirandola's Encounter with Jewish Mysticism*. Cambridge and London, 1989.

Wolfson, E. R. "Anthropomorphic Imagery and Letter Symbolism in the *Zohar*." *Jerusalem Studies in Jewish Thought* 8 (1989): 147–82. In Hebrew.

———. "Beautiful Maiden without Eyes: *Peshaṭ* and *Sod* in Zoharic Hermeneutics." In *The Midrashic Imagination*, edited by M. Fishbane, 155–203. Albany, 1993.

———, ed. *The Book of the Pomegranate: Moses de León's Sefer ha-Rimmon*. Atlanta, 1988.

———. " 'By Way of Truth': Aspects of Naḥmanides' Kabbalistic Hermeneutics," *AJS Review* 14 (1989): 103–78.

———. *Circle in the Square: Studies in the Use of Gender in Kabbalistic Symbolism*. Albany, 1995.

———. "Circumcision and the Divine Name: A Study in the Transmission of Esoteric Doctrine." *Jewish Quarterly Review* 78 (1987): 77–112.

———. "Circumcision, Vision of God, and Textual Interpretation: From Midrashic Trope to Mystical Symbol." *History of Religions* 27 (1987): 189–215.

———. "Female Imaging of the Torah: From Literary Metaphor to Religious Symbol." In *From Ancient Israel to Modern Judaism*

Intellect in Quest of Understanding: Essays in Honor of Marvin Fox, edited by J. Neusner, E. S. Frerichs, and N. M. Sarna, 2:271–307. Atlanta, 1989.

———. "God, the Demiurge, and the Intellect: On the Usage of the Word *Kol* in Abraham ibn Ezra." *Revue des ètudes juives* 149 (1990): 77–111.

———. "The Image of Jacob Engraved on the Throne: Further Speculation on the Esoteric Doctrine of the German Pietists." In *Massuʾot: Studies in Kabbalistic Literature and Jewish Philosophy in Memory of Prof. Ephraim Gottlieb,* edited by M. Oron and A. Goldreich, 131–85. Jerusalem, 1994. In Hebrew.

———. "Images of God's Feet: Some Observations on the Divine Body in Judaism." In *People of the Body: Jews and Judaism from an Embodied Perspective,* edited by H. Eilberg-Schwartz, 143–81. Albany, 1992.

———. "Letter Symbolism and Merkavah Imagery in the Zohar." In *ʿAlei Shefer: Studies in the Literature of Jewish Thought Presented to Rabbi Dr. Alexandre Safran,* edited by M. Hallamish, 195–236. Bar-Ilan, 1990. English section.

———. "Merkavah Traditions in Philosophical Garb: Judah Halevi Reconsidered." *Proceedings of the American Academy for Jewish Research* 57 (1990–1991): 179–242.

———. "Meṭaṭron and Shiʿur Qomah in the Writings of Ḥaside Ashkenaz," to be published in the proceedings of the conference Mystik, Magie und Kabbala im Aschkenasischen Judentum, Dec. 9–11, 1991, Frankfurt am Main, Germany. Edited by K. E. Grözinger.

———. "The Mystical Significance of Torah Study in German Pietism." *Jewish Quarterly Review* 84 (1993): 43-78.

———. "The Theosophy of Shabbetai Donnolo, with Special Emphasis on the Doctrine of *Sefirot* in His *Sefer Ḥakhmoni." Jewish History* 6 (1992): 281–316.

———. *Through a Speculum That Shines: Vision and Imagination in Medieval Jewish Mysticism.* Princeton, 1994.

———. Woman—The Feminine as Other in Theosophic Kabbalah: Some Philosophic Reflections on the Divine Androgyne." In *The Other in Jewish Thought and History: Contructions of Jewish Culture and Identity,* edited by L. Silberstein and R. Cohn. New York, 1994.

———. "Yeridah la-Merkavah: Typology of Ecstasy and Enthronement in Ancient Jewish Mysticism." In *Mystics of the Book: Topics, Themes, and Typologies*, edited by R. A. Herrera, 13–44. New York, 1993.

Yaari, A. "Two Foundational Editions of the Shivḥe ha-Besht." *Kiryat Sefer* 39 (1964): 249–72, 394–407, 559–61. In Hebrew.

Youtie, H. C. "A Gnostic Amulet with an Aramaic Inscription." *Journal of the American Oriental Society* 50 (1930): 214–20.

Yuval, I. J. *Scholars in Their Time: The Religious Leadership of German Jewry in the Late Middle Ages*. Jerusalem, 1988. In Hebrew.

Zak, B. "On the Commentaries of R. Abraham Galante: Some Notes on Their Relationship to the Writings of His Teacher." In *Misgav Yerushalayim: Studies in Jewish Literature*, 61–86. Jerusalem, 1987. In Hebrew.

———. "The Exile of Israel and the Exile of the Shechina in 'Or Yaqar' of Rabbi Moses Cordovero." *Jerusalem Studies in Jewish Thought* 4 (1982): 157–78. In Hebrew.

Zandee, J. "Die Lehren des Silvanus. Stoischer Rationalismus und Christentum im Zeitalter der frühkatolischer Kirche." In *Essays on the Nag Hammadi Texts in Honour of Alexander Böhlig*, 144–55. Leiden, 1972.

———. " 'The Teachings of Silvanus' (NHC 7, 4) and Jewish Christianity." In *Studies in Gnosticism and Hellenistic Religions Presented to Gilles Quispel on the Occasion of his Sixty-Fifth Birthday*, edited by R. van der Broek and M. J. Vermaseren, 498–584. Leiden, 1981.

———. *The Teachings of Sylvanus (Nag Hammadi Codex 7, 4)*. Leiden, 1991.

Zimmer, E. "Poses and Postures During Prayer." *Sidra* 5 (1989): 89–130. In Hebrew.

Zunz, L. *Literaturgeschichte der synagogalen Poesie*. Berlin, 1865.

◆ INDEX ◆

References to contemporary scholars are limited to occurrences of their names in the main body of the text.

Azriel of Gerona, 65, 86, 118n, 187n, 191n, 208n, 221n
Azulai, Ḥayyim Joseph David, 147n

Baḥya ben Asher, 118n, 122n, 152n, 155n, 175n, 182n, 223n
Baruch of Miedzyborz, 224n
Baruch of Tulchin, 108–9
Benjamin bar Samuel, 143n
Berachiah, 6
Bogomils, 64, 189n

Campanton, Judah ben Solomon, 120n, 122n, 126n, 129n, 145n, 152n
Catharism, 64, 189n
chariot (*merkavah*), angels unworthy of seeing, 17; and the cherub, 129n, 157n; desire of, 13, 57; distinction between supernal and second, 15; entry before, 32; erotic union in the realm of, 55; God descends from, 58; identified as Jacob, 157–58n; and Jacob's ladder, 130n; letters of, 143n; Meṭaṭron identified as, 16–17, 128–29n; of the Presence identified as the bed, 126n; Patriarchs identified as, 115n, 148n, 155n; separated from the glory, 123n; *Shekhinah* identified as the work of, 125n, 128n; structure of in the form of an anthropos, 120n; symbolized as a nut, 2; used metaphorically to refer to a woman, 172n; visionary ascent to, 17
cherub, androgynous nature of, 179–80n; assumes anthropomorphic dimensions of the *Shiʿur Qomah* tradition, 11, 61, 62; and the attribute of mercy, 40; called the lesser Lord, 156n; characterized as having a small face, 15, 32, 33, 34, 35, 36, 43, 121n, 155n, 156n; compared to the eyes, 39; compared to the face of Joseph, 122n; comprises two cherubim, 51; designated as *malkhut*, 201n; distinguished from the *Shekhinah*, 11, 12; divine names inscribed upon the forehead of, 39, 45, 46, 49, 50; eight cherubim surround face of Jacob, 155n; emanated from the Splendor, 15n; face of contrasted with human face, 9, 15, 121n; face of refers to the youth who sins and repents, 120n; female imagery of, 160n; glory mentioned in proximity to, 51; God enthroned on, 171n; God rides upon at the Red Sea, 37, 38, 160n, 161n; identified as the divine chariot, 173n; identified as the four creatures of the chariot, 10, 11; identified as the enthroned glory, 10, 12, 54, 55, 59, 60, 61, 123n; identified as the image of God, 11; identified as the image of Jacob engraved on the throne, 3, 34, 35, 36, 37, 38, 39, 40, 43, 50, 51, 52, 54, 59, 60, 61, 62, 135n, 155n; identified as the intellect that moves the ninth sphere, 134n; identified as the lower glory, 3, 15, 39; identified as Meṭaṭron, 128–29n, 135n, 187n; identified as the one creature that comprises all of the chariot, 11, 123n; identified as the throne, 35, 61, 157n; and the increase of procreation, 43; intention of prayer directed to, 156n; manifests the appearance of the glory, 39, 44, 157n; masculine and feminine nature of, 43, 51, 57, 179n; mounting of the glory upon, 48, 51, 54, 55, 56, 172n; and the names of God, 43–44, 45, 46, 47, 48, 50, 51, 167n, 173n; name of God inscribed on crown of, 169n; object of prophetic vision, 11; patriarchs identified as, 155n; and the Primal Ether, 179n; removal of the glory from, 54; replaced the image of the ox on the chariot, 121n; serves as tabernacle for God, 123n; sexual nature of, 166n; splendor of the, 184n; and the study of Torah, 169n;